D1104586

Indigenous Struggle at the Heart of Brazil

Seth Garfield

INDIGENOUS STRUGGLE AT

THE HEART OF BRAZIL

State Policy,

Frontier Expansion, and

the Xavante Indians,

1937–1988

Duke University Press   *Durham & London*   *2001*

© 2001 Duke University Press   All rights reserved
Printed in the United States of America on acid-free paper ∞
Designed by C. H. Westmoreland   Typeset in Minion by Wilsted & Taylor, Inc.
Library of Congress Cataloging-in-Publication Data appear
on the last printed page of this book.

Portions of chapters 1 and 2 appeared in " 'The Roots of a Plant that
Today Is Brazil': Indians and the Nation-State under the Brazilian Estado
Novo," *Journal of Latin American Studies* 29 (1997): 747–68, and is reprinted
with the permission of Cambridge University Press. Some of the material in
the introduction and chapters 6 and 7 appeared in "Where the Earth Touches
the Sky: The Xavante Indians' Struggle for Land in Brazil, 1951–1979,"
Hispanic American Historical Review 80 (2000), and is reprinted
with permission of Duke University Press.

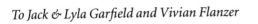

To Jack & Lyla Garfield and Vivian Flanzer

Contents

List of Maps, Tables, and Illustrations

Acknowledgments

Funding for various stages in the research and preparation of this book came from the J. William Fulbright Foreign Scholarship Board, the Mellon Foundation in the Humanities, the Yale Council on Latin American Studies, the Yale Program in Agrarian Studies, the Yale Center for International and Area Studies, the Smith-Richardson Foundation, the Bowdoin College Faculty Research Fund, and the National Endowment for the Humanities Summer Institute in Brazil.

My heartfelt gratitude goes to Emilia Viotti da Costa, my dissertation director. Her intellectual guidance enhanced my scholarship and her acquaintance enhanced my life. The input and support of Gil Joseph was also invaluable in the writing of this book. Any research on the Xavante owes an intellectual debt to the pioneering ethnographic work of David Maybury-Lewis. I am grateful as well to Aracy Lopes da Silva at the Universidade de São Paulo, who shared her intellectual insight and personal experiences regarding the Xavante, fielding the endless questions of a feckless *gringo* with patience and humor. Antonio Carlos de Souza Lima greatly facilitated my research at the Museu Nacional and indicated pertinent reference material, as did Maria Lúcia Pires Menezes and Iara Ferraz. For their professional guidance and collegiality, I thank Jeff Lesser, Barbara Weinstein, Mona Lyne, Barbara Sommer, John Manuel Monteiro, Allen Wells, Lidia Santos, Laura Graham, Raquel Casas, Chris Sterba, and Marshall Eakin. For assistance with the preparation of the manuscript and the design of the maps, I thank Charlotte Magnuson, Sylvia Targoff, and Kirsten Boettcher, respectively. I thank Marco Antônio da Rocha, Nilza Waldeck, Marisa Leal, and others at the Fulbright Commission of Brazil for their assistance. Thanks to Henrique and Rosa Flanzer for their hospitality in Rio. Valerie Millholland at Duke University Press deserves special praise for her unyielding support for this project.

My plunge into the history of Brazilian indigenous policy began at the Museu do Índio and I thank the staff there that came to my rescue: José

Levinho, Rosely Rondinelli, Penha Ferreira, and, in particular, Carlos Augusto da Rocha Freire. At the FUNAI archive in Brasília, Luiz Otávio Pinheiro da Cunha deserves kudos for his remarkable efforts to gather and preserve historical documentation. He went out of his way to help me with my research, as did his assistant, Cícera dos Santos, who fished documents from an archival jumble. FUNAI administrators Odenir Pinto de Oliveira, Claudio Romero, Jaime Mattos, and Elias Bigio generously shared their knowledge.

In central Brazil, the Salesian Fathers Bartolomeu Giaccaria and Pedro Sbardelotto offered invaluable information about Xavante history, as did Ismael and Sara Leitão. I would especially like to thank Carlos Dumhiwe and Renato Tsiwaradza of the Xavante village at Parabubure for their collaboration in documenting their community's history. They asked, among other things, that their story be told to the world, and I hope that I have served them.

I thank my parents, Jack and Lyla Garfield, for the many trips to the Dominican Republic that birthed my dearest childhood memories and my affinity for Latin America; I am forever grateful for their love, generosity, and support. Jane Frank has been an inestimable lifelong friend. I thank Alice Garfield and Bob Garfield for their encouragement. Martin Berger offered endless advice, and commiseration, with both compassion and humor. Finally, I thank my wife, Vivian Flanzer, for her love, dedication, and collaboration. She assisted in my fieldwork among the Xavante and has continued to provide thoughtful commentary. With her anthropological eye and spirit of adventure, she has made my life much happier.

Introduction

Indians and the Nation-State in Brazil

On the night of July 17, 1994, I joined hands with Xavante Indians in their village of Parabubure in central Brazil as they celebrated a festive occasion with song and dance. Ringed in a circle, the Indians stomped the earth at the center of the village in graceful rhythm, chanting sonorously in their Gê tongue. As men pounded their feet in one step and women in another, the gendered spheres of Xavante society were ritually enacted. The remoteness of Parabubure from Brazilian settlements shrouded the ceremony in eerie seclusion, the starlit Mato Grosso sky offering the only illumination. Had their forebears been resurrected for an instant and accompanied the performance, they might have thought that little had changed, that the Xavante remained undisputed masters of their territory, faithful preservers of ancestral custom.

But they would have been deceived. Whereas the Xavante once danced on land that extended "to where the earth touches the sky," they now trod on the confines of a reservation, demarcated by the Brazilian government a decade and a half earlier. Decrepit buildings, the administrative skeletons of a defunct cattle agribusiness, marred the natural tapestry of sprawling shrub, the familiar backdrop for communal ritual. Worn-out clothing draped muscular bodies once bared publicly with neither reproach nor shame. Moreover, the Xavante were not honoring an ancient tradition nor performing a long-standing rite. They were commemorating Brazil's victory in the World Cup.

Earlier in the day, the Xavante were not celebrating much at all. They were struggling, like other historical actors, to make the most of their circumstances. As their village lacked electricity, the Indians had hoped to view the final soccer match on the public television in the central plaza of Campinápolis, the nearest town, which was a two-hour drive away. On the dirt road to town, the Indians would pass a succession of cattle ranches whose fenced-off pasture land once served as hunting ground for wild pig, anteater, deer, and peccary. With shattered pride but determination, the progeny of a onetime warrior nation could take their rightful place in the Campinápolis square, brooking the racism and condescension of ranchers and townspeople.

Cirilo, the Xavante driver, planned to chauffeur many of the eighty or so members of his community in the truck that the Fundação Nacional do Índio (National Indian Foundation, FUNAI) had provided some time ago. He regularly transported fellow villagers to town to buy foodstuffs, clothes, and basic household goods, as well as to receive medical treatment and social security payments. But with each attempt by Cirilo to rev the engine, frustration mounted as the Indians sensed that the trip would be canceled.

The Xavante might have radioed FUNAI regional headquarters to send a mechanic. Based on long experience, though, they knew that state assistance would not be forthcoming for days or even weeks. Besides, the radio was broken as well, informed Carlos, a Xavante who headed the FUNAI post in the village and earned his pay as an agency employee. For the final match of the World Cup, a portable radio would have to suffice, and we all huddled around to await the momentous showdown between Brazil and Italy. The nation's triumph on the soccer field electrified the indigenous community. During that nighttime revelry, their cynicism (and that of other Brazilians) regarding state capacity and national potential appeared to dissipate.

Less than half a century earlier, the Xavante were as much in the dark as the countryside around them that night regarding soccer, trucks, radios, researchers, reservations, the Indian bureau, and nationalism. In short, they knew little about Brazil, whose victory they now cheered. Nor did they have very much interest, for that matter. Had my grandfather ventured off in his youth to a Xavante village to learn about the interplay between state policy and indigenous political culture, he might have witnessed a more "traditional" lifestyle. He also likely would not have lived to tell the tale.

From the second half of the nineteenth century to the mid–twentieth century, the Xavante defended an enormous stretch of territory in northeastern Mato Grosso against Indian and non-Indian alike. Male warriors bludgeoned interlopers to death, strewing their naked corpses as testaments to Xavante supremacy, xenophobia, and masculine prowess. A history of resistance to Portuguese and Brazilian expansionism and defense of sociopolitical autonomy fueled Xavante belligerence.

The Xavante: A Brief Historical Overview

According to Xavante oral histories, the first contact with non-Indians occurred far from their present home in central Brazil, in a region situated "near the sea." The earliest documentary reference to the Xavante, a map drawn by Francisco Tossi Colombina in 1751, placed the Indians' domain between the Araguaia and Tocantins Rivers in what was then the northern region of the captaincy of Goiás, today the state of Tocantins.[1] Along with the Xavante, Goiás was home to numerous indigenous groups, such as the Kayapó, Karajá, Krahô, and Canoeiro.

Like other areas of central Brazil under Portuguese colonial rule, the captaincy of Goiás experienced a boom during the 1720s with the discovery of gold by slaving expeditions (*bandeiras*) from São Paulo.[2] As ranchers drove livestock from the northeastern *sertão* to provision the growing mining centers, northern Goiás was also transformed into a cattle-grazing region. The *goiano* frontier, as Mary Karasch has shown, consisted of a multiethnic population: Luso-Portuguese adventurers and priests, men and women of African ancestry both enslaved and free, and assimilated Indians as well as Tupi speakers who had fled Portuguese exploitation on the coast. Census data from the late eighteenth century indicate that Luso-Brazilian whites comprised only 17.4 percent of the population of Goiás. White females, and free women in general, were particularly scarce.[3]

The Portuguese crown endeavored to protect natives from settler depredation, to create sedentary laborers and loyal Christian vassals, and to safeguard gold extraction from indigenous sabotage. Royal legislation, inspired by Jesuit campaigns, barred Indian enslavement in 1655, recognized indigenous rights to land in 1680 (as "the original and natural lords of it"), and regulated the allocation and remuneration of native labor. Settler opposition, indigenous offensives, and divided loyalties of the crown, however, stifled royal efforts to ensure humane treatment of Indians. Colonists, dependent on coerced native labor for their livelihood as well as for defense against hostile indigenous groups, revolted against Jesuit enforcement of protective legislation. In retreat, the crown would hastily reintroduce legalized Indian slavery under the terms of "rescuing" Indian prisoners of intertribal warfare condemned to death, or "just wars," in which an "infallible" threat to Portuguese rule existed. In fact, slaving raids would proceed indiscriminately.[4]

On the eighteenth-century goiano frontier conflict raged as bandeirantes plundered indigenous villages in search of slaves and gold. Competition for female labor and sexual companionship was a constant source of violence, with Luso-Brazilian raids capturing indigenous women and children to serve as slaves or retainers.[5] The Xavante sought to repel settlers, on four different occasions destroying the mining camp of Pontal, founded in 1738 within their territory. In 1762, Captain General João Manoel de Mello organized a retaliatory mission comprised of five hundred men, and two decades later the Captain General received royal authorization to wage "offensive war" against the Xavante.[6]

During the decade of the 1770s, as part of the Pombaline reforms aimed at revitalizing a sagging colonial economy, the Portuguese crown sought to promote trade on the Araguaia River and to concentrate local indigenous groups in official villages, or *aldeias*, where they could supply labor and provision food to settlers and riverine travelers.[7] By 1788, Captain General Tristão da Cunha had resettled two thousand Xavante at the aldeia of Pedro III or Carretão, survivors of bandeira raids and settler attacks. Smaller contingents of Xavante were congregated at other settlements, although many never submitted to the aldeias.

The aldeias, administered by military officials and tended to by missionaries, failed to convert the Xavante into agricultural laborers and loyal vassals. Cunha Mattos, a visitor to Carretão in 1823, noted: "The Indians who live here number 200 instead of the 5,000 who were once here. There is an indigenous commander (*capitão-mor*) and almost all of his subjects belong to the Xavante nation and a few Caiapós. . . . These Indians are peaceful, speak Portuguese poorly, are baptized, lazy, drunkard, and are presently useless to the whole world."[8]

Indeed, several factors sapped the aldeias, rendering the Indians "useless to the whole world." Epidemics such as smallpox and measles decimated the settlements and prompted survivors to flee. Funding for the aldeias, never bountiful, dried up with the region's economic downturn after the decline of the mines in the 1780s.[9] The Indians, physically abused with chains and whips, abandoned the aldeias and resumed violent attacks—armed with knowledge of European weaponry and greater familiarity with settlers' ways.[10] The Xavante's travails mirrored those of other indigenous groups under Portuguese colonial rule: between 1500 and 1800 the native Brazilian population of at least two and a half million was reduced by probably three quarters.[11]

In 1811, the royal government in Rio de Janeiro authorized another "just war" against the Xavante, Karajá, Apinayé, and Canoeiro Indians. The following year, Xavante and Karajá joined forces to destroy the presidio of Santa Maria do Araguaia.[12] By 1849, there were only seventy or eighty Xavante remaining at Carretão.[13] The first official effort to "civilize" the Xavante had collapsed.

Nonetheless, the havoc wreaked by warfare, disease, enslavement, and forced migration or tense coexistence reconfigured Xavante society. A definitive split occurred within the group sometime during the first decades of the nineteenth century.[14] One contingent, which came to be known as the Xerente, settled in the vicinity of the Tocantins River (in the present-day state of Tocantins) and maintained "peaceful" contact with outsiders. Those rejecting rapprochement, who came to be known as the Xavante, migrated westward toward the Araguaia River. The river, an important waterway for north-south trade, was viewed by settlers in Goiás as the boundary line between "civilization" to the east and the "wilderness" of Mato Grosso to the west.[15] Retreating from settler advance, the Xavante crossed the Araguaia to Mato Grosso sometime before 1862.[16]

Like other Gê social structures, the Xavante's capacity for fission and fusion may have originated in the pre-Columbian period from the necessity to mobilize for war against the Tupi-speaking populations on the Atlantic coast in order to occupy these more favored regions. Since the Portuguese conquest, this social structure proved much more adaptable in resisting the impacts of colonialism, chronic warfare, and epidemic than that of the more sedentary coastal populations.[17] Over the course of the next three-quarters of a century, the Xavante found refuge in the *cerrado*, or tropical savannah, of northeastern Mato Grosso. Expelling Karajá and Bororo Indians, the Xavante carved out an extensive domain. The unity that marked their foray into Mato Grosso soon dissipated, more the product of expedience than custom. Prizing political autonomy and access to natural resources, groups splintered off to stake their territorial claim.

As capital accumulation in Mato Grosso was clustered primarily in the southern and western portions of the state—maté near the Paraguayan border, rubber in the Guaporé valley, and cattle in the Pantanal—the Xavante remained relatively unfettered in their pursuits.[18] But in the first decades of the twentieth century, as settlers trickled across the Goiás border or south from Pará into the Xavante area in search of cattle pasture and farmland, violent conflicts erupted with growing frequency. In the early

1940s, the Brazilian state, committed to settling and developing the nation's western frontier, undertook a concerted effort to establish peaceful contact with the Xavante and to restructure their way of life. Over the next half-century, as this book documents, the Indians' political economy and cultural identity would be dramatically altered—as would the course of Brazilian state formation.

As in the past, the Xavante continue to hunt and gather, albeit on less expansive territory but more diversified treks. In 1990, the erstwhile lords of the Mato Grosso cerrado were divided among six reservations, with a population numbering approximately six thousand. The Indians now besiege bureaucrats, politicians, missionaries, and visitors with requests for trucks, tractors, satellite dishes, and monetary handouts. Their cultural benchmarks, scripts, and audiences have likewise broadened. Xavante songs are chanted in their villages, but are also marketed on compact discs sold at Brazilian music stores. Oral traditions are recounted by elders to youths in the Xavante language, and published in indigenous-authored books in Portuguese. Today the Xavante revere not only their ancestors but Brazilian soccer heroes as well.

Revisiting the History of Indigenous-State Relations in Brazil

This book raises several questions regarding the incorporation of indigenous peoples into the Brazilian nation-state. How did the processes of state formation and western frontier expansion in twentieth-century Brazil unleash such dramatic change among an indigenous people? And how did indigenous people such as the Xavante strive to mediate such change? How, despite the chronicle of their death foretold, have Xavante adapted to dominant society while honoring ancestral customs? What has been the nature of indigenous struggle at the geographic, cultural, and political heart of Brazil?

My study looks at the political, legal, and ideological interventions by different forms of the Brazilian capitalist state to subjugate and reconstitute an indigenous people. It analyzes the evolving material and cultural factors bearing on the subordination of the Xavante and the protocol and symbols through which social relations of power have been articulated and experienced. While examining state formation in twentieth-century Brazil, capital accumulation on the frontier, and social constructions of ethnicity, this book chronicles patterns of Xavante sociocultural adaptation and political mobilization. It probes how dominant signs and material practices were contested and embraced, undermined and amended by the indigenes.

The incorporation of indigenous populations and territories into the nation-state was fundamental to the growth of Brazil's regional and national economies and its emergence as a continental power. Indigenous peoples, moreover, have had great symbolic importance in the construction of Brazilian national identity. And Brazil's foreign relations, much to the government's chagrin, have been rocked by accusations of mistreatment of native peoples. Yet, though anthropologists and sociologists have produced illuminating studies of indigenous-state relations in Brazil, historical research remains embryonic.[19] The marginalization of Indians within Brazilian historical narratives subsequent to the early colonial period stems from several sources. The indigenous no-show or typecasting in Brazil's national roll call conforms to the broader hemispheric tradition in which Native Americans have been depicted as folkloric curiosities rather than ongoing producers and products of historical outcomes.[20] The shadow of social Darwinism and positivism, which preached the imminent, inevitable, or actual demise of indigenous peoples, has extended farther than admitted. But the lacuna derives from trends more specific to Brazilian historiography as well. The myth of racial democracy, celebrating interracial mixture in smoothing the nation's sociocultural formation—although debunked by researchers—undoubtedly has managed to obscure indigenous realities (as it has elsewhere in Latin America).[21] Moreover, for the postcolonial period, historical research has overwhelmingly focused on Brazil's southeastern and northeastern regions, due to their preponderant political, economic, demographic, and intellectual importance in shaping national development. The central western and northern regions—in 1990, home to more than half of the nation's small native population of approximately 235,000—have been given short shrift, rendering indigenous history less visible.[22] The political projects, research agendas, and cultural blinders that stripped Brazilian history of Indians also have stripped Brazilian Indians of history in distorting, if not overlooking, analysis of indigenous socioeconomic engagement.

In recent years, historians have begun to retrieve the Brazilian indigenous experience, revisiting the archives to reinsert the disappeared into regional and national historical narratives.[23] To be sure, these inroads trail recent contributions to Spanish American historiography, which have stressed the intricate and conflictual relations between indigenous peoples and the state.[24] This book seeks to bring Brazil's blurred indigenous past further into focus.

Of State Formation, Frontier Expansion, Race and Ethnicity

Several narrative strands thread this study. The dominant one explores how the Brazilian state since the Estado Novo dictatorship of Getúlio Vargas (1937–1945) crafted a political project and cultural discourse to exercise dominion over indigenous groups and their territories. Brazilian state officials had long pondered the daunting challenge of consolidating rule over far-flung regions, and the diverse, multiethnic populations that were to constitute "the nation." As a dynamo of state consolidation, the Estado Novo—marked by political centralization, pronounced intervention in civil society, inward-oriented economic growth, and nationalist bent—signified an important watershed in relations between the state and indigenous peoples and between the political center and periphery. The Vargas regime, extending its determined if weak arm to the Mato Grosso backlands to promote capital accumulation, colonization, and national integration, intensified the process of western expansion that would transform Xavante lifestyles.

Indeed, the "development" of the western and Amazonian hinterland would remain a political project of potent nationalist symbol long after the Estado Novo. From the construction of a new capital, Brasília, smack in the central western *planalto* under the administration of Juscelino Kubitschek (1956–1961), to the pharaonic roadbuilding and colonization projects of the military governments (1964–1985) in Amazonia, images of the western frontier and its populations were indelibly stamped on the nation's political and cultural consciousness. So, too, the west's natural resources remained inextricably linked to bureaucratic planners and investor portfolios.

The Brazilian frontier was demarcated neither by geographic line nor cultural boundary, enveloped by process neither unilateral nor unilinear. Rather, the frontier was splotched by zones of multiple, intermittent, and complex interpenetrations among social groups endowed with unequal power in contest over territorial space, resource allotment, and cultural primacy.[25] Although constructed in binary terms as an ideological foil for core areas ("civilization" vs. "barbarism"), the frontier may be better conceptualized in terms of networks of social linkages and understandings, a large proportion of whose relations, experiences, and meanings transcend bounded notions of place.[26] Critically, frontier regions have been marked by the state's tenuous ability to exercise hegemony through mechanisms of consensus and consent and to monopolize the use of violence. Political disarticulation of the bourgeoisie, lopsided patterns of capital accumulation, environmental barriers, technological constraints, and sociocultural resistance traditionally have accounted for such fragmentation. (It should be noted that Brazilians refer to the vast interior of the country as the *sertão* or *interior* rather than the Portuguese cognate *fronteira*, which connotes a boundary line or border.)

Brazilian frontier expansion is a historically specific process of occupation (and contestation) of lands and their integration into the national economy.[27] Since the 1930s, as Brazil experienced rapid industrialization, urbanization, and labor surplus, the frontier expanded in response to capital accumulation and demands within the national economy. As the Brazilian economy deepened in industrial and financial centers, it widened through the accumulation and appropriation of frontier surplus and the integration of "unexplored" regions. Frontier land served to expand production of agricultural staples for a growing urban population and industrial economy; surplus labor, denied access to land under a monopolistic system of tenure and displaced by mechanization, moved onto the frontier to meet this demand. (This trend, then, is not reducible to earlier models of export-oriented or "moving" frontiers, whose economic activities were directed to the world market.)[28]

Joe Foweraker rightly notes the central role of the Brazilian state in ensuring accumulation on the twentieth-century frontier and its reproduction of capitalist social relations through the use of legal mechanisms, bureaucratic agencies, and violence.[29] Yet institutions of state are also cultural forms whose activities, routines, and rituals serve to constitute and regulate social identities.[30] In analyzing efforts employed by Brazilian state officials and elites to establish hegemony over indigenous peoples, we may touch briefly here on the structural and ideological components of nation building: the cult of nationalist developmentalism, the reification of the state, and the construction of "Indianness."[31]

Since the Vargas era, the Brazilian state defined and legitimized its link to the "nation" by overseeing a developmental project aimed at transforming a neocolonial agro-export economy into an industrial power. As changes in the international capitalist economy had rendered the process of Latin American industrialization distinct from that of the North Atlantic, state planning and leadership were upheld as indispensable in managing basic industries and infrastructure, regulating imports, and controlling wages to nurture the domestic private sector.[32] The overall growth of state power in the period under study is impressive. The developmental policy of import-substitution industrialization, which engendered a long period of economic growth and structural transformation from the 1930s to the late 1970s, entailed heavy state involvement in economic planning, regulation, and financing. Frontier expansion was championed by state officials as a means to supply staple foods for the growing urban population by expanding agricultural production, as well as a means to rectify regional imbalance, social inequality, and national defense.

Brazilian state-led developmentalism also served, to adapt Partha Chatterjee's reflections on postcolonial India, as an effective tool for containing and resolving class conflict in a large and heterogeneous country and controlling dispersed power relations to further capital accumulation. Corporatist structures linking workers to the state and governmentally authorized forms of group representation and consultation served to shape and give meaning to the very notion of "politics."[33] Development was conjured as a linear progression premised on a collective will, transcending regional and particular interest and benefiting all members of the "nation."[34] State officials presented Brazilian nationality as a constituted entity that was threatened by "feudal" modes of production and ethnic separatism; in fact, the very emergence of that national identity was contingent on the reproduction of capitalist social relations and the elimination of cultural differences.[35]

As Eric Hobsbawm succinctly asserts, "Nations do not make states and nationalisms, but the other way around."[36] The recasting of the Brazilian "nation" from an amorphous social mass represented one of the long-term successes of state officials. Still another enduring legacy of Vargas was his promotion of the *idea* of the state as a consolidated and unified entity. For the image of the nationalist state masked more than the actualities of class power in Brazil:[37] as Philip Abrams has noted, the state itself serves as a mask, a message of domination whose unified symbol camouflages profound division and lack of cohesiveness within the political realm.[38]

The cult of statism and nationalist development converged in policy making and pronouncements toward indigenous people. To promote accumulation, the developmentalist state constituted objects of planning as objects of knowledge, mapping out the physical resources, capabilities, and propensities of its economic agents.[39] State planners sought to define and regulate indigenous territorial boundaries, modes of production, and civic capacity. Yet, as James Scott points out, state "maps," in attempting to render societies more manipulable, simplify and misrepresent complex local social practices, depicting only those aspects that interest official observers and monitors from the center.[40] Thus, land that the Xavante used as hunting, foraging, and agricultural grounds was surveyed by planners in terms of cash crop and livestock potential. Land providing cultural sustenance and historical reference was pinpointed by military strategists as national security zones or as safety valves for the nation's dispossessed. Intricate modes of production and kin networks structuring communities were disregarded or oversimplified by officials intent on "rationalizing" indigenous production and organization.

Enjoining indigenous peoples to surrender territorial control and political autonomy in the "national" interest, state planners affirmed exclusive know-how and capacity to engender *better* Indians: sedentary agriculturists, disciplined rural laborers, market consumers, and patriotic citizens. The Brazilian state, like its mid-twentieth-century hemispheric counterparts, claimed mastery of indigenous uplift through noncoercive and enlightened methods—methods "respectful" of indigenous cultures yet adequately propulsive of a transformational and nonreturnable journey into the socioeconomic mainstream. As a linchpin in this agenda of domination, elites employed biologically and culturally deterministic notions of "Indianness" to legitimize power and naturalize social inequalities.

Long before the state reached the Xavante's doorstep, ideologues sidelined indigenous peoples on a field of power demarcating social entitlement, status, and identity. To a modernizing state promoting capital accumulation and national homogenization, indigenous territorial dominion and cultural difference was anathema. Yet, for the nationalist authoritarian Estado Novo—coincident with statist, chauvinist, and nativist regimes worldwide—indigenous people also held great symbolism as primordial citizens and markers of national exceptionalism. Indians thus were classified as raw material rather than finished products of nation building: noble savages and/or mental deficients who required "protection" and refashioning by the state; social isolates who would biologically and culturally fuse with other Brazilians.

Numerous contradictions fractured these images. As progenitors of Brazilian nationality, Indians were ceremoniously offered a seat of honor in the national pantheon; yet, as dim-witted children, they were reprimanded. As cultural gems, Indians represented an asset to nation building; yet, as idlers and resisters, Indians constituted a drag. As past and future contributors to the process of *mestiçagem* (or racial mixture) in Brazil, Indians stood as equal partners in a national project; yet, as wards of the state steered on the right track by *"civilizados"* (or whites), Indians were relegated to the back seat. Elites had essentialized indigenous peoples as an ethnic "other": paragons of morality, valor, and generosity, or of simplemindedness, deviance, and sloth.

All collective social identity, whether indigenous or nonindigenous, is founded on opposition toward "others." Ethnicity, however, as conceptualized by John Comaroff, consists of the stereotypic and hierarchical assignment of social groupings to niches within the division of labor, originating in historical processes surrounding "the *asymmetric* incorporation of structurally dissimilar groupings into a single political economy." At the apex of this socially constructed hierarchy of opposed ethnic identities lies "race," whose identification by ancestry or physical appearance is belied by inconclusive bases of genetic differentiation and the lack of universal apprehension of phenotypical variation.[41] Yet, although structural forces form the root of ethnicity, ideologies are irreducible and mutually constitutive aspects of material reality, with the capacity to reproduce and/or alter the character of that social order.[42] Thus, cultural constructions of Indians represented and enacted structural inequalities in Brazilian society through the signs and symbols of everyday practice and acquired relative autonomy to impact those structures.

The Vargas regime, of course, did not invent these dual images of Indians; rather, it mobilized certain variants of feelings that already existed and that could operate on the macropolitical scale to conform with a "new" nation-state.[43] Yet, in imposing, rewarding, or "encouraging" certain sociocultural practices and forms of expression while suppressing, marginalizing, or undermining others, Brazilian state power would serve to conscribe indigenous agency and representation.[44]

The implications of the state's message were patent. Indians, as the primordial Brazilians, would (or should) embrace present-day western expansion; indigenous communitarianism would buttress the political economy of the frontier; Indian prowess would strengthen the nation; racial mixture would eliminate social conflict. The benevolent state would regenerate the innate potential of the Indian, and the innate benevolence of the Indian would regenerate national potential. Through biological mixture and cultural assimilation indigenes would further meld a mestiço nation. Fashioned painstakingly on an elite assembly line, Brazilian Indians had been destined for ultimate demolition. This curious fate, in fact, conforms to Gerald Sider's insight that "the historical career of ethnic peoples can [thus] best be understood in the context of forces that give a people birth and simultaneously seek to take their lives."[45]

The Janus-faced ideology articulating race, racial mixture, and nationality is not unique to Brazil. In Colombia, for example, the celebration of racial mixture glorifies the convergence of three races on neutral ground, yet the ideology of *blanqueamiento* (whitening) envisages a future in which blacks and Indians are eliminated, giving rise to a *whitened* mestizo nation.[46] In tracing the tangled economic and ideological webs that enmeshed an indigenous people since the Vargas regime, this study seeks to broaden our understanding of the nexus among state formation, frontier expansion, and ethnic identity in twentieth-century Brazil.

Hegemony and Its Malcontents:
The Brazilian State and Indigenous Engagement

State capacity and autonomy in implementing policy is not only historically variable but typically uneven across sectors, dependent on factors such as administrative-military control of territory; financial means and staffing; the organization, interests, and advantages of socioeconomic groups; and transnational structures.[47] Indeed, the process whereby structures and ideologies become hegemonic, or accepted as the natural, universal, and true social order, is never total.[48] As such, hegemony is a process that constantly has to be constructed and may be unmade, and whose resilience varies from one regime to another.[49]

The Brazilian developmentalist state—which historically prioritized industry over agriculture, city over countryside, and southeast over west—would be hard-pressed to execute indigenous policy and to restructure the sociopolitical dynamics and economic course of the west. As state policy for indigenous people was both ambitious and ambiguous—contacting and "protecting" hostile groups; teaching Portuguese and civic-mindedness while preserving indigenous "virtues"; inculcating new modes of production and demarcating indigenous reserves—it impinged on not only the Indians but the interests of regional oligarchs, missionaries, corporate investors, and domestic and international advocacy organizations. Consequently, various social groups mobilized to influence and reformulate policy. Struggles between national and subnational officials or among federal bureaucracies, reflective of these competing interests, further adulterated the officially prescribed dosage for indigenous integration. As this study documents, "the state" did not unilaterally nor uniformly determine the fate of indigenous communities, lands, and identities in the Brazilian west. Rather, outcomes evolved out of the conflicts and negotiations among government officials, indigenous peoples, local elites, missionaries and church leaders, peasants and squatters, journalists and intellectuals, foreign governments and human rights groups in a dynamic interplay that shifted over time from one regime to another. Whereas celebratory and revisionist analyses reify state power, I explore the contingency of Brazilian state structures to understand the course of indigenous policy.[50]

My lens focuses on Xavante engagement of the socioeconomic structures and cultural mechanisms that sought to redefine their political economy and identities. Xavante postcontact history—haunted by death, exile, territorial loss, and cultural violence—proves no major exception to most postconquest Native American experiences. Yet, while decrying such victimization, we need not reduce Indians to ciphers. Heeding Marshall Sahlins's admonition against equating colonial history simply with the history of the colonizers, we must explore how disciplines of the state are internalized and resisted.[51] My secondary line of inquiry, then, seeks to investigate how one indigenous group navigated paths of integration into the Brazilian nation-state, and the legacy produced for Indians, state, and society.

For too long the study of indigenous people in Latin America was reduced to a catalogue of cultural change or continuity that embodied essentialist notions of ethnicity and offered scant explanation of indigenous history. One scholarly tradition, informed by modernization and world system theory, conceptualized indigenous integration as a game of billiards in which one cultural trait or stage was consecutively knocked out by capitalist expansion, rather than as an uneven, multifaceted, and contradictory process.[52] Of course, many indigenous peoples and their cultures *have* perished in Brazil and elsewhere in Latin America—as the result of genocide, epidemic, territorial usurpation, and social assimilation.[53] Yet recent scholarship has illuminated how indigenous engagement with dominant society has engendered varied historical outcomes.[54]

A countervailing approach has viewed subaltern politics as an "autonomous" domain, a cultural cocoon that has allowed for, in Ranajit Guha's words, "dominance without hegemony."[55] Among Latin Americanists, such a concept is best embodied in the notion of "the Andean" (*lo andino*), whereby Andean peoples' histories are gauged and validated by supposed continuities with precolonial Inca rule and resistance to Westernization.[56] Although such insight underscores the importance of endogenous beliefs and practices in resisting hegemonic control, it straitjackets indigenous cultural authenticity in the mantle of continuity and restricts postcontact history to an exercise in negation. Indeed, in obscuring the creative and contradictory processes whereby dominant symbols and meanings are filtered, absorbed, and reworked by indigenous peoples, such a methodological approach impoverishes our understanding of the history of indigenous-state relations.[57]

Ethnic cultures, born of resistance and adaptation to domination, must be seen as transformative and relational rather than timeless, capsulized essences.[58] I do not imply here that indigenous peoples lacked group consciousness or identities based on sociocultural difference prior to incorporation into Brazilian society; rather, such identities changed as the social and material boundaries marking this opposition shifted in the course of economic and political processes.[59] For example, it meant one thing to be Xavante living on the sparsely populated Mato Grosso frontier in the early 1940s using sheer force to defend extensive territory and entertaining the overtures of a wobbly central government bent on rearranging matters. It meant quite another to be Xavante in the late 1970s, fenced in by whites, beholden to state power, swept up in swirling national and international debate over the rights of Brazilian Indians, and engulfed by the mass media. Indeed, what must be probed is the violent and convoluted process whereby the Xavante, stripped of autonomy, *learned* and articulated that their ethnicity was a political marker that restricted or accorded them rights and obligations as indigenous peoples and Brazilian citizens. For just as state formation hinders, it enables, with capitalist political and cultural forms restricting certain capacities while developing others.[60]

In schools, civic ceremonies, and public discourse, government officials and missionaries conveyed to Xavante notions of state power, indigenous rights, and political representation. These ideological weapons were not furnished ready-made to the Indians; rather, the Xavante adapted them from a dizzying montage assembled by dominant actors to showcase normative forms of behavior and identity. Thus, we must explore how indigenous tactics of resistance to external domination derive from the very institutions and doctrines that the colonizers imposed to ensure subordination.[61] Withstanding the sociocultural avalanche of state power, the Xavante selected, remolded, and hurled back fallen debris in their defense. Xavante leaders stormed the political arena, an elite bastion, reinforcing yet realigning the framework of Brazilian law. Portuguese, a vessel of cultural-linguistic subjugation, was reworked by the indigenes into a language of protest. "Indianness," a subordinative classification, was refitted by the Xavante into a social identity and organizational medium for mobilization.

Of course, the Xavante also harnessed endogenous social patterns and historical experiences for battle: a political culture that enshrined aggressiveness and daring in its leadership, communal organization amenable to strategic dispersal, and a collective memory of episodes of violent confrontation as well as "peaceful" engagement with Brazilian society. Parlaying "traditions" into statements of political dissent and entitlement,

Xavante communities sought to temper and contour patterns of socio-economic domination. The indigenous past, then, would serve as a way to mediate a culturally specific mode of change.[62]

In their quest for greater autonomy *and* access to Brazilian accoutrements of power, Xavante villages pursued polyvalent strategies: deferring to agents of dominant society while cherishing—or discarding—alternative visions; gauging the strengths and weaknesses of the state (which evolved with *its* stages of "integration"); forging cross-cultural alliances for political expediency; revealing pent-up grievances or "hidden transcripts" only at propitious moments.[63] These tactics engaged elites on the very legal, political, and cultural grid that had been plotted for indigenous subordination.

The Research Methodology and Agenda

As this text examines the relationship between Brazilian state formation and indigenous political engagement, certain caveats must be set forth. In examining state policy toward indigenous peoples, this work does not offer a traditional political history focusing on parties, congressional debates, and judicial proceedings, nor an institutional history of the Indian service.[64] Rather, it seeks a broader picture of the material and cultural interface between indigenous policy and indigenous politics. Though critical of Brazilian state policy toward indigenous peoples, this work is not intended as a blanket indictment of state power and planning nor as an apologia of neoliberalism. It critiques, following James Scott, state hegemonic projects that disregarded the values, aspirations, and objections of indigenous peoples and marginalized native know-how and input in the process of frontier expansion and nation building.[65]

On the other hand, this work does not offer a "thick" ethnography or detailed ethnohistory of the Xavante, nor does the analysis of Xavante interaction with outsiders exhaust all facets of indigenous consciousness and representation, whether historical, mythical, or a combination thereof.[66] It does endeavor, in tracing the larger material and cultural forces impacting on the Xavante, to document experiential nuance within and among communities.

My focus on the Xavante as a case study for analyzing the Brazilian state's indigenous policy stems from several factors. In many ways, the Xavante epitomized "the Indian" spotlighted by twentieth-century Brazilian government officials and intellectuals and conjured in the popular imagination: truculent, nomadic, "uncorrupted," and Amazonian. Moreover, Xavante adaptation to and subversion of dominant political institutions and cultural norms reveal an indigenous people's strategic engagement of Brazilian society. The Brazilian indigenous population is estimated at no more than 0.2 percent of the national total of more than 160 million. Although numerically small, the Xavante constitute one of the larger indigenous groups in Brazil and the largest in Mato Grosso. Of the 206 different indigenous peoples in Brazil speaking approximately 170 distinct languages, nearly half have only 200 to 500 members; only ten groups, including the Xavante, have a population exceeding 5,000.[67] My specific findings on the Xavante do not encapsulate the trajectory of all Brazilian indigenes, whose variegated patterns of socioeconomic integration, cultural practice, geographic distribution, and historical experience defy pigeonholes. My research is intended to provide a comparative reference point for historical inquiries into Indian-state relations in twentieth-century Brazil and Spanish America and broader questions of ethnicity and postcolonial nation building.

This book illuminates not only the implications of Brazilian state policy for indigenous groups but the implications of indigenous groups for state policy. For although skewed by sharp imbalance, power dynamics between Indians and the Brazilian state must be viewed in dialectic terms. The historical foundations of this relationship are explored in chapter 1, which examines the construction of the Indian under the Estado Novo (1937–1945). As a vestige of primordial Brazil—a living archaeological relic—the Indian stood as a valuable symbol for a state whose political legitimacy rested on its nationalist developmental project. Indigenous people and the western hinterland epitomized "Brazilianness": redemption of the nation from a traditionally subordinate role in the Atlantic world as agro-exporter and industrial and cultural importer. Indians were consecrated as a precious national resource who had inestimably enriched the Brazilian sociocultural makeup since the arrival of the Portuguese. Gendered variations on the theme featured the intrepid Indian man who had helped the Portuguese tame the natural environment, and the sexually accommodating Indian woman who lovingly begat the mestiço population. This demigod could still be found uncorrupted in the pristine west, habitat of the nation's "authentic" Indians. The celebration of the Indian further served to deflect racist aspersions cast from the North Atlantic that impugned the potential of a nation with a large nonwhite population.

Yet, simultaneously, Brazilian state officials depicted indigenes as slackers and incompetents who required discipline to learn the meaning of "work," the importance of "rational" resource management, and the evils of "nomadism." The noble savage, elites charged, was socially underdeveloped and economically unproductive; for their betterment, Indians required state oversight to manage their land and resources and to regiment their labor. In the context of western frontier expansion, state discourse and policy, which defined Indians as both "others and brothers," could naturalize arrogation of indigenous territory and socioeconomic subordination.[68]

Chapter 2 looks at state efforts to "pacify," or peacefully contact, the Xavante to regiment the process of accumulation and settlement on the central western frontier. State officials would be vexed by violent resistance from the Indians, opposition from homesteaders, and competition from missionaries. The state's triumphs were piecemeal and fragmentary and served to provoke a schism between government officials and elite sectors who advocated integration and those who advocated preservation of uncontacted (or recently contacted) indigenous groups.

Chapter 3 looks at the shortcomings of state policy toward the Xavante in the early postcontact period. It explores the political economy and social structure of the Xavante, which had been systematically devalued or overlooked by state planners in their transformative mission. The Indians' mixed subsistence economy, based on hunting, gathering, and agriculture, had been adapted to a forbidding natural environment, and village politics was marked by factionalism. State officials, bent on stamping out nomadism and harnessing indigenous labor, sought to co-opt Xavante leaders with consumer goods; indigenous leaders, however, viewed access to state largesse as a mechanism to achieve factional supremacy rather than a recompense for abandoning foraging. The disjuncture between state and indigenous expectations, and between state objectives and capabilities, exploded in internecine strife on the Mato Grosso frontier.

The federal government's challenge in reserving territory for the Xavante, faced with stiff opposition from Mato Grosso elites, is explored in chapter 4. Land politics in Mato Grosso, marked by violence, fraud, and clientelism, paved the way for the commodification of Xavante territory and the assault on their communities. The federal Indian bureau, hobbled by juridical, administrative, and fiscal constraints as well as patronage and corruption, offered scant defense. Indeed, the chapter explores how Mato Grosso land policies served as a site of both contest and compromise among state and subnational governments that undergirded the Brazilian postwar democratic system (1946–1964).

Chapter 5 probes the difficulties Xavante communities experienced with forced subordination to dominant society. At government posts and religious missions, Indians were pressured to modify their political economy, social norms, and cultural mores. Xavante communities would demonstrate disparate responses to outside intervention, responses that were also fractured by age and gender. While maintaining sociocultural differences, they demonstrated an eagerness to master the political and economic structures and symbolic codes that served to subjugate their communities. From this apprenticeship, Xavante would assay the political value of their ethnic culture as a banner of entitlement, and would acquire the linguistic skill and rhetorical weaponry to brandish these claims with measured success.

Chapters 6 and 7 examine the dramatic intensification of state power, capital accumulation, infrastructural and demographic growth, and environmental destruction in Amazonia precipitated by two decades of authoritarian rule after 1964. To induce corporate capital to the Amazon, the military government lavished investors with generous fiscal incentives and tax breaks and expanded transportation and communication networks. Military officials viewed the economic development, colonization, and integration of northern Mato Grosso and other areas of Legal Amazonia as imperatives of national security. Indigenous policy would be targeted by state officials—endowed with far greater capacities under military dictatorship—avid to promote economic development, agricultural modernization, and supremacy over regional oligarchs.

Although the military endeavored to corral Indians on small reserves, the Xavante mobilized to challenge the territorial and political confines imposed by an authoritarian government. To recover usurped territory the Xavante engaged in persistent "lobbying" of state officials and outreach to key sectors of civil society; extralegal measures and mock violence; and skillful manipulation of indigenist discourse, the law, and the media. In their struggle, the Indians benefited from and breached the boundaries of a newly liberalized political system established by the military government.

Chapter 8 explores the impact of a state-sponsored development project implanted in Xavante communities with various objectives: forging self-sufficiency through agricultural modernization, consolidating state power, and quelling indigenous militancy. State planners in Brasília devised the high-input agricultural project without consulting the Indians and with little concern for local know-how, capabilities, and realities. Although the project faltered from the outset, it degenerated into a morass of patronage and corruption as state officials and Xavante leaders became coupled in an unseemly and uneven alliance. From this tense patron-client relationship, a disheveled state agency and a dependent indigenous people emerged, and the boundary between indigenous policy and indigenous politics further muddied.

In the conclusion, I explore changes in the legal status of indigenous peoples brought about with redemocratization and the Constitution of 1988. Moreover, I reflect on the legacy of indigenous-state relations in twentieth-century Brazil and propose a redefinition of the role of the state and its ties to indigenous peoples and other members of civil society.

It should be noted that I use the term "Indian"—which does not have a pejorative connotation in Brazil—as defined by Brazilian legislation, to refer to an individual who is a descendant of pre-Columbian peoples and who identifies with and is identified as belonging to an ethnic group whose cultural characteristics are distinct from national society. These "cultural characteristics," as this book shows, are not fixed, but rather relational and malleable. In interethnic settings, the terms *civilizado* (civilized) and *branco* (white) are often used interchangeably by both Indian and non-Indian alike. This popular usage is retained in the text, although these classifications, of course, are social constructs as well. I also follow the Brazilian custom of referring to indigenous leaders by their first name (either in Portuguese or Xavante). The spelling of Xavante (sha-VAN-te) has varied in Brazil and in English transliteration; I use the current Portuguese version, but retain alternative spellings in citations. The orthography of Xavante words, whose phonetic notation was developed by Summer Institute of Linguistics missionaries in the 1970s, has historical variants; in this study I have employed the spelling most commonly found in primary documents.

The relationship between the Brazilian state and the Xavante since contact illustrates William Roseberry's point that "what hegemony constructs, then, is not a shared ideology but a common material and meaningful framework for living through, talking about, and acting upon social orders characterized by domination."[69] This study, highlighting the struggles of Brazilian government officials, Indians, missionaries, elites, politicians, intellectuals, and social activists, looks at the way men and women lived through, talked about, and acted on state policy toward indigenous peoples. What follows is a multidimensional account of Brazilian political history that reveals the material and cultural foundations of the state, the contested and common ground on which it stands, and the breaches and patch-ups in the national edifice. It is an account in which indigenous people emerge as agents as well as victims of Brazilian nation building.

1

"The Base of Our National Character"

Indians and the Estado Novo, 1937–1945

In August 1940, Getúlio Vargas flew twelve hundred miles from the presidential palace in Rio de Janeiro to visit the Karajá Indians in Central Brazil. The Karajá, a responsibility of the federal Indian bureau, Serviço de Proteção aos Índios (SPI), received the presidential delegation with great pomp and ceremony at their village on Bananal Island. They performed "traditional" rituals and, with great patriotic flourish, sang the hymn to the Brazilian flag. Vargas, in turn, distributed knives, axes, and other tools to the Indians. Consonant with his image as "Father of the Poor," the president held a Karajá baby tenderly in his arms.[1] Observing the "simple lifestyle" of the Karajá, Vargas pondered how his government might "make use" of the Indians.[2]

With a trailblazing spirit, the president rode by horse around Bananal Island, cruised the Araguaia River, and camped along its shore. His search for adventure unquenched, Vargas announced his desire to reconnoiter the territory of the "extremely ferocious Xavantes." In the environs of the Araguaia and the Das Mortes Rivers in northeastern Mato Grosso, the Xavante, since the mid–nineteenth century, had killed encroachers and plundered their goods, terrorizing travelers, homesteaders, and indigenous groups such as the Karajá and Bororo. Vargas, the twentieth-century "pioneer," could dispense with worries. From the safety of his bimotor army plane, the president, with binoculars in hand, viewed the large thatch houses of an uncontacted Xavante village. The wonders of aeronautics facilitated journeys to places once inaccessible from the center of state power—although Vargas did claim that the Indians greeted the latest uninvited guests with a familiar response: shooting arrows and brandishing clubs.[3]

Undeterred by the Xavante's "ferocity" or the Karajá's "simple lifestyle," the president outlined his ambitious plans for transforming the west and its inhabitants. He vowed to demarcate indigenous reserves as mandated

Map 1. Central-Western Brazil and Indigenous Populations

by the Constitution of 1937, to parcel out land to *caboclos* (a polysemous term encompassing deculturated Indians, ethnically mixed populations, and local peasants), and to create agrarian colonies for homesteaders. Indigenous people, defined by the Civil Code of 1916 as "relatively incapable" in civil matters, would be shielded by the state from exploitation. The spi would scrupulously exercise its statutory guardianship or *tutela* over the Indians (administered since 1928), ensuring indigenous territorial defense and fair terms of labor and exchange.[4] In teaching Indians as well as caboclos to "understand the necessity of work" and "fixing men to the land," the state would groom productive and patriotic citizens.[5] The "problems" of isolation, indiscipline, and lack of civic-mindedness, after all, afflicted not only Indians but all who subsisted in the nation's hinterland.[6]

Vargas was the first Brazilian president to visit an Indian area, or the central western region of the country for that matter. Three years earlier, in 1937, he had dismissed Congress and disbanded all political parties, proclaiming an Estado Novo (New State) committed to national integration under the firm hand of the central government.[7] To undermine regional interests and oppositional elites, Vargas appointed *interventores*, federally designated state governors endowed with legislative powers. In 1938, Vargas instituted the Departamento Administrativo do Serviço Público (Administrative Department for Public Service, DASP), a central personnel agency for the federal civil service that sought to eliminate cronyism through competitive entrance examinations and that provided him with greater personal control over federal administrations.[8] The following year, he created the state's Departamento de Imprensa e Propaganda (Department of Press and Propaganda, DIP), entrusted with disseminating the ideological directives of his regime through cultural production and censorship.[9]

A master of political pageantry, Vargas embarked on his escapade to the Indians to codify the emergence of an all-powerful central government, much as he had presided over a public ceremony in which all local state flags were burned. As part of his multifaceted project to construct a new nation—more economically independent and inward-oriented, politically consolidated and socially unified, militarily fortified and geographically integrated—Vargas set his sights on its aboriginal inhabitants. A DIP cameraman who accompanied Vargas on his western junket filmed the images enshrined by the nationalist authoritarian regime: the long arm of the state extending into the backwoods to spearhead economic development while ensuring social justice; robust Indians, emblematic of native Brazilian stamina, uplifted by industrial goods yet tradition-bound; camaradarie between Indian and white on the western frontier (with Vargas the paragon of the *homem cordial*, or Brazilian bonhomie).[10]

That Indians had been summoned to the political stage by Estado Novo officials signified their symbolic importance for the regime. Indigenous people constituted a minuscule percentage of the Brazilian population: though Brazilian census statistics are notoriously flawed, of a total population of 41 million in 1940, only 58,000 individuals affirmed speaking an indigenous tongue at home.[11] Furthermore, they lived predominantly in the western and Amazonian hinterland—where many had fled to seek refuge from domination. This chapter examines some of the factors prompting their subpoena: the Estado Novo's effort to consolidate state power, commodify western territory, and foster national unity; elite invention of a historical narrative mapping the nation's origins and destiny; and preoccupations over Brazil's present-day racial makeup and military preparedness. All would have a bearing on the state's formulation of a cultural identity for Indians and a policy for their integration. For the state had assigned a momentous task to the Indians: to render the backlands productive, to thwart imperialist designs, and to safeguard Brazil's "ethnic formation."

The Lure of the West

The spotlight on the Xavante and their territory formed part of the Vargas regime's effort to popularize the March to the West, a state-led project to settle and develop Brazil's central western and Amazonian regions. Unveiled on the eve of 1938, the march mirrored other programs of the Estado Novo in its far-reaching and regimented endeavors at nation building. Despite immense national territory, Brazilian demographic concentration was overwhelmingly clustered near the littoral, with over 90 percent of Brazilians occupying roughly one-third of the country. The vast hinterland, principally the northern region (comprising the states of Amazonas and Pará and several federal territories in the Amazon region) and the central west (Mato Grosso and Goiás), remained sparsely populated. In Vargas's words, the march embodied "the true sense of Brazilianness," a remedy to the nation's skewed demographic distribution and uneven economic development.[12]

Several culprits accounted for the nation's lopsided condition. To start, a lack of navigable rivers and passable roads, conjoined with exorbitant overland transportation rates, isolated the central west from more economically dynamic areas and mired the region in poverty. Coastal mountains, extending from the northeast to the south, presented a serious obstacle to overland communications with the interior. Indeed, interior settlement of importance existed only in areas that were relatively accessible, located at the intersection of trade routes or in regions possessing readily marketable, high value-to-weight goods, such as the mining regions. Insalubrious conditions served as a disincentive as well.[13]

But the Brazilian west's economic stagnation owed to human as well as nature's ungenerosity. The Portuguese, unlike the Spanish in Mexico or Peru, did not inherit a native overland transport network, and few strides had been taken during the colonial period to build a trafficable series of roads.[14] The Portuguese mercantilist system, an alliance between commercial capital and the Crown, implanted a system of trading monopolies and privileges linking Brazil to the mother country. In the quest to export tropical commodities, the internal market lagged behind. Colonial cities, located principally along the coast, served as centers for the export of primary products and the import of manufactured goods, as well as military posts for defense and seats of civil and religious authority.[15] A mining boom in the central west in the eighteenth century contributed to demographic growth and urbanization in the interior, but with the exhaustion of the mines the region's economic and political importance faded.

With independence in 1822, little changed in Brazil's social structure. Under the empire (1822–1889), the nation continued to be controlled by groups linked to the export-import economy: landowners, merchants, slavetraders, and their clients. The features of traditional colonial society—slave labor, the patronage system, small urban populations concentrated in the main ports, and a predominantly rural population—remained firmly entrenched. With the abolition of the slave trade in 1850, a land law was enacted to ensure future access to labor by landowners. In mandating that public land could be acquired only through purchase—rather than traditional forms of acquisition such as squatting and royal grants—the imperial government restricted legal ownership of land in the west.[16] Hostility from uncontacted indigenous groups deterred western expansion as well.

The federalist system and liberal economy of the republic (1889–1930), which replaced the empire, further skewed regional growth. Under the highly decentralized political structure of the republic, individual states held sole control over the export tax, contracted foreign loans without federal approval, and gained jurisdiction over all public lands (aside from those deemed necessary for national defense) and subsoil rights. Coffee-producing states such as São Paulo and Minas Gerais, profiting handsomely from export taxes, prospered under such a system. By 1930, São Paulo, Minas Gerais, and Rio Grande do Sul accounted for almost 70 percent of all state revenues and had a per capita tax income more than three times that of the remainder of the country.[17] Mato Grosso and Goiás, whose volume of trade lagged far behind and whose population was too sparse to have electoral weight in the political deal making of the republic, sulked as poor cousins, federalism's castaways. In 1930, for example, only the southern region of Mato Grosso was accessible by rail from Brazil's more economically dynamic southeastern region, whereas the vast northern area of the state was bereft of such links.

In the aftermath of World War I and over the decade of the 1920s diverse sectors of society became disillusioned with the republic. The weakness of the central state, overwhelming dependency on coffee for export earnings and skewed economic development, pervasiveness of electoral fraud and patronage, absence or ineffectiveness of social welfare legislation, unpreparedness of the national army, and cultural obsequiousness to European styles spawned growing disaffection among disparate social groups. With the onset of the Great Depression, the export-oriented growth model based on the liberal principle of comparative advantage foundered in Brazil and other areas of Latin America. The republic came to an end with the revolution of 1930, led by Getúlio Vargas and comprising a diverse coalition of regional elites resentful of São Paulo's dominance in national politics, coffee growers disgruntled by the lack of government compensation for falling prices, and junior army officers discontent with the nation's limited military-industrial capacity.[18]

Over the course of the 1930s, the Brazilian state under Vargas would seek to centralize political power, assume greater responsibility for economic development and social welfare, and tighten control over regional elites.[19] From the crisis of oligarchic hegemony and fissure within the dominant class triggered in 1930, a more powerful state would emerge, allying with the bourgeoisie and, in particular, the industrial bourgeoisie, to ensure and expand relations of accumulation. The institution of the Estado Novo dictatorship in 1937 accelerated the process of political centralization, state-led industrialization and inward-oriented growth, with Vargas lashing out at the "evils" of both Marxism and liberalism. Through corporatist legislation and repression, federal intervention in local affairs, promotion of import-substitution industrialization, and placation of landed interests, the authoritarian regime sought to impose priorities and policies throughout national territory.[20] The incorporation of the west, spearheaded by the state-led March, embodied the Estado Novo's thrust toward "nationalist development."

To be sure, Vargas was not the first Brazilian political leader preoccupied with western expansion and national integration. At the time of Independence, Brazil's "founding father," José Bonifácio de Andrada e Silva, had advocated relocating the capital from Rio de Janeiro to the interior to open up roads, communication networks, and commerce. The republican Constitution of 1891 designated land in the central Brazilian planalto for the implantation of a new federal capital. Geographic remoteness, inadequate capital and technology, and political factionalism, however, anesthetized the project for nearly seven more decades.[21] If unsuccessful in uprooting the capital from its coastal perch, the republic could boast of linking Rio de Janeiro by telegraph to far-flung corners of the nation. From 1890 to 1915, the Comissão das Linhas Telegráficas, under the leadership of army engineer Cândido Mariano da Silva Rondon, would lay down lines connecting Rio de Janeiro to Mato Grosso and Amazonas.[22] During World War I, in a patriotic outpouring, national defense leagues were organized to protect the hinterland from foreign attack.[23]

The Estado Novo, rearticulating the relationship of the state to civil society, outstripped the republic's fledgling attempts at western expansion. Industrialization and the extension of social legislation to urban workers provoked increased urbanization as rural workers, denied access to land under Brazil's monopolistic landholding system, migrated to cities. Faced with the challenge of provisioning agricultural staples, rechanneling surplus labor, and quelling urban unrest, the Vargas regime promoted settlement of the western frontier. Indeed, since the Revolution of 1930, the state had sought to spearhead agricultural colonization through various political interventions aimed at resettling domestic workers and recontouring immigration policy.[24] The Departamento Nacional de Povoamento, created in 1930, sought to relocate unemployed urban workers to the interior, and the Constitution of 1934, constricting the entry of foreigners by quotas of national origin, granted preferential treatment to agriculturists.[25] In 1938, the Divisão de Terras e Colonização of the Ministry of Agriculture was formed, promoting agricultural colonization by Brazilian workers, or *trabalhadores nacionais*.

As Vargas stated, the nation need look no further than its own forgotten backyard, "to the vast and fertile valleys" of the west, to forge the "instruments of our defense and our industrial progress."[26] For Mato Grosso and Goiás, Estado Novo officials envisioned the creation of agrarian and livestock cooperatives comprised of the "recognizably poor."[27] State extension of credit, education, health care, and transportation networks would sustain western colonization, stanch rural exodus, and consolidate the nation as an organic whole. Its imposing presence in the west would mold "disciplined" workers and patriots.[28] The colonist, whose productive labor contributed to economic growth, would become a true citizen, endowed with social rather than political rights, and an esteemed member of the national community.[29] Founded on more egalitarian social bases, the settlement of the west would serve to offset the power of the traditional landed elite, offering the central government further leverage against oligarchic particularism.[30]

On his return from Bananal Island, Vargas met with the minister of agriculture, taking initial measures for a state-led colonization project in Goiás, one of six such Colônias Agrárias Nacionais founded in the central western, northern, and northeastern regions during the Estado Novo.[31] Through radio broadcasts, the Vargas regime's soapbox, officials encouraged settlers to go west.[32] In 1943, Vargas created the Instituto Agronômico do Oeste, an institute dedicated to improving agronomic techniques for Mato Grosso, Goiás, and Minas Gerais through research and instruction.[33]

The colonization of the sparsely populated hinterland fulfilled aspirations of the military, a key buttress of the Vargas regime. The revolution of 1930, backed by junior officers disillusioned with the republic's poor military-industrial capacity and weak central state, had triggered a turnover of the officer corps with rapid advancement of Vargas's supporters. Under the influence of European-trained officers and the experience of World War I, Brazilian military leaders held that modern wars would be "total wars," waged between nations rather than armies and requiring the mobilization of the entire population.[34] Axis expansionism led the military to envision the outbreak of another major international war, while, closer to home, the Chaco War between Bolivia and Paraguay (1932–1935) as well as a border dispute between Peru and Colombia (1932–1933) and skirmishes between Ecuador and Peru (1941) led military leaders to view anxiously the nation's unfortified hinterland.[35]

General José Pessoa applauded the March to the West, calling for a stronger military presence in Mato Grosso, whose "defenseless" borders with Bolivia and Paraguay rendered the region vulnerable in the case of war. He urged Vargas to deploy army engineers and air force officials to construct military barracks, roads linking the army command to the borders, and schools and clinics.[36] In *Projeção continental do Brasil*, Mario Travassos wrote of the geopolitical importance of western expansion in securing access to strategic headwaters in the Amazon basin and River Plate.[37] With the Estado Novo, the relationship between the armed forces and the Vargas government was further strengthened as the military bolstered the dictatorial regime and assumed a growing role in planning commissions, bureaucracies, and other state organs.[38]

The March to the West, as Alcir Lenharo has argued, conjured the image of a nation united, neutralizing or transcending conflicts of race, class, and region in its westward advance. Yet the reality was far less festive. To begin with, popular participation in the march, as in other regime initiatives, was restricted and regimented by government directives.[39] Moreover, in endorsing frontier colonization rather than agrarian reform and rural unionization, the march refrained from a frontal attack on entrenched power structures in the countryside. For although Vargas sought to subordinate the rural oligarchy to the central government, he appreciated the importance of agro-exports in financing industrialization and of landowners' exertion of social control during a period of socioeconomic flux. Rural workers were endowed under the Estado Novo with the rights to a minimum wage, annual paid vacations, labor contracts, and syndicalization, but limited enforceability of social welfare legislation and restrictive parameters for union organization vitiated such legal advances.[40] And although regime rhetoric about western expansion was overgenerous, fiscal investment in it was not: state expenditures privileged the southeastern urban industrial sector. These less glamorous aspects of Vargas's stylized "Western"—immunity of the rural oligarchy from structural change, authoritarian heavy-handedness, minimal funding for the march, and arrogation of indigenous and squatter territory—were kept out of the spotlight.[41]

Although the March to the West conformed to the Estado Novo's overall goal of centralizing power to promote capital accumulation while reconciling social conflict, its uniqueness lay in the populations and territories targeted as subjects of study, discourse, and control. Vargas had incorporated central Brazil and its peoples into the ideological repertoire of his regime—with music accompanying the show ranging from a Villa-

Lobos composition to a 1939 carnival song, "March to the West."[42] As always, Vargas received top billing. Without an audition, Indians were cast as heroes—albeit in need of a whiteface makeover for this national production.

Myth Making and Nation Building: Images of Indians and the West

The invention of historical traditions underlay state efforts to popularize the March to the West and to forge among Brazilians a shared memory of a heroic past. In grand theatrical style, the march commanded a staff of gifted scriptwriters such as Cassiano Ricardo, the DIP director in São Paulo. In his principal work, *Marcha para Oeste*, published in 1940 to great acclaim, Ricardo streamlined popular legends about the Brazilian frontier, crafted others, and stamped them all with the imprimatur of an authoritarian government bent on scavenging myths of origin for its nationalist project. Ricardo extolled the colonial bandeirantes, adventurer bands from São Paulo, whose territorial expansionism into the backlands—in search of gold and Indian slaves—represented the only authentic Brazilian "ideology." In contrast to the socially rigid, "feudal" coastal sugar plantations, Ricardo argued, the multiracial bandeirantes had helped construct a racially harmonious society based on small holdings and cooperativism.[43] Ricardo lavished special praise on Indians for helping lay the foundations of nation building. In imparting the keys to "nomadic" living and environmental adaptation, indigenous people ensured the expeditionaries' survival. Furthermore, Ricardo noted the role of indigenous women who had helped bridge "racial and social distances" through sexual relations with Luso-Brazilians.[44]

In idealizing the indigenous contribution to Brazil's sociopolitical formation, Ricardo showcased Indians as a valuable component of the national heritage. Nevertheless, in offering the bandeirantes as an inspirational model for present-day westward expansion, the DIP ideologue did not obscure his authoritarian and racist bent. Although he celebrated racial and cultural mixture, Ricardo insisted that the bandeirantes had succeeded because of the hierarchy maintained by the white man, whose "spirit of adventure and command" prevented his cohorts from slipping into anarchy.[45] Reflective of the Estado Novo's political project, Ricardo reviled the separatism of uncontacted Indian villages (and maroon communities) as "racial cysts" endangering the socioeconomic health of the nation.[46]   .

The state project to glamorize and subordinate the Indian found an eager proponent in Cândido Rondon as well. Rondon, the army engineer who headed the Comissão das Linhas Telegráficas and served as the first director of the SPI at its inception in 1910, took heart in the state's newfound concern with Indians and their "problems."[47] In 1939, Vargas appointed Rondon head of the Conselho Nacional de Proteção aos Índios (National Council for the Protection of Indians, CNPI), which was entrusted with promoting public awareness of native culture and state policy and serving as intergovernmental liaison for indigenous affairs.[48]

In a 1940 speech entitled "Bound for the West," disseminated by DIP, Rondon rhapsodized about Indians and the invaluable role the Brazilian state played in their integration. In Rondon's appraisal, "Of all the precious things that befall us in this new march to the West, all relevant to the greatness of Brazil, none surpasses the Indian." Friend, lover, guide, and warrior, the Indian had provided vital aid to the Portuguese in the settlement and development of Brazil. For example, recounting the seventeenth-century war against the Dutch in northeastern Brazil, Rondon underscored that Indians and their mixed-blood progeny had confronted not only the invaders but a craven Portuguese crown wont to surrender sacred Brazilian terrain. "They have given us the base of our national character," he exulted; "resistance, bravery, generosity, and modesty, contributed by the Indian to the formation of our people, is what we consider precious, as much in the past as it still is in the present."[49] The March to the West would allow Brazilians to mine from the uncontacted (hence uncorrupted) Indians their cultural essences: forbearance, chivalry, pride, cooperativism.

Both Rondon and Ricardo wove together myth and history in their grand narratives to naturalize present-day patterns of accumulation, social hierarchy, and state control. Bandeiras *had* been ethnically mixed, but there was scant historical substantiation that their commanders were pure "white." Indigenous people *had* fought in the colonial war against the Dutch, but others sided with the Dutch and, on Holland's withdrawal, bewailed their abandonment.[50] Indians *had* provided invaluable assistance to the Luso-Brazilians as trackers, hunters, porters, rowers, scouts, and sexual partners, yet this was only one aspect of Brazilian interethnic history.[51] Both Estado Novo officials glossed over or attenuated the violence that saturated frontier society. Ricardo downplayed the enslavement and relocation of indigenous peoples, touting the benefits of social "incorporation."[52] Both men recast as interracial love what, in reality, often consisted of the rape of indigenous women.[53] Both depicted indigenous interaction with outsiders as historically invariant rather than protean. Such truths were neatly swept under the carpet by government officials: they were unbecoming of the image of the noble savage, the benevolent state, and social harmony on the present-day frontier.

Eric Hobsbawm defines "invented tradition" as a set of practices that seeks to inculcate values and norms of behavior by repetition and implied continuity with a suitable historical past. He notes that the invention of tradition occurs more frequently when a rapid transformation of society weakens or destroys the social patterns for which "old" traditions had been designed.[54] The Vargas era, marked by import-substitution industrialization, political centralization, labor populism, rural-urban migration, frontier expansion, and World War II mobilization, offered fertile ground for the invention of historical traditions.[55] In romanticizing indigenous history—a history of struggle and collaboration, accommodation and resistance—Estado Novo officials employed one such artifice to legitimize the envelopment of Indian communities and territories.

The Cultural Production of Indianness:
The Return of the Native

Through formalization and pageantry, Estado Novo officials and intellectuals signified the cultural identities of both Indians and the state. New rituals and devices were invented, while older images were extended or adapted for new purposes. In 1943, consecrating a national icon, Vargas decreed 19 April the Day of the Indian. Over the following years, the Day of the Indian occasioned numerous civic events and public ceremonies. In a cultural blitz, the DIP organized museum exhibitions, radio programs, speeches, and films about the Indian.[56] The SPI created a film department to document indigenous traditions and transformations, and the CNPI (established by Vargas in 1939) assembled an ethnographic team to gather artifacts for a future Indian museum.[57] The ethnographic excitement regarding indigenous culture was noteworthy given its weak historical precedent in colonial and much of nineteenth-century Brazil.[58] The "anthropological" research of João Batista Lacerda, head of the National Museum in Rio de Janeiro from 1895 to 1915, had been limited to cranial measurements of Botocudo Indians that affirmed their purported intellectual inferiority and limited aptitude.[59] Of course, alongside the wonders of indigenous culture, the Estado Novo showcased the "benevolence" and expertise of the state in acculturating natives.

The Brazilian state was far from alone in these pursuits. Governments throughout Latin America championed *indigenismo*, a political and cultural movement aimed at fostering ethnographic understanding of indigenous peoples and noncoercive projects for their socioeconomic integration into the nation-state. The Day of the Indian, for example, had been promoted at the Pátzcuaro Congress in 1940, an international convention sponsored by the Mexican government. Indeed, the imposing monument of the Aztec leader Cuauhtémoc, given to the city of Rio de Janeiro by the Mexican government in 1922, inspired Brazil's own Day of the Indian festivities. But if Mexico spearheaded the continental indigenista movement, most notably with the organization of the Instituto Indigenista Interamericano, that movement found adherents as well as innovators in Brazil.[60]

A cluster of Indianist texts published in Brazil during the Vargas era reflects vigorous homegrown interest in indigenous peoples. Such intellectual production was facilitated by the reduced import capacity caused by progressive currency devaluations and the disruption of international trade, fueling expansion of the domestic book market.[61] But the publication of Indianist texts during a period of state intervention in all aspects of cultural production and conservation reveals political as well as economic bolsters.

In 1943, Angyone Costa, an archaeology professor at the National Historic Museum, published *Indiologia*, a paean to indigenous peoples. The Indian, according to Costa, had imparted to Brazilians "tameness, a delicateness in treatment, a certain irony that we dispense to people, kindness for animals, an acuteness for all things. To us also came strength in suffering, a contemplative tenderness for the land, excessive fondness for children, the sensitivity in which we become involved in our sympathy for the world that surrounds us."[62] But the historic claims extended further as intellectuals grappled with Brazil's national identity, questioning historic subordination to North Atlantic economy and culture and struggling to excavate the "real Brazil" from superimposed economic and political structures.[63] Zoroastro Artiaga, the director of the historical museum of Goiás, contended that the Brazilian Indian originated in the New World rather than the Old.[64] Affonso Arinos de Mello Franco argued that the egalitarianism of Brazilian Indians had contributed to the birth of political liberalism over which Europeans now claimed sole paternity.[65] In Brazil, as in other areas of Latin America, urban intellectuals ascribed indigenous identities and influenced the formation of political positions about Indians.[66]

A historical irony tinged such depictions: Indians, whose appellation had been ascribed by Europeans to people they believed to be Asians, were now being celebrated for their Americanness. Consecrating the native American, members of the intelligentsia during the Estado Novo muddied the Eurocentric conceptions of the nation's history and culture traditionally held by elites. The essence of Brazilianness had been redefined; it no longer flowed from across the Atlantic but oozed from the nation's soil, from its flora, fauna, and primordial inhabitants, and from the biological and cultural hybrids spawned there.

The ideological switch was hardly original. In the nineteenth century, authors José de Alencar and Antônio Gonçalves Dias trumpeted the birth of a distinctly national culture, with highly romanticized accounts of Indians and their coupling with whites.[67] Likewise, the award-winning essay presented by German naturalist Karl von Martius to the Instituto Histórico e Geográfico in 1844 highlighted the fusion of whites, Indians, and blacks as the foundation of Brazilian nationality.[68]

More recently, in the aftermath of World War I and the Week of Modern Art in São Paulo in 1922, modernist artists had rediscovered the Indian, albeit of a different stripe. Tarsila do Amaral had embraced the man-eating indigene in her painting *Abaporu* (1928), and poet Oswald de Andrade launched the "Anthropophagous Manifesto" that same year, assaulting imitativeness of European styles in Brazilian art and endorsing a synthesis of the autochthonous and the foreign.[69] Literati of the right-wing Verdeamarela movement, such as Plínio Salgado (future head of

Brazil's fascist Integralista Party), Menotti del Picchia, and Cassiano Ricardo "rejected" the European past altogether, penning nativist writings that glorified preconquest societies, endorsed the study of the Tupi language, and upheld the Indian as a national symbol.[70] In 1933, Gilberto Freyre hailed the indigenous contribution to Brazilian cultural formation and racial democracy in his highly influential *Casa grande e senzala*.[71]

Brazil, then, had a trend of paying tribute to the Indian that political leaders and nationalist thinkers during the Estado Novo could adapt to construct a nation.[72] Indeed, the very success of any government in forging a patriotic agenda derives from its ability to build on already present unofficial nationalist sentiments.[73] The Vargas regime, in fact, would incorporate or co-opt many intellectuals into the expanding state bureaucracy—such as Cassiano Ricardo, Menotti del Picchia, and Affonso Arinos de Mello Franco—imbuing the authoritarian regime with an aura of ideological legitimacy (and furnishing intellectuals with financial stability and political clout).[74]

Nevertheless, what specific nationalist purpose did Estado Novo rhetoric serve in hailing Brazil's small indigenous population and its contributions to Brazilian "national character"? Surely, as the motives behind Brazilian celebrations of the Indian varied over time, so too did their tone and timbre. Nineteenth-century nativism boasted separatism from Portugal, and romantic Indianist literature may have aimed to cloak the institution of African slavery.[75] During the Estado Novo, images of the Indian served to justify the arrogation of indigenous land and sociocultural subordination in the context of western frontier expansion. Moreover, the images allayed elite fears regarding the nation's racial composition and military unpreparedness during a period of world war, which Brazil would formally enter in 1942.

Situating Brazil outside of "Foreign Frameworks":
Celebration of Indians and Mestiçagem

In constructing images of the Indian, Estado Novo ideologues and intellectuals grappled with the legacy of scientific racism, which had been widely accepted by elites with slight moderations from 1888 to 1914.[76] During World War I and its aftermath, a patriotic surge led many to question or repudiate beliefs in the inferiority of nonwhites and the degeneracy of mixed bloods that boded so poorly for their nation. Confronted by the virulent scientific racism of Nazi Germany, Brazilian thinkers assailed compatriots who still affirmed white supremacist ideas.[77] In 1935, twelve prominent Brazilian intellectuals issued a manifesto against racism, which was seconded by the Brazilian Society of Anthropology and Ethnology in 1942.[78]

With Brazil's overwhelmingly multiracial population, Estado Novo officials were loath to broadcast an ideology demonizing all nonwhite Brazilians in its nation-building project—particularly when many influential families lacked lily-white pedigrees. As Angyone Costa taunted, regardless of the obsequiousness and pretensions of the elite, all Brazilians were considered by Europeans "as a people situated slightly above Negroids, below Yellows, and infinitely distanced from Whites." He called on the nation to forsake "foreign frameworks" and to cherish its indigenous roots.[79]

The nonwhite Brazilian would be defended, the immutability of race rejected, and the process of racial mixture celebrated. Upholding the character (and perfectibility) of the Brazilian Indian, the SPI clamored, "The indigenous soul is subject to the same passions to which is subject the European soul, displaying, however, superiority in temperance, in patient energy and even, we will say, in truth, even justice and charity."[80] Tributes to indigenous men lauded their "physical hygiene, comparable to the masculine beauty of the Greeks of the Olympics."[81] Out of the indigenous admixture to Brazil's bicultural makeup emerged a stonger nation. As anthropologist Roquette-Pinto asserted, "To contradict the opinion of those who believe in the bad influence of mixture for racial vitality, we will point to, among other examples, the population of Northeastern Brazil (Ceará, etc.), a region of big and strong families of courageous and active men, conquerors of the Amazon forest, all with some Indian and white blood."[82] Or, as *Cultura Política*, the mouthpiece of the Estado Novo, affirmed, "The constitutive traits of our character help us: we have the marks of all peoples and we will not be confused with any of them. It is possible that in Brazil a new man (*homem novo*) will emerge and with him a new age."[83]

Despite claims to homegrown authenticity, the racial discourse of the Estado Novo revealed quite the opposite, owing a great deal to "foreign frameworks." Just as the regime had borrowed heavily from a fascist corporatist model in its efforts to reorder labor relations, so too the Estado Novo retained a racialist paradigm that ascribed innate characteristics to social groups based on biological descent. But in an age-old practice, Brazilian elites adjusted "foreign frameworks" to domestic realities.[84] Reconfiguring doctrines of scientific racism, Estado Novo officials redefined which racial and ethnic groups were irremediable. The threat to national progress and defense lurked in the "inassimilable immigrant" who resided in Brazil (or might attempt to), hopelessly "imprisoned to their traditions of origin, with their flags, their anthems, and their use of customs . . . perturbing its [the nation's] ethnic formation."[85] Or it festered in "famished nations" searching for a dumping ground for their "excess population" in the Brazilian hinterland.[86] Indigenous people, on the other hand, had fortified Brazil since the Portuguese conquest through sexual and military alliances.[87] Indeed, Rondon and other army officials who staffed the spi championed military service as an "ideal" means to turn the Indian into "an efficient citizen."[88] Given the Indian's "love for his piece of land," love for Brazil was but "a simple extension."[89]

Herein was the Estado Novo's spin on indigenous incorporation within the context of frontier expansion and nation building. The Indian offered a sociocultural arsenal, a national asset at a time when Brazilian officials spoke of the nation's strength determined by the "proportion of men endowed with greater energy."[90] But the *better* Indian upheld by state officials would share these essences with other Brazilians through biological and cultural mixing, while welcoming the whitening influence of state power—including territorial arrogation. The state plan for indigenous populations was, therefore, segmentary. Protecting indigenous peoples from extermination, the spi would "impede the abnormal [premature] disappearance of the Indians through death, so that Brazilian society, in addition to the obligation to care for them, can receive in its breast the precious and integral contribution of indigenous blood."[91] This would allow the spi to achieve its ultimate goal: "We do not want the Indian to remain Indian. Our task has as its destiny their incorporation into Brazilian nationality, as intimate and complete as possible."[92]

The Indigenous "Problem" and the Solution

For all their nationalist cachet, Indians presented a thorny problem for government officials and elites. Hostile groups, such as the Xavante, thwarted capital accumulation on the frontier. Those beyond the grasp of the state bedeviled its fundamental functions to consolidate power and transform society through territorial control, taxation, conscription, and prevention of rebellion.[93] Indians predated the nation-state and, whether in theory or practice, challenged its institutions and traditions with alternatives to dominant socioeconomic structures and cultural values.[94] To commodify land and regulate Indian lifestyles, state officials sought to naturalize territorial usurpation and indigenous subordination by embracing Indians as proto-patriots. Another ideological tack of domination consisted in defining indigenous peoples as indolent children or potential turncoats requiring supervision.

The Indian's "brain is slightly evolved," asserted Army Colonel Themístocles Paes de Souza Brazil, "not being in satisfactory condition to assimilate in a complete way the education and other demands of our civilization."[95] Indeed, military concern with regulating indigenous communities in sensitive border areas most likely precipitated the transferral of the SPI to the Ministry of War between 1934 and 1939 (when it was returned to the administrative jurisdiction of the Ministry of Agriculture).[96] On a similar note, Ildefonso Escobar, onetime member of the Conselho Nacional de Geografia, railed that the Indian remained "naive and lazily contemplating Nature while all other Brazilians . . . work for the progress of the Nation."[97] The depiction of Indians as slouches was particularly damning under a regime enshrining an ideology of work, or *trabalhismo*, as constitutive and determinative of citizenship.[98]

The Civil Code of 1916 had defined indigenous peoples as "relatively incapable," ostensibly to provide oft-needed legal protection against fraud and exploitation. Yet such paternalism easily degenerated into condescension and abuse. Government pronouncements during the Estado Novo harped on the purported infantilism of Indians, whose full maturation would come about only through civic and vocational instruction. Consider, for example, the SPI's pronouncement in 1939: "The Indian, given his mental state, is a kind of big child to educate, very susceptible to receiving advice, praise, gifts, and other stimuli, to live and 'do well' and modify noxious habits. As in general they have good sense and are very reasonable to the people in whom they trust, it is almost always possible to convince them and improve them."[99] The infantilized Indian featured prominently as well in popular literature and pedagogical texts published during the Estado Novo.[100]

The transformation of the Indian from "a kind of big child" into model citizen was heralded by positivism, whose tenets informed many military as well as nonmilitary officials within the SPI. Upholding a hierarchical and paternalistic social order—epitomized in the maxim "Dedication of the strong to the weak, veneration of the weak for the strong"—positivism championed "scientific" authority, spiritual freedom, and elevation of the subaltern through education.[101] Positivism affirmed the ineluctable progression of societies from so-called stages of "fetishistic" primitivism to "scientific" rationalism. As Rondon, an orthodox positivist, stated: "The transformation of the savage is very slow . . . because time and careful dedication are required so as not to violate the natural laws which rule human life. The transformation of the fetishistic mentality to the theological and from the latter to the positivist demands a moral and social environment capable of acting on the soul of the catechized with moderation, without profound shock."[102]

The SPI proposed to shepherd the Indians on their evolutionary journey, employing suasion rather than coercion and vigilance rather than indifference to avoid "profound shock." Thus, the agency denounced colonial resettlement policies as traumatic to the indigenous "soul," endorsing reservation of ancestral land. With its incrementalist and pseudoscientific bent, the SPI envisioned nurturing the Indian in a hothouse: industrial goods and wisdom would be filtered in incrementally, the Indian would flourish and cross-pollinate with other Brazilians, and the most honorable and vigorous crop of humanity would be produced.

Nevertheless, SPI patience and "respect" for indigenous ways had its limits. Indigenous territorial claims and autonomy would have to be conscribed, sacrificed in the national interest. The nomadic lifestyle of hunter-gatherers had to give way to "rational" market-oriented activities, such as cattle raising and agricultural cultivation, and indigenous recourse to violence stanched. In defining indigenous identity and culture as immature and transitory—an evolutionary stage—the SPI could dispense with reserves adequate to sustain effectively the Indians' way of life and commodify outlying areas.[103]

Rondon presaged that in the golden future "emancipated Indians" would divide their reservation lands into individual parcels or even reside with non-Indians on the agrarian colonies that the government would establish as part of the March to the West.[104] Boaventura Ribeiro da Cunha, a member of the CNPI, elaborated on such a vision in *Educação para os selvícolas*. Cunha affirmed that the colonization and defense of the Brazilian hinterland required the collaborative effort of trabalhadores nacionais and indigenous peoples.[105] He endorsed the creation of agricultural colonies composed of separate but adjacent settlements of "Brazilindians" and peasants. Indian youths "overtaken by the spirit of imitation and curiosity" would inevitably seek to emulate their peers. Colonists, however, would aspire to the social cohesiveness allegedly regnant in Indian communities.[106] Ultimately, the "natural fusing" of Indians and "national ethnic elements" would contribute to the "solidification of the Brazilian social edifice."[107]

The Dual Legacy of Vargas

The Vargas regime, proponents cheered, had redeemed the downtrodden of the backlands, meriting the highest praise for its commitment to rural productivity, social welfare, and national integration.[108] At long last the Indians—"the modest but dedicated jungle worker, the true sentinel of the frontier, the vigilant soldier of the nation"—would be "comprehended and utilized" and "incorporated definitively as laborers for national grandeur."[109] Strong central government under the Estado Novo promised a new era of state assistance for "the most genuine Brazilians," hailed SPI Director José Maria de Paula in 1944.[110] As a daily reminder, a photograph of Vargas holding the Karajá toddler beamed from every Indian post in Brazil.[111]

Such protectionist language and imagery reflected the Estado Novo's pattern of conferring notions of citizenship and entitlement to previously disfranchised or marginalized social groups.[112] In this spirit of paternalistic goodwill, the Vargas regime ennobled the state's wards, imparting social and cultural prestige to Indian groups through their consecration as primordial Brazilians.

On the other hand, in promoting western frontier expansion, the regime would intensify invasion of indigenous land. State expenditures on indigenous education, health care, and land demarcation lagged far behind the rhetoric proclaiming indigenous uplift. Even the state's symbolic embrace of the Indian represented more of a bear hug. Smothered by government rhetoric, Indians struggled to articulate their material and cultural needs. Indeed, on the flip side of tutela and other paternalistic policies endorsed by the Vargas regime lurked the specter of government heavy-handedness. The state's redemption of indigenous people, dwelling on their putative infantilism and sloth, allowed for the appropriation of indigenous land and labor. The system of guardianship, fashioned to defend indigenous rights, easily gave way to the systematic disregard of Indian concerns in the formulation and implementation of state policy and attached to Indians the social stigma of immaturity and incompetence. This humiliating status could be legally removed only when Indians became "adapted to the civilization of the country."[113]

Despite the existence of over two hundred indigenous groups in Brazil, with varied histories, languages, cultural ecologies, political economies, and relationships to dominant society, the state had affixed to all a collective political/cultural identity as "Indians." In ascribing to indigenous peoples innate qualities as "Indians" based on biological determinism and cultural essentialism, Estado Novo officials continued to feature race (or to equate it with ethnicity) as an independent factor operating alongside distinct historical factors in shaping human capacities.[114] In retaining race as an explanatory device and autonomous determinant of sociocultural behavior, the very regime theoretically committed to racial and ethnic mixture had concretized a differential and stereotyped identity of "Indianness." The history of Indian-state relations under Vargas, then, confirms Gerald Sider's trenchant observation: although it is often believed that the expansion and consolidation of modern state power destroys or undermines prior cultural distinctiveness or generates distinctions in the context of seeking to divide and conquer, in fact ethnic group formation is often the product of "a much more complex, less specifically planned, and far more resistance-permeated process that we might call 'create and incorporate.'"[115]

Indigenous peoples would contend with the ambiguous images and policies popularized under the Estado Novo, the foundational era of the Brazilian national state, for decades to come. Though rich in ideological symbolism and contradiction, these constructions were belied by the historical and contemporary realities of most indigenous peoples. So, too, the self-styled image of the leviathan masterminding western expansion was wildly overinflated. Brazilian state formation on the frontier hurtled in a bumpy and conflictual process, snarled by limited state capacity, local elite opposition, missionary rivalry, and indigenous resistance. Indeed, contacting the "ferocious" Xavante was but one in a series of challenges faced by the developmentalist state in its project to reorder the sociopolitical landscape of the west.

2

"Pacifying" the Xavante, 1941–1966

Government efforts to contact the Xavante gained urgency with the deployment of the Expedição Roncador-Xingu (Roncador-Xingu Expedition), the centerpiece of the March to the West. Unveiled by Vargas in June 1943, the Roncador-Xingu Expedition was entrusted with various tasks: opening up lines of communication to the Amazon through central Brazil, building airstrips and roads, and establishing settlements along the headwaters of the Xingu River. Vargas decreed the expedition, organized by the war-time board Coordenação da Mobilização Econômica (Coordination of Economic Mobilization, CME), of "military interest" to the nation.[1]

The expedition was led by Colonel Flaviano de Mattos Vanique, chief of the presidential guard, as well as Antônio Basílio, a captain in the Força Aérea Brasileira (Brazilian Air Force, FAB). Established in 1941 along with the Ministry of Aeronautics, the FAB sought to establish an overland aerial route linking Rio de Janeiro to Manaus and Miami.[2] As part of its planned 1,800-kilometer trajectory from the Goiás–Mato Grosso border northwest to Santarém, Pará, the Roncador-Xingu Expedition projected the establishment of a camp on the banks of the Das Mortes River and a trek through the Sierra do Roncador—a region inhabited by Xavante.[3]

In October 1943, the Roncador-Xingu Expedition was placed under the aegis of the newly created Fundação Brasil Central (Central Brazil Foundation, FBC). The FBC mandate called for the construction of schools, hospitals, roads, and airstrips in central Brazil. As an *autarquia*, a semi-autonomous federal bureau, the FBC enjoyed independent resources and decision-making capacity and jurisdiction over land that had been ceded by state governments for up to ten years. The FBC sought to persuade São Paulo industrialists to create private companies in the region to develop local resources and promote immigration. Four enterprises, including a river boat line for eastern Amazonia, were eventually established under the foundation's auspices.[4] The agency's budget in 1945 would be CR$23 million.[5]

Vargas appointed João Alberto Lins de Barros FBC president. Two decades earlier, *tenente* Lins de Barros had marched through central Brazil under different circumstances: as a member of the "Prestes Column" of rebellious junior army officials retreating from Republican forces after an uprising in São Paulo against the oligarchic government in 1924.[6] Lins de Barros had been struck by the potential of Goiás and Mato Grosso, lamenting that its "cheap and abundant land" lay idle because the region lacked "men with initiative."[7] Now, as president of the FBC, he stood poised to change the region's destiny.

With great fanfare, the small, fifty-man team of the Roncador-Xingu Expedition—recruited in São Paulo, Rio de Janeiro, and the central west—set out for a hinterland "more distant than Africa."[8] In a festive sendoff from São Paulo, the expeditionaries received generous donations of canned meat, fuel, and camping equipment. *Paulista* women bestowed on them a Brazilian flag hand-sewn with gold trim, which they were enjoined to set atop the "legendary Sierra do Roncador," a modern-day "ceremony of possession" of indigenous territory.[9] In September 1943, the expedition established camp at Barra Goiana, a small gold-mining settlement at the juncture of the Araguaia and Garças Rivers on the Goiás–Mato Grosso border; in a gesture symbolic of the state's efforts to redefine the cartography of central Brazil, Lins de Barros renamed the location Aragarças.[10] From Aragarças, the expedition proceeded en route to the Das Mortes River (see Map 2).

The adventurers experienced many of the hardships of their colonial predecessors: hunger, sickness, inclement weather, pesky critters, and infighting. Patriotic pep talks roused the team to proceed in their overland trek, yet several deserted.[11] To boost morale, the adventurers composed songs: one ballad vowed, "Upon crossing the Sierra do Roncador / if I meet the Xavantes / I will show my valor."[12] The opportunity would soon arrive. By February 1944, having cleared nearly three hundred kilometers of trail through the shrubbery of Mato Grosso, the expeditionaries had reached the Das Mortes River. They named their camp Xavantina in homage to the fearsome Indians lurking across the river in the region surrounding the Sierra do Roncador—a region they would soon traverse.[13]

The Xavante's local reputation was legendary. Because the Indians ambushed interlopers, people feared to camp overnight on the west bank of the Araguaia from Bananal Island to the Garças River.[14] As a Protestant

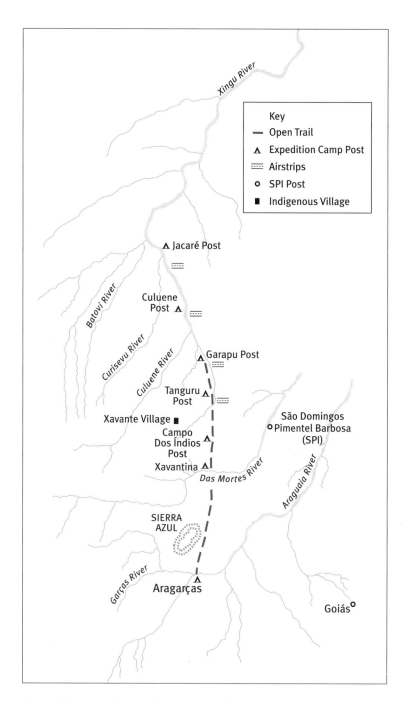

Map 2. Itinerary of Roncador-Xingu Expedition

missionary who traveled down the Araguaia in the 1920s registered: "They are a constant menace to travellers on the Araguaia and lately a man and a woman were clubbed to death while gathering honey on their side of the river. Their hand is against every man's and no one has ever fallen into their power and come back to tell the tale."[15] In 1930, Alencarliense Fernandes da Costa, the SPI inspector in Goiás, spoke of the grave danger to travelers on the Araguaia as well as to "our Karajás," attacked near the government post at Bananal Island. Da Costa lamented that the shortage of funds hampered the SPI from resolving the "anguishing problem of pacifying the Xavantes."[16]

But if Indian belligerence had obstructed central Brazil's development, the nation need fret no longer. The Estado Novo, whose functionaries rushed in where others feared to tread, had now arrived with the panacea for the backlands. Besides, "ferocious" Indians like the Xavante were not really so deep down (had not Indians, as Rondon stated, "given us the base of our national character"?); they had been transmogrified by "white" cruelty. As Lins de Barros noted, "Probably it is the whites' fault that the Xavantes withdrew from civilization, to which they have never returned until this day."[17] With proper ("white") polish, applied by state officials, the Indians' pristine essence would sparkle anew. The first step was the delicate task of "pacification," the term used by the SPI to denote the establishment of peaceful contact with a hostile indigenous group.

This chapter explores the historical context surrounding the "pacification" of the Xavante, which catapulted the Indians from local notoriety to national and even international renown. As the objectives of federal intervention in the backlands were multifold—the elimination of interethnic violence, the commodification of indigenous land, and the centralization of state power—the historical verdict on state policy remains divided. Official accounts celebrate the martyrdom of public servants who sacrificed their comfort and even lay down their lives to defend Indians from settler attack; revisionists decry the subordination of indigenous land claims and lifestyles to state domination, insidiously couched in protective language.[18] This chapter assesses the merit of traditional and revisionist accounts, yet challenges the monumentalization of the state present in both. It probes the myriad sites of contestation on the Mato Grosso frontier and in the corridors of state power.

The centralized state touted by Vargas masked more than misalignment among federal agencies; it glossed over the nitty-gritty of local politics. The SPI effort to consolidate power in northeastern Mato Grosso would prove fitful, challenged by the Xavante, local settlers, and missionaries. Although the state could claim some success, the difficulties encountered foreshadowed challenges to its hegemonic aspirations. Indeed, the very cohesiveness of the SPI's integrationist project would erode as critics bemoaned the sociocultural impact of state-led western expansion on indigenous peoples and clamored for their cultural preservation.

"Pacification" and the Mato Grosso Frontier

The SPI prided itself on mastering the art of "pacification" through nonviolence, even at the cost of self-sacrifice. The agency's motto, frequently incanted, was "Die if necessary; never kill." The "pacification" of the Xavante would follow standard procedures. First, the SPI would establish "attraction" posts in the vicinity of the Xavante to contact the Indians and to bar or remove from the region civilizados with "vices and antisocial habits."[19] Such interlopers, according to the SPI, derailed the delicate process of attraction, as the Indians, unable to distinguish between evildoers and well-wishers, would shun all forms of contact. Next came the protracted *namoro*, or "courtship," of the Indians. The SPI would provision crops and distribute tools, knives, combs, mirrors, and other gifts, "facilitating and giving comfort to the life of the tribe."[20] Apprehending the goodwill of the state, the boons of Brazilian society, and the reward for renouncing violence, the Indians would sue for peace.

To be sure, the SPI's insistence on peaceful contact and gradual integration diverged from official indigenous policy employed by other Latin American nations during late nineteenth- and early twentieth-century frontier expansion. The Argentine army, during the "Conquest of the Desert" in 1879–1880, destroyed Indian communities, dispersing inhabitants and seizing captives to serve households in Buenos Aires.[21] The Mexican government's "pacification" of the Yaqui would culminate under the dictatorship of Porfirio Díaz with the massive deportation of the Indians from Sonora; most would end up as virtual slave laborers on the henequen plantations of the Yucatán.[22] Notwithstanding, the Brazilian state's official commitment to nonviolence and gradual integration was predicated on command of resources, authority, and political consensus on the frontier. In fact, SPI functionaries, laboring in remote areas with poor infrastructure and limited funds, contended with settler hostility, missionary rivalry, and indigenous resistance.

Long before Getúlio Vargas appropriated the west in a state-led nationalist crusade, others had begun marching to Mato Grosso to the beat of a different drummer. Indeed, political initiatives by the state had never been indispensable in promoting migration to the frontier, given the socially unjust patterns of land and labor in Brazil.[23] Since the eighteenth century, settlers had arrived in the region in search of gold and cattle pasture as well as refuge from slavery. More recently, after a long economic downswing since the late colonial period, northeastern Mato Grosso began a slow recovery in the first decades of the twentieth century with the discovery of diamonds in the Garças River. In 1924, a group of *garimpeiros*, or miners, set up camp at Barra do Garças, to the south and east of Xavante territory, and later that year the first commercial firm arrived.[24] In 1936, the state government officially recognized Barra do Garças as a town, appointing its first judge and notary.[25] To be sure, Barra do Garças was a rough-and-tumble place where many arrived with inflated hope and left with broken dreams—and limbs.

In 1935, Armando de Arruda Pereira, a paulista industrial engineer and member of the Rotary Club of Brazil, sailed down the Araguaia River to scout out its commercial potential, recording his impressions of the area. Sparse settlements dotted the river's banks in northern Mato Grosso, composed predominantly of migrants from the northeast and the neighboring states of Pará and Goiás. Some planted crops and raised cattle, but most subsisted primarily on fish and wild game; all lacked access to education and health care. From the exchange of animal skins, settlers acquired salt, sugar, cigarettes, coffee, bullets, fishing hooks, and clothes from riparian travelers and peddlers.[26] Although Pereira envisioned the Araguaia region transformed by fluvial trade and communication, the backwater portended no such grandeur.

One settlement along the river was located in the midst of territory claimed by the Xavante. In 1934, a group of eleven men, led by Lúcio da Luz, sailed upstream from Pará in search of pasture, establishing the settlement of Mato Verde, to the west of Bananal Island. Twenty-three families—relatives of the original settlers—arrived thereafter with livestock.[27]

Yet Xavante attacks harried the scattered population of peasants, ranchers, goldminers, missionaries, and other Indian groups in northeastern Mato Grosso. In 1935, the Xavante killed the eleven-year-old son of a worker at the Salesian mission at Merure.[28] In retribution, the child's father and grandfather, together with a gang of eighteen men, shot three Indians to death and set their village afire.[29] Similarly, the SPI accused Luz of killing Xavante as well as other homesteaders whose deaths he attributed to the Indians. Clearly, these settlers had their own notions of how to "pacify" Indians.

To establish peaceful contact with the Xavante, the SPI ordered the withdrawal of Luz, charged with inciting interethnic violence as well as usurping indigenous land. The agency asserted that Luz had seized land that "maybe the Indians would prefer for their future concentration."[30] In 1942, the SPI succeeded in removing Luz provisionally from the area. Although he telegraphed an appeal to Vargas bemoaning his persecution by SPI officials, he was rebuffed.[31]

The SPI's efforts to defend the Xavante from Luz highlight the agency's role in safeguarding Indian communities from settler attack. Revisionist works harping on the repressive nature of Brazilian state power overlook or downplay the importance of such protection for indigenous communities. Yet, notwithstanding commitment to the physical safety and integrity of indigenous communities, the state's defense was far from openended. The SPI's indictment of Luz is telling. Luz had violated the orderly process of frontier expansion and capital accumulation envisioned by the state. For only *after* the Xavante received "reserved and secured areas for farming" would the state and the civilizados "become owners of the excess lands of extreme wealth which they [the Indians] had dominated and defended with bravery."[32] Indigenous "preference" would dictate the "future concentration" of communities in their ancestral regions, a token of the state's "respect" for indigenous peoples. Yet, in "concentrating" indigenous people on small reserves and commodifying outlying areas, the state discounted larger land claims; it dismissed the importance of an extensive territorial domain—or, as anthropologists have termed it, a habitat—in sustaining an indigenous community's welfare. "Pacification" thus entailed more than the state's monopoly over violence on the frontier: it signified the repudiation of indigenous lifestyles and territorial claims as well.[33]

Rivals for Glory: The Lure of "Pacification"

Interethnic violence presented the SPI with a dilemma: although strife legitimized the SPI mandate, its persistence tarnished the agency's image. Consequently, successful conflict resolution gravely concerned the SPI, as its reputation hinged on it. Chronically strapped for funds, the beleaguered SPI faced adversity on all fronts: aside from hostile Indians, there were ill-disposed local elites, nettlesome missionaries, and vociferous skeptics.

With its corps of military officers and engineers, the SPI claimed exclusive knowledge of the "backland and military operations of defense" that the "pacification of Indians demanded."[34] These "scientific" methods to establish peaceful contact with indigenes were hardly SPI innovations. In fact, since the colonial period missionaries and government officials had employed nonaggression and gift-giving to contact and subordinate indigenous people.[35] But SPI self-congratulation served various purposes. It reinforced the image of an omnipotent and benevolent state whose know-how and capability alone could ensure the Indians' well-being and the orderly process of frontier expansion. Successful "pacifications," feathers in the SPI's cap, were brandished when detractors accused the agency of ineffectualness.[36] Furthermore, for the sertanistas ("backlands experts") in the SPI, such undertakings glorified their manliness and increased their "symbolic capital."[37] Implicit in sertanista swagger was that "pacification" represented a manly art and the backlands a masculine domain where real men could prove their mettle.[38] Indians—feminized by the SPI language of courtly love as well as by the Civil Code (which collapsed them with married women as "relatively incompetent")—could not but surrender their maidenhead to such unremitting advances.

Following the revolution of 1930 that first brought Vargas to power, the SPI budget had been more than halved. However, with the March to the West, the agency assumed greater importance for the Vargas regime. By 1944, its annual budget was CR$3.7 million, the second highest in its thirty-five-year history.[39] Indeed, tax jurisdiction, revised by the Constitutions of 1934 and 1937, succeeded in increasing the federal government's share of public sector revenue from 51.2 percent in 1930 to 55.7 percent in 1945.[40]

Nevetheless, SPI officials faced rivals who also sought to contact the Xavante, threatening to steal the agency's thunder. In the 1930s, Hermano Ribeiro da Silva and Willy Aureli led different bands of paulista adventurers to the Xavante region seeking renown, publishing various sensationalist books on their raids and exploits.[41] But the SPI's most persistent challengers were the Salesian missionaries.

Since their invitation in 1894 by the Mato Grosso government to proselytize the Bororo Indians, the Salesians had received large tracts of public land at Merure and Sangradouro, to the southwest of Xavante territory, and acquired considerable influence in the state. Aside from the prospect of converting the Xavante, the Salesians expressed interest in the economic potential of their territory.[42] Moreover, the Xavante had clashed with Bororo and attacked the mission at Merure.[43]

In 1933, two Salesians—João Fuchs, a Swiss, and Pedro Sacilotti, a Brazilian—established a station at Santa Terezinha within Xavante territory to contact the "warrior and sanguinary tribe." Separating from "relatives, friends, and nation to obey the manifest will of God," Fuchs and Sacilotti braved hunger and thirst to contact the "heathen."[44] Plying the environs of the Das Mortes River, the missionaries erected wooden crosses and sprinkled gifts to broadcast their message of salvation and goodwill. For more than a year the Xavante eluded them, until one day, in November 1934, they spied from their boat two indigenes drinking water at the river's edge. When the Indians retreated into the bush, Fuchs and Sacilotti hurried after them. The fathers never returned. The subsequent day, the missionaries' assistants found their bodies stripped naked with their skulls crushed. One Xavante community had sent a stern message to encroachers, but the Salesians reveled in such martyrdom. "Their blood," the order vowed, "will be a fecund seed" for the "conversion of these very Xavantes."[45]

Hipólito Chovelon, a French Salesian, took up the banner of his slain comrades, establishing a hut at a site he named São Domingos on the east bank of the Das Mortes River. Appealing to federal and state officials for assistance in "making the Xavante Indians friends and good Brazilians," Chovelon emphasized his contribution to the March to the West.[46] In 1940, the Ministry of Education and Health gave the Salesians a subsidy of twenty contos de reis for the purpose of contacting and educating the Xavante.[47] The following year, the state of Mato Grosso ceded land to the mission in the Das Mortes region with tax exemption for ten years. In 1941, Foreign Minister Oswaldo Aranha presented to Vargas a proposed accord between the Brazilian government and the Vatican, granting religious missions tax exemption, authorization to acquire lands in border areas, and an expanded role in the process of indigenous integration.[48]

The warming of church-state relations, after decades of ill will under the republic, was one of the hallmarks of the Vargas era. Whereas the Constitution of 1891 had officially stripped the Catholic Church of political privilege, sociocultural authority, and state subvention, Vargas pursued strategic alliance with church leaders, manipulation of Catholic iconography, and harnessing of clerical anticommunism to shore up political legitimacy. Although the Constitution of 1934 maintained the division between church and state, it granted far greater clerical influence over marriage, education, and the military and allowed for state subvention of the Church "in the collective interest." Under the Estado Novo, the Vargas regime continued to formalize and deepen the close relationship between church and state.[49]

The missionary advance, however, was anathema to the SPI. Brazilian law did not bar missionaries from catechizing Indians, but the SPI retained strict control over access to indigenous populations. The presence of the Salesian missionaries—many of whom were foreigners—among indigenous peoples had never sat well with leading SPI officials, with their nationalist mission, positivist anticlericalism, and hegemonic pretensions.[50] (Other government bureaus displayed less antagonism toward missionaries, belying the professed unity of "the state" in policy making toward indigenous peoples.) Assailing the proposed treaty with the Holy See as an affront to national sovereignty, the SPI prevailed on the Foreign Ministry to scrap the plan. But the nuisance of the Salesians, ogling the Xavante and appealing to other government ministries for funding, still had to be confronted.

Officials at the SPI seized on bungled "pacification" efforts to shore up their anti-Salesian arsenal. Impugning missionary masculinity and truthfulness, one SPI report noted: "Any trips down roads commonly traveled even by women, the Salesians transform into ['pacification'] expeditions and describe emotionally the suffering of the 'Missionaries' who dare to carry them out."[51] Blaming the death of Sacilotti and Fuchs on their "imprudence, negligence, and tactlessness," Alberto Jacobina, the

SPI inspector in Goiás, asserted that the Salesians lacked the "necessary moral disposition, that is the caution and humility which any functionary of the Official Service [SPI] customarily employs." He also railed that SPI efforts would now be hampered because the Xavante, fearing retribution, would evade contact with civilizados.[52]

Charges against the Salesians mounted. The SPI challenged the ability of foreign missionaries, with their "racial prejudices against Indians and against Brazil" and their belief in "the superiority of their Nation," to instill in the Indians "feelings of Brazilian nationality."[53] Just as Estado Novo officials questioned the patriotism of German clergy in southern Brazil, SPI officials argued that missionaries could never be entrusted with "nationalizing" the Indians.[54] In fact, the history of Salesian commitment to proselytizing Indians suggested otherwise. Pedro Malan, the Salesian inspector in Brazil earlier in the century, yearned to see Indians fortify "the nation, of which they are the true owners, and which they will come to love, defend and illuminate."[55]

The SPI further accused the Salesians of appropriating indigenous lands. The charge was not baseless, as missions were often granted indigenous territory by state governments, although the SPI showed like-minded disregard for indigenous land claims.[56] But the SPI's conclusions were alarmist and incendiary: "the assault of Father Chovelon" formed part of "the plan to take possession of Brazil by the Vatican proceeding through the Jesuits, the Salesians, and other religious orders especially linked to the Pope."[57] Branding missionaries ne'er-do-wells who stymied contact, incited violence, and usurped indigenous land, the SPI would exclude the Salesians from official "pacification" efforts on the Das Mortes River.

In fact, SPI officials overestimated state capability and underestimated missionary resolve, not to mention indigenous agency. A decade later the SPI would concede its limitations in controlling interethnic violence and fostering capital accumulation on the Mato Grosso frontier, delegating to missionaries (Catholic and evangelical) a more prominent role in "civilizing" the Xavante. Indeed, Xavante would enlist missionary backing in defense of their communities' well-being and exploit the rivalry between bureaucrat and cleric to leverage consumer goods and greater autonomy.

In the meantime, the SPI had its own image to patch up. In 1941, a small SPI team, headed by Genésio Pimentel Barbosa, set out to "pacify" the Xavante. The contingent, which included two Xerente Indians who served as interpreters, established their base at Chovelon's disused hut at São Domingos. Crossing the Das Mortes River into the Sierra do Roncador, the team consistently deposited tools, clothes, and other goods for the Indians.[58] Undoubtedly, they took heart when the Xavante began to retrieve the offerings. But the glory of "pacifying" the Xavante was not to belong to Pimentel Barbosa either. In November 1941, he and five of his assistants were bludgeoned to death by the Indians.[59] In a chilling rebuff, the Xavante had signaled opposition to the state's intrusion on their terrain and antipathy toward their Brazilian "brothers."

Like the Salesians, the SPI beatified its fallen. Pimentel Barbosa had died true to the SPI's nonviolent credo, victim of a humanitarian mission.[60] Under no circumstance were reprisals against the Indians warranted. Yet how would government officials who spoke of indigenous affability and interethnic harmony explain such belligerence? Like his noble counterpart, the ignoble savage too had a long history in Brazil dating back to the Portuguese conquest.[61] The dichotomy stemmed from Europeans' ambivalence toward their own societies which they projected onto indigenous populations—as well as from the varied response of indigenous peoples toward Europeans.[62] Both figures continued to command credibility among the Brazilian populace.[63] The Vargas regime, in fashioning the image of the Indian as primordial Brazilian citizen awaiting state redemption, would adapt these tropes to its political project.

When the SPI acknowledged the "ferociousness of our Indians," such as the Xavante, it blamed civilizados for provoking indigenous aggression. As Rondon stated, following the murder of Pimentel Barbosa, "The Indian is a docile creature of primary intelligence, who only requires mild methods to surrender to our appeals. I can only, therefore, attribute the thoughtless gesture by the Xavantes to some reprisal . . . which has made them declare war on civilizados."[64] Such a viewpoint protected the hallowed image of the noble savage: by nature "tame and affectionate," the Indians could not tolerate what "in their understanding constitutes an affront or a lack of respect."[65] Yet in reducing the conflictual manner of frontier matters to a matter of conflictual frontier manners, the state stripped Indians of the complex socioeconomic and political directives that marked their interaction with outsiders. Indigenes were ciphers, either deranged by civilizado malevolence or redeemed by its kindness.

The March to the West Confronts the Xavante Roadblock

In 1944 the SPI assigned a seasoned sertanista, Francisco ("Chico") Meireles, to the Das Mortes region to oversee the "pacification" of the Xavante.[66] Establishing camp on the Das Mortes River at São Domingos (renamed Pimentel Barbosa in memory of his ill-fated predecessor), Meireles was accompanied by a small team that once again included several Xerente. To dispel Xavante fears of retaliation, Meireles chose the very site of the massacre to leave offerings of industrial goods. The team's work, however, was not easy: transportation links were precarious and supplies, shipped by boat, were often lost or delayed and invariably expensive. Forlorn in the cerrado, facing inadequate finances and a hostile indigenous group, the SPI's "pacification" team could not perform miracles overnight.

By the time the Roncador-Xingu Expedition stood at Xavantina on the banks of the Das Mortes River poised to blaze a trail through Xavante territory, the SPI had still not established peaceful contact with the Indians. Anxiety gripped the expedition. Colonel Vanique enjoined his men never to wander off alone. A chronicler of the expedition, Acary de Passos Oliveira, attributed its first fatality to a gunshot wound precipitated by a heated discussion between nervous team members about the likelihood of a Xavante attack.[67]

The volatility of the situation worried the SPI. A horde of individuals from a much publicized, nationalistic undertaking would be encroaching on Xavante territory, untrained in the SPI's "pacification" tactics.[68] The SPI was under intense pressure to establish peaceful contact with the Xavante, and lots of people were watching. In June 1945, Vargas would return to the central west, visiting FBC bases at Aragarças and Xavantina in the company of top government officials and the press. The president praised the "fearless patriots, who felled impenetrable sertões, the goldminers and sertanistas, who conquered wild regions, transforming them into promising nuclei."[69] But despite the chauvinistic rhetoric, "promising nuclei" were unassured so long as the SPI failed to achieve its goal of "pacifying" the Xavante.

In a mutual agreement, the SPI secured the technical assistance of the FBC to contact the Indians, while the Roncador-Xingu Expedition pledged adherence to the agency's policy of nonviolence before proceeding.[70] Members of the expedition would experience tense moments in July 1945 while clearing a path through Xavante territory. In one incident recounted by Cláudio and Orlando Villas Bôas, the expedition's most renowned participants, two startled men fired shots into the air on meeting up with a band of Xavante warriors; the Indians reciprocated with a volley of arrows. Three days later, the contingent also fired overhead shots to ward off a surprise attack by twenty to thirty Indians.[71]

The logistic support provided by the FAB facilitated SPI efforts to pinpoint the location of Xavante villages, avoid casualties, and plot a strategy for contact. Aerial reconnaissance offered invaluable assistance to ground teams, distinguishing the March to the West from previous patterns of western expansion.[72] Since 1930 three aircraft assembly plants had been installed in Brazil, and the Correio Aéreo Militar was founded in 1931 (consolidated into Correio Aéreo Nacional in 1941).[73] Moreover, FAB would receive more than three hundred airplanes from the United States under the war-time Lend-Lease program.[74]

Aeronautics also offered new possibilities for the media, which accompanied the Roncador-Xingu Expedition in its foray into Xavante territory and projected the Indians from local to nationwide legend.[75] The most eye-catching accounts were the photojournalistic spreads of David Nasser, a Brazilian journalist, and Jean Manzon, a French photographer, which were published in the magazine *O Cruzeiro* and worldwide.[76] Manzon's photographs, shot from an FAB plane, captured all of the requisite images: intrepid state officials trekking through the Mato Grosso wilderness, and Xavante warriors—described alternately as "bronze giants" "red devils," and "the last unknown savage tribe of Brazil"—hurling projectiles at the aerial invaders.[77] Indeed, air power undoubtedly disquieted the Indians, whose testimonies recall: "When we saw the airplane for the first time, the children were scared and hid in the grass . . . fleeing into the river also. They were frightened. Really frightened."[78]

In his 1945 report, Meireles noted that the Xavante had gathered manioc from the SPI's plot and kept free of overgrowth the area where gifts had been deposited.[79] In August 1946, after nearly two years of sustained SPI "courtship," Xavante men "of extraordinary athletic" build beckoned to Meireles's team. On hand were SPI photographers to immortalize the climactic moment when "the Indian warrior" contemplated face to face "the fearless pacifier," a testament to interethnic harmony and state supremacy.[80] A "medicine man" sprinkled the SPI team with a strange white powder and "the Chief," Apoena, offered Meireles three arrows and cotton necklaces as a token of friendship. Meireles, motioning to the Indians, pledged "any assistance they might require," whereupon the Xavante began "wrangling over our knives, axes, sickles, cauldrons, pots and other objects which roused their attention, such as cameras, revolvers, wrist watches, hats and matches."[81]

The first peaceful contact between the SPI and the Xavante occasioned the greatest deluge of literature on the Indians in their history. The journalist Lincoln de Souza, who accompanied the initial encounters with the Xavante, penned two books on his experiences; his colleague Sylvio da Fonseca published another; and the filmmaker Genil Vasconcelos produced a one-hour documentary in homage to Chico Meireles and other "bandeirantes of the twentieth-century" containing footage of the "pacification" and subsequent interactions.[82] The Xavante had become the first Brazilian indigenous group marketed by the mass media.

Although Vargas had been deposed by the military in October 1945 amid calls for redemocratization, he could nevertheless take pride in the transformations that the Estado Novo had wrought. An article published in *Time* noted that, after a century of war, the Xavante had been conquered by the government's "patience, suffering, and love," no longer standing "in the path of Brazil's great dream: 'the March to the West.'"[83] In an essay published in the journal of the Interamerican Indigenist Institution, *América Indígena*, SPI old-timer Amilcar Botelho de Magalhães exulted that the "glorious victory" of "pacification" echoed throughout Brazil and the world in proving "the efficacy of the suasive methods of attracting Indians to live together with us, without useless and inhuman violence."[84] Flush with victory, the SPI predicted that "sooner or later on a tall and narrow flagpole, erected on Xavante lands, the green-and-yellow [Brazilian] flag will be hoisted, to the sound of the national anthem sung by dignified and proud Xavante children, on a day of national commemoration."[85]

Crowning years of federal intervention and propaganda, the festivities surrounding "pacification" overstated the state's achievements and potential. To begin with, in deeming the exchange between Apoena and Meireles the "pacification" of the Xavante, the Brazilian government reinforced the idea that the Indians lacked their own initiatives for contacting outsiders—whether bureaucrat, missionary, or settler.[86] Apoena's community certainly saw things differently: they believed that *they* had "pacified" the whites.[87] How else could the turnabout of events be explained whereby after decades of unbridled hostility by the *waradzu*, as non-Xavante were referred to, small bands of peacemakers suddenly offered up gifts? Surely it had been the power of the Xavante's *rómhuri* ("magic") that had elicited such goodwill from the waradzu.[88] The interface between Xavante and waradzu presaged future cultural misalignment and political cross-purposes (discussed in chapter 3).

State propaganda misled further because Meireles had not established peaceful contact with "the Xavante." For, although sharing a common language and cultural practices, the Xavante did not constitute a political unit. Divided into autonomous, often rivalrous communities dispersed across northeastern Mato Grosso, the Xavante lacked a centralized political structure.

According to Xavante oral histories, after crossing the Araguaia River into Mato Grosso in the nineteenth century, the Indians established a large village named Isõrepré in the area of the Das Mortes River. Due to infighting, however, over the course of the 1930s the village of Isõrepré hemorrhaged. One faction migrated to the area near the Couto Magalhães River ("Lagoa"), over two hundred kilometers to the southwest; another migrated north approximately one hundred kilometers to the region of Marãiwatsede. These new settlements subdivided as well (see Map 3). Yet another splinter group from Isõrepré established the village of Arõbõnipó in the Das Mortes region; it was this community, led by Apoena, that the SPI contacted in 1946.[89]

Meireles, then, had "pacified," in fact, only one Xavante community,

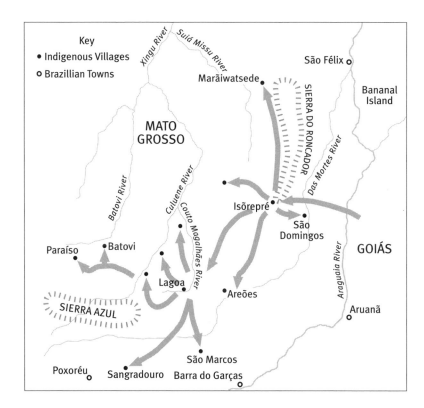

Map 3. Xavante Migrations

living in the Das Mortes region. The Brazilian flag would not be hoisted for several years in the Xavante region of Norōtsu'rā, nestled between the Couto Magalhães and Culuene Rivers.[90] The community at Marāiwatsede, where the Salesians had been murdered, would only be "pacified" in 1966. The process of contact would be chaotic, violent, and spottily mediated by the state, which proved incapable of protecting all Xavante communities or demarcating reserves for their "future concentration."

Indigenismo Fractured

The initial "pacification" of the Xavante did help engender an interesting plot twist: a fissure in indigenous policy as support for the spi's integrationist project eroded. In fact, all along there were naysayers who criticized the March to the West's objective of contacting the Xavante. Following the death of Pimentel Barbosa, the writer Austregésilo de Athayde stated, "We must adopt, faced with these Brazilians, a different policy which consists in leaving them in their huts, without any initiative of protection or understanding." Yet others could not hide their admiration for the Indians' indomitability, "a virtue which during these times should be well imitated by all of us."[91] Skeptics wondered if "civilizing" the Xavante was desirable or feasible, given the squalor of "contacted" Indians and the backland population in general.[92]

After the "pacification" of Apoena's village, as violent clashes between settlers and Xavante erupted, skepticism mounted. Critics contended that the March to the West stoked rather than stanched interethnic violence in the west by unleashing the invasion of indigenous territory. The governor of Goiás, Jerônimo Coimbra Bueno, impugned the state's mission and capabilities in a letter to the SPI director and the Minister of Agriculture. After witnessing the massacre of hundreds of Krahô Indians in 1941 in his own state, Coimbra Bueno questioned the SPI's ability to fulfill its obligation to protect the Xavante. As the goiano governor admonished:

It is not possible to police the virgin zones occupied by the Xavantes, living as they are segregated from our civilization. . . . The service of attraction, theoretically meritorious, in practice will be nugatory, as has happened with smaller tribes, if [the Xavante are] left accessible to the adventurous herd whose coexistence contaminates the Indians with sicknesses, principally the women, and reduces the Indians to a situation of physical misery, decimating them in a few months.

Coimbra Bueno argued that a more fitting measure would be "to leave them like they are, limited to the territories they occupy, until the country, after the rehabilitation of illiterate and unproductive whites in the sertão . . . can dispose of resources not only to attract the Indians, but, above all, to duly assist them."[93] His concerns were echoed by Herbert Baldus, chief of the ethnology section of the Museu Paulista and a professor at the Escola Livre de Sociologia e Política in São Paulo.[94] Baldus asserted that the Brazilian government lacked the capacity to incorporate Indians through a proper "scientific" process, and urged the temporary isolation of the Xavante and other Indian groups with little or no contact with outsiders.[95] The role of the SPI—which Baldus lambasted for its positivist underpinnings—should consist primarily in defending Indians against "all outside aggressors, whether whites or neighboring tribes."[96]

In 1949, Vasconcelos Costa, a federal deputy from Minas Gerais, delivered a speech in the Brazilian Congress in which he called for the creation of a "national park" in the Xavante region: "The region of Central Brazil where the Xavantes are located, between the Das Mortes and Culuene Rivers, which encompasses the Sierra do Roncador, is one of the most beautiful in this country and until now, one of the most unknown. . . . One has the impression that it is a paradise there, such is the beauty of the land, the robustness of the man who lives there, and his happiness will never be exceeded in exchange for civilization." His discourse consecrated the image of the pristine Indian that had formed part of the Estado Novo propaganda—but whose preservation was unintended. In a matter of years, Vasconcelos Costa feared, roads would facilitate transportation to the region, shattering this fragile menagerie. The creation of a national park, however, would safeguard the land, "with its primitive lords and the variety of game and fish so abundant there," and ensure the "historical and geographical patrimony for future generations."[97] Were not the Xavante, after all, "the entrails of their native country," the last vestige of pre-Columbianism, "the last Brazilian Indian"?[98]

The campaign by Brazilian state officials and intellectuals to preserve "authentic" Indian culture revealed what anthropologist Renato Rosaldo has termed "imperialist nostalgia," whereby agents of colonial domination long for the very forms of life they have altered or destroyed.[99] It is noteworthy how official rhetoric helped lay the groundwork for this preservationist shift. The SPI had waxed ecstatic about Indian valor, dignity, and virtue. It had fetishized the brave warrior, communal dweller, and primeval Brazilian. Of course, these images provided myths of origin for the Brazilian nation, narratives of "progress," and notions of racial democracy—if not superiority. But the exotic images of the Indian nurtured romantic visions that refused to wither because the SPI had declaimed the inevitability of the march of "civilization." Perhaps this brave, noble, valiant being, so idealized by the government as a building block for the nation, was too precious a material to be calcified in the process. Perhaps the state had neglected its duties or erred in its focus. Perhaps the Indians could be preserved in their habitat and the March to the West rerouted.

A "New Redemption" for the Xavante?

Vasconcelos Costa's plan to establish a national park encompassing Xavante territory foundered, but contemporaneously a movement with greater élan and support from disparate elite factions coalesced around the creation of a national park in the Xingu region in northern Mato Grosso. Spearheaded by a diverse alliance—academics and scientists; media moguls; officials from the SPI, CNPI, and FAB; and sertanistas Orlando and Cláudio Villas Bôas—the proposal for the Xingu park endorsed the creation of a large protective buffer for indigenous groups.[100] "Representatives of pristine Brazil," the various groups from the four major aboriginal language families (Tupi, Arawak, Carib, Gê) living in the Xingu region would be safeguarded in their habitat; they would serve to showcase the conditions in "which the first society of European tradition was successfully implanted in the tropics: Brazilian society." The original plan for the park, introduced in the federal Congress in 1952, included part of the territory inhabited by then uncontacted Xavante.[101]

Although elites continued to depict Indians as ahistorical subjects, the proposal for the Xingu National Park broke new ground in Brazilian legal history. Rather than conceiving of indigenous land in narrow terms of physical occupation, the park envisioned an integrated habitat capable of sustaining a community's physical as well as cultural well-being.[102] Integration into Brazilian society would be gradual and limited.

A schism cleaved Brazilian indigenous policy (as elsewhere in Latin America) between advocates of integrationism and of preservationism—although neither side was marked by purism.[103] While SPI director José Maria da Gama Malcher supported the creation of the park, Chico Meireles demurred.[104] According to Meireles, Indians ultimately craved to live like whites and to become "people, the way we are people"; after years of peaceful coexistence, they would realize that whites lived with greater comfort and would seek to emulate them. It was the state's duty, therefore, to assist the Indians "in their just longing and facilitate everything for them . . . because if we do not proceed this way, we are being inhuman and practicing a clamorous racial discrimination."[105]

When the Brazilian Congress finally approved the creation of the Xingu National Park—nine years after the first proposal had been submitted—

the reduced area no longer included Xavante territory (see chapter 4).[106] The state did not cordon off the Xavante in Xingu, but rather sought to demarcate small reserves where the Indians would be transformed into small agriculturists. Buoyed by industrial goods, the Indians ideally would renounce not only violence but ancestral land claims as well.[107]

The March to the West had left its imprint on the backlands of Mato Grosso. The state, dynamized by the centripetal force of the Vargas regime, had established peaceful contact with a Xavante contingent after nearly a century of unbridled hostility by the Indians toward encroachers. It had also succeeded in protecting the Indians from attack by Lúcio da Luz. In disarming Indians and settlers, the Brazilian state had advanced its claim to monopoly over the legitimate use of force. And in excluding the Salesians from the official "pacification" process, the SPI had affirmed the supremacy of state over church in indigenous affairs.

Yet, a host of factors would cramp state efforts to place the Xavante and the western landscape under heel. Just as the process of "pacification" had been fitful, contested, and incomplete, so were efforts to convert the Xavante into reservation-bound agriculturists and servants of the nation. As the next two chapters illustrate, efforts by the central government to reorder political dynamics and social relations in the west were riddled with Xavante initiatives, opposition from Mato Grosso elites, and sabotage by SPI officials. Peaceful contact between Xavante and government officials did not signify, as the SPI declared, "a new redemption" for the nation-state and the Indians.[108] It signified new types of conflict and accommodation.

3

"The Father of the Family
Provoking Opposition"

State Efforts to Remake the Xavante, 1946–1961

In January 1954, Rio de Janeiro was graced by the presence of eight esteemed visitors: an entourage of Xavante Indians escorted by Francisco Meireles. The whirlwind tour of the nation's capital included meetings with President Getúlio Vargas (elected to office in 1950), Cândido Rondon, and the Minister of Agriculture. It also featured a promenade on Copacabana beach as well as a soccer game at Maracanã stadium. Ever the media's darlings, the Xavante were accompanied by a reporter from the newspaper *O Globo*. At last, one commentator noted, cariocas could view firsthand authentic Indians—"like the Tupis that Cabral saw" when he arrived in Brazil in 1500—instead of the "decadent" ones always milling about their city.[1]

Speculation abounded regarding the motivations behind the Indians' visit to Rio. Some alleged that the Indians, angered by the invasion of their lands, had been on the brink of war until Meireles convinced them to seek legal redress by meeting with the "great chief of the civilizados."[2] Others lambasted the trip as a media circus catering to Meireles's megalomania.[3] Though such explanations are credible, the visit most likely served other purposes as well. It would inform the Indians where the fulcrum of power lay in Brazil, while showcasing the boons of "civilization."

Like other indigenous groups maintaining only sporadic contact with outsiders, the Xavante knew little about the world beyond their region. In the early 1950s, demographics on the sparsely populated Mato Grosso frontier, which an estimated several thousand Xavante called home, gave the Indians a different sense of who was the ethnic minority and social subordinate in Brazil. Indeed, the Indians did not even refer to themselves as Xavante, a name of unknown origin coined by outsiders and apparently applied indiscriminately to indigenous groups in the Brazilian hinterland. They called themselves A'uwẽ, which in their tongue, a branch of the Gê linguistic family, signified "the people." Other groups could not lay claim to such humanity. The ethnocentrism of spi officials had met its match. A trip to the nation's capital would disabuse the Indians of their superiority complex. Should the "great chief of the civilizados" fail to dissuade the Xavante from violence (and "nomadism"), perhaps a flexing of the white man's muscle would.

It is unlikely, however, that the Xavante had been dragged along on this odyssey. According to Meireles's brother, Silo, the Xavante had implored government officials for permission to visit "their village."[4] The prospect of exploring uncharted territory, netting novel commodities from well-wishers, and discovering more about waradzu culture had its allure. As an spi official noted of the initial visits by other Indians to large cities, "Upon returning, the Indians enjoy themselves gathering, every night, people from the tribe, to tell what they saw and did not see. And, sometimes, they keep narrating their adventures, quite fantastical, for months."[5] The admiration—and envy—inspired in peers by such forays into the murky world of the waradzu rivaled that of the adventurers, missionaries, and sertanistas who embarked on the opposite journey.

One noteworthy Xavante visitor to Rio that January was "Chief" Urubuenã. A strapping man, resplendent in Western clothes only several years after "pacification," Urubuenã cut an impressive figure. Speaking to the press, with Meireles as translator—and undoubtedly embellisher—Urubuenã pronounced: "We wish to live in peace and collaborate with the whites. We know that among us many bad elements exist, those who disrespect the laws of their chiefs, but among the whites the same things are verified."[6] Gone was the implacable foe of the white man—thanks to spi endeavors—and in his place stood the peaceful Indian whose values, it appeared, were really not too different from those of Brazilians.

The spi viewed native chiefs as cornerstones in the process of indigenous integration. As the state eschewed reserving extensive territory for the Xavante, it sought the assistance of chiefs in regimenting indigenous labor and stamping out nomadism to commoditize outlying areas. As the spi urged, "The respect, authority, and prestige of the chief among his tribe should be maintained, by having the benefits of civilization distributed to them by the chief."[7] In Urubuenã, it appeared, the spi had found its man.

Urubuenã's visit to the capital in 1954 was so fruitful that three years later he returned for an encore. On this trip, he was accompanied by Walter Velloso, the SPI post chief responsible for his community. Velloso boasted of measures to convert the Indians from hunter-gatherers into sedentary agriculturalists and of the cozy relationship he had forged with Urubuenã. At SPI headquarters, Urubuenã was duly rewarded with presents before returning home.[8] For government officials, the heralded course of indigenous integration seemed on track: erstwhile hostile Indians consorted with post chiefs; the Xavante were hooked on industrial goods and the Brazilian way of life (but returned contentedly to their rural enclaves); the public remained apprised of the grand transformations wrought by the SPI; and all was quiet on the western front. Nevertheless, constructed on faulty foundations, government policy toward the Xavante soon crumbled.

During their visit to Rio, the Xavante entourage had foreshadowed that the process of indigenous integration would be more conflictual and erratic than the SPI projected. Reporters had been puzzled when Urubuenã shoved another Indian aside as photographers tried to assemble a group portrait. Four years later, in May 1958, while visiting a dissident Xavante community, it was Urubuenã's turn to be manhandled. Only this time, he was bludgeoned to death. Bedlam ensued as internecine strife ravaged Xavante communities, the SPI post was abandoned, and a stream of Indian refugees poured into the town of Xavantina and threatened to overwhelm it.[9] The press went wild with tales of pandemonium on the Mato Grosso frontier, and critics lambasted the state's failure in ensuring the well-being of its tutelados (or legal wards).

This chapter explores some of the difficulties bedeviling SPI endeavors to build "better" Indians—the small farmers, sedentary dwellers, and law-abiding citizens, who retained their indigenous "virtue." On one hand, SPI shortcomings stemmed from the dissonance between state expectations and Xavante objectives. Officials at SPI hoped to persuade Xavante communities to renounce nomadism and practice intensive agriculture, rewarding indigenous chiefs to do their bidding. In the agency's estimate the makeover appeared simple enough: Indians craved to live like whites but merely required proper instruction; indigenous chiefs, presiding over communitarian harmony, would serve as emissaries. From the indigenous perspective, however, things looked somewhat different.

Although solicitous of Western commodities, Xavante were loath to sever their historical relationship to the natural environment, a relationship meticulously calibrated to survive nature's vagaries. Indigenous leaders, uneasily straddling the factious world of village politics, exploited SPI patronage to reward supporters and punish foes and were unassured of communitywide assent. Intraethnic conflict, fissure, and dispersal ensued, derailing the orderly process of indigenous integration and frontier expansion projected by state officials.

On the other hand, the SPI fell short because of the disjunction between state goals and capabilities. Scarce resources, poor infrastructure, and disgruntled or wayward employees hamstrung the potential of SPI posts to overhaul Xavante society. Its outreach to indigenous communities teetered as funds dwindled and post officials smarted from frustration. The Xavante, who negotiated and demanded backing from state officials (and missionaries), would resent its suspension.

Xavante and state officials would come together on what Richard White has termed "the middle ground": a place between cultures where diverse peoples adjust their differences through a process of creative misunderstandings, and from whose misunderstandings arise new meanings and new practices; a place where neither Xavante nor waradzu could ignore each other any longer, but where neither could completely impose their will.[10] To begin our analysis, we must examine aspects of the Xavante political economy in the early postcontact period. Native culture would provide the template for stasis and change, accommodation and resistance, adaptation and redefinition, in engaging the world of the waradzu. For, as Sherry Ortner has noted, "Pieces of reality, however much borrowed from or imposed by others, are woven together through the logic of a group's own locally and historically evolved bricolage."[11]

The Ecology of the Cerrado

The cerrado, the tropical savanna zone inhabited by the Xavante, is characterized by temporal variability and geographical patchiness. Covering one fifth of Brazil's surface, the cerrado is marked by a relatively short dry season, from May through August, followed by a rainy season with heavy precipitation. But temporal fluctuations may be considerable: average interannual rainfall can range 15–20 percent from the norm, with short dry spells during the rainy season further increasing unpredictability. Dense low scrub with twisted trunks and boughs and thick corky bark predominate in the region, but its vegetation varies substantially, ranging from closed-canopy (or gallery) forest to grass with or without trees and shrubs. Most cerrado soils are moderately to highly acidic, low in nutrients, high in aluminum, and toxic to most crops—far from the Eden depicted in March to the West propaganda. Without the use of tractors, limestone, and chemical fertilizers or sophisticated organic farming methods, only the narrow strips of the gallery forests, located near rivers, naturally provide conditions for agricultural cultivation.[12]

Consequently, slash-and-burn agriculture remained a seasonal resource for the Xavante, a subsistence strategy of secondary importance. The Xavante planted maize, beans, and pumpkins in the gallery forest, usually more than a day's walk from their villages in the cerrado scrubland. Such crops, which could be harvested quickly, were favored because they did not tie the Indians to their village. Indeed, the Xavante customarily dedicated no more than three weeks to a month of the year to agriculture: one week, after the first rains, to plant the seeds; a second week to harvest the corn; and a third to harvest the beans and pumpkins.[13] These crops were valued for ceremonial usage, such as the male initiation rituals when the Indians feasted on cakes baked from corn.[14]

To provide their nutritional mainstay, the Xavante, like other indigenous inhabitants of central Brazil, foraged for plant foods and hunted game. On treks, indigenous women might collect tubers, hearts of palm, the fruit of the *buriti* and babassu palms, carob pods, *piqui*, mangoes, *genipapo*, and wild roots.[15] Foraging yielded the bulk of indigenous sustenance but netted more than food. Gourds served to store water or seeds; bark for bandages; cotton and beads for necklaces; *urucum* for corporal decoration and anointment prior to sexual intercourse (to favor conception); roots for treating snake bites and gastrointestinal ailments; straw for baskets; razor-sharp grass to cut hair.

Hunting, carried out by Xavante men, took place on both an individual and a collective basis. Some hunts were composed of all members of an age group, and the meat divided among their various households; others were undertaken by solitary hunters or small groups.[16] Xavante men returning to their village with peccary, wild pig, tapir, anteater, or deer would be greeted with great cheer.[17] Indeed, the better visibility and marked seasonality of the cerrado (facilitating prediction of the behavior of game) made it much more advantageous for hunting than tropical forests.[18] To forestall the depletion of soil and game, the Xavante would abandon their base villages after several years, often returning only a decade later.[19] Even while at a base village, where concentration ensured greater defense and success in a collective hunt, the Xavante undertook numerous treks annually to maintain socioeconomic equilibrium.[20]

Although trekking was extensive, it was never random, aimless, or scattershot. Xavante routes, sites, and destinations were structured and guided by keen environmental knowledge and sense of territorial domain.[21] David Maybury-Lewis observed of the Xavante:

> They were nomads, but not in the sense that their home was wherever they happened to be at a given moment. They had their villages, which they thought of as semi-permanent settlements. Such settlements might be abandoned without too much difficulty and similiar half-circles of huts erected on a new site; but they did not generally abandon them without good reason and would do so as infrequently as possible, in order to spare themselves the labour of erecting new huts. Yet they spent little time in these base villages. For much of the year they were out on trek. A trek starts from the base village and may last as little as six weeks or as much as three or four months. It is deliberately planned by the elders in the men's circle so that the community may move over certain country with a view to exploiting specific resources.[22]

Clearly, the Xavante lifestyle necessitated territorial expanse, versatility, and great physical endurance. It also entailed strategic modification of the natural environment: burning of the savanna to attract game and of the gallery forest for swidden agriculture. The notion of the Indian as innately preservationist, stylish in contemporary environmental politics, is ethnographically complex and historically contingent.[23]

Because of their "nomadic" lifestyle, Gê groups, such as the Xavante, were stigmatized as vagrants and "veritable beasts, in a constant struggle for daily food constituted of wild fruits and raw meat."[24] As jurist Rodrigo Otávio asserted, Brazilian Indians lived "without normal work habits, from the fruits they gather, from hunting and from fishing."[25] The Brazilian state (like most others) historically condemned nomadism—irrespective of its practitioners' ethnicity—for mobility bedevils political domination and social control.[26] In the context of western expansion, indigenous "nomadism" thwarted the orderly process of land commodification and capital accumulation heralded by government planners. Yet for the Xavante, the mixed subsistence economy based on hunting-gathering and agriculture was a creative adaptation to a forbidding and unpredictable environment that they were unwilling to surrender following "pacification."

Gender, Age, and the Kin-Ordered Mode of Production

To triumph in their daily contest with the environment, villagers pooled labor and shared territorial resources and knowledge.[27] The success of such kin-ordered economies stemmed from the ability to manage conflict through consensus formation and informal sanctions as well.[28] It was also a society marked by a strict division of labor based on gender and age, divided into a number of age sets arranged in hierarchical order of seniority. Formal village politics remained the exclusive domain of *predu*, or mature men (married men living with their wives); it excluded age sets of younger, uninitiated, or recently intitiated men and all women. The women's realm resided firmly in the household.[29] Nevertheless, as political discussions occurred outside the formal arena, including in the household, women might have indirect impact on decisions.[30]

The protocol governing hunting and the distribution of meat illuminates mechanisms designed to forge cooperation and generosity while buttressing the gendered and age-based spheres structuring Xavante society. In communitywide hunts, normally held during the dry season, all able-bodied men participated. Embodying the masculine ideals of physical endurance, alertness, speed, and agility, hunting served to delimit and reinforce the sexual division of labor. Igniting the shrubbery of the cerrado in a horseshoe of flames, Xavante men congregated at the opening and slaughtered fleeing game with clubs and arrows. The meat would then be allocated equally to all households, whose elders would oversee distribution.

In hunts carried out by smaller parties, the rules varied but still sought to bolster masculine pride, collaboration, and deference toward elders.

Meat belonged to the hunter who first spotted the game (rather than the man who killed it), but it was not properly his for very long. On returning to his place of residence (the house of his in-laws, as Xavante society is ux-orilocal), he would deliver the meat to his wife, who, in turn, would hand it over to her mother for distribution within the household. Leftover meat was given to the hunter's parents.[31] Age, then, conferred prerogative within Xavante society as elders were entitled to the fruit of youths' labor and the distribution of food.[32]

Although territory was controlled and defended collectively, the Xavante possessed more restricted notions of household property.[33] Agricultural plots, for example, were tended by individual households—cleared by the men, cultivated by the women, and the produce distributed by the elder women for consumption. A Xavante woman wove cotton and made her own baskets of palm fiber, and a man produced his own bows and arrows and sleeping mats. Yet the existence of proprietary notions did not foster acquisitiveness. Not only did the natural environment limit accumulation, but Xavante mores guarded against it as well.

Worldly belongings were buried with the deceased, eliminating the possibility of inheritance. Indeed, Xavante disregard for the quantification of commodities was reflected in their native language, which lacked numbers greater than five; anything above was simply termed "many." Systems of exchange further militated against acquisitiveness by adhering to fundamental criteria: goods offered for barter were to be proportional to the capability of the traders; a request should never be refused; and compensation need not take place immediately. The contravention of principles of reciprocity stigmatized the transgressor as *tsotidi*, or a "socially dangerous" person, and, tellingly, served as the only impediment to marriage in Xavante society.[34]

Like other subsistent rural dwellers—regardless of ethnicity—the Xavante tailored a way of life to the natural environment's geographic and fluvial contours, flora and fauna, and seasonal variations. And like other rural subsistence dwellers, the Xavante would suffer government disapprobation for a lifestyle defying "rational" planning and capitalist logic.[35] Like other indigenous peoples, the Xavante mined natural resources for corporal decoration and festive occasion from a landscape mastered through perseverance and saturated with historical memories. And like other indigenous peoples, the Xavante would confront a state that viewed cultural differences as "ethnic cysts," defined community in national rather than kin-based terms, and surveyed ancestral land in the interest of commodification and national defense.

Political Dynamics in Xavante Villages

In its effort to "settle" Xavante communities (via blandishment of their chiefs), the SPI stumbled onto difficult terrain. Xavante communities were temporary arrangements prone to constant rifts and reconfigurations, nucleations and dispersals. They were racked by warfare that issued from village politics and kin relations, culturally patterned beliefs and attitudes, population pressure on ecological resources, and interaction with Westerners.[36] As in many precapitalist societies, violence and conflict buffeted Xavante communities—as would occur, with modifications, over the course of integration into the Brazilian national economy.[37] Xavante communities were far from the utopias that government officials and intellectuals preened would be readily convertible into agricultural cooperatives.

Riven by dualisms and factionalism, the Xavante inhabited a patrilineal society composed of agamous and exogamous moieties, *poridza'ono* and *ōwawé*, and lineages.[38] Theoretically, members of one moiety relied on solidarity and support from each other, while brooking hostility from individuals of the opposite moiety. In actuality, however, lineages formed the organizational nuclei for village politics, demanding strict allegiance from their members; dissenters might seek alliances with another lineage or become adopted by it. Lineages formed the core of factions, the axis of Xavante politics. Permeating day-to-day affairs, factionalism reigned from the council of elder men, the central political forum of the Xavante, to the household, the basic unit of the village economy formed by the fusion of exogamous moieties.[39]

Feuds, often sparked by accusations of sorcery, frequently precipitated the fissuring of villages and the dispersion of Xavante communities' factions across northeastern Mato Grosso.[40] The death of an individual often was attributed to an evil spell cast by a man from an opposing faction within the community, usually an affine of the deceased. Sorcery, a masculine activity, dramatized tensions among categories of Xavante males, with intrinsic political overtones.[41] In the fallout the entire village might become embroiled as charges against an individual inevitably involved his faction, unless it were to disown him. Narratives by Xavante at Pimentel Barbosa recall ancestral intraethnic conflict; in one feud, two Xavante were killed in retaliation for the murder of a villager at Isõrepré. The community mobilized for war: "There were those who favored vengeance. . . . It was hand to hand combat." Ultimately, those who left migrated north to Marãiwatsede.[42]

Xavante society did contain mechanisms to forestall conflict and breakup. A system of age sets divided Xavante society laterally, grouping men from opposing exogamous moieties to cooperate in tasks and rituals.[43] Furthermore, certain individuals, *wamaritede'wa*, served as community peacemakers, offering corn cakes and other presents to mollify the lineage of the deceased.[44] But no organization or professional can ensure consistent success, and if conciliation failed and the accused stayed put, he might risk death by those clamoring for vengeance. One solution, then, was to seek refuge in a dissident village or, together with his allies, establish a new one.[45] The memory of past injustices, sustained by refugees' tales and dissidents' thirst for vengeance, might keep feuds alive for years.[46]

The Xavante did maintain ties with hostile communities. Marriage patterns led young men to leave their village to find a wife from an opposite exogamous moiety; furthermore, a weaker faction within a particular community might maintain an alliance with another village where members could find haven in case of persecution by the dominant faction. Nevertheless, the great distance between Xavante villages (up to at least a day's walk from each other) ensured a tentative peace—although conflicts might rage as a result of contact during trekking or raids on another community's territory.[47]

Competition over natural resources undoubtedly triggered intra- and intercommunal strife. Indeed, violence, rather than an autonomous cultural value, most likely served as a tactical element to defend territory and ward off attack.[48] With growing encroachment by waradzu on their territory over the course of the 1950s and 1960s, intraethnic conflicts probably intensified as Xavante came into increased contact with each other in competition over dwindling resources, access to Western goods, and efforts to exclude rivals from Brazilian trade networks.[49] Certainly, contact with outsiders imprinted new patterns on Xavante political leadership.

The Role of the Chief

In this context of inter- and intraethnic clash and negotiation, we can explore the evolving role of the "chief" in Xavante society. Like other indigenous groups of central Brazil, Xavante society lacked a supreme political or religious head.[50] Leadership was not hereditary nor marked by an inauguration ceremony nor endowed with unique prerogatives or tributes.[51] Chiefs were, more accurately, leaders of factions, bound by the same kinship arrangements regarding distribution and accumulation as other community members. Because various factions existed within a given village, at any time several chiefs might vie for power.

Policy making in Xavante villages did not issue from a chief, but rather was hammered out in the warã, the council of elder men, which served as the most important public political arena. In the warã, a leader seeking to influence public opinion and command wider authority would brandish his oratorical skills and cunning, with the backing of his faction. Concurrence, however, was not ensured. The warã might endorse a particular suggestion (usually after modification), but also might rebuff a leader's exhortations. Until the council ratified the suggestion of an influential factional leader it remained nothing but that.[52]

Aspirants to leadership needed to demonstrate charisma, generosity, valor, and prowess. One leader might attain supremacy over others as the result of various factors: mastery of skills; preponderance of offspring and their installation as leaders within their respective age sets; the elimination of rivals through execution or migration. Most important, the chief required the constant backing of his faction, the ultimate source of his power. Yet, to maintain widespread support, a Xavante leader had to embody and fulfill larger community aspirations: presiding over communal hunts and the distribution of meat, overseeing the clearing of land for cultivation, and serving as master of village ceremonies (under the careful direction of village elders). Although the chief's exercise of power varied from one village to another—depending on, inter alia, the strength of the diverse factions—one thing remained almost certain: if he disregarded the interests of members of opposing factions, he risked the breakup of the community and the concomitant socioeconomic destabilization.[53]

The position of the chief, then, was fraught with contradictions. His immediate source of power emanated from his faction, but he had to display neutrality in symbolically representing the interests of the entire community. And although his prestige derived from his embodiment of the kin order, he was also bound by its strictures.[54] With contact, such power dynamics could easily be skewed, particularly because Brazilian government officials sought to redefine the role of chief. In gaining access to government largess, a Xavante leader could bolster his prestige (and the SPI's) by distributing food and industrial goods to his community. But, if he kept the lion's share for himself and his faction, he could undermine the customary kinship mode of production and foment resentment.

Various ethnographies have highlighted the role of SPI post officials in anointing chiefs ("caciques" or "tuxauas") of indigenous communities.[55] The Brazilians were hardly pioneers in this: as Eric Wolf has noted, Europeans historically bestowed the term of chief on native persons believed capable of favoring or thwarting colonial objectives.[56] The Brazilian state's success in transforming Xavante political economy through such clientage can be gauged comparatively in the trajectories of two chiefs, Urubuenã and Apoena, and their respective communities.

"Pacification" and the Mato Grosso Landscape Revisited

Urubuenã and Apoena were leaders of rivalrous factions.[57] Both lived in the Das Mortes region, but their fates diverged dramatically. Apoena's group had relocated from Isõrepré to Arõbõnipó, establishing contact with the Brazilian government in 1946. Apoena's community benefited from the SPI post at Pimentel Barbosa, which provided commodities and rudimentary health care. The post's regular provisioning of industrial goods, relatively inaccessible prior to contact (other than through raids), eased painstaking tasks. Xavante testimonies, for example, recount the difficulty of felling trees without axes.[58] Matches effortlessly set fires to clear bush; guns and knives offered new possibilities for hunting.

The post also received a steady stream of beneficent visitors. An air force plane would provision the post with goods, which often included tools and hunting gear. On special occasions, high officials in the Brazilian Armed Forces would visit Pimentel Barbosa to have their photographs taken with the recently "pacified" Indians, lavishing presents in exchange.[59] And in return for the directorial cues of filmmakers and journalists eager to document the rituals of Indians who had not already become "too acculturated," the performers could expect—and demand —payment in kind.[60] Visitors to Apoena's village were told to return soon—and to bring more ammunition, fishhooks, clothes, and other offerings.[61]

Unassisted by the SPI, Urubuenã's group, which Lopes da Silva speculates had remained in Isõrepré, was guaranteed none of this.[62] Given his enmity toward Apoena, Urubuenã could not turn to the Pimentel Barbosa post for support; nor, given the SPI's limited allocations for outreach to indigenous communities, had a new post been established. In 1951, Urubuenã and his community of approximately two hundred migrated to the surroundings of the FBC base in Xavantina in search of handouts, food, and medical care. Over the next five years, the Indians remained in the environs of Xavantina, receiving intermittent assistance from the FBC. Clashing with rival Xavante communities displaced by ranchers from the Couto Magalhães region, Urubuenã's group sought refuge closer to town.[63]

As Urubuenã's group descended on Xavantina, helping themselves to merchandise and food, settlers despaired. One inhabitant of Xavantina recalled: "The Xavante robbed a lot. They would say give me those eyeglasses, this bracelet, these clothes. . . . But you couldn't give, because if you gave to one, then ten wanted. They didn't like it. They got very mad and cursed us."[64] The role reversals could not but offend residents' sensibilities: civilizados were supposed to sally forth into indigenous territory, arrogate their resources, and remodel their lives, not vice versa. Towns, even those whose names paid homage to indigenous people, were open to Indians only on a contingent basis.

The chaos threatened Xavantina, the showcase of state-led western expansion established with great fanfare in 1944 during the Roncador-Xingu Expedition. Xavantina's air base, administered by FAB, served as an important point in the great aerial diagonal linking Rio de Janeiro to Miami. Inhabited until the mid-1950s largely by civil servants, Xavantina had failed to attain agricultural self-sufficiency. For basic foodstuffs, it relied on aerial supply—few and far between during the rainy season. The appropriation of scarce resources alarmed residents, who summoned the SPI to remove the Indians from town.[65] In a classic scenario, the agency charged with protecting Indians required a full-blown crisis to mobilize—tellingly, one that discomfited non-Indians arguably more than Indians. In 1956, the SPI established a post at Capitariquara—120 kilometers from Xavantina down the Das Mortes River—and convinced Urubuenã and his followers to settle there. Shortly after the transfer to Capitariquara, approximately half of the Xavante, led by Zé Tropeiro, defected; the dissidents ultimately came under the aegis of an American evangelical Protestant missionary, Robert Butler, who established a settlement at Areões on the Das Mortes River. Several years earlier, when the Xavante had first arrived in the environs of Xavantina, another faction of sixty-five Indians, led by Jorure, had parted ways with Urubuenã, relocating to the Salesian mission established at Santa Teresinha.

A comprehensive explanation for these fissures may never be achieved. Had Jorure accused Urubuenã of sorcery in the death of his kin? David Maybury-Lewis, for example, found that the chief at Santa Teresinha in 1958, Tomõtsu, antagonized kinfolk of two of his wives who died within a short time of each other. The aggrieved, however, apparently recognized that Tomõtsu's tenure was secured by the Salesians and opted for relocating to Capitariquara.[66] What appears most likely is that outside intervention engaged, redefined, and rechanneled Xavante factional disputes. Indeed, the firsthand observations of one Salesian suggest a significant and enduring source of enmity toward Urubuenã: "We could see from Urubuenã's behavior that he was very selfish because he always kept for himself and his family the best presents, and gave what he did not want to the others, leaving some with nothing."[67]

A Tale of Two Posts: Capitariquara and Pimentel Barbosa

Walter Velloso was the SPI post chief, or *encarregado*, assigned to Capitariquara. The SPI directorate placed great faith in its ground crew's ability to transform Indians into agriculturalists and cattlemen.[68] Agency memos enjoined post chiefs to "teach the Indian to work," as Indians lacked "systematic habits" to "take advantage of their land."[69] Nevertheless, most encarregados were ill-prepared for the job. The son of SPI photographer Nilo Velloso, Walter had taken a UNESCO-sponsored course on grassroots education for rural communities, but had little feel—or concern—for Xavante culture.[70] To be sure, the post chiefs' lot was often not a happy one: they struggled with nature's inclemency, meager funding, inadequate supplies, poor communication and transportation networks, hostile settlers, contrary Indians, a lack of ethnographic training, and an onerous solitude. No matter how well-intentioned, encarregados could not perform miracles.

The reports of s p i encarregados—one of the few extant written sources detailing daily life at the post—are minefields of historical inaccuracy, rife with self-aggrandizement, distortion, misinterpretation, and omission. Notwithstanding, Velloso's reports, compared with those issued from the Pimentel Barbosa post, shed some light on a series of issues: varied approaches by post chiefs to reduce the Indians' mixed subsistence economy to sedentary agriculture; struggles among government officials, missionaries, and Xavante over the pace and nature of indigenous "integration"; and modes of accommodation reached between Xavante and waradzu.

Walter Velloso's project to convert Urubuenã's community into agriculturalists and cattle grazers was ambitious. To "fix definitively" the Indians to the land, he instituted a daily nine-hour work schedule for the Indians—four hours in the morning and five in the afternoon—except for Saturdays and national and religious holidays.[71] The Xavante's precious "internal organization, habits and institutions," which Velloso defined as cooperativism, would be harnessed for agricultural production. Where suasion and respect faltered, the specter of starvation compensated: the post threatened to provide food only to Xavante who pitched in and worked their plots.[72]

Never mind that the s p i's agricultural blueprint discounted indigenous notions and rhythms, or that cattle raising, which historically had not been practiced by the Xavante, required capital and care. So be it if such temporal regimentation made little sense to the Indians, or that their nutritional intake plummeted with the reduction in game and the scarcity of wild fruits in the region. No matter that the s p i had located the post in a region marked by geographical elevations (unlike the typical flat terrain that the Indians favored for their villages) that lacked the buriti palm that Xavante men used to confect sleeping mats and women used to make baskets to transport infants, food, and wood. Or if the Indians bristled at the presence of garimpeiros nearby.[73] The s p i stood firm in its role of "the father of a family provoking the opposition of his children for attempting, in their interests, to impose upon them restrictions they do not understand."[74]

Capitariquara's agricultural experiment came with a price tag. For 1957, the cost of sustaining operations at the post ran to CR$550,000. Velloso, however, viewed this as a provisional outlay to guarantee indigenous self-sufficiency. He insisted that by the following year the Xavante would be able to market their surplus and, with the profits, purchase clothes and other commodities.

Velloso's ideas were not the ravings of a crazed bureaucrat hatched in the heart of darkness of the Mato Grosso frontier. He was implementing state policy, with all of its biases and contradictions. Efforts to eradicate hunting and gathering conformed to agency directives against indigenous "perambulation."[75] Indeed, such acculturationist measures adhered to guidelines set forth in the United Nations International Labor Organization Convention 107 of 1957, which called for governments to introduce "modern methods" of production among indigenous and tribal populations to ensure economic development and "progressive integration."[76]

Velloso toed the line, as well, in his concern with profit margins. Because of its financial insolvency, the SPI sought to convert indigenous posts into commercial enterprises through regimentation of indigenous labor and "rational exploration of natural resources."[77] By 1957, during Velloso's tenure as post chief, the SPI had instituted a policy of renda indígena, or indigenous proceeds, whereby revenues generated at a particular post would be transferred to the larger patrimony administered by the agency and applied, at the discretion of SPI leadership, to indigenous communities throughout Brazil.[78] Finally, Velloso's sentimental insistence on retaining Xavante "habits" and "institutions" (despite revolutionizing their day-to-day routine) reflected the agency's arbitrary validation of "traditions" worthy of preservation.[79]

Velloso contrasted his methods with the "paternalistic" and "obsolete" policies of Ismael Leitão, the encarregado at the Pimentel Barbosa post. Whereas Velloso exchanged goods for services, Leitão nurtured dependency by doling out clothes, medicine, and other commodities. Whereas Velloso took steps to train the Indians in husbandry, Leitão allowed "the tribe to continue in that routine of hunting and gathering, ever more difficult to sustain." As proof of his colleague's shortcomings, Velloso pointed to the migration of Indians from Pimentel Barbosa to Capitariquara "in search of a different type of life more in accord with their interests and actual necessities."[80]

The situation at Pimentel Barbosa certainly contravened s P I invectives against "perambulation" and dependency. Although the post provided the Xavante with tools in exchange for handicrafts, Leitão consistently failed to convince the Indians to stay put, renounce hunting and gathering, and diversify cultivation from their aboriginal crops. In 1954, Apoena's village of more than six hundred, which lay sixty kilometers from the post, lacked all that the agency hoped to implant in an indigenous community: intensive agriculture, cattle, and commerce. In 1958, the s P I regional inspectorate ordered Leitão to secure the "immediate return" of Xavante "wandering" in the Araguaia region, "causing annoyance" and failing to "respect the property of others."[81]

Leitão, who had directed the post since 1950, used "various insinuations" to convince Apoena's community to intensify agricultural production for future self-sufficiency, lamenting their "advanced state of primitivism."[82] Yet a report by Amaury Sadock, a physician dispatched by the s P I to Apoena's community in 1954, elucidates the encarregado's predicament. Sadock noted that the Indians' seminomadic lifestyle, affording "everything they need for their consumption," accounted for the absence of "nutritional deficiency" among either men or women. Although he supported the s P I's goal of "turning the Indian into a better Indian," as a physician he could not but comment on the Xavante's "beautiful physical appearance" and well-balanced diet providing protein, carbohydrates, fats, mineral salts, and vitamins. In fact, he upheld the Xavante's physical health as an ideal standard for all Brazilians.[83]

When David Maybury-Lewis conducted fieldwork at Pimentel Barbosa in 1958, not much had changed. The Indians had moved their base village closer to the post but, even so, spent only several weeks of the year there. Despite s P I exhortations to remain sedentary, the community would trek, splitting up to maximize access to resources. Post efforts to promote crop diversification, in the hope of dispensing with the Indians' need for more extensive territory, foundered. Banana trees planted by post personnel were left to wither or inadvertently burned down in clearing undergrowth. Although the Xavante acquired a hankering for manioc (cassava), they refused to cultivate it themselves because of the modifications implied for trekking; instead, they preferred to, literally, beg, steal, or borrow it from Brazilians from miles around.[84]

The resilience of Apoena's community owed to territorial control, salutary health conditions, and the backing of the s p i post and its illustrious guests. From their position of strength, Apoena's group could modulate integration into the Brazilian economy, welcoming commodities from post officials and visitors while retaining their seminomadic lifestyle. Leitão was hamstrung in "fixing" the Indians to their plots.[85]

This does not imply that the s p i post failed to influence power dynamics within Apoena's community, or vice versa. Leitão relied on Apoena to persuade community members to perform necessary tasks—say, clearing shrubbery to maintain the post airstrip—in return for "payment." In turn, Apoena counted on Leitão to strengthen his faction's position vis-à-vis others, circumventing established kin modes of production and distribution. Indeed, Maybury-Lewis noted that the encarregado feted Apoena, ensuring that he never went away empty-handed when he came to visit. (Likewise, Apoena and his kinsmen divided up the best knives, Norwegian fishhooks, and ammunition that Maybury-Lewis offered in return for his stay, distributing the remainder to fellow villagers.)[86]

Out of such negotiation, new systems of exchange emerged whose meaning differed for each party. Officials of s p i offered commodities to stanch interethnic violence and to persuade Apoena to regiment his community for husbandry and post upkeep. Apoena, on the other hand, exploited this patronage to resolve internal struggles. The accommodation that evolved certainly strayed from the agency's stated intentions and objectives. For example, the first time s p i officials were invited to enter Apoena's village—in 1950, four years after official "pacification"—it was to broker an internal dispute.[87] Later that year, Apoena and his allies murdered, in one night, eight members of an opposing faction in the village whom he blamed for casting a spell that caused his brother's death. Although hardly inured to violence, the Xavante were shocked by the carnage, unusual in scale and method. Many alleged that Apoena used the .22 rifles received from the s p i to carry out the bloody deed.[88] Leitão proved unable or unwilling to interfere in the Xavante's fratricidal strife, although one of the few instances when the agency officially sanctioned interference in indigenous cultural affairs ("through suasive means") was to modify "antisocial" habits.[89] With the flight of many of the deceased's kin to other villages, Apoena's faction was strengthened.

In sum, members of Apoena's village arrived at Capitariquara for reasons other than a desire to live the high life, as Velloso alleged. Indeed, Velloso would soon appreciate the perils of clientelism, the volatility of Xavante factionalism, and the difficulties of rooting out indigenous "perambulation."

Capitariquara's Woes

Urubuenã's community was undoubtedly more vunerable than Apoena's to SPI heavy-handedness: its numerical strength had been sapped by the defection of Jorure and Zé Tropeiro's contingents; it suffered a number of attacks from the Xavante at Couto Magalhães; it endured a more tumultuous interaction with waradzu while in the vicinity of Xavantina for several years; and the environs surrounding Capitariquara were less propitious for foraging. Urubuenã's village suffered from malaria, poor nutrition, and scabies. In less than a year since the post had been founded, twelve Xavante children, all under the age of three, had died. Of course, the encarregado was not entirely to blame for such calamities (although he conveniently hid them from his superiors).[90]

Velloso, nevertheless, proved no more successful in "fixing" the Indians to their plots, regimenting labor, or containing "antisocial" behavior. Nobue Miazaki, an anthropologist from the Paulista Museum who spent two months in 1957 at Capitariquara, reported on the difficulties at the post. Language barriers stymied communication, as only one of the post officials spoke Xavante and only several of the Indian youths were conversant in Portuguese; yet the problems were more than linguistic. The Xavante performed their chores "contrarily," she noted, and were "never disposed to pick up their metal instruments and dedicate themselves daily to agricultural labor." As João Gomes, who assisted SPI officials, recalled, "Velloso had to plant the crops for the Indians. We had to do it for them. If you gave them a sickle, they would break it when you turned your back."[91] Indeed, Xavante "cooperativism" manifested itself in ways uncelebrated by Velloso: while some Indians slept on the job, others stayed on the lookout for an approaching post official. Moreover, the Xavante would abandon their tasks whenever the alarm of wild game sounded.[92]

To exert influence over the community, Velloso, with agency encouragement, privileged the chief. Miazaki noted that Urubuenã frequently requested goods from Velloso and, based on his cache—two rifles, a wristwatch, several suitcases, fine clothes, and a flashlight—probably succeeded in his endeavors. At mealtime, Velloso seated Urubuenã together with post employees, while the rest of the Indians ate at their own table.[93] Velloso himself complained that some of the Indians at Areões—the dissident group led by Zé Tropeiro—"feel an enormous aversion towards me," which he attributed to preferential treatment shown to Urubuenã and others, particularly youths.[94] Then there was Urubuenã's second trip to Rio de Janeiro in 1957, on which he was personally accompanied by Velloso. But the visit might have been a last-ditch attempt for both men to keep the patron-client relationship alive.

To furnish food and material to the Indians, the post had incurred hefty expenditures. As bureaucratic lassitude and mismanagement bogged down disbursement of funds from agency headquarters, Velloso turned to Xavantina merchants to provision the Indians and pay his staff.[95] (Velloso did not suffer alone: visitors to Pimentel Barbosa in 1961, for example, noted that Leitão had not been paid in the prior five months and that the post had little to offer the Indians.)[96] In time, the merchants suspended credit to Velloso, spelling disaster for the Indians and the post officials. Several spi employees abandoned the post after months without payment.

For Urubuenã, the post's insolvency meant that goods would not be delivered—or delivered as promised. For example, as Maybury-Lewis recounts, Velloso had vowed to provide Urubuenã with *balas*, or bullets —which were quite expensive in Central Brazil—for his rifle. When Urubuenã began to pester Velloso to follow through, the post chief resorted to subterfuge: he delivered a bag full of candies, which in Portuguese are also called *balas*. Urubuenã did not find the pun the least bit amusing.[97] Velloso ultimately was transferred to spi's educational sector, where he penned articles encouraging "gifts" to native chiefs and their kin as the means to expedite indigenous integration![98] His successor, Alberico Soares Pereira, took up residence in Xavantina rather than at the post (for which the spi suspended pay for ten days).[99]

Given the Indians' resistance to intensive agriculture and sedentarism, Capitariquara's failure to sustain goods and services undermined whatever legitimacy the spi post commanded. The situation of Zé Tropeiro's community at Areões, tended to by the American Protestant missionary Robert Butler, provides an interesting counterpoint. On her visit to Areões, Miazaki noted that Butler too sought to curtail hunting and gathering, instituting strict work hours and exchanging food for labor. Like Velloso, Butler faced steep resistance, as the Xavante "for any motive of dissatisfaction whatsoever stop work." But the Xavante at Areões were "well-appointed" and enjoyed good health, with the sick tended to by a nurse. She also noted the reverend's personal participation in the Indians' daily activities.[100] Furthermore, Butler enjoyed material support from his mission that Velloso did not command from the SPI.[101]

The Xavante at Capitariquara, who had come to expect government beneficence and medical assistance, were outraged by their abandonment. As Terence Turner noted of the Kayapó, once "pacified" and settled at the post, the only means for warrior nations to compel the SPI to provide support consisted of threats of violence against post personnel and buildings or the threat to abandon the post entirely.[102] Certainly, there was not much else to keep the Indians satisfied at Capitariquara.

Crisis Reborn

In 1958, Urubuenã set off to speak with rival leaders of the community at Areões. According to David Maybury-Lewis, Urubuenã sought to recruit Zé Tropeiro's assistance in attacking the SPI post at Capitariquara.[103] Pedro Sbardelotto, a Salesian missionary, affirmed that Urubuenã merely hoped to convince the dissidents to rejoin his group in an effort to buttress its strength.[104] In any event, entering enemy camp was a bold and unorthodox move. Urubuenã's efforts to forge ethnic unity met with a fatal rebuff. His pan-Xavante pitch, and his life, were cut short by his foes, who accused him of murdering their kin.

Xavante factionalism exploded. When the Indians at Capitariquara learned of Urubuenã's death, his brother, Sebastião, mobilized the community for battle, killing several Xavante at Areões. In a follow-up attack, they forced members of Zé Tropeiro's community to abandon Areões and flee to the Salesian mission at Santa Teresinha. The two factions subsequently clashed again. Xavante at Capitariquara regrouped their forces near Pimentel Barbosa, allied with Apoena, and carried out an attack on Santa Teresinha in 1959 in which one Xavante was killed and several injured. Under threat of further attack, Zé Tropeiro's group abandoned

Santa Teresinha and headed for Xavantina; the Salesians, left without their flock, were forced to close the mission. Sebastião's group would ultimately disperse to the Salesian missions at Sangradouro and São Marcos.[105] In sum, the post at Capitariquara, as well as the missions at Santa Teresinha and Areões, had been abandoned by the Xavante.

The SPI leadership revealed ignorance, if not disingenuousness, in the wake of the Xavante bloodletting. Director José Luis Guedes stated, "We receive the news of the death of the cacique Urubuenã with much surprise because it is known that the Indians only kill people from other tribes, and even then only when they are at war. . . . Within the same group, they never discuss orders nor fight for power."[106] In another press interview, he categorically denied that the SPI might have contributed to the fracas by "taking sides among the Indians," glossing over the fact that SPI patronage had tinkered with leadership roles and capabilities.[107] Scapegoating proved a more effective tactic. Guedes pinned the blame on the Protestant missionary at Areões, accused of arming the Indians with rifles.[108]

A decade after Urubuenã's community first flooded Xavantina, a tattered band of Xavante had now returned, piquing criticism. Orlando Villas Bôas, a sertanista critical of integrationism, lambasted the SPI for the Xavantes' plight:

> They live now, more than one hundred of them, from alms, in the vicinity of Xavantina. In rags, because ["white"] man demanded that they go clothed and did not furnish clothing; famished, because ["white"] man insisted that their cultivation methods were primary and did not furnish either the instruction, the seeds or the tools. Abandoned to their own destiny, infected by diseases which cause them irreparable harm, the Xavantes are going to disappear.[109]

At the end of 1961 the SPI removed the Indians from Xavantina to Areões, converting the abandoned mission buildings into a government post.

Strewn in the wreckage lay years of government efforts to transform the Xavante into "disciplined" workers and agriculturalists. Xavante leaders had welcomed and assimilated commodities proffered on "pacification" but objected to efforts to redesign their subsistence patterns. Indigenous resistance, conjoined with inadequate and misapplied state resources, doomed initial SPI efforts to reorder the Indians' political economy. The clientage of indigenous chiefs, nurtured by SPI officials to facilitate social control, yielded mixed results. Chiefs such as Apoena could fulfill spi requests in persuading community members to perform tasks for the post; but chiefs, contending with internal village politics, had their own agendas in affiliating with post officials. Through such alliances, they might reward their faction or settle scores with opponents. Discord, fragmentation, violence, and dispersal ensued, to the consternation of state officials pining for stability and order. The "middle ground" on which Indians and post officials had come together was rocky terrain indeed.

The failure of the spi to transform the Xavante from forager-farmers into full-time agriculturalists was not the only kink in its project for frontier expansion. The spi would be tested in its constitutional mandate to reserve indigenous land, for Mato Grosso state officials and their clientele challenged the "father of the family" to a showdown.

4

"Noble Gestures of Independence and Pride"

Land Policies in Mato Grosso, 1946–1964

With the advent of the March to the West, the commodification of land in northern Mato Grosso intensified. In 1960, the SPI noted that Xavante lands, "which, in 1940, had no price, were acquired for forty-three cruzeiros an *alqueire* [5.98 acres] in 1943, and today are worth nearly four hundred. And, with the collusion of the Mato Grosso police, the Xavante are being shot at by land grabbers, land transactors."[1] Although the SPI never endorsed reserving extensive territory for the Indians—merely "areas sufficient for fixing and maintaining the Xavante nation"—the unsuccess in reserving even a modicum of land for the indigenes after "pacification" was jarring.[2] As the SPI lamented, the agency "continues to complete its sad fate, fattening the frog for the snake to eat!"[3]

In fact, the SPI's shortcomings toward the Xavante rang all too familiar. Since its inception in 1910, the SPI had been shackled by juridical and political constraints in demarcating indigenous land. The Republican Constitution of 1891, which dismantled the centralized political structure of the empire, transferred dominion over *terra devoluta* (public land) from the federal to local state governments.[4] It also omitted mention of indigenous land.

Subsequent legislation made slight inroads into clarifying the status of indigenous land rights. The Constitutions of 1934, 1937, and 1946 explicitly recognized the right of indigenous people to land where their communities were "permanently located." Nevertheless, jurisdictional squabbles, juridical biases, and limited enforceability vitiated such legal protection.[5] For example, if Indians were guaranteed lands only where they were "permanently located," how would the territorial claims of nomadic groups be honored? According to which criteria would the boundaries of indigenous reserves be devised? Moreover, sticky issues of jurisdictional competence between the federal and state governments hampered SPI defense of indigenous territory. For although since the seventeenth century Indians enjoyed the legal right to their land, the (untitled) territory they occupied prior to demarcation was often classified de facto by state governments as terra devoluta, which remained since the Constitution of 1891 under their jurisdiction. The delimitation of indigenous reserves suffered so long as local state governments violated Brazilian law, failing to distinguish either knowingly or unwittingly between indigenous territory and terra devoluta in their eagerness to commodify "public" land. Officials at SPI appealed to state governments to respect Indians' constitutional right to land, but local elites typically shrugged.[6]

There had been several attempts at the federal level to iron out some of these problems. In 1944, SPI Director José Maria de Paula drafted legislation for regulating constitutional guarantees to indigenous land, and a decade later, then SPI official Darcy Ribeiro elaborated a similar congressional bill. Both proposals defined indigenous lands as those presently inhabited, historically granted, or occupied uninterruptedly for twenty years by Indians—even if acquired by others. Ribeiro's bill stipulated that the SPI would determine the boundaries of indigenous reserves based on the status, resources, subsistence needs, and developmental potential of each group. Lacking congressional support, neither bill passed into law.[7]

This chapter focuses on efforts by Mato Grosso officials and elites in the postwar democracy to commercialize public and indigenous lands and the abortive efforts of the SPI to delimit Xavante reserves. In poor states such as Mato Grosso, land represented a source of power and prestige, a means to cement political deals and electoral backing, and a speculative hedge for investors against inflation. In response to growth and demand within the national economy, frontier land offered new venues for the expansion of capital and accumulation of surplus. The Brazilian legal system served to foster unresolvable procedural complexity in land conflicts, promoting illegal practices and extralegal solutions.[8]

The SPI's dismal performance in demarcating reserves owed to limited capacity stemming from infrastructural deficit, juridical handicap, and administrative overload. Yet, as this chapter argues, the SPI was enfeebled by patronage, corruption, and *empreguismo* (bloated bureaucracy), which particularly infected certain sectors of the Brazilian civil service. Indeed, clientelism and patronage, party alliances and trade-offs, and bargaining between federal and state officials were the sinews of Brazil's newly democratic system. For the Xavante, Brazil's "experiment with democracy" from 1946 to 1964 would be fateful.

Mato Grosso: The Awakening Giant

Arquimedes Lima, editor of the daily *Estado de Mato Grosso*, resembled many matogrossense elites in his drive and frustration. In his 1941 book, *Problemas matogrossenses*, Lima exhorted the "businessmen and men of initiative" of his state to commercialize its natural bounty of gold, lumber, rubber, babassu palm, ipecac, and pasture land."[9] A colossus of 1,477,041 square kilometers, Mato Grosso at the time was Brazil's second largest state. Its territory (which included the present-day state of Mato Grosso do Sul) exceeded all other South American nations except Argentina, and surpassed that of France, Poland, Italy, Denmark, Portugal, and Hungary combined.[10] Divided into twenty-eight counties, five of which stretched over 100,000 square kilometers each, the state had a population, according to 1939 estimates, that numbered only 403,000 (excluding the indigenous population), or 0.3 inhabitants per square kilometer.[11]

Alas, the sparse population, Lima noted, was only one of many grave problems conspiring to "retard and impede our progress."[12] Another was the near absence of overland transportation networks, which stymied trade and communication.[13] The capital, Cuiabá, located in the northern region of the state, lay forlorn since the decline of the gold rush in the eighteenth century. Linked to the south of the state by precarious roads, the capital was inaccessible by railroad and navigable from the southern city of Corumbá only when conditions on the Paraguay River permitted.[14]

Indeed, a considerable part of the state's non-Indian population, 66 percent of whom lived in rural areas in 1950, subsisted through "antiquated processes" with little participation in the market economy.[15] As Raymundo Santos, the mayor of a Mato Grosso county, complained in a letter to Vargas in 1942: "We are practically isolated from our State and from the Nation. . . . and everything else because we do not have roads. Due to the isolation here, we partake, Your Excellency Mr. President, without exaggeration, of a quality of life a little bit above our Cabixi, Pareci, and Nambiquara [Indian] brothers."[16] Poor epidemiological conditions blighted the state as well. A 1941 report found that leprosy, tuberculosis, malaria, and yellow fever afflicted swaths of the population.[17]

By 1955, little had improved. The state's road network, none of which was paved, covered only 14,734 kilometers and was often impassable during the rainy season.[18] Freight companies charged exorbitant rates to

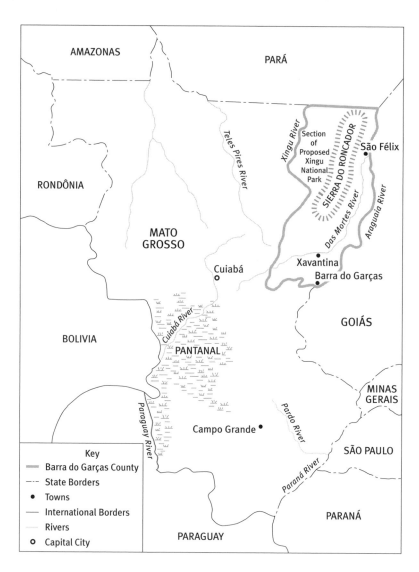

Map 4. Mato Grosso State and Barra do Garças County, 1958

transport cargo over tortuous hauls. Although more dynamic, fluvial commerce suffered from vessels unsuited to the peculiarities of mato-grossense rivers, which varied in water volume and current.[19] The enormous distances between counties, not to mention financial and industrial centers of Brazil, frustrated the growth of the state's economy.[20] The perennial ills of an underdeveloped region, ranging from meager state revenues and lack of local capital to the brain drain of skilled professionals, backed Mato Grosso into a cul-de-sac.[21]

Out of their peripheral vision, Mato Grosso elites forged a strong regional identity and political mythology. Long-suffering stepchildren abandoned by the central government, matogrossenses remained, nevertheless, unwavering in patriotic spirit while awaiting redemption. With pride, elites recounted how their ancestors had braved the wilderness to secure national territory, and how they had resisted and suffered under enemy occupation during the Paraguayan War (1861–1865)—the sole instance of foreign invasion of Brazilian soil since Independence. "Daughter of uprooted bandeiras," affirmed matogrossense José de Mesquita, "my people are engraved in fire and blood in our nation's history, the most beautiful and noble pages of ardent civic-mindedness and Brazilianness."[22] With bitterness, elites lamented how the central government, under the Republic, had punished them with dereliction and, more recently, under Vargas, with dismemberment of the territories of Guaporé (the present-day state of Rondônia) and Ponta Porã.[23] Notwithstanding such hard knocks, matogrossenses embraced the image of law-abiding citizens and rugged patriots. As Mesquita noted of the "matogrossense spirit": "It is intolerant of authoritarianism, of power unsupported by law and reason. It applauds all noble gestures of independence and pride."[24]

In fact, Mato Grosso had very little to applaud, as its "noble gestures of independence and pride" consisted of separatist revolts, elite infighting, banditry, violence, and lawlessness.[25] Between 1930 and 1937, Mato Grosso changed its head of state nine times, convulsed by political turmoil.[26] The clan politics of *coronelismo* fractured Mato Grosso as rural bosses struggled for territorial control and regional supremacy through violence, fraud, and factional alliances.[27] For example, the mines of the Garças-Araguaia region, located south of the Xavantes' territory, were racked in the 1920s by armed battles between two *coronéis*, José Morbeck and Manuel Balbino de Carvalho, and their clientele of northeastern migrants.[28]

Separatist movements festered in the south, whose demographic and economic growth, deriving primarily from livestock and maté, outstripped that of the north, based on sugar and rubber.[29] Resentment by southerners toward the political domination of Cuiabá erupted in a series of revolts; in 1932, rebels from southern Mato Grosso, seeking secession from the north, collaborated with São Paulo forces in an abortive uprising against the federal government.[30] Small wonder that Mato Grosso elites, dogged by economic hardship and political instability, were limited in their ability to exploit the state's natural resources.

Yet how tantalizing were the "opulent lands" of the gigantic county of Barra do Garças, home to the Xavante and other indigenous groups (see Map 4). In 1936, Virgílio Corrêa Filho, a Mato Grosso historian, spoke of the county's rich potential for pasture and lumber, untapped by its minuscule non-Indian population, which he estimated at 3,787.[31] Indeed, regardless of geographic location, ideological conviction, or political allegiance, Mato Grosso elites shared in their understanding that land was a primary avenue to wealth and power.[32] In its agrarian policies, Mato Grosso's "noble gestures of independence and pride" would entail gross violations of articles of the federal constitution that protected indigenous lands, barred land sales near international borders (the domain of the federal government), and mandated Senate ratification for the sale of plots greater than ten thousand hectares (1 hectare = 2.471 acres).

The Politics of Land in Mato Grosso:
The March to the West and Its Aftermath

In 1938, the federal interventor in Mato Grosso, Júlio Müller, had brimmed with optimism: "The 'March to the West,'" he proclaimed, "is our salvation."[33] At long last, the central government not only declared the region's economic development a nationwide crusade but had christened its denizens national heroes. To their cries of distress came federal agencies such as the FBC to implant roads, schools, hospitals, airstrips, and agrarian colonies; the FAB to provide aerial support; and a fortified SPI to "pacify" Indians.

If the March to the West fell like manna from heaven on Mato Grosso, it particularly benefited those elites graced by Vargas's backing. The Müllers, a Cuiabá-based oligarchy, had been boosted over rival elites: as interventor, Júlio enjoyed full executive and legislative powers; his brother, Filinto, was appointed chief of police in Rio de Janeiro. By "federalizing" local elites, Vargas aimed to gain greater leverage over Mato Grosso affairs.[34] Under Müller, the state of Mato Grosso granted land to the SPI to establish "pacification" posts for the Xavante, as well as all land fifty kilometers to each side of the trajectory of the Roncador-Xingu Expedition.

And in 1945, the interventor issued a decree-law ceding extensive territory in northern Mato Grosso to the FBC for the implantation of agrarian colonies.[35]

With the demise of the Estado Novo, both Vargas and Müller were removed from office. The presidential election of Eurico Dutra and the promulgation of a new constitution in 1946 signaled the restoration of liberal democracy and competitive politics, the diminution of federal power, and the invigoration of laissez-faire economic principles.[36] In 1947, the government of Mato Grosso, assailing federal control of large tracts of state land, rescinded Müller's decree-law.[37] Instead, elites called for private enterprise to promote colonization. The territorial dispute with the FBC augured poorly for another federal agency: the SPI. The Indian bureau would be hard-pressed to convince Mato Grosso officials to disaggregate indigenous territory from the mass of public lands that elites viewed as commodities and emoluments. Mato Grosso elites pegged their "political survival" on eliminating federal competition over land policies.[38]

In 1949, the Mato Grosso congress passed a new land code that outlined procedures for privatizing public lands. The code priced public lands by category—pasture, farming, or extractivism—yet in all cases the cost paled in comparison to land in São Paulo or even Goiás.[39] The prospects for land speculation were inviting, given the vagaries of the Brazilian economy. Mato Grosso's lack of a cadastre—another liability of the financially strapped gargantuan—only further paved the way for rampant commodification of federal and indigenous territory, land fraud, and violence.

The land code did mandate that territory be ceded "as judged necessary" to "Indian villages," yet the state government's commitment was clearly halfhearted. For example, in March 1950 Governor Arnaldo de Figueiredo issued a decree setting aside an impressive 2.4 million hectares in the county of Barra do Garças for the Xavante, based on an aerial survey of indigenous territory undertaken jointly with the SPI. There was, however, one important proviso: the SPI was granted only two years to demarcate the extensive reserve before the land would revert to the state.[40] The SPI failed to meet this and subsequent deadlines set by the Mato Grosso government (for reasons that will be explored). Yet, given that the federal constitution protected indigenous land, delimitation could not be contingent on a deadline. (Moreover, the prospective reserve would have only encompassed Xavante communities in the Das Mortes region, excluding those in the Couto Magalhães–Culuene zone.)[41]

The land transactions triggered under Figueiredo's successors signaled the vulnerability of Xavante land to matogrossense political intrigue and frontier speculation. With the 1950 gubernatorial election of Fernando Correa da Costa, head of a rival political faction marginalized since the Estado Novo, a binge on public lands ensued by latecomers to the smorgasbord of state and indigenous patrimony. During Correa da Costa's five years in office, the Mato Grosso government transferred nearly 4,210,000 hectares of land in the north of the state—more than one third of which were in Barra do Garças county—to eighteen colonization companies based primarily in São Paulo and Paraná.[42] Aside from the colonization companies, each conceded areas of 200,000 hectares or more, millions of hectares were sold to a handful of private investors.

Correa da Costa contended that such transactions did not violate the constitutional ban on the sale of tracts greater than 10,000 hectares without Senate approval, as his administration had not transferred the land in toto to the companies; rather, the companies would sell plots no larger than 2,000 hectares to colonists. The companies, he argued, promised the infusion of scarce capital, infrastructure, and expertise. Furthermore, he insisted, in validating and regularizing land titles, the companies would protect buyers against fraud as Mato Grosso lacked a rural cadastre.[43]

In fact, the land transactions were tainted by numerous irregularities. The state of Mato Grosso doled out land without competitive bidding; Correa da Costa dealt directly with all of the colonization enterprises, personally housing directors of the companies when they visited Cuiabá.[44] Furthermore, no measures were taken by the companies to develop infrastructure in the region. What state officials touted as frontier development was merely an exercise in land speculation. For indigenous communities, it meant a license for usurpation. Millions of hectares ceded or sold by the Mato Grosso government were located in the proposed area of the Xingu Park.[45] For example, the Colonizadora Norte de Mato Grosso Ltda., headed by Décio Franco de Almeida, acquired 400,000 hectares that included land reserved for Xavante communities in the pending bill on the Xingu National Park.[46] In 1952, reports surfaced that surveyors from Almeida's company had clashed with an "uncontacted" Xavante community.[47]

The bazaar of public lands in Mato Grosso, with its indiscriminate violation of indigenous rights, bankrolled the state's prosperity. After six lean years of state deficits, Correa da Costa ushered in an era of plenty. In 1952, for example, public land sales totaled over CR$16 million; in the subsequent year they yielded over CR$30 million, slightly less than 20 percent of all state revenue.[48] Although barred from consecutive reelection, state governors sought to maintain political machines and prepare for future electoral runs.

As Mato Grosso lacked industry, infrastructure, and public works, state officials manipulated land policies to reward electoral supporters and convert skeptics.[49] In 1954, state congressmen from Correa da Costa's party, União Democrática Nacional (UDN), canvassed support from opposition deputy Gerson de Oliveira to appoint a UDN congressman as house leader. In return, Oliveira was promised that a colonization company to which he was linked would be granted an area of 200,000 hectares; as a bonus he would receive 5,000 hectares of public land.[50] Clientelism would be adapted to a political landscape transformed by the growth of parties, voters, state expansion, and economic development.[51]

Land policies also served to court voters, as politicians, operating under the competitive party system of the postwar period, confronted the massive expansion of the electorate resulting from the enfranchisement of women in 1934 and the electoral reforms of the early 1930s. Indeed, with the end of the Estado Novo, the new registration of voters in 1945 created an electorate of 7,306,995 in Brazil, compared with 1,466,700 for the Constituent Assembly of 1933.[52] Indigenous people, however, did not earn the right to vote until 1966. (Even then, given their small population, Indians would have limited electoral influence.) The judiciary, generally favoring state over federal rights in land matters, offered little recourse for legal redress. Disenfranchised and disadvantaged, Indians stood little chance of having their rights vindicated in a political environment where, in the words of one SPI director, "the law of the strongest, the most armed, the most politically and financially backed, overshadowed the principles defended by the SPI."[53]

The Politics of Racism

The pursuit of economic gain and political clientelism do not fully explain the violation of indigenous land rights. Racism was another factor.

Mato Grosso elites disdained Indians as wasteful, unproductive, and debauched. As one matogrossense author noted, "In Rondonópolis, a civilized city, the seat of one of the most prosperous counties of eastern Mato Grosso, the Bororo live from public charity and waste the majority of their alms in the purchase of *cachaça* (liquor)."[54] Surely, such parasites contributed little to local or national well-being. Indians were no more than a "racial concept and a stage of civilization" destined for extinction.[55]

Imbued with racist and ethnocentric beliefs, it is not surprising that Mato Grosso elites viewed the defense of indigenous land rights as a benevolent gesture rather than a constitutional obligation. In their view, only the industrious "white man" merited state assistance in occupying lands "legally" acquired.[56] It already galled many state officials that areas to the north and northeast of the capital, because of Indian dominion, remained "practically uninhabited" (i.e., by "white men") as late as 1955.[57] Now, the bugbear of indigenous reserves, tax-exempt tracts immobilizing marketable land, haunted them. Correa da Costa and his cohorts railed against the proposed Xingu Park as "another enormous area for the aborigine" that violated the state's "territorial integrity."[58] In a clever—if unoriginal—sleight-of-hand, matogrossense elites had inverted the nature of their relationship with Indians: the victimizer had now been recast as the victim. Unlike SPI officials who consecrated indigenous difference (at least in the present and the immediate future) to legitimize power, local elites sought to demonize and dispense with Indianness to skirt constitutional guarantees.

Elite Infighting: Same Cases, Different Faces

Correa da Costa's agrarian policies met resistance not only from Indians and SPI officials but from disgruntled Mato Grosso elites. For example, federal Senator Filinto Müller, a rival of the governor from the Partido Social Democrático (PSD), inveighed in the press against the sale of lands in the proposed Xingu Park. He rallied behind a 1955 parliamentary inquest into land policies in Mato Grosso, which inculpated the state government for the unconstitutional sale of federal land.[59] Yet, closer scrutiny of Müller's party cohorts reveals that dissent often was aimed at discrediting political foes rather than sanitizing matogrossense land policies.

Few denounced the "grave damage" of irregular land sales to Mato

Grosso's reputation more vociferously than João Ponce de Arruda, the PSD candidate who swept the gubernatorial election in 1955.[60] In a chastening address to the Mato Grosso legislature, Ponce de Arruda lambasted his predecessor for unlawfully conceding fiefdoms to the colonization companies and rescinded their contracts. To signal a clean break, Ponce de Arruda closed the state's Departamento de Terras e Colonização (Department of Land and Colonization, DTC), whose jursidiction extended over northern Mato Grosso. The DTC had been so deluged by land transactions—12,253 bids had been filed in 1952 and 15,529 in 1953 alone—that the governor vowed to reopen the office only after at least half had been processed.[61] Ponce de Arruda also vowed to promote sales to individuals rather than companies and to abide by constitutional guidelines.[62] And he pledged to honor indigenous territorial rights. In December 1956, Ponce de Arruda signed a law authorizing the creation of a Xavante reserve of over one million hectares. The new law likewise granted the SPI only two years to demarcate the land before it reverted back to the state of Mato Grosso (which the agency once again failed to accomplish).

Notwithstanding Ponce de Arruda's sermonizing, his commitment to constitutional principles quickly flagged. Even prior to the expiration of the two-year grace period, the state proceeded to title land in the prospective indigenous reserve.[63] The bulk of Xavante territory would be titled in 1960, at the end of his administration. Ismael Leitão, the post chief at Pimentel Barbosa, discovered in 1960 that not only had Xavante land been sold by the government of Mato Grosso but so too had the "lands where for 19 years the Indigenous Post of Pimentel Barbosa has been situated"![64]

Ponce de Arruda's administration thrived on cronyism, corruption, and land speculation, which his embittered political rivals were all too happy to denounce:

After the "shakedown" in all the bureaucratic channels, the price (thirty cruzeiros per hectare) had already risen 300%. Some politicians and businessmen in the region [Cuiabá] have already begun driving automobiles of the latest model since the "boom" of land sales began, and have increased the frequency of their visits to apartments and luxury hotels in Copacabana. . . . The [Cuiabá] hotels are full of real estate agents coming from all parts of Brazil. They sit on their front porches drinking beer or cachaça and speak in terms of thousands of hectares. Maps are unfolded and the boundaries are sketched for extensive areas.[65]

The film noir evocation indeed captured the shady dealing surrounding the speculative real estate boom during Ponce de Arruda's tenure. A federal investigation in 1964 of illicit land sales in Mato Grosso sheds light on how state officials cannibalized public and indigenous patrimony to strengthen partisan interests and political coalitions. State officials openly acknowledged to investigators the violation of indigenous rights, the circumvention of constitutional restrictions on excessive landholding, the abuse of public office for personal gain, and the "divvying up of the bureau [DTC] to cohorts." Roger Assef Buainain, who served for two years as Ponce's Secretary of Agriculture, admitted that he had "signed titles in areas reserved for Indians." Hélio Ponce de Arruda, entrusted with announcing public land sales in the Mato Grosso *Diário Oficial,* confessed he had used his position to acquire 128,945 hectares in proxy for paulista investors and 9,000 hectares for himself.[66]

Governor Ponce de Arruda boasted in 1959 that a revamped DTC had isssued temporary title to 1,793,539 hectares and permanent title to 2,637,142.[67] Land transactions intensified at the end of his term, undoubtedly a last-ditch effort to garner electoral funds and support and, following the victory of Correa da Costa in the 1960 gubernatorial race, to make a final sweep before relinquishing power.[68] Yet Antônio de Arruda Marques, director of the DTC in 1964, affirmed that, fifteen years after the land code had been instituted, his office still lacked standardized titling procedures, adequate records, and cadastral plans that "correspond with reality."[69]

Fraud and Violence on the Frontier

The network of *grilagem,* or land grabbing, that swallowed up indigenous territory extended from the centers of political and economic power to the field. Land surveyors, enjoined with informing the DTC and the SPI of the presence of Indians (which would impede sales), often failed to do so. Some performed their job perfunctorily and left others to contend with the consequences; others received payoffs, acted as real estate agents, and even became large landowners in their own right.[70] In 1952, two Xavante from the Culuene region died in a clash with a land surveyor, Wilson Furtado; four years later, Furtado himself was registered as a landowner in the region.[71] Fellow conspirators in the usurpation of indigenous territory included the staff of local county registries (*cartórios*) where titles were often doctored in return for payment.[72]

Along with fraud, violence continued to serve as a tried and true method of accumulation and domination on the Mato Grosso frontier. In 1951, an expedition of *fazendeiros* (landowners) and their thugs set out from the town of Barra do Garças to attack Xavante in the region between the Couto Magalhães and Culuene Rivers. The area was home to ten different Xavante villages, still uncontacted by the SPI. Raiding the village of Parabubu, the assailants killed several Xavante, wounded scores, and set fire to the houses.[73] Over the following years, villagers from Parabubu were ravaged by an epidemic spread apparently by contaminated clothing that they had received from fazendeiros. In 1956, when Xavante refugees were brought by a local landowner to Cuiabá to seek assistance from the governor, they were turned away.[74]

By 1958, the entire Xavante population in the Couto Magalhães–Culuene region had been forced into exile. Some of the communities fled to SPI posts in outlying regions; others sought haven at the Salesian missions (see chapter 5). Uprooted from their lands, exiles from the Couto Magalhães–Culuene region retained nothing but memories, scars from gunshot wounds, and the faint hope of returning home one day (see chapter 7).[75] The state of Mato Grosso sold off much of the Xavante territory in the Couto Magalhães–Culuene region in 1960.[76]

To be sure, the Xavante at Couto Magalhães–Culuene attempted to repel invaders, as they had for decades. Two years prior to the attack on Parabubu, the Xavante slaughtered another band of invaders.[77] Similarly, Claudio Martins, a land surveyor, reported to SPI officials in 1953 that his team had not fared well either: the Xavante living near the Noidori River had killed one of its members.[78]

Indeed, conflict raged between another uncontacted Xavante group, those at Marãiwatsede, and residents of São Félix do Araguaia, a town founded on the banks of the Araguaia River by Severiano Neves (brother-in-law of Lúcio da Luz). In 1950, Neves, now subprefect, complained that the "population was seized by panic" as the Xavante were "destroying crops, [and] taking tools from the small farmers residing here."[79] Local SPI officials and residents of São Félix called for the establishment of another "attraction" post to establish peaceful contact; the Indians at Marãiwatsede, rivals of Apoena's faction, would not relocate southward to the government post at Pimentel Barbosa. The SPI directorate vetoed the idea, citing a shortage of funds.[80]

Over the next decade hostilities intensified. In 1951, the Xavante carried out two attacks in which five settlers were bludgeoned to death.[81] The settlers of São Félix hardly sought succor alone in their town's patron saint. In 1953, a local resident, Antônio Cardoso de Melo, wrote to Rondon and SPI Director José Maria da Gama Malcher of a massacre of Xavante allegedly masterminded by Neves: "I am well known along the banks of the Araguaia for thirty years, but I have never seen barbarities like those that Severiano [Neves] did to the Indians."[82] Cardoso de Melo expressed hope that "justice one day will be meted out to Severiano for the death of the Indians."[83] It never was.

The final blow to the Xavante at Marãiwatsede would come from paulista corporate investors who established a large-scale cattle enterprise, the Suiá-Missu ranch, on their territory. The ranch initially offered the Xavante food and knickknacks in return for services in clearing trails and an airstrip. But as tension mounted, the Xavante of Marãiwatsede were rounded up in 1966, placed on air force jets, and deported to the Salesian mission hundreds of kilometers to the south.[84] Like the Xavante communities of the Couto Magalhães–Culuene region, those of Marãiwatsede had been violently forced into exile. The subordination of Marãiwatsede, the last Xavante contingent to be subjected to external rule, signaled the final surrender to waradzu domination.

Trials and Tribulations of the SPI:
Funding, Patronage, and Corruption

Federal officials since the March to the West had envisioned the delimitation of indigenous reserves as part of an orderly process of frontier expansion. But in light of this multipronged assault on indigenous territory, the SPI's challenge in reserving Xavante lands can be understood. Mato Grosso elites and public servants violated Xavante land rights; speculators devoured indigenous territory; loopholes and contested competences defanged the SPI; and judicial impunity blessed wrongdoers. Yet, to what extent was the federal agency haunted by its own demons: patronage, corruption, inadequate funding, and misspending? Why did the SPI, authorized by the government of Mato Grosso to demarcate Xavante lands, founder on two separate occasions? How can such shortcomings be further explained?

In November 1958, one month before the expiration of Ponce de Arruda's deadline to demarcate Xavante lands, the agency's director, Colonel José Luis Guedes, appealed to the governor for a two-year extension. The SPI directorate cited meager finances and Herculean responsibilities, but the Mato Grosso governor, unmoved, denied the request.[85] Guedes's argument was credible, however, given the structural inequalities militating against the agrarian sector and the west in general, and indigenous policy in particular.

The SPI was subordinate to the Ministry of Agriculture, which had low priority in a developmentalist state committed to import-substitution industrialization. For example, between 1956 and 1960, agriculture received only 4.7 percent of total government expenditures, and only 2.9 percent between 1961 and 1965. Indeed, the policy of import-substitution industrialization, with its urban-oriented state subsidies, worked heavily to the detriment of the countryside. Within the rural sector, state policy showed marked regional and class bias: the majority of resources were channeled to modernize large-scale agriculture in the south and southeast of the country to underwrite these dynamic centers of industrial growth.[86]

Within the Ministry of Agriculture, the redoubt of regional oligarchs, the SPI held secondary importance. In 1960, for example, the SPI's budget was CR$17 million. Even if earmarked solely for the 60,000 Indians directly under the agency's tutelage—rather than, say, for administrative purposes—this sum represented CR$283.33 expended per Indian, at the time less than the price of a pair of pants.[87] Of this total, only a sum of CR$1 million had been proposed annually for demarcation between 1960 and 1962.[88] With more than one hundred posts nationwide, SPI's resources were stretched thin. Administrative and financial burdens crushed SPI regional offices, or inspectorates, entrusted with the demarcation of reserves, topographical studies, post construction, and maintenance for all indigenous communities under their jurisdiction.[89] The SPI was a poor guardian of the Indians in more than character: its meager funding reflected the marginal status of Indian protection in federal policymaking.

Consider, then, the difficulties faced by even the most well-intentioned

SPI employee in defending Xavante land. As the state of Mato Grosso lacked an adequate cadastre, SPI officials had long complained of the difficulty of ascertaining whether lands for sale encroached on Indian territory.[90] To complicate matters further, the SPI inspectorate overseeing Xavante communities in the Das Mortes region was responsible for Karajá, Apinayé, and Krahô communities as well; moreover, the office was located in another state capital, Goiânia. The journey to Xavante posts and Mato Grosso administrative bureaus was interminable during the rainy season, when bridges washed away, roads flooded, and vehicles became disabled. As the inspectorate reported on the difficulty of defending indigenous land, "the most elementary legal processes, whether issuing citations, calling witnesses, etc., because of delays—owing to the great distances—becomes almost impossible."[91] The hostility of uncontacted Xavante communities presented another obstacle to land surveyal and demarcation.

In a feeble attempt to stanch titling of indigenous lands, the SPI dispatched one of its employees, José Vieira da Silva, to monitor transactions in the DTC.[92] Likewise, in August 1956, the SPI inspector in Cuiabá, Octaviano Calmon, implored the DTC director not to grant title to forty-three prospective investors seeking to purchase Xavante land.[93] Reliant on headquarters for funding and local elites for goodwill, inspectors could often count on neither. The weak institutional presence of the federal government in the central west thwarted effective authority over land policies.

Although poorly funded, the SPI misused or squandered scarce finances. Corruption long plagued the SPI. José Maria da Gama Malcher, who served as director from 1951 to 1955, presided over numerous internal audits and investigations, yet from the fruits of his labor only one employee was removed.[94] Malcher's outspoken defense of indigenous rights, according to newspaper accounts, led instead to his dismissal.[95] In 1964, a Brazilian congressional investigation of the SPI found that under the administration of Moacyr Ribeiro Coelho (1961–1963), renda indígena obtained from the sale of post cattle wound up in the pockets of the director and his cronies.[96]

Misspending stemmed, on the other hand, from the nature of federal budgetary allotment, which bogged down in congressional wrangling and negotiation. Funds would often be disbursed to the SPI late in the year, bedeviling attempts at rational planning and allocation. Agency officials administered resources wantonly—failing to register goods, maintain inventories, or pursue competitive bids for services—fearful that the upcoming budget would be slashed otherwise.[97]

Post employees, occupying the lowest rung on the SPI administrative ladder but a vital link for indigenous communities, particularly suffered from such financial disarray. Because salaries were low and arrived months late, post officials often turned to local "agents," or *procuradores*, who advanced payment in return for a fee. Dependence on the very elites often most hostile to the indigenous cause surely compromised the loyalties of some.[98] If principled, encarregados served as the Indians' defenders; if unscrupulous, they stood poised like a fox guarding the henhouse. Through complicity or dereliction, Indian land might be seized, cattle sold off, resources embezzled, and the cry for justice muffled.[99] Such malice or delinquency was not universal, nor restricted to the lower levels of the SPI administration. A good number of post chiefs were probably neither knight nor knave; in the tradition of patronage permeating the Brazilian public service, many simply lacked will or merit.

Indeed, patronage and empreguismo waylaid legal defense of indigenous land. The bloating of SPI headquarters in Rio de Janeiro, remote from the Xavante and most indigenous communities under its guardianship, bespoke these trends. From 1953 to 1960, the number of employees in Rio de Janeiro nearly tripled, from twelve to thirty-four, while all but one regional office, or inspectorate, atrophied, with an overall decrease of seventy-two employees. Malcher lambasted the SPI's clique of "semi-illiterate teachers, radio transmitters who have never seen a transmitter and motor technicians in the same situation, great being the number of functionaries at the Directorate without any function."[100]

The bane of empreguismo and *pistolão* (patronage) was not novel nor confined to the SPI. It proliferated throughout the Brazilian civil service in the postwar period, albeit in marked sectoral concentration. The growth of public sector expenditures in postwar Brazil under the developmentalist state—from 17.7 percent of the GDP in 1947 to 29 percent in 1960—allowed politicians to build a base for large-scale patronage.[101] Furthermore, with population growth, urbanization, and insufficient employment in the private sector, jobs in public service cushioned Brazil's expanding workforce and provided security during a time of rapid economic change.[102] In 1940, 1 out of every 132 actively employed Brazilians was in the federal bureaucracy; by 1960 it was 1 out of every 65.[103]

During the Estado Novo, Vargas had created the DASP to forge a technocratic cadre of public servants for effective planning and implementation of state policy. The agency classified civil servants in three categories: permanent functionaries, who were required to pass competitive entrance examinations; "interims," whose tenure was (purportedly) limited to one year; and "extranumeraries," lower-level employees only partially covered by the provisions of the civil service law.[104] However, with the demise of the Estado Novo and the emergence of a decentralized political system based on a mass electorate and party politics, Vargas's administrative reforms (which had never eliminated patronage entirely) assumed a purely formalistic character.[105] They were incompatible with the demands of a representative and competitive political system, where parties, divided along regional lines, allocated public office to bring together diverse interests and to reward electoral supporters. Although DASP continued to administer public service examinations and to appoint career civil servants, under the Second Republic (1946–1964) departmental guidelines were routinely bypassed: interim and extranumerary employees were appointed on the basis of personal or political considerations and were entitled to job tenure after several years of seniority.[106] Indeed, DASP reported in 1961 that an investigation of 300,000 federal civil servants uncovered that only 15 percent had been admitted through public examination.[107]

Under the presidency of Juscelino Kubitschek (1956–1961), the Ministry of Agriculture, which oversaw the SPI, fell particular prey to pistolão. Kubitschek, like Vargas, promoted state-led development and appreciated the importance of increasing competence in the civil service. However, because of his narrow electoral victory and tenuous support based on a political alliance between his own party, the PSD, and the Partido Trabalhista Brasileiro (PTB), Kubitschek relied on patronage appointments as well. Whereas the state economic planning and development agencies were relatively insulated from patronage, the Ministries of Agriculture and Labor served as strategic reserves.[108] In his memoirs, Darcy Ribeiro attributes the SPI's decline in the late 1950s to Kubitschek's carving up of the Ministry of Agriculture to political supporters from the PTB.[109] Under the administration of President João Goulart (1961–1964), whose political base was even weaker than Kubitschek's, patronage continued.

While patronage and corruption plagued (unevenly) the Brazilian public service, their implications were particularly pernicious for indigenous peoples. As wards of the federal government, Indians relied entirely on the SPI to defend their constitutional rights. Betrayal by state officials constituted a grievous offense. In 1963, a special congressional inquest of the SPI concluded, "This Service, instead of serving for protection of the Indian, serves for persecution."[110] The investigation, however, failed to rectify the structural problems plaguing the SPI and yielded little substantive change for the Xavante. The diffidence of the congressional panel, two of whose six committee members were from Mato Grosso, undoubtedly stemmed from reluctance to alienate vested interests and electoral supporters.[111]

The SPI, Matogrossense Elites, and Indigenous Land

In praising the protectionist ideal of Brazilian *política indigenista* (indigenous policy), anthropologist Darcy Ribeiro posited an antinomy between urban enlightenment and backland brutality: "The population of the Brazilian cities, distant not only geographically but historically from frontiers of expansion, could no longer accept the traditional treatment of the indigenous problem. History had opened up an abyss between the urban mentality and that of the backlands."[112] Most matogrossenses did hold highly negative beliefs about indigenous peoples, devoid of any of the paternalistic romanticism of some metropolitan compatriots. Yet, this chapter suggests that the dichotomy between town and country should not be overdrawn nor *mentalités* abstracted from structural realities. With the extension of urban financial and corporate capital into the central western frontier, the boundaries between core and periphery had become more porous and the "abyss" increasingly filled.

Moreover, the emergence of a competitive party system and expansion of the electorate led politicians at both the national and subnational levels to rely heavily on public office and expenditures to build a patronage base for electoral support. Matogrossenses were more intimately involved in the usurpation of Xavante lands through violence and fraud. Land policies in Mato Grosso, promoting speculation by largely extraregional capital, fueled state capacity and postwar economic growth. Racist beliefs served to legitimize the violation of indigenous rights. Yet, the SPI, in many respects, complemented (and, at times, abetted) such malfeasance, prompting even Ribeiro to denounce corruption of the SPI's higher calling.

Both federal and state officials appropriated resources rightfully befitting or belonging to indigenous people. Whether in Rio de Janeiro, Cuiabá, or Barra do Garças, the pursuit of personal gain and political advantage steamrolled Xavante constitutional guarantees. As with other aspects of policy making, the jurisdictional ambiguities, malleable competences, and jural irresolution regarding indigenous territorial rights conjoined with cronyism, corruption, and legal impunity to lubricate the political bargaining of the Brazilian democratic machine between 1946 and 1964.[113] In the cross fire and compromise between federal and state officials and the larger class interests they represented, indigenous land rights remained largely indefensible, and the fate of their communities hung in the balance.

Aerial photograph of Xavante village. Xavante villages traditionally comprised large thatch houses arranged in a horseshoe format. Courtesy of Museu do Índio.

Getúlio Vargas (left) and Cândido Rondon (right), 1940. With the March to the West, the "indigenous question" would gain greater urgency for state officials. Courtesy of Arquivo Nacional.

Xavante warriors. Through sheer force, Xavante warriors had dominated outsiders, keeping invaders at bay for nearly a century. Courtesy of Museu do Índio.

Contact between Xavante and s p i attraction team. The Brazilian government celebrated its success in peacefully contacting, or "pacifying," the Xavante on the Das Mortes River in 1946. In fact, the process of contacting other villages would stretch out another two decades. Courtesy of Museu do Índio.

Francisco Meireles and a Xavante Indian. Meireles was one of Brazil's most renowned *sertanistas*. His wife and child are in the foreground of the photograph. Courtesy of Museu do Índio.

Getúlio Vargas and Xavante Indians at Catete Palace, 1954. A visit to the "big chief" was the highlight of the Xavante tour of Rio de Janeiro. Urubuenã stands to the left of Vargas, who holds a cigar. Courtesy of Arquivo Nacional.

Xavante Indian with knife at Pimentel Barbosa Post. State officials relied on industrial goods to ingratiate themselves with the Xavante, who valued knives and other tools for their utilitarian purposes. Yet, to their consternation, such influence would not signify the ability to reconfigure indigenous society as envisioned. Courtesy of Museu do Índio.

Urubuenã and Walter Velloso at Capitariquara Post. Velloso's experiment in acculturating natives would be derailed by indigenous factionalism and resistance, as well as official dereliction. Courtesy of Museu do Índio.

Celestino descends on FUNAI headquarters in Brasília, 1980. Over the course of the late 1970s and 1980s, Xavante leaders routinely traveled to Brasília to pressure FUNAI officials to demarcate their reserves and to assist their communities. To "lobby" government officials, Celestino arrives with traditional war paint and club, as well as an attaché case. The media, freed of government censorship during the final years of military rule, served as an important ally for indigenous peoples in disseminating their struggles. Courtesy of *O Globo*.

5

"Brazilindians"

Accommodation with Waradzu, 1950–1964

In 1960, President Juscelino Kubitschek inaugurated the nation's new capital, Brasília, in the central west. Brasília marked the most dramatic symbol of state-led western expansion since the Roncador-Xingu Expedition. Like Vargas, Kubitschek embraced developmentalist nationalism, upholding Brasília as a marker of inward-oriented growth, national integration, and the triumphant march westward. So, too, Brasília touted the promise of frontier development, rather than structural change, as a solution to the nation's inequitable distribution of land and wealth.[1] The Brasília-Belém highway, built in 1960 with loans from the World Bank, stretched 2,230 kilometers through the sparsely populated interior of Goiás and Pará; by 1971, one million people would settle along its trunk.[2] Land values rose in northeastern Mato Grosso and the entire Araguaia region.[3]

Xavante communities, once at the nation's economic periphery, were being increasingly encompassed by statist development and the extension of capital from core financial/industrial regions. Their prospects were uncertain. Anthony Smith, member of a British scientific team invited by the Brazilian government to Mato Grosso in the late 1960s to study the environmental impact of the Xavantina-Cachimbo highway under construction, saw little hope for the Xavante at Areões. Whereas in the past, Smith noted, the Xavante had hunted jaguars to extract claws for necklaces, macaws for feather ornaments, and rubber-tappers for supplies, they now dressed in rags and seemed mere "remnants of their shattered culture." Xavante lands had been invaded, their birthrate had plummeted, and anomie paralyzed once vibrant communities. In the town of Xavantina, twenty-five miles from their village of two hundred persons, a few Indians worked, some came to beg for fishhooks, tobacco, and handouts, and yet others loitered. As Smith gloomily concluded, "They are neither Indians nor Brazilians. They are twilight people, existing between two worlds, begging from the twentieth century and retreating into the past. . . . They have an enclave of their own, but it will not last for long."[4]

Xavante communities had sustained seismic changes since contact. Inter- and intraethnic warfare ravaged villages. Exile and territorial loss deprived them of access to natural resources and historical guideposts. Epidemic, high infant mortality, and settler attack did indeed endanger the physical survival of many groups. Cultural conflict with civilizados sapped Xavante of resolve, and shame stripped them of self-confidence. Anthony Smith undoubtedly was correct: dejection permeated Xavante communities as the brutal realities of frontier expansion set in.

Although Smith ably diagnosed many indigenous ills, he underestimated prospects for recovery. Cultural blinders led him to view the irreconcilability of his subjects remaining Xavante and becoming Brazilians. In other words, the notion of a Brazilian Indian was an oxymoron. Like many observers of non-Western peoples, Smith privileged tradition over transition as constitutive of ethnic authenticity; its demise signified ethnic extinction.[5] The onslaught of development doomed indigenous culture and identity, because Xavante who hunted with less frequency, wore Western clothes, and traveled to towns were no longer *real* Xavante. In his renowned *Tristes Tropiques*, Claude Lévi-Strauss likewise bewailed the cataclysmic change battering Brazilian indigenes, "wretched people who will soon, in any case, be extinct."[6]

Ethnographic mourners who pinned the preservation of cultural distinctiveness on geographical and social isolation underestimated the role of social interaction in sustaining ethnic difference. For as Fredrik Barth has noted, ethnic ascription and categorization are not determined by fixed cultural practice; instead, ethnicity (self-defined or imputed) derives from and depends on the maintenance of a boundary of difference and serves as a social vessel.[7] Moreover, in viewing interethnic friction as a Manichaean showdown between indigenous peoples and dominant forces rather than a complex intercultural zone, observers failed to appreciate how differences were resolved through political and economic practice. Thus the error in focus: cultural "authenticity" in fact resides in the specific ways that indigenous societies adapt to historical change.[8] Many Xavante, however, would come to understand that selective cultural adaptation offered the best insurance for defending their land and communities and for modulating their relationship with the dominant society.[9]

This chapter examines the series of shocks that buffeted Xavante communities following contact: the restrictions imposed by resettlement around religious missions and government posts; low birthrate and high child mortality; apprenticeship under the capitalist system; and instruction in Portuguese and civic education. Yet, reducing Xavante postcontact experience to a laundry list of cultural loss, retention, or mutation without exploring *political* ramifications impoverishes analysis of indigenous and Brazilian history. This chapter, then, also explores how a range of experiences in the 1950s and 1960s served to reshape indigenous modes of political consciousness, representation, and mobilization. How would new frameworks imposed by waradzu proscribe, but also provide, prospects for indigenous communities to safeguard their communities and lands? These historical components comprise sections of a larger puzzle I wish to piece together: How did the A'uwē come to represent themselves to outsiders as "Xavante" or as "Brazilian Indians"? How did their leaders come to straddle the purportedly unbridgeable worlds of their communities and the national polity as Indians *and* Brazilians? In short, how did the course of indigenous policy reconfigure indigenous politics, and vice versa?

Mapping Postcontact Xavante Communities

All Xavante communities experienced the loss of territory and autonomy following contact, yet the nature and extent of this loss, as Lopes da Silva has pointed out, varied significantly.[10] The Xavante communities at Pimentel Barbosa and Areões both lived in the precontact Das Mortes region directly under the aegis of the SPI. Both communities, however, had witnessed the drastic reduction of territorial domain and concomitant sociocultural change. Whereas in 1958 the Xavante at Pimentel Barbosa had refused to plant manioc because it would compromise trekking, four years later they had relented in acknowledgment that hunting and foraging could no longer ensure their sustenance. By 1962, hunting was no longer the primary topic of conversation among adult men in Apoena's community; discussion more likely revolved around travel plans to a Brazilian town to acquire manufactured goods.[11] The community at Areões, visited by Anthony Smith, had even more sustained contact with outsiders, given its proximity to Xavantina.

Other Xavante communities were uprooted entirely from their pre-contact territory. Some fled as a result of settler attack and disease or were induced by government officials or missionaries to resettle else-where. One such community had resided before contact near the Culuene River when members were "attracted" by the SPI in the late 1940s to an area several hundred kilometers west of their lands. There, near the Para-natinga River, the Culuene Xavante split into two groups: one settled at the SPI post of Simões Lopes, which already served the Bakairi Indians (who had a much longer history of contact with Brazilian society); the other Xavante group settled near the Batovi River (see Map 3). At Batovi and Simões Lopes, the Culuene Xavante were proselytized by evangelicals from the South American Indian Mission and the Summer Institute of Linguistics, who exploited enforced dependence to reorder cultural be-liefs and practices.

Still other Xavante exiles fled to the Salesian missions. Approximately one hundred Xavante from the Couto Magalhães region, driven out in the aftermath of the Parabubu massacre, epidemic, and other skirmishes, sought asylum at the Salesian mission at Merure (home to the Bororo In-dians) in 1957. The group, led by Chief Dutsan, had barely settled at Me-rure—to the discomfort of the Bororo—when a rival faction from Couto Magalhães of nearly two hundred, led by Apoena (not of Pimentel Bar-bosa), arrived there as well. Apoena's group, guided to the mission by a lo-cal landowner, narrowly escaped death at the hands of another fazendeiro, Manuel Garcia Azambuja, who had planned to give the famished refugees poisoned meat.[12] The Salesians coaxed Dutsan's group to relocate to their mission at Sangradouro, while establishing in 1958 a new mission at São Marcos, forty kilometers away from Merure, for the remaining Xavante[13] (see Map 3).

With the subsequent arrival of different factions at São Marcos, the Xa-vante community grew under the folds of the Salesians. In 1961, a group migrated from Pimentel Barbosa. Three years later, eighty Xavante left the Batovi region to settle at São Marcos. Finally, in 1966, São Marcos shel-tered 263 Xavante from the region of Marãiwatsede after their expulsion by the Suiá-Missu ranch. By 1969, São Marcos contained 798 Indians or 37 percent of the estimated total Xavante population; Sangradouro ac-counted for 367 Xavante or 17 percent of the total. In other words, over half of the estimated total Xavante population of 2,160 were living outside their precontact territory.[14] If state officials had once decried missionary oversight of indigenous integration, they now conceded its utility in buffering interethnic violence, paring spi expenditures, and safeguarding accumulation on the Mato Grosso frontier.

Tending to the Xavante's Physical Health

It is difficult to quantify the precise impact of contact on Xavante health, given that precontact medical histories are fragmentary; even following contact, indigenous posts often failed to keep meticulous records. Medical researchers conducting physical examinations on the Xavante in the early 1960s, however, found the adult population relatively free of chronic or degenerative disease. The men were of "exuberant health and vitality"; the women, though healthy, showed signs of premature aging probably due to a more strenuous lifestyle.[15] The researchers did find a high frequency of antibodies to a variety of nonendemic diseases, such as measles and whooping cough, as well as endemic agents such as salmonella, poliomyelitis, arboviruses, and a wide variety of intestinal parasites. The presence of antibodies to introduced diseases led them to speculate that the Xavante might have experienced serious epidemics in the recent past or, alternatively, that such diseases and immunological competence had been endemic among the Xavante and neighboring Indian groups for a considerable period of time.[16]

It appears, though, that increased infant mortality from nonendemic diseases occurred during the late 1950s and 1960s.[17] At Simões Lopes, the Xavante suffered an epidemic of whooping cough and pneumonia in 1960 and measles two years later, with sixty-two child deaths recorded between 1958 and 1963.[18] At Pimentel Barbosa, anthropologist Nancy Flowers found that 67 children of the total 129 babies born between 1957 and 1971 had died, with girls accounting for a disproportionate number. During crisis, Flowers speculates, males might have received more care or the Xavante might have engaged in female infanticide, although the Indians deny its practice. Overall, the Xavante demonstrated a concomitant low birthrate. Xavante women spoke of "losing their will to have children," a trend corroborated by researchers who have correlated low fertility to stress.[19]

The Xavante's distress undoubtedly allowed missionaries and government officials to curry favor with communities procuring medical assistance for their children. Robert and Helena Crump, from the South American Indian Mission at Batovi, chronicled how they had ingratiated themselves with their flock. One day in 1959 a Xavante couple came to the missionaries from their village across the Batovi River, which housed 250 indigenes, in search of medical assistance for their son. The Crumps administered penicillin injections and the child recovered. The grateful family spent one week with the missionaries before returning to their village.[20]

Yet, if settlement around mission and government post provided the Indians with physical refuge and access to medical treatment, it also served as a breeding ground for disease that, in the past, dispersal may have stanched. A measles outbreak ravaged the Xavante who first arrived at São Marcos, killing a great number of children as well as adults. Ninety of the Xavante from Maraiwatsede, approximately one-third of the refugees, died in a measles epidemic at the mission shortly after their arrival.[21]

Willy-nilly, high infant mortality increased the Indians' day-to-day contact and dependence on the missionaries as well as the SPI. One visitor to the Salesian mission at Sangradouro noted, "When the children get sick, as they did with measles, they were tended to, whenever possible, in the beds of the Mission. . . . The Indians appreciate our medicines a lot, including the application of injections, even faking being sick, just to take injections."[22] As with other aspects of intercultural contact, however, health care might easily degenerate into struggle and standoff. James Neel, a geneticist who carried out medical research among the Xavante in 1962, recounts that when a newborn baby died, he stood accused for having laid hands on the mother's abdomen and administering medication just before her labor. For two days his research came to a grinding halt as the village deliberated and tension filled the air. Although he was ultimately allowed to continue examining the Xavante men, when treating an illness of any severity he was careful to explain that malevolent spirits were clearly at work and that the village "shaman" should also be consulted.[23]

Life at the Missions and the SPI Posts

The ideological bent of those most immediately overshadowing the Indians' lives clearly nuanced each Xavante community's historical experience. Missionaries, more proscriptive of indigenous ritual and sexual mores than were government officials, sought to suppress or alter customs and introduce new belief systems and behavioral codes. Moreover, on a more fundamental level, missionary emphasis on individual conscience and salvation clashed with the Xavante cultural understanding of the person as a collective social product, which underlay their communal ceremonial system.[24] Protection from physical harm would come at the expense of cultural violence.

To facilitate conversion, extirpate native beliefs, and exert greater social control, missionaries sought proficiency in indigenous languages. To be sure, proselytizing "inhabitants of the reign of Satan" was not simple, given the Indians' resistance to conversion. Thomas Young, of the South American Indian Mission, described his faltering efforts among the Xavante at Batovi:

> I have tried to utilize the services of a civilized Indian who knows the language well, however, not being a believer (*crente*), he is little interested that his listeners come to understand the Gospel. We have sufficient vocabulary regarding material goods of daily life, however to preach the Word of God, we need much more than mundane expressions. Pray with us that the day will not be too distant when the Xavantes will hear the message of God in their own language.[25]

A similar challenge was faced by members of the Summer Institute of Linguistics (SIL), another U.S.-based missionary group, committed to the Christianization of native peoples worldwide through the translation of the Bible into indigenous languages. The SIL placed teams among the Xavante at Simões Lopes and Batovi as part of its strategic penetration of the Brazilian Amazon in the late 1950s.[26] The Brazilian government granted the SIL carte blanche among the indigenous population for various reasons. The SIL's linguistic expertise, unparalleled at the time in Brazilian universities, was deemed indispensable in registering the nation's diverse indigenous languages (prior to "extinction").[27] Government officials might have viewed the SIL, armed with an impressive radio network and airplane fleet, as a buttress for the SPI or even a check on its growing corruption.[28] Ultimately, the missionary-linguist project complemented that of the state: though the SIL devised a written alphabet for indigenous people and offered literacy training in their mother tongue, such measures were merely intended to expedite the transition to Portuguese and integration into the national society. Neither Xavante language nor culture was valued in itself. Instruction was conducted by non-Indians, although the SIL sought to train indigenous monitors, most likely in an attempt to legitimize its activities. Significantly, the SIL's bilingual educational method would be formally adopted by the Brazilian government in 1970.

Missionaries strong-armed Xavante to abandon their religious beliefs and to replace veneration of "spirits" with monotheistic ideals.[29] Their condescension toward native culture and religion rang out in vows to lead the Xavante "from death to life, from the death of their beliefs and sins, to the new life of Jesus Christ."[30] Indigenous marital patterns, sexual mores, body ornamentation, and cultural norms suffered clerical reprobation. Missionaries inveighed against polygyny, a traditional prerogative of many men. Marriages involving prepubescent females—the result of older men taking multiple wives, which consigned newly initiated males to betroth young girls—were likewise denounced. The Salesian missions sought to suppress the *wai'a*, an important male ceremony that involved the ceremonial rape of select women by the officiating male age set.[31] The women's naming ceremony, which involved extramarital sexual relations, was phased out after contact in all but the community at Pimentel Barbosa.[32] Whereas prior to contact, Xavante women went about naked and initiated men covered themselves with only a penis sheath, missionaries draped the Indians in clothing, seeking to inculcate Christian notions of modesty. The ear piercing of Xavante men—the rite of passage to adulthood—was scorned by evangelicals as unmanly, and males at Simões Lopes and Batovi forsook wearing ear plugs for over a decade.[33]

At the São Marcos and Sangradouro missions, the Salesians' efforts to "make the Indian a man, in the plain sense of the word, a citizen of the world and a member of the Church," entailed separating Xavante children from their families through the *internato*, or boarding school.[34] Here, the Salesians sought to replicate their educational "successes" with the Bororo at Merure. Barred from speaking their native language and performing ancestral rituals, the Bororo had been "redeemed" through religious conversion, labor regimentation, sedentary living, and civic-mindedness.[35]

Xavante parents, leery of the priests' intentions, initially refused to allow the Salesians access to their children. Indigenous pedagogy, based on the collective inculcation and apprehension of skills in a broad social panorama, clashed with the waradzu method in which education was ministered in a socially segregated space by a select (and alien) individual.[36] Xavante society, divided by hierarchical age sets, traditionally placed all boys from the age of approximately seven to ten years for five years in the hë, or "bachelors' hut," where they learned from elders the requisite skills and ceremonial competences for initiation into adulthood. Nevertheless, it was most likely the food and medicine offered to the Xavante children that changed their parents' minds, along with the perception that education offered a key to empowerment. As a visitor to Sangradouro noted, "The parents like to send their children, because they have confidence in the priests, principally because of the medicine they give them."[37]

The Salesians soon convinced the Xavante to locate the bachelors' hut at the mission. At São Marcos, boys were fed at the mission, and one of the lay brothers slept in the bachelors' hut for closer "supervision."[38] The Salesians educated other age sets, as well as Xavante girls, who were schooled separately. During the early years at the mission, literacy training was provided to children as well as adults in Portuguese, with Latin reserved for liturgy. The Salesians did not endorse education in the Xavante tongue.[39] In 1962, four years after the Xavante had arrived at São Marcos, visitors to the mission noted that the Indians could tell time, converse minimally in Portuguese, and sing hymns and patriotic songs.[40]

The missionaries instructed young Xavante women in domestic service and agricultural husbandry. Young men were apprenticed as carpenters, cowhands, shoemakers, agriculturists, and machinists; they operated tractors, threshers, and trucks, and labored in the brickyard, in construction, and on hydraulic works to supply the mission's electric power.[41] The Salesian fathers supervised the indigenous men, who mustered their respective age grades, as well as the women, to their respective tasks. Such instruction was imparted through wage incentives as well as heavy-handed methods. The Salesians instituted a remunerative system whereby Xavante men and women received vouchers of various colors corresponding to the value of services performed. The scrip was redeemable at the mission store for consumer and industrial goods: tools, fishing hooks and hunting gear, needle and thread and fabric, and cooking supplies such as salt, sugar, and oil.[42] Xavante testimony bemoans, as well, the missionaries' use of physical punishment to discipline children—a trend not uncommon in religious or public schools in Brazil but unheard of among the Xavante—and the exploitation of their labor.[43]

The transformations wrought by the Salesians were dramatic. As the chief of the spi Eighth Inspectorate marveled in 1966: "The work carried out by the Xavante with the assistance of the missionaries is really notable: large plots planted, a brickyard, diverse wooden constructions. All demonstrate work, order and the spirit of organization."[44] Needless to say, religious indoctrination, educational training, and labor discipline all served to crimp communal undertakings and ceremonies requiring broader preparation and participation. The Xavante hunted with less frequency, and youths educated by the missionaries (who disapproved of trekking) resisted their parents' efforts to take them away.[45]

In 1971, Father Bartolomeu Giaccaria, director of the Sangradouro mission, praised the "spontaneous" participation of the Xavante in the labor regimen established by the Salesians, "with all agricultural produce, directly or indirectly, utilized by the students, children, and elders of the village." Nevertheless, he also hinted that such spontaneity stemmed less from choice than from necessity. As he noted, land for the Indians had become increasingly "insufficient for hunting, fishing, and gathering of wild fruits."[46] With their earnings lacking buying power outside the mission, the Indians' dependency on the Salesians—who also commercialized the Indians' handicrafts and their crops—was further entrenched.[47]

Missionary influence and proscription also contributed to new forms of representation—if not self-perception as well. Xavante youths at the Salesian mission, swaggering about in city-made snakeskin belts and speaking a few sentences of pidgin Portuguese, proudly told David Maybury-Lewis that, unlike the community at Pimentel Barbosa, they no longer practiced "sorcery" or murder.[48] In a similar vein, a mission Indian responded to a São Félix shopkeeper's taunt by declaiming, "Xavante not savage . . . Xavante not kill Christians!"[49]

Missionaries cheered Xavante submission to religious dogma and labor regimentation. A report by the sil in 1967 noted that "physically, morally, economically, educationally, and spiritually in all aspects of their life, the Xavante are much better today than in the period of their pacification only some 13 years ago." This owed, in their estimation, to the Indians' "great acceptance of Christianity" and their access to the Bible now that "a number of Xavantes can read their own language and are beginning to read Portuguese."[50] Likewise, the South American Indian Mission boasted that 150 Xavantes had been baptized in the villages of Batoví and Paraíso.[51] At the Salesian missions, the "spirit of religiosity of these Indians" glowed with daily prayers offered in both Portuguese and Xavante. So, too, did their loyalty to the Salesians, with the Indians "reacting violently against those who refer disapprovingly to the missionaries or who want to interfere in their lives."[52]

It is interesting to compare the experience of missionized Xavante with those under the direct domination of the spi. In a book showcasing the Brazilian government's indigenous policy, Darcy Ribeiro touted its enlightened pedagogical methods, which ensured "the moral elevation of the Indian, based on the values of his own culture, and acceptance of tribal customs."[53] Ribeiro was one who "referred disapprovingly" to Salesian methods, assailing the internato for breeding "marginals and misfits." Segregated in missionary schools, Indian youths had been deprived of the socialization provided by village life and had been transformed into "professional Indians," social pariahs dependent on spi assistance.[54] Indeed, spi officials had long lambasted missionary education, whose "sterilizing prayers and devotions" instilled in Indians "a weakened spirit" that stripped them "of the pride which the conquistadores were not able to dominate." Education in spi schools, contoured to the Indians' heritage and respective degree of acculturation, would nurture feelings of self-worth, cushioning the painful process of integration and producing better servants for the nation.[55]

Though less restrictive of social mores than were the missionaries, spi respect for tribal custom was less open-ended than apparent. Ribeiro himself considered it "foolish romanticism" to imagine that the cultural practices of indigenous groups could be preserved after contact. The spi schools sought to prepare the Indian "for the life he will live as a wage laborer." Indian boys were to be schooled in carpentry, shoemaking, and leatherworks, and girls were to be trained as seamstresses—more a reflection of Brazilian than indigenous gendered division of labor.[56] Like the missions, spi posts targeted children, viewed as more impressionable, promising, and accommodating of change.[57]

Through Portuguese instruction, literacy training, and civic lessons, the post labored to instill "a more general and accurate notion about the Nation and the tribe itself."[58] (Until 1970, state officials rejected literacy training in the native tongue or even bilingual education, alleging the infeasibility of preparing alphabets and grammar books in Brazil's nearly two hundred indigenous languages.)[59]

Indeed, neither bureaucrat nor missionary questioned the basic mission of remaking the Xavante.[60] Both discounted the political economy of the Xavante and disregarded the sociocultural importance of the land, redoubling efforts to convert the Indians into agriculturists and wage laborers. Both viewed Indians as indolent, backward, and slow-witted.[61] If the missionaries meddled in indigenous affairs, the SPI pried "through suasive means." And if missionaries spread the message of God, the SPI preached the gospel of order, progress, and nationalism.[62]

Perhaps more significant than differences in educational outlook between missionary and government official were those in input. In general, primary education never topped the list of government expenditures in Brazil and remote rural areas particularly suffered the brunt of such dereliction. Nor was education given priority by the SPI, stymying the retention of staff and provision of pedagogic, technical, and material resources.[63] Lamenting the spotty school attendance record of Xavante children, encarregado Agapto Silva noted that his post had managed to provide meals for the students only four times over the preceding year.[64] Indeed, the Xavante were well aware of the disparity between the pedagogical messages of the SPI—such as compensation for labor—and the agency's track record. In 1965, the encarregado at Pimentel Barbosa, Eurides Radunz, remarked that the Indians refused to work for the post based on "the exhange of conversation or promises," demanding immediate "payment in specie."[65]

Of Day-to-Day Resistance, Accommodation, Adaptation

As José de Souza Martins has memorably noted, indigenous people are compelled to live "a life of duplicity," shielding certain elements of their culture from scrutiny and revealing only that behavior sanctioned by their dominators.[66] Outward signs of religious observance or social compliance, then, should not be taken as signs of uniform or unswerving submission to waradzu hegemony, nor as categoric rejection of native practice. Dominant forms, imposed on the Indians, would commingle with, confront, or overlay indigenous practice.

In an effort to reproduce cultural values, rights and obligations, and modes of exchange that traditionally had ordered their lives and defined their identities, the Xavante retained the age-set system, exogamous moieties, uxorilocal residence, and communal institutions. The replication of cultural forms and patterns served as a means of empowerment, allowing social persons and their communities to embrace ideals that made life meaningful amid the sweeping changes that had uncontrollably enveloped them.[67] Because certain communal ceremonies apparently bore little connection to theistic beliefs, they did not clash head-on with missionary doctrine, although specific rites suffering clerical condemnation came under greater strain.[68]

As Laura Graham has shown, through discursive and expressive ceremonial practices, the Xavante fostered a sense of cultural resilience in the midst of tumultuous historical circumstances. Xavante fathers continued to summon their sons to their sleeping mats in the afternoons to relate bits of family history through oral transmission; likewise, elders of the senior age grade, in the quest for immortality, passed on memories to the youth, promoting and perpetuating a cultural identity and sense of agency as Xavante. The cyclical recurrence of age-set names engendered an illusion of continuity and renewal as younger Xavante men were linked to their forebears, just as forms of singing, name giving, and ritual were passed from seniors to youths. The deceased, viewed as immortals watching over the living, revealed themselves to Xavante men in dreams shared and performed collectively. This connectedness with the past was further signaled in the Indians' forms of singing and in their cycle of rituals, such as *uiwede*, buriti log relay races held during the rainy season that pit the members of one agamous moiety against the other. In linking themselves to the past through myth telling and performance and celebration of the power of their ancestors and creators, the Indians replicated cultural forms, promoted feelings of persistence, and affirmed a distinctive Xavante identity.[69] Indeed, when Maybury-Lewis inquired as to the significance of their ceremonies, Xavante responded simply that they were *wẽ da*, "to make beautiful."[70]

Although indigenous cultural performances conjured long-standing traditions, their content and meaning varied according to the changing circumstances and creative innovation of community members.[71] As Joanne Rappaport notes, commemorative ceremonies not only remind participants of events but *re-present* them, lending an instrumentality to history by shifting its locus from the past to the metaphysical present.[72] Moreover, though the Xavante endeavored to kindle feelings of continuity with the past, these efforts at cultural reproduction were neither smooth nor seamless, but rather prone to conflict and contestation, as undoubtedly occurred prior to contact.

As the Xavante struggled to temper enforced dependency, they engaged in other acts of defiance. The Indians balked, malingered, dissembled, dragged and voted with their feet, and played missionary and indigenista against one another. Although the exploration of the "weapons of the weak," or day-to-day forms of resistance, lies outside this work, numerous incidents suggest their pervasiveness during the years following contact.[73] For example, efforts to refine indigenous gastronomy, a longtime marker of "civilization," foundered.[74] In a meeting with Apoena at the Pimentel Barbosa post, Air Force Brigadier Aboim recoiled when his companion casually snacked on roasted grasshoppers from a straw basket. With noblesse oblige, he offered Apoena a tin of saltines. Nibbling cautiously on a cracker, the Xavante chief winced, dumped out the contents of the tin, and placed the grasshoppers in his newfound container.[75]

Missionaries met similar challenges in tackling indigenous social mores. Researchers examining marriage patterns at Pimentel Barbosa, Simões Lopes, and São Marcos in 1963 and 1964 found polygyny widely practiced in all three villages, with over 40 percent of the 184 men studied married to more than one wife. Missionaries might have been more successful in curbing "child marriages"—nearly 30 percent of the marriages reported at Pimentel Barbosa involved prepubescent girls, whereas only one such marriage was acknowledged at Simões Lopes and none at São Marcos—but this difference may have reflected the strategic concealment of such betrothals from the clerics.[76] Likewise, J. R. Amaral Lapa, a visitor to Sangradouro, noted that notwithstanding Salesian efforts to clothe the Indians, "When far from the priests, in the natural life of the village, men and women do not use, in general, even feathers as a covering. They go about entirely naked."[77] With duplicity or temerity, Xavante struggled to defend certain native cultural practices from being refashioned or rooted out by outsiders.

For historically seminomadic and factionalized communities, dispersal and relocation (or its threat) offered another recourse to temper external domination. In a stunning rebuff to missionary intervention, a handful of Xavante, under the leadership of "Chief" Benedito Loazo, abandoned the mission at Sangradouro in the early 1960s and returned to their precontact (and now mostly titled) lands in the Couto Magalhães region.[78] Loazo's group would turn to the SPI and local ranchers as a counterweight to missionary assistance.

Yet, at other times, community members conformed selectively to new restrictions and opportunities or sought to make the most of their contradictions. While welcoming industrial and consumer goods to satisfy new tastes and needs, Xavante readily forgot admonishments against becoming "professional Indians." With poor conditions besetting the post, particularly the chronic lack of medical supplies and personnel, Indians traveled to the inspectorate in search of handouts.[79] But then, had not SPI Director Tasso Villar de Aquino, on a visit to Pimentel Barbosa in 1961, discussed with the Indians, "particularly the caciques," the agency's commitment to community health care and agricultural production?[80]

While highlighting forms of Xavante resistance, we must avert a tendency to overstate the cultural impermeability or unitary consciousness of subaltern groups.[81] Like other indigenous peoples after contact, members of Xavante communities demonstrated a range of responses to their subordinate position within Brazilian society.[82] Apoena, it should be recalled, had proudly savored his grasshoppers, but he also clearly preferred the tin box as a receptacle. In fact, exposure to Brazilian practices and values shamed many Indians, who sought to conceal or jettison aspects of precontact culture. Many avidly donned clothing and Brazilian hairstyles to discard "savage" traces.[83] At Sangradouro, Xavante no longer constructed houses in traditional circular style arrayed in a crescent, but rather built oblong Brazilian-style abodes laid out in rows. At São Marcos, both men and women developed a passion for a new recreational form: soccer.[84] Indeed, indigenous imitativeness might even be reprimanded by missionaries or government agents if its precipitancy riled their moral sensibilities or acculturationist timetable. Thus, Salesian missionaries urged the Xavante at Sangradouro to retain their original hairstyles, "one of their most beautiful and appreciable peculiarities," in combating the Indians' "imitative instinct which has given them the desire to cut their hair like the whites."[85]

Nor should it be surprising, given Xavante social segmentation by age and gender, that disparate sectors responded differently to external domination.[86] We have already examined how Xavante youths were more amenable or vulnerable than elders to missionary admonishments to forsake hunting. Gendered variations emerged as well. Although the wai'a might have been an important male ritual—symbol of masculine hierarchy, virility, and aggression—for some women it was clearly no cause for celebration. An elaborate ceremony carried out in conjunction with male initation, the wai'a culminated in the ceremonial rape of select women from each moiety by all men of the officiating age set. While serving to stanch rivalry among men, the wai'a undoubtedly struck terror in many women. Intervention by outsiders offered women some recourse. At the Salesian mission, one Xavante woman fled her consigned fate and sought asylum with the church fathers. In subsequent wai'a, other women followed suit. As a result of female resistance and their strategic alliance with Salesians, Xavante men would be hard-pressed to carry out the wai'a while at the mission, although they continued to perform it on trek.[87]

Of course, Xavante adaptation of waradzu forms did not necessarily signify that a given object, symbol, or mode of behavior had the same meaning or relevance for the Indians. For example, when Xavante attended school their expectations diverged markedly from their teachers'. Whereas educators offered vocational training as a consolation prize for socioeconomic subordination, the Indians aspired to positions of power held by government officials, technicians, and white-collar professionals they encountered.[88] A report from one SPI teacher noted:

> The Xavante Indians have a mistaken idea regarding the knowledge that the school will give them. They believe that in a short time they will be able to learn how to make tractors, cars, airplanes or radios, and other materials whose elaboration is difficult and even we do not know how they are made. Or they believe that they will leave the school as doctors and will learn in a short period of time how our society functions. These ideas are shared at times by the Chief of the Community, who hopes firmly that the school will provide this knowledge.[89]

Schools, then, became another contested arena for waradzu and Xavante, each armed with conflicting notions regarding educational capabilities and objectives.

Ultimately, dependency on outsiders, though restrictive of Xavante political economy and cultural expression, did not generate defeatism.

Rather, the Xavante assessed that through mastery of the sociopolitical codes of the waradzu they could regain greater autonomy over their lives *and* access to Western goods. For the Xavante the price of becoming a Brazilian Indian entailed territorial loss, infant mortality, and cultural violence, yet potential redress lay in the rights of citizenship and indigenous entitlement. Through the acquisition of Portuguese and apprehension of Brazilian civic culture, Xavante leaders (whether subordinate to cleric or bureaucrat) would embrace newfound forms of political interlocution and identification to secure control over territory, communal affairs, and Western commodities. A key component in this strategy entailed the deployment of "traditional" practice in the service of sociocultural change.

A New Political Language

Xavante acquisition of Portuguese evinces strategic appropriation of an armature of conquest. Portuguese had long been upheld by state officials as a marker and determinant of Brazilian nationality. Just as Vargas clamped down on foreign-language schools and periodicals during the Estado Novo, enthusiasts of the March to the West noted the "paradox of maintaining the *true Brazilians* speaking different languages from ours."[90] Indigenous tongues, then, were seen as a hindrance to national unity, whereas Portuguese was upheld as a cultural glue and ethnic anesthesia.

Estado Novo officials valued indigenous tongues not for their present-day usage but for their historic contribution to the formation of a "Brazilian language."[91] Francisco Campos, the framer of the Constitution of the Estado Novo, asserted that indigenous and African influences in Brazil had converted Portuguese from the pedantic material of "dust-covered books" into a "rebellious and amorous language, picturesque and full of malice, the language of our people."[92] Thus, when Minister of Education Gustavo Capanema proposed in 1943 the instruction of Tupi-Guarani at the Federal University of Rio de Janeiro, he trumpeted its cultural-linguistic importance in the colonial period rather than contemporary parlance of its linguistic derivatives by various indigenous groups.[93] The celebration of a fossilized native language dovetailed better with the state's nationalist tribute to (hierarchical) racial mixture and indigenous disappearance.

Observers held dichotomous views regarding Indians who lacked proficiency in Portuguese. Some, like Ildefonso Escobar, argued that retention of indigenous language signaled categorical rejection of dominant society, as "the tribes, speaking different dialects, seek to avoid contact with the Brazilians." Others, like Darcy Ribeiro, envisioned that the Indians would one day speak Portuguese "without an accent," a sign of their transformation into true-blue Brazilians.[94]

Like other facets of interethnic relations, linguistic engagement defied such binary vision. Within their communities, Xavante continued to speak their native tongue (while incorporating Portuguese words into their vocabulary). They also insisted on learning Portuguese. Giaccaria and Heide have argued that Xavante consider language a generative force and therefore clamored for the waradzu to teach the secrets of their language so that they too might be empowered. Withholding Portuguese instruction—and, initially, even promoting bilingual education—was decried as obscurantist.[95] Like other speakers of vernacular languages worldwide, many Xavante understood that monolingualism shackled its interlocutors in engaging the world around them.[96]

Efforts by Xavante to acquire Portuguese, whether at the mission or SPI post, resembled a strategy of colonized peoples worldwide who have appropriated the imperial language to master its cultural codes, often to subvert them.[97] Brazilian Portuguese, a cultural-linguistic artifact marshaled by Estado Novo elites to forge pan-Brazilian unity and to challenge the legacy of colonial rule, would be reworked by Xavante as a cultural-linguistic artifact of pan-Indian protest and a challenge to the legacy of Brazilian rule.[98] With very marked accents, indigenous leaders used Portuguese to denounce the violation of their constitutional right to land, to assert entitlements to social welfare, and to negotiate greater autonomy over community affairs.

Of course, Portuguese instruction had multiple and uneven effects on Xavante communities, as language and expression are constituted by and constitutive of social thought.[99] If Portuguese, for example, had one word for bee honey, Xavante coined scores, reflecting its centrality in the Indians' precontact pursuits. If Xavante lacked numbers greater than five, Portuguese, articulating a culture of acquisitiveness, boasted infinity.[100] Moreover, proficiency in spoken and written Portuguese, skills prized by the dominant society, altered dynamics of power within Xavante communities. Participation in formal political affairs had been limited to "mature" men; recent initiates into adulthood were barred from political debate in the warã, or council of elder men, until they achieved fatherhood and mastered oratorical skills. However, as chiefs increasingly looked to waradzu for assistance, they came to rely on younger assistants (later known as "secretaries") more proficient in Portuguese and savvy about Brazilian political culture.[101] The emergence of younger men as political power brokers in negotiations with outsiders, if not a tell-tale indication of hierarchical strain, represented an elevation in the former's stature within the community. Moreover, Xavante men attained greater proficiency in Portuguese than did women, owing to and facilitating increased interaction with waradzu.

Aside from Portuguese instruction, the Xavante gleaned new forms of political engagement and protest from civic lessons administered by missionaries and SPI officials. At SPI posts, the teacher (often the wife of the post chief) taught Xavante students about the nation's history, geography, and political system. To inspire the Xavante to "always love, respect and defend our nation," Lucy Soares da Silva, a teacher at the Simões Lopes post in 1960, recounted momentous episodes such as the Portuguese "discovery," the abolition of slavery, and the founding of Cuiabá. "I make them sing the National Anthem with me at the beginning of class," Silva boasted, and "every Sunday we raise the Flag to rehearse because the Xavante need lots of rehearsing."[102]

Violeta Tocantins, who taught at Simões Lopes in 1965, sought to inculcate in her students an understanding of their rights and responsibilities as Indians and Brazilian citizens. Her students learned that "Brazil is a democracy, that is, a nation in which all are equal before the law and where the government is elected by the people. Those who were born in our Nation or under our nationality are Brazilian citizens, entitled because of this to enjoy the rights conceded by our constitution, where the basic laws of Brazil are found."[103] Tocantins's lesson was passé: the democracy had been quashed a year earlier by the military. Moreover, indigenous people would be granted the right to vote only by a Supreme Court decision of 1966, the following year.[104] Nevertheless, she had clearly articulated notions of "citizens' rights" to liberty, education, and safety as well as their responsibilities to "work for the greatness of Brazil."[105] At Pimentel Barbosa, post officials informed the Xavante of their constitutional right to land, assuring, "This is your land—when you die it will be for your children."[106]

Educators also lectured their students on "the" indigenous past. A third-year student's examination, forwarded by Tocantins to the SPI inspectorate, reveals the pedagogic thrust. When the Portuguese arrived in Brazil, wrote the student, "Brazilindians lived almost naked. They wore a feathered loincloth on their waist and a crown of feathers on their head. They painted their body, and used necklaces from beads and animal teeth. They managed on game, fish, fruits, roots, etc. The Brazilindians did not have religion, they worshipped the sun, the moon and the stars and they feared thunder which they called Tupã." This historical rendition, concocted by whites, erased cultural distinctions among indigenous peoples, branding all patriotically (and anachronistically) as "Brazilindians."[107] Indeed, the curricular emphasis on the pan-Indian historical experience and sociocultural integration was featured right in the classroom: the Xavante at Simões Lopes, for example, studied together with Bakairi children as well as those of post officials and local residents.

Yet, although educators distorted and devalued Xavante history, they provided raw material for future political deployment. As the nation's aboriginal citizens—"Brazilindians"—Xavante could clamor for the delimitation of their precontact territory. Through pan-Indian appeals, Xavante could reach out to indigenous "brethren" as well as nonindigenous sympathizers.

The SPI posts bolstered both civic-mindedness and notions of Indianness through celebrations such as the Day of the Indian and Rondon's birthday. Superimposed on traditional Xavante notions of time, these festivities sought to convey "how beneficial the union existing between civilizados and Indians is, a friendship which ought to be encouraged whenever possible."[108] Thus, at the Simões Lopes post, the Day of the Indian was commemorated in 1960 by a crowd of Xavante, Bakairi, and civilizados who sang the national anthem and the hymn to the Brazilian flag while standing before a portrait of Rondon. A Bakairi and a Xavante student recited poetry, and the Xavante entertained the group with a traditional dance. But as faithfulness to indigenous tradition was not really the order of the day—or of government policy in general—festivities were capped with a reprise of the national anthem.[109] In a similar vein, the hundredth anniversary of Rondon's birth was commemorated in Cuiabá in 1965 with a dance ceremony featuring fifty Xavante and fifty Bororo "showing their physical strength and paying their respect" before a stadium of eight thousand onlookers.[110]

Staged for Brazilian audiences, these spectacles were designed to symbolize indigenous acquiescence to state power. State officials authorized—and encouraged—the Xavante "traditions" performed on the Brazilian political stage. Body ornamentation, chants, and dances were lovely to behold; "nomadism," "sorcery," and violence were better off squelched. Indigenous "folklore" was quaint; extensive territorial claims were not. Brazilian racial democracy was to be displayed, but indigenous socioeconomic marginality obscured. These celebrations reflected contradictions in indigenous policy as well. Despite the official emphasis on acculturation, indigenous tributes in civic commemorations and history lessons, however inauthentic or unrepresentative, upheld a distinct "Indian" identity as an integral part of the nation's heritage.

The ideological nuance would not elude the Xavante. They soon surmised the symbolic capital of indigenous difference—traditional, ascribed, or a combination thereof—as a mechanism to advance territorial claims and sociocultural empowerment. The dominant discourse regarding indigenous people offered numerous tropes to enlist state (or missionary) assistance: Indian as protopatriot, racial partner, endangered species, defenseless child, and exotic other. Of course, the Xavante response to external domination was not entirely improvised or fabricated from scratch. The Indians, for example, did not need waradzu to teach them that their rituals were special or "beautiful"; of this most Xavante were long convinced. They also understood that native memory, narrative, and performance engendered a sense of control over externally imposed change.[111] Rather, from interaction with outsiders the Indians would apprehend that their rituals were not only "beautiful" but *political* as well.[112] They would publicly reckon their ancestors not only as immortals but as "Brazilindians." These new ideological weapons, much like the war clubs of the past, would be brandished at dominant society in the struggle for power and autonomy. Rather than signifying a utopian return to primordial ways, Xavante "traditions" would embody and empower culturally specific modes of adaptation.[113]

"Brazilindians"

In the aftermath of contact, Xavante had experienced a painful loss of life, territorial domain, and cultural autonomy. Several communities suffered violent attack and exile, and infant mortality surged. Missionaries and government officials offered protection from physical harm and, in varying degrees, health care, civic education, Portuguese instruction, and access to Brazilian commodities. Yet these agents of dominant society exploited indigenous vulnerability to root out sociocultural practices deemed objectionable. Moreover, they ascribed to the Xavante a legal and cultural identity as "Brazilindians": naïfs who required oversight and discipline, yet protopatriots whose cultural difference glorified the nation's heritage.

The Xavante responded to enforced dependency through selective adaptation. Although external domination placed great strain on Xavante communities, the Indians struggled to sustain communal institutions, structures, and ceremonies that reproduced the cultural values that ordered their lives and identities. Through discursive or expressive practices, the Indians linked themselves to the past, generating a sense of empowerment amid such sweeping change. Yet outsiders' taunts also shamed Xavante into abandoning or disguising certain traditional modes of behavior. The Indians demonstrated enthusiasm for Brazilian goods and recreational forms and aspired to attain proficiency in Portuguese and positions of power valued by dominant society. Of course, not all members of Xavante communities, riven by factions and segmented by age and gender, responded identically to outside intervention, given that their traditional roles and historical experiences had varied.

Although territorial loss and cultural change bred woe and confusion among Xavante communities, it did not engender hopelessness. Rather, the Xavante increasingly sensed that strategic engagement of dominant society offered the prospect of regaining usurped land and autonomy as well as continued access to Brazilian goods. From civic lessons and commemorations the Xavante surmised that indigenous "tradition," endogenous or imputed, offered a valuable tool in the struggle for greater power. With white proscriptions and expectations dictating modes of behavior in interethnic settings, the Xavante were pressed to expand their political repertoire, adapting, reworking, or inventing cultural traditions. Civic education and Portuguese, material imparted by elites to cement consensus, would be transformed by Xavante leaders into a language of dissent engaging state power. The "traditional" Indian showcased by the Xavante in the Brazilian political arena surfaced in acts of mobilization and protest. For the Xavante, becoming Brazilian and becoming Indian did not represent a bane of territorial dislocation and sociocultural domination; it represented a balm. As "Brazilindians," the Xavante braved a political climate transformed by military rule and a natural landscape reconfigured by corporate investment, large-scale migration, and environmental degradation.

6

"Where the Earth Touches the Sky"

New Horizons for Indigenous Policy under

Early Military Rule, 1964–1973

In 1964, the Brazilian armed forces deposed President João Goulart, ushering in twenty-one years of military rule. During Goulart's presidency, the nation had been wracked by high inflation, stalled production, and other strains caused by structural limitations of import-substitution industrialization, as well as by mounting political polarization.[1] Members of the industrial and agrarian elite, who feared losing control of national political institutions under a populist democracy, encouraged military intervention. The military purged leftists from government and repressed peasant and labor movements, but did not relinquish power as soon as some elites had hoped. The military's blueprint to stabilize and reform financial markets, rectify sectoral and regional imbalances, and shore up national security occasioned a significant reconfiguration of Brazilian politics.

The military government sought to modify the inward-oriented development model, promoting and diversifying manufacturing and agricultural exports. Through tax incentive schemes, tightened credit, and wage squeezes, the infusion of foreign capital through official and private loans and direct investment, and state investment in infrastructure, the military endeavored to stimulate capital accumulation. Political repression was key to the implementation of this developmental model.[2]

Unlike counterparts in the Southern Cone, the Brazilian bureaucratic authoritarian regime did not eliminate representative institutions entirely. Although it abolished all existing political parties, the military organized a pro-government party, Aliança Nacional Renovadora (ARENA), and allowed the creation of an opposition party, Movimento Democrático Brasileiro (MDB). Regularly scheduled elections were permitted. Nevertheless, the restrictive parameters and repressive climate established by the military clearly sought to centralize and depoliticize policy making. Through numerous "institutional acts," "complementary acts," and repression of political opposition, the military strengthened the executive while weakening the legislature, and bolstered the national over subnational government. Presidentially proposed bills and constitutional amendments could be approved with a smaller congressional majority and within a shorter time frame; the executive was further empowered to bypass Congress altogether in enacting legislation by decree.[3] Emasculating the legislature, purging leftist as well as traditional politicians, quashing popular opposition, and impaneling hundreds of new councils and state enterprises, the regime sought to give free rein to a technocratic corps of economists, engineers, administrators, and military officers to formulate and execute state policy. For indigenous people, wards of the federal government, the centralization of state power under an authoritarian regime committed to frontier development signaled a historical watershed.

The military's developmental project for the region of Amazônia Legal (Legal Amazonia), home to the majority of Brazilian indigenous groups as well as the majority of the nation's territory, aimed to promote industrialization, agricultural modernization, and infrastructural expansion to address regional disequilibrium, and "national security." Sprawling over five million square kilometers, Legal Amazonia covered nearly two-thirds of Brazilian territory (see Map 5). With its sparse population, precarious infrastructure, tenuous links to the nation's economic and demographic core, and unfortified international boundaries, Legal Amazonia was viewed by military officials as vulnerable to foreign appropriation and communist infiltration. National security ideology premised Brazilian defense on industrialization, effective utilization of natural resources, and "national integration" through extensive transportation and communication networks.[4] To protect Amazonia from "possible paths of penetration" and internal subversion, General Golbery Couto e Silva, an influential military theorist, endorsed settling the "frontier areas starting from the advanced base that is to be constructed in the Center-West and following a coordinated and planned strategy of development along the large river."[5]

Moreover, the military viewed the creation of a modern agro-export sector as a priority in boosting economic performance and industrial out-

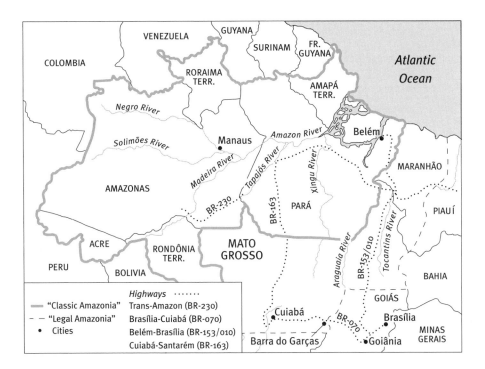

Map 5. Amazonia

put. Agricultural "rationalization" would overcome the food crises and economic bottlenecks of the early 1960s, promoting cheaper food for cities, new markets for industry, and export diversification for sustained growth. Through a dramatic increase in subsidized rural credit, export incentives, and reduced import tariffs on machinery and other inputs, the military sought to transform latifundios into rural enterprises and a select group of small farmers into dynamic entrepreneurs. Expansion of agricultural production into the Amazonian frontier would further stimulate economic growth and stem increased rural to urban migration.[6]

The boundaries of Legal Amazonia, devised according to sociopolitical criteria, expanded federal jurisdiction over the western frontier: whereas the "classic" or geographic definition of Amazonia historically employed by the Instituto Brasileiro de Geografia e Estatística (Brazilian Institute of Geography and Statistics, IBGE) comprised Amapá, Acre, Roraima, Pará, Amazonas, and Rondônia, Legal Amazonia augmented the area by over one-third by including the northern regions of Mato Grosso and Goiás and western Maranhão[7] (see Map 5). Xavante territory, located in northern Mato Grosso, would thereby fall under the jurisdictional domain of Legal Amazonia, subject to the military's developmental project for the region.

Efforts to transform the central western and northern hinterland, of course, had dogged Brazilian state officials (and the military in particular) since earlier in the century. Most notably, during the Estado Novo, Vargas had sought to rearticulate state-society relations in the region with the March to the West. Although the central government had been put on the defensive by regional oligarchs in the postwar period, the legislative framework remained in place. The Constitution of 1946, for example, had earmarked 3 percent of total federal tax revenues for Amazonian development. In fact, the boundaries of Legal Amazonia were established in 1953 under the democratic rule of Getúlio Vargas by Law 1806, which also created the Superintendência do Plano de Valorização Econômica da Amazônia (Superintendency for the Economic Valorization of the Amazon, SPVEA), a federal agency overseeing agroindustrial development and infrastructural growth. Budgetary weakness, political fragmentation, and corruption hamstrung the SPVEA, although it could count the construction of the Belém-Brasília highway, the first major roadbuilding project in the Amazon region, as a significant achievement.[8] Under the military—blessed with greater technological and fiscal capability than the Estado Novo, faced with stronger pressure and backing from private capital, and unhampered by the political and juridical constraints of its populist predecessors—Amazonian development would intensify as the state strengthened its institutional presence on the frontier (and throughout the Brazilian countryside).

For the Xavante, as this chapter explores, the most significant changes issued from rapid state-sponsored capitalist growth in northern Mato Grosso and increased federal jurisdiction over indigenous and regional affairs. Like other Brazilian Indians, the Xavante suffered a massive onslaught on their communities under military rule, "victims of the miracle" of economic development.[9] Yet, a closer examination reveals that the "miracle" did not descend smoothly from the mount. Rather, state policy was combated, negotiated, amended, and even embraced, at times, by the Xavante, who grappled with its multifaceted nature.

New Directions in Amazonian Development:
SUDAM and "Operation Amazon"

Military officials, attributing Amazonia's laggard development to its extractivist economy, weak capital markets, and oligarchic cronyism, sought to remedy all at one fell swoop.[10] The solution entailed an alliance of the state with multinational and domestic corporate capital. To compensate for the apprehensiveness of the former and the weakness of the latter in spearheading Amazonian development, the government assumed a central role in regulatory planning, production, international borrowing, and infrastructural investment, and in extending fiscal incentives to private capital in Amazonia.[11] In 1966, the military government replaced SPVEA with the Superintendência do Desenvolvimento da Amazônia (Superintendency for the Development of the Amazon, SUDAM) to plan and implement regional developmental policies. Nearly $2 billion was earmarked over the following five years for infrastructural development of transportation networks and public utilities and research and exploration of natural resources in the Amazon.[12] To lure private investors, the military government of General Humberto Castelo Branco unveiled "Operation Amazon," a cluster of legislation passed in 1966 and 1967, which offered generous tax breaks and fiscal incentives.

Law 5174, passed in October 1966, stipulated that up to 50 percent of corporate tax liability could be invested in agricultural, ranching, or industrial ventures approved by SUDAM in Legal Amazonia. Projects backed by SUDAM were further entitled to up to 75 percent of total investment costs financed by tax credit funds, as well as below-market loans by the Banco da Amazônia (BASA), SUDAM's financial agent. To sweeten the offer further, all SUDAM-backed ventures established in Legal Amazonia prior to 1972 (later extended to 1975) were exempt from income tax, and those established prior to 1982 would enjoy a 50 percent reduction. Local states and counties proffered additional inducements through tax breaks.[13]

In light of the military government's commitment to political centralization, agricultural modernization, frontier settlement, and national security, we can explore the decision to overhaul indigenous policy. To foster accumulation on the Amazonian frontier, government planners apprehended the importance of reserving indigenous land to safeguard title holders from contentious claims and conflict.[14] Multilateral lending institutions, such as the World Bank and the InterAmerican Development Bank, extending credit for agricultural development applicable to the Amazon, promoted regularization of rural cadastres and land titles to stimulate future investment and production.[15] Furthermore, violence stemming from Amazonian land conflicts prompted concern by military officials attentive to national security threats.[16] One of the divisions of the Conselho de Segurança Nacional (National Security Council, CSN) conducted studies, elaborated reports, and formulated policy on matters concerning indigenous populations, Amazonian settlement, and land conflicts.[17] Xavante lands, almost entirely unreserved by the late 1960s, were but the tip of the iceberg.[18]

Through enactment of legislation and strengthening of the federal bureaucracy, the military state assumed a more interventionist role in mediating socioeconomic relations in Amazonia, including indigenous affairs. Arrogating control over indigenous lands, heretofore claimed by local governments as terra devoluta, the state circumscribed the power of local elites. Dismissing indigenous claims, the military strove to delimit minimal reserves in the interest of promoting capital accumulation.

Notwithstanding political centralization and repression, the military would face numerous challenges in its project for Amazonian development. The feared foreign assault on the Amazonian hinterland would come—not in the form of armed invasion but in a welter of worldwide condemnation of indigenous policy. At the grassroots level, the situation remained equally rancorous. For investors and politicians in Mato Grosso, no indigenous territory reserved by the federal government was small enough. For the Xavante, no reserve was big enough. And neither side was disposed to surrender.

The Figueiredo Report and Its Ramifications

The military signaled its intent to overhaul indigenous policy in 1967 when Attorney General Jader Figueiredo was entrusted with investigating corruption in the SPI. Malfeasance in the SPI was not a secret—given an earlier congressional inquest and the litany of internal investigations—

but the military resolve to clean up the agency bespoke commitment to change. Although a "mysterious" fire at the Ministry of Agriculture hobbled Figueiredo's investigation—destroying SPI correspondence, financial records, and confidential reports—the attorney general proceeded through inquiries, interviews, and visits to Indian posts. In March 1968, he held a press conference to publicize the findings of his twenty-volume, 5,115-page report.

Evidence had been found not only of massive corruption, land grabbing, and labor exploitation but of massacres, enslavement, rape, torture, and biological warfare against the indigenous population. The abuse stemmed from the dereliction and, at times, collusion of SPI officials, although there was no evidence of systematic state-backed efforts to eliminate indigenous peoples.[19] Figueiredo concluded, however, that through lack of assistance, the SPI had "persecuted the Indians to the point of extermination."[20] Of the 700 employees of the SPI, 134 were charged with crimes, 33 removed, and 17 suspended.[21] In December 1967, the military dismantled the SPI and created the Fundação Nacional do Índio (FUNAI), subsumed under the Ministry of the Interior.

The investigation of the Indian agency conformed to military efforts to "rationalize" the bureaucracy to eliminate corruption, clientelism, and leftist "infiltration."[22] What is curious, however, is the military's decision to divulge rather than muffle the shocking findings of the Figueiredo Report, thereby risking international opprobrium. In part, the Figueiredo Report staged a perfect morality play to legitimize authoritarian rule in spotlighting corrosion of the public sector under the populists. Military officials apparently also wagered that in publicizing crimes against Indians they would earn kudos for salvaging Brazil's sacred racial harmony. One month after the release of the Figueiredo Report, the Ministry of the Interior impressed on a skittish Ministry of Foreign Relations that denouncing these atrocities "could only strengthen abroad the Brazilian image with regard to racial democracy" and demonstrate that military rule was "incompatible, in its spirit, with the process of human degradation."[23]

The decision to publicize the report backfired. Condemnations of government-backed genocide—which was factually unfounded—blanketed the Brazilian press.[24] Notwithstanding the military's sanctimoniousness, few believed that long-neglected Indian rights were suddenly being safeguarded by the most unlikely of heroes: a military regime committed to the rapid development of the Amazon. For opponents, the controversy offered an opportunity to challenge the military and enlist foreign support. Politicians from the MDB, the legal opposition party, threatened to appeal to the United Nations to place Brazil's indigenous populations under international guardianship—one of the regime's dreaded nightmares.[25]

To the military's chagrin, the accusations ricocheted into the international arena and provoked an avalanche of censure. An embarrassed and offended Brazilian government would spend years fending off charges of genocide as scathing denunciations of Brazilian Indian policy appeared in the European press.[26] The Ministry of Foreign Relations rushed to aid bedraggled Brazilian diplomats, disseminating bulletins that highlighted official measures to safeguard indigenous rights; the Brazilian delegation at the United Nations was enjoined to combat any resolution in the General Assembly charging the government with genocide.[27] The demon of genocide, first conjured up by military officials, refused to disappear. In 1970, the International Red Cross, on the invitation of the Brazilian government, partook in a three-month fact-finding mission to twenty different indigenous groups, including one Xavante community, to investigate these charges. Other foreign delegations followed: in 1972 the London-based Aborigines Protection Society visited Brazil, issuing a report on the condition of indigenous peoples.[28]

International and domestic pressure on the Brazilian government opened new horizons for indigenous peoples in their struggle to secure land. Government officials, bristling at worldwide disapprobation, vowed everything possible to "remove the indigenous problem from the headlines of Brazilian and foreign newspapers." In July 1968 and April 1969 Minister of the Interior Albuquerque Lima met with the Xavante, Bororo, Karajá, and various Xingu communities to affirm governmental determination to reserve as well as to recover indigenous lands.[29] In July 1969, it was President Arthur da Costa e Silva's turn: in the footsteps of Getúlio Vargas nearly thirty years earlier, the military president visited Bananal Island, where he met with a delegation of Xavante, Karajá, Kayapó, and Kamaiurá Indians.

As on Vargas's trip in 1940, the Indians entertained Costa e Silva with "traditional" song and dance. But things were not quite the same. The president's pan-Indian audience was a tell-tale sign of how much had changed since the March to the West, when the "ferocious" Xavante were mortal enemies of the Karajá. So, too, was the response of the Xavante, who decades earlier knew little about the nation-state but now summoned the discourse imparted by missionaries and government to strike a responsive chord. In the "name of all the Xavante tribe," Humberto Waomote, an Indian from the São Marcos mission, thanked the president for his efforts to "improve the life of the Brazilian Indian."[30] Similarly, at the Salesian mission at Sangradouro, a Xavante proclaimed to Minister of the Interior Albuquerque Lima, "We are all Brazilians. We, the Xavantes, arrived first."[31]

Albuquerque Lima, impressed by the Xavante's "courageous" leaders, vowed to restore territory in the Couto Magalhães region, from which many had been expelled years before.[32] But decades-old promises to the Xavante would not be easy to fulfill in the name of developmental planning, social justice, or foreign relations. Federal officials were well aware that title holders to Xavante land and matogrossense politicians showed "systematic opposition" toward FUNAI and the Indians.[33]

FUNAI and the Indian Statute:
New Promises and Problems for Indians

Like the state agencies entrusted with rural development, colonization, and road building, FUNAI embodied the federal government's growing hegemony over the countryside and its efforts to foster capitalist growth and defuse social conflict through bureaucratic administration.[34] An amalgam of three previously separate entities entrusted with indigenous affairs—the SPI, CNPI, and Xingu National Park—FUNAI commanded greater power than any of its predecessors. To start, the military greatly enhanced federal revenues by enacting a sweeping fiscal reform package in 1966 (later incorporated into the 1967 Constitution), part of its project to wrest control of state spending from regional oligarchies. Between 1965 and 1975, the federal government increased its share of public service revenue from 63.9 percent to 72.9 percent.[35]

Moreover, FUNAI enjoyed greater legal jurisdiction as well. The Constitution of 1967, drafted under military rule, designated indigenous land as federal territory, with Indians granted permanent possession. Under the SPI, demarcation of indigenous reserves had been contingent, in practice, on excision by state governments of Indian territory from terra devoluta. State governments, however, had often failed to do so, unlawfully treating Indians as de facto occupants of terra devoluta. The military government's constitution deemed Indians the de jure possessors of federal territory. The federal government would be less beholden to local politicians compromised by electoral deals and vested interests in reserving indigenous land. A 1969 constitutional amendment undoubtedly struck further fear in investors whose hearts were set or feet were planted on indigenous territory: private titles to Indian land (federal property) were void and their holders ineligible for indemnification.[36]

Indigenous policy was codified in the Estatuto do Índio of 1973, which presented both promises and problems for the native population. On the one hand, the statute recognized the indigenous right to permanent possession and usufruct of land, a "habitat" adequate for self-sustenance and the maintenance of "custom and tribal traditions." It defined as indigenous lands those areas presently or historically occupied by Indians, or any region of national territory so mandated by the federal government. The statute called for FUNAI to delimit all indigenous land within five years, empowered the armed forces and federal police to assist the agency, and banned the leasing of Indian territory, common under the SPI.

But on the other hand, the Indian Statute honored existing leases, sanctioned the relocation of Indians by presidential decree for the sake of "national development," endorsed the commercial orientation of the indigenous post through promotion of renda indígena, and allowed the state to contract third parties for prospecting or mining on indigenous land. Moreover, the statute retained the legal status of Indians as tutelados subordinate to state power and upheld an acculturationist framework envisioning the eventual extinction or "emancipation" of indigenous communities.[37] Indeed, the administrative subordination of FUNAI, entrusted with Indian protection, to the Ministry of the Interior, mastermind of Amazonian development, spoke volumes.

For the Xavante, the state's fortified power represented a double-edged sword. In promoting Amazonian development through the extension of transportation networks and infrastructure, tax incentives, and colonization projects, the military intensified occupation and deforestation of Xavante land. Yet, with increased jurisdiction over indigenous land, the state offered new outlets for the Xavante in their struggle for territorial control. With the state armed as potential bodyguard or bully, the Xavante sought to curry favor through dramatic appeals and ultimatums. That the new and ambiguous rules of the political game might somehow redound to their benefit depended, in no small part, on indigenous forbearance and resourcefulness. For as the battle waged over the decade of the 1970s proved, the Xavante had something very different in mind from the government and investors regarding the fate of their lands.

The Cerrado Transformed into Cattle Pasture

Investors in Legal Amazonia represented segments of powerful industrial and agroindustrial capital from the domestic as well as the multinational sector (the latter concentrated more heavily in mining than ranching).[38] Between 1968 and 1975, 95 percent of all tax credit options in Legal Amazonia were held by extraregional interests, with corporations based in São Paulo accounting for 60 percent.[39] Corporate capital pressured the military government to subsidize cattle ranching, whose lower labor and infrastructural requirements were deemed more suitable to the region than agriculture or industry, given sparse population, services, and transportation networks.

Unlike older ranchers in the Amazon, who arrived in the region often in response to deterioration of land or labor at their place of origin and who lacked collective political representation capable of framing public policy (relying instead on the local police and regional authorities), the new corporate capital engaged in sophisticated lobbying of state bureaucracies.[40] As Fernando Henrique Cardoso has noted, with the emasculation of the legislature and political parties, instruments through which the elite had traditionally wielded power, interest representation became dependent on alliances with the military and technocrats (or "bureaucratic rings") who controlled the state apparatus.[41] Clientelism had not been excised from the body politic by the military; it had merely taken new forms in a highly regulated environment.

The mouthpiece of corporate capital in Legal Amazonia was the Association of Amazonian Entrepreneurs (Associação dos Empresários da Amazônia, AEA), formed in 1968. Headquartered in São Paulo, the AEA boasted solely cattle-ranching enterprises until 1976 and a board of directors culled from large national and multinational firms. Hermínio Ometto, a well-known paulista industrialist who served as first president of the AEA, was a "pioneer" in the Amazon: he had established the 600,000-hectare Suiá-Missu cattle ranch on Xavante lands at Marãiwatsede in 1961, three years before the military coup.[42] As head of the AEA, Ometto lobbied SUDAM to subsidize cattle ranching, sponsoring a visit of state ministers and top Amazonian policymakers to the region.[43] For until 1968, the bulk of government fiscal incentives in the region went to industrial ventures, and less than 40 percent benefited agricultural or livestock projects.[44] Corporate capital, exerting concerted pressure on a state dependent on its collaboration, would redraw the contours of government policy in the Amazon.

State planners endorsed the AEA's pitch for ranching as a primary pathway of Amazonian development. Fiscal incentives earmarked by SUDAM for livestock projects skyrocketed from CR$29.8 million in 1968 to CR$75.7 million in 1969 and CR$170.1 million in 1970, where they would hover for the next four years (see Table 1). By 1978, 503 cattle projects had been approved by SUDAM in Legal Amazonia, and approximately $1 billion invested in these ranches. To be sure, the World Bank and the InterAmerican Development Bank strongly backed cattle ranching in Brazil as a sound developmental option, with total direct livestock support between the late 1960s and 1970s summing $1.3 billion. Cattle ranching was trumpeted as a means to diversify exports and increase foreign revenue, although most Amazonian livestock would ultimately serve domestic consumption. Furthermore, by increasing cattle production, military officials sought to ensure low beef prices to the urban working class, shoring up support from a sector hard hit by the regime's wage freezes, economic stabilization policies, and political repression.[45]

State fiscal incentives and road-building projects precipitated an avalanche of investment and settlement in Xavante territory, as private capital savored northern Mato Grosso for cattle ranching and migrants came to the frontier in search of land. Between 1966 and 1970, SUDAM approved sixty-six agribusiness projects in the counties of Barra do Garças (home to the Xavante) and Luciara alone, with nearly CR$300 million awarded in fiscal incentives.[46] Banco do Brasil and BASA established branches in

Table 1.   SUDAM Fiscal Incentives, 1965–1973
(in CR$)

Year	Cattle/ Agricultural Sector	Industrial Sector	Basic Services Sector	Total
1965	—	1,101,418	—	1,101,418
1966	1,170,254	8,249,541	—	9,419,795
1967	10,493,518	20,197,647	53,941	30,745,106
1968	29,890,865	37,474,553	13,044,382	80,409,800
1969	75,724,743	67,963,073	6,336,321	150,024,137
1970	170,130,339	123,242,390	37,570,161	330,942,890
1971	168,269,558	134,947,091	30,406,970	333,623,619
1972	180,304,280	116,869,017	27,774,376	324,947,673
1973	174,198,128	153,713,637	12,464,624	340,376,389
Total	810,181,685	633,240,758	127,650,775	1,601,590,827

SUDAM Incentives by Yearly Percentage

Year	Cattle/ Agriculture	Industry	Basic Services
1965	—	100	—
1966	12.42	87.58	—
1967	34.13	65.69	0.18
1968	37.17	46.60	16.23
1969	50.48	45.30	4.22
1970	51.41	37.24	11.35
1971	50.42	40.48	9.10
1972	55.48	35.97	8.55
1973	50.27	46.51	3.22
Total	50.39	41.50	8.11

Source: Fernando Henrique Cardoso and Geraldo Müller, *Amazônia: Expansão do capitalismo* (São Paulo: Brasiliense, 1977), 160.

the town of Barra do Garças, and the AEA opened a regional office to defend members' interests. Indeed, the disproportionate investment in eastern Amazonian states of Mato Grosso and Pará (where 90 percent of the total projected investment in livestock was concentrated), reveals the unevenness of regional growth.[47]

Public expenditures on infrastructure promoted accumulation and labor migration. The Departamento Nacional de Estradas e Rodovias (National Highway Department, DNER), which received a total of $400 million in loans between 1968 and 1972 from the InterAmerican and World Bank, oversaw construction of a federal highway linking Brasília to Cuiabá between 1969 and 1973, and a road linking the town of Barra do Garças to São Felix do Araguaia.[48] Indeed, funding for the military's Amazonian development project, like other aspects of the state's "economic miracle," came heavily from international lending institutions and foreign banks: in 1972, Brazil became the largest borrower from the Export-Import Bank and was the major debtor to the World Bank, with foreign debt climbing to $12.5 billion in the following year.[49]

In the county of Barra do Garças vertiginous land transactions subdivided, reconfigured, or agglomerated plots.[50] As a visitor to Barra do Garças in the late 1960s noted, "The selling and reselling of lots is prodigious," notwithstanding that the "names on the [cadastral] map do not correspond to actual owners."[51] Indeed, by 1971 the cadastre of Barra do Garças county showed that the immense area home primarily to Indians, squatters, and goldminers decades before had been nearly completely subdivided and titled. The location of Barra do Garças in eastern Amazonia, with greater access to interregional highways and economic markets, undoubtedly lured capital, with promoters touting the county's extensive size and inexpensive pastureland.[52] Local governments complemented federal initiatives: in 1971, for example, municipalities in the center west spent 30.3 percent of public service expenditures on transportation and communication.[53] Privately, investors were assured of cooperation in repressing subaltern protest from the oligarchic cliques who controlled the county's civil administration, police force, and notarial office.[54]

By 1970, the population of Barra do Garças county numbered 28,403.[55] Yet land tenure patterns within northern Mato Grosso in the 1970s reveal the inequitable distribution spawned by expansion of the ranching sec-

Table 2.   Cadastral Statistics for Barra do Garças County, 1972

Property Type	Total	Total Area (Hectares)	Cultivatable Area	Uncultivated Area
Minifundio	290	71,026	11,216	5,431
Rural Enterprise	60	143,455	68,867	5,690
Latifundio by Use	2,024	9,957,924	6,051,991	3,748,521
Latifundio by Dimension	4	948,711	519,005	291,700

Source: INCRA, Sistema Nacional de Cadastro Rural, *Recadastramento, 1972.*

tor: 6.7 percent of landholders contolled 85 percent of the private sector lands, while almost 70 percent of the remaining farms owned merely 6 percent of the area.[56] Whereas cattle ranches in southern Brazil measured typically between 800 and 900 hectares, those established in Barra do Garças averaged 20,000 to 30,000.[57] Moreover, the majority of fazendas in the region failed to make effective use of extensive holdings. A 1972 survey by the Instituto Nacional de Colonização e Reforma Agrária (National Institute for Colonization and Agrarian Reform, INCRA) classified 2,028 properties in the county of Barra do Garças as latifundio and only 60 as rural enterprises (see Table 2).

The low returns on livestock due to higher operating costs in the Amazon and government price controls might have discouraged ranchers. More likely, however, such considerations were secondary. Investors prized land precisely for its exchange worth, which granted access to tax breaks and other fiscal incentives, rather than its productive value.[58] For example, the price for pastureland in Barra do Garças and other counties of northern Mato Grosso increased at an annual rate averaging 65–70 percent per year (or about 38 percent annually in real terms) between 1970 and 1975, whereas for Brazil in general the average rate increased around 25 percent. Any investor who purchased average pastureland in northern Mato Grosso in, say, 1970 and sold it in 1975 unimproved would have realized a 504 percent gain on initial outlay.[59]

Projected cattle ranching ventures served little more than to conceal the time-worn practice of land speculation as an inflationary hedge, albeit this time with the bonus of federal fiscal incentives generating handsome untaxed capital gains. Nor did these properties generate long-term employment possibilities: one study found that 46 percent of SUDAM-backed ventures relied on seasonal and part-time labor, failing to sustain employment.[60] Land speculation and concentration crimped Brazilian economic productivity and dashed the long-standing promise of allocating frontier land to the nation's disadvantaged.

It was during this period of frontier boom that Fazenda Xavantina, ranging over 100,000 hectares, was consolidated on Xavante land in the Couto Magalhães–Culuene region (and encompassing the former village of Parabubu). Between 1966 and 1968, two North Americans, James Phillips and Edward Harstein, bought up title to eleven landholdings and amalgamated them into Fazenda Xavantina. All but one of the eleven properties, each measuring slightly less than 10,000 hectares, had been originally sold by Mato Grosso's land department (DTC) between 1958 and 1960, subsequent to the Xavante's expulsion from the area.[61] In 1969, Fazenda Xavantina was sold by the North Americans to Clovis Ribeiro Cintra, who headed Amurada Planning and Engineering Inc., a Brazilian-owned transportation firm based in the southern state of Paraná.

Landowners Confront "the Indigenous Question"

For investors streaming into northern Mato Grosso and other areas of Legal Amazonia, the region's vast space nevertheless teemed with vast complications. Buyers purchased land deeds that were often imprecise, fraudulent, superimposed (often multilayered), or contested by others. Yet, regularized title was essential for bank credit.[62] Thus, property owners endeavored to reconcile titular rights with de jure claims or de facto occupation by indigenous groups, long-term squatters, or even small towns.[63]

Irregular titles had circulated in the northern Mato Grosso real estate market since the 1950s and early 1960s but had not fazed their holders: many owners hardly, if ever, stepped foot on lands purchased for speculation; others, less pressured for precision by lending institutions, government agencies, or industrious neighbors, simply made do with indefiniteness. With investment and settlement in the region snowballing in response to state policy, the rush to regularize titles intensified, as did conflict. For, to honor all of the titles issued and claims staked, the governor of Mato Grosso stated in the 1970s, "it would be necessary to invade the neighboring states."[64] Indeed, the state of Mato Grosso shut down the discredited DTC entirely between 1966 and 1977, abdicating to federal bureaucracies and local notarial offices responsibility for land titling.[65] (In 1976, two policy directives were drafted by the Conselho de Segurança Nacional and issued by INCRA to address the problem of fraudulent land titles in Legal Amazonia. In the interest of promoting regional "development," Directive 005 honored existing titles to private property in the Amazon as legal "even though constituted through devious, reprehensible practices, constituting a breach of law and order"; Directive 006 recognized the claims of long-term residents of the region, granting title to up to three thousand hectares if they had effectively occupied the land for ten years.)[66]

Indigenous land represented a particular problem. Private title to indigenous land (federal property) was invalid and, subsequent to the 1969 Constitution, ineligible for indemnification as well. Furthermore, in 1969, SUDAM adopted a policy that required title holders seeking fiscal incentives to obtain from FUNAI a *certidão negativa* (negative certificate), a document avouching the nonexistence of Indians in the area. Moreover, so long as the delineation of indigenous reserves languished, the region remained prone to violence and financial risk. Indeed, as early as 1966, a São Paulo firm complained to the SPI that the Xavante at Areões had destroyed forty meters of its ranch's barbed-wire fence; the complainant demanded the immediate demarcation of the Indians' territory to avoid further skirmishes.[67] Yet the creation of indigenous reserves also hung like a Damoclean sword over the heads of fazendeiros who stood to lose their capital investment depending on the area delimited. In contradistinction to ethnographers, investors fretted not over the impact of the market on the Indians but over the impact of the Indians on the market.[68] They tackled the "indigenous question" very strategically.

Fazendeiros in the Xavante region, like others throughout Brazil, took various tacks to buttress authority and quash subaltern protest. Violence, whether extralegal or state-backed, most brutally ensured indigenous subordination. Yet, fazendeiros in Mato Grosso also wove paternalistic webs that enmeshed the Xavante through employment, technical assistance, "favors," and handouts. Fazenda Xavantina offered to provide medicine and construct a clinic for Benedito Loazo's group at Couto Magalhães; paid twenty-two Indians "the same price as 'civilizados'" to plant pasture; and ceded thirty-eight alqueires for the Xavante to plant rice and corn.[69] Likewise, Ometto "compensated" for the expulsion of the Xavante from Marãiwatsede and their resettlement at São Marcos by donating a tractor as well as monthly payments for one year to the mission.[70] Medicine provided here to assist infirm Xavante; tools and fertilizers provided there to help with the harvest; a cow sacrificed to appease a famished community; a lift to the nearby town to scour assistance or commercial transactions—all placed a fig leaf over raw power and domination.[71]

Landowners profited from the precarious conditions at the indigenous posts that fostered dependency. The post at Couto Magalhães, located 269 kilometers from the nearest commercial center and 1,000 kilometers from the regional office of FUNAI, invariably leaned on Fazenda Xavantina. Indigenous men's growing reliance on wage labor to purchase goods and to compensate for shrinking resources further cemented ties.[72] Finally, the complicity of government officials and some indigenous leaders maintained the status quo. Elite "benevolence" helped glue together social relations fraught with tension and distrust. Paternalism lulled fazendeiros into thinking of "their" Indians as complacent and loyal. For the Xavante, it ameliorated the bitter pill they were forced to swallow in witnessing their lands invaded and deforested.

To be sure, tension brewed. José Aparecido da Costa, a paulista rancher, informed the Minister of the Interior that in May 1969 a group of armed Xavante had threatened the lives of seventeen employees, "immediately taking possession of the area already deforested [20 alqueires], barring access by me and my employees to the area in question until today."[73] As a solution, FUNAI proposed to resettle the Areões Xavante on 35,000 hectares of forestland in the state of Minas Gerais, enlisting the mediation of Father Pedro Sbardelotto, who years earlier had helped negotiate the removal of the Marãiwatsede Xavante to the Salesian mission. The Xavante did not take kindly to Sbardelotto's latest entreaty. Recalling the epidemics that claimed the lives of scores of kin as a result of the last mass transfer, the Indians at Areões "practically expelled him from the village."[74] The FUNAI shelved the plan.

With FUNAI's disinclination to relocate the Xavante, investors endorsed their next best option: delimitation of small, undesirable areas. Minister of the Interior General Costa Cavalcanti did not need to be strong-armed.

After meeting with AEA representatives in 1969 he asserted, "The Indian has to remain with the minimum necessary."[75] Landowners in Barra do Garças were personally assured in a letter from the Ministry of the Interior, "FUNAI is clarifying that in accord with the thought of the Minister [of the Interior], the areas to be reserved for the Indians will not prejudice the property of third parties, especially where there are agricultural/ranching and industrial properties."[76]

Relegating the Xavante to "the Minimum Necessary"

Initial efforts to reserve Xavante lands reflected "the minimum necessary" policy—as well as some of its challenges. In September 1969, the president decreed three reserves for the Xavante, at Areões, Pimentel Barbosa, and Couto Magalhães. The outcome, however, satisfied neither landowner nor Xavante. The Xavante protested that the areas reserved were inadequate; for example, the reserve at Couto Magalhães encompassed only a fraction of the Indians' precontact territory. Moreover, the decree neglected altogether to reserve land for the Xavante at the Sangradouro and São Marcos missions. Many Xavante at the missions now viewed their refuge as their home, with precontact areas serving more as a source of identity and symbolic reference than as a place of return.[77] For their part, landowners howled that the reserves impinged on "productive" lands and had been foisted on unsuspecting title holders. Less than one month later, the decree establishing the reserves was revoked and FUNAI vowed to devise new boundaries.

But FUNAI responded to the political stalemate with dilatory tactics. The federal government would linger three years before decreeing new reserves in September 1972. In fact, government "inaction" fronted intense political activity favoring the cycle of capitalist gain in the Barra do Garças region and Legal Amazonia as a whole.[78] This was perhaps most evident in FUNAI's indiscriminate issuing of the certidão negativa. The certidão sought to safeguard indigenous land rights, yet, in practice, its doctoring served to reward the military's corporate clientele in Legal Amazonia and offered bureaucratic rent seeking. In 1971, FUNAI issued a certidão negativa to one ranch, Cristalina Agro-Industrial Ltda., located within the Xavante's precontact region of Couto Magalhães–Culuene.[79]

(In five months alone during 1970, FUNAI issued 150 such certidões throughout Legal Amazonia.)[80] Testifying in 1977 to a Brazilian parliamentary committee investigating the invasion of indigenous lands, then-president of FUNAI General Ismarth Araújo de Oliveira acknowledged the numerous irregularities surrounding the furnishing of certidões negativas.[81]

The lethargy in delimiting Xavante territory owed to other reasons as well. New reserves demanded added studies and expenditures and, notwithstanding FUNAI's greater financial and legal muscle, many of the old problems of the SPI persisted. FUNAI's responsibilities remained extensive and far-flung: in 1971, the agency administered 142 indigenous posts throughout Brazil, yet only 11 reservations existed (even so much as on paper).[82] Furthermore, of the CR$13.5 million allotted to FUNAI by the Ministry of the Interior in 1970, only CR$1.6 million were earmarked for demarcation of indigenous lands.[83] Patronage and corruption within the agency, which persisted under military rule, took its toll as well (see chapters 7 and 8). The stalled demarcation of Xavante lands would be jump-started by the military in response to international uproar as well as local violence.

The New Impetus to Reserve Xavante Land

In the early 1970s, the nature of federal involvement in Legal Amazonia shifted somewhat as geopolitical concerns with national integration and territorial occupation mounted. In 1970, Decree-Law 1106 established the Plano de Integração Nacional (National Integration Plan, PIN), which pledged over $1 billion between 1971 and 1974 for the construction of an east-west Trans-Amazon highway linking the northeast to the Peruvian border, and a north-south highway linking Cuiabá to Santarém.[84] The PIN also called for massive settlement of the Amazon in a state-led colonization project that targeted the relocation of more than 5 million people on plots along the Trans-Amazon. The PIN was a showcase of the regime of General Emílio Garrastazu Médici (1969–1974), a highly repressive period of military rule, marked by the abrogation of civil rights, torture of political prisoners, and media censorship.[85]

To bolster his legitimacy, Médici made extensive use of propaganda emphasizing Brazil's superpower potential through westward expansion ("O Brasil Grande") and the impressive growth occasioned by the "economic miracle" of 1968–1973.[86] Rehashing themes popularized since the March to the West, the Médici government emphasized that the colonization of the Amazon would solve the nation's demographic imbalance and social tensions; it would also protect the region from the alleged threat of "internationalization," most recently "detected" in the suggestion by members of the U.S.-based Hudson Institute to dam the Amazon River to provide cheaper electrical energy and improved transportation.[87]

The FUNAI estimated that five thousand Indians from twenty-nine different groups lived along the Trans-Amazon and Santarém-Cuiabá highways; twelve had sporadic contact with Brazilian society. As swaths of roadway were cleared in lands inhabited by semicontacted or hostile Indians or areas reserved for indigenous groups, FUNAI confronted a whole new set of challenges. Many indigenous peoples, such as the Parakanan and Kreen-Akraore (Panará), were ravaged by disease or forcibly relocated as a result of these public works.[88] Facing criticism, FUNAI President General Oscar Jerônimo Bandeira de Mello (1970–1974) thundered that the Indian was not "a guinea pig, nor the property of half a dozen opportunists," and that nothing could stop the course of Brazilian development.[89]

Barbs aside, FUNAI remained preoccupied with its public image, particularly abroad, as an effective conciliator of interethnic and territorial conflict. Bandeira de Mello created a public relations department "to establish an accurate image of FUNAI in the country and abroad, eliminating distortions purposefully disseminated by subversive elements," and closely monitored press coverage of Indians and indigenous policy.[90] The Xavante would benefit from the international pressure on behalf of indigenous communities.[91]

Meanwhile, at the grassroots level, the Xavante mobilized for battle. In light of previous expulsions, the Xavante refusal to relocate to Minas Gerais bespoke unwillingness to buckle to state pressure and a growing sense of political empowerment. Of course, their successful standoff owed ultimately to government moderation in resolving this particular Amazonian conflict. With road building, mineral extraction, and other "megaprojects" undertaken in the name of national development and security, military officials showed no misgivings in dislocating other indigenous groups.[92] Darcy Ribeiro's observation underscoring the diversity of indigenous historical experience according to regional patterns of capital accumulation remains most pertinent.[93]

Emboldened by promises of land demarcation, Xavante lowered their facade of compliance and raised cries for justice. In 1970, members of the Areões community seized food, batteries, tools, and horses from a nearby ranch. Chief Saamri, confronted at gunpoint by one fazendeiro, threatened that a hunting expedition of thirty-five Indians "would burn the ranches remaining in the area and expel their residents."[94] Stunned by such insolence, ranchers lashed out at FUNAI officials and missionaries, whose "recognized ill-will" had "aggravated the relationship between whites and Indians."[95] Yet landowners clearly muddled the distinction between intent and consequence: FUNAI officials and missionaries had never set out to sour interethnic relations or incite Indians to direct action. On the contrary, FUNAI sought to defuse social conflict and political activism through bureaucratic administration. In what Guha has termed "the prose of counterinsurgency," landowners attributed revolt to agents of the state and church, denying historical agency to Indians who had seized on the prospect of greater institutional backing to reshape political and socioeconomic boundaries.[96]

The Xavante's Reservations

Officials of FUNAI, alarmed by the "grave problem" of conflict in the Xavante region, called for "an urgent and definitive solution which satisfied both the Indians and the ranchers, establishing the limits of the reserve."[97] In September 1972, more than twenty-five years after official "pacification," the Brazilian government reserved five territories for the Xavante. But for the Indians, the ordeal of gaining effective territorial possession was still far from over. Until FUNAI officials physically demarcated the areas and removed invaders, the reserves remained paper tigers. Furthermore, although this decree delimited land for the communities at Sangradouro and São Marcos, all of the reserves were inadequate in size and caliber. The Xavante at the Couto Magalhães reserve received 23,000 hectares of miserable quality that lacked adequate quantities of buriti palm, which the Indians used to weave baskets, sleeping mats, and roof thatch, and whose trunks served for ceremonial races.[98] No reserve at all was created in the Culuene region. Fazenda Xavantina and other landowners usurping Xavante precontact land in the Couto Magalhães–Culuene region emerged largely unscathed. So, too, the Suiá-Missu ranch retained full territorial control as the government failed to delimit land in Marãi-watsede. The new decree reserving Xavante land, blunting indigenous territorial claims, indeed reflected the military's promise to relegate Indians to "the minimum possible."

To bury indigenous land claims (and historical memory), the military government proposed hypnosis through increased market participation and acquisition of industrial goods.[99] In his October 1971 report, José Carlos Alves, the FUNAI post chief at Couto Magalhães, waxed ecstatic about the "advanced process of assimilation" of the seventy-six Xavante residing there under the leadership of Chief Benedito Loazo (who had led back the original five from the Salesian mission in 1961). Alves boasted of the group's proficiency in Portuguese, devotion to Catholicism, and passion for soccer. Although he mentioned that "armed conflict" had nearly erupted between the Indians ("who say that they arrived first to the locale") and the employees of the neighboring Fazenda Xavantina, Alves brushed aside indigenous territorial demands. Instead, he called for a vocational school to train Xavante men in mechanics and masonry and sewing machines for Xavante women. With an optimism bound to please his superiors, he concluded, "These Indians are exceptional and all FUNAI can do to invest in them will be sufficiently profitable and will yield one further happy initiative for FUNAI."[100]

Xavante were not averse to market participation or acquisition of Western goods, but they did not view them as quid pro quo for territorial surrender. For the Indians, land held the promise of greater socioeconomic and cultural autonomy and represented a wellspring of historical memory.[101] Military officials and landowners who hoped that the Xavante would resign themselves to the legal and territorial confines imposed by the state found their hopes dashed. In November 1972, 150 Indians from the São Marcos mission migrated to the Couto Magalhães reserve, unshaken by appeals from a FUNAI official, a Salesian missionary, and a Xavante leader to turn back. With the Couto Magalhães reserve engorged by the return of exiles, the Xavante faced a crisis in health care and food supply.[102] In December 1972, the post chief at Couto Magalhães, whose model

Indians had been praised a year earlier, fretted over their dissatisfaction with the newly decreed reservation:

> The Indians, notwithstanding our explanations, reaffirm that their lands go until "where the earth touches the sky," that they do not want cerrados or capoeiras (brushwood) which do not have their principal source of nourishment, animal game. They demand lands that have bush where they can carry out their hunting, gathering, and above all good lands for agriculture. With the proximity of Fazenda Xavantina we receive daily complaints that the Indians knock down coconuts, uproot manioc, potatoes, etc., but what is to be done? Try to explain, we do, but much remains for them to understand what the notion of property is. Formerly all of these lands were theirs, and for them that is enough.[103]

Because "all of these lands were theirs," the Indians' greatest challenge loomed in pressuring state officials to enlarge their reserves. Whereas prior to contact the Xavante secured their lands through sheer force, indigenous communities would be pressed to diversify strategies to safeguard or reclaim land. Violence—a touchstone for conflict resolution in rural Brazil—would continue to be employed by the Indians, albeit in highly stylized form. But after roughly two decades of subordination to the waradzu, the Xavante understood that storming the Brazilian political system, with the rights and privileges extended to Indians therein, ensured the most viable means for securing their lands and socioeconomic well-being. Surely, the apprenticeship had been painful, as the Indians were forced to adapt time-tested behavior and to learn novel forms of expression to solve problems both old and new.

An Indigenous Struggle for Land in Legal Amazonia

Expanded state power in Legal Amazonia under authoritarian rule catalyzed infrastructural expansion, economic investment, demographic growth, environmental degradation, and indigenous dislocation. The reconfiguration of political dynamics and socioeconomic interests under the military also enabled the state to delimit reserves for the Xavante and other indigenous groups. In compliance with large-scale private capital—key partners and beneficiaries of the state's developmental project in

Legal Amazonia—the military government sought to corral Indians on small plots of land.

Over the next decade, Xavante communities would struggle to amplify reserves and expel invaders, encountering fierce opposition. The Indians charged into political battle with ancient valor and bellicosity, as well as with allies and accoutrements their ancestors never would have imagined. Through various forms of political mobilization—moral appeals, extralegal actions and mock violence, bureaucratic "lobbying," domestic and international alliances—the Indians engaged an authoritarian regime to modify its developmental project. The Xavante dressed up their appeals—and their bodies—with the signs and symbols of indigenous "tradition" that elites had consecrated as integral to the nation's cultural heritage. Traveling to the nation's capital down the same roads constructed to commodify their territory, indigenous leaders arrived to strong-arm state officials. In short, with similar determination, pomp, and media coverage, the Xavante inverted the pilgrimage led by Vargas that had catapulted them to national attention. With Brasília as their mecca, the "true sense of Brazilianness" for the Xavante lay in the March to the East.

7

The Exiles Return, 1972–1980

If the Xavante of Couto Magalhães believed that their lands reached to "where the earth touches the sky," others insisted they extended no further than the 23,000 hectares that the government had reserved in 1972. In 1974, General Clovis Ribeiro Cintra, head of Fazenda Xavantina, sent a stern letter to the Ministry of the Interior recounting a deal that he had struck two years earlier with then-Minister Costa Cavalcanti and FUNAI President Bandeira de Mello.

According to Cintra, the ranch had ceded 5,000 of its 114,922 hectares to enlarge the Couto Magalhães reservation then under study. In return, Xavantina received a certidão negativa from FUNAI, which allowed access to generous fiscal incentives. (Indeed, between 1972 and 1977, FUNAI issued nineteen certidões negativas to title holders whose lands lay within the Xavante's precontact region of Couto Magalhães–Culuene.)[1] Moreover, Cintra claimed, FUNAI had vowed to block future Xavante migration to the reserve and to congregate those Indians already at Couto Magalhães at Chief Benedito Loazo's village.[2]

Fazenda Xavantina's apprehensions mirrored those of other title holders in the Xavante region whose lands were embedded in the newly created reservations or occupied contested areas excluded by the decree.[3] One strategy to contain Xavante land claims consisted in appeals to government influentials; another in the co-optation of indigenous leaders. Fazenda Xavantina's insistence on centralizing leadership under Benedito Loazo, whose village lay twelve kilometers from its headquarters, had little to do with concern for communal harmony. Rather, it reflected efforts to buttress the authority of Loazo, whom the ranch paid monthly "protection" money to dissuade Indians from attacking cattle or demanding territorial annexation.[4]

Over the decade of the 1970s, however, the uneasy accommodation among Indians, landowners, and the state in northern Mato Grosso collapsed as the alignment of power shifted at the local and national level. During the presidential term of General Ernesto Geisel (1974–1979), the military goverment would oversee a process of *distensão*, or political "decompression," aimed at taming hardliners, controlling leftist "subversion," and regulating the return to democratic rule. Geisel's project for political liberalization aimed at shoring up the military government's legitimacy, undermined by a faltering economy and mounting opposition to human rights abuses. Indigenous leaders, along with human rights and grassroots social activists, would seize on this political opening to test the limits of military rule.[5]

At the local level, the Xavante struggle for land gained urgency as demographic growth, territorial occupation, and deforestation intensified in northern Mato Grosso. In September 1974, Geisel launched the $1 billion Polamazônia Program in which fifteen "development poles" in Legal Amazonia, including the region of Barra do Garças, were targeted for investment in livestock, timber, mining, and other economic sectors of perceived comparative advantage.[6] The II Plano de Desenvolvimento da Amazônia 1975–79 (Second Development Plan for the Amazon)—responding to corporate pressure against state-led, small-scale settlement entailed in the PIN—endorsed private colonization projects.[7] By the end of the 1970s, over 2 million hectares in Mato Grosso had been transferred by INCRA to private companies, with 24 of the state's 55 colonization ventures located in the county of Barra do Garças.[8] Spontaneous, or "unofficial" migration, which characteristically far surpassed formal colonization in Legal Amazonia, contributed to rapid growth as well. Between 1970 and 1978, the population of Barra do Garças county quintupled from 26,000 to 135,000.[9]

From the southern states of Rio Grande do Sul, Paraná, and Santa Catarina hailed thousands of small farmers and tenants dispossessed by mechanization or relegated to *minifúndio* in the military's sweep to promote agricultural modernization.[10] By 1978, more than one thousand families from southern Brazil had resettled on over 500,000 hectares in Barra do Garças county, where average land cost one-tenth of the price in Rio Grande do Sul.[11] Most colonists in Barra do Garças cultivated rice on lots averaging four hundred hectares, receiving special credit through long-term, low-interest loans extended through the federal Programa de Redistribuição de Terras (Program for the Redistribution of Lands, PROTERRA).[12] Three of the colonization projects—Canarana, Água Boa, and Serra Dourada—encroached on or adjoined areas contested by the Xavante at Pimentel Barbosa, and another was located in the vicinity of the

Couto Magalhães reserve.[13] Migrants from the northeast arrived in the region in search of land as well, albeit with less startup capital than many of their southern counterparts.

Among Xavante communities despair raged as the Indians, confined to small reserves, witnessed the systematic invasion and destruction of the natural environment. With the indigenous population swelling from a high birthrate and lower infant mortality, the prospect of self-sufficiency dimmed. As one visitor to Couto Magalhães noted, the Xavante "are revolted in watching, in front of them, on the other side of the creek, which does not belong to them, the relentless felling of the only, but excellent, bush existent, by the axe of the peons and hands of the local small fazendeiros. Meanwhile, on the indigenous side, every month alimentary difficulties multiply because productive lands do not exist . . . for the ever growing population."[14] The settlers' scorn for the Indians, denigrated as savages and social parasites, only stiffened indignation.[15] As Hipru, a Xavante from Pimentel Barbosa, charged, "We respect their place. Why don't they respect our territory? They only think of taking our land. We didn't leave here to take their land. You can see. They think that they are the only ones who exist in the world."[16]

This chapter examines how Hipru and other Xavante transformed moral outrage into political action. Employing dramatic spectacle, indigenista rhetoric, exhortatory appeal, and confrontational tactics, the Indians pressured state officials to honor land claims and to enlarge reserves. In this battle, they would joust with landowners and squatters, matogrossense and federal officials, but would gain newfound allies among state functionaries and sectors of civil society invigorated by a thaw in military repression. It was during this period of political flux and uncertainty, frontier boom and transformation, that landowners in northern Mato Grosso, such as Fazenda Xavantina, and the military government would be confronted by Xavante mobilization.

The Return to Couto Magalhães–Culuene Begins

From the outset, reining in the Xavante at the Couto Magalhães reserve proved more difficult than landholders, government officials, and missionaries hoped. Indeed, Fazenda Xavantina's letter to the Ministry of the

Interior bespoke frustration at the state's failure to uphold the ban on Xavante migration. The return of 150 Xavante exiles from the São Marcos mission to the Couto Magalhães reserve in November 1972 was only the beginning.[17] In December 1973, twenty years after dispersing from the Culuene region, thirty-four Xavante abandoned their resource-poor reserve at Batovi (Marechal Rondon) and resettled in the environs of the Culuene River near the western border of the Fazenda Xavantina (see Map 6).

The government had not reserved land for the Xavante in the Culuene region under the 1972 decree. The untoward resurrection of the Xavante alarmed state officials as well as landowners and squatters who had acquired title or settled in the Culuene region. Smallholders like José Cândido Ferreira and Célio Mascarenhas blanched as the Indians seized crops, vowed to slaughter livestock, and announced the arrival of an additional three hundred relatives by the following May.[18] Other fazendeiros retorted with threats of violence, bragging to the Indians and local FUNAI employees of assassins in their employ.[19] Federal officials "innumerable times" admonished the Indians against the "irregularities" of their return to Culuene.[20] Impressing on local FUNAI employees the determination to remain, the Xavante

> showed themselves to be aggressive and threatening. We were obliged to use all of our abilities and know-how acquired in our training as indigenistas to dominate the impetuousness of the aforementioned Indians, especially the Indian Tomaz, who even armed himself with a club and rifle, resorting to intimidation and bedeviling the success of our mission. He remained unflinching when we counseled him to withdraw together with the other Indians to their reservation of origin.[21]

The Xavante had resorted to direct action in occupying unreserved territory. Yet leaders from Culuene ultimately traveled to FUNAI headquarters in Brasília to legitimize their case.

The director of FUNAI's Departamento Geral de Operações, Colonel Joel Marcos, groped for a solution at Culuene. He agreed to allow the Xavante to stay at Culuene until harvest time in mid-1974, whereupon he offered to transfer them, with their consent, to the Xavante reserve at Pimentel Barbosa. The plan never materialized. It was not solely that the exiles were inextricably bound to their precontact territory. After all, not all

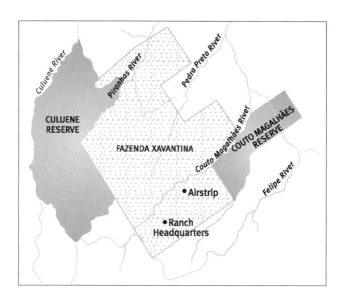

Map 6. Culuene and Couto Magalhães Reserves, 1976

of the Xavante from Batovi returned to Culuene. Rather, the existence of long-standing conflicts with the community at Pimentel Barbosa militated against resettlement as well. In acceding, the state once again exercised restraint toward the Xavante that was denied to other indigenous groups obstructing hydroelectric, road-building, and mining projects viewed as indispensable to "national security."

With a foothold established in the Culuene region, indigenous reinforcements arrived. In March 1974, four Xavante families from the Paraíso post (Simões Lopes) migrated to Culuene and, soon thereafter, the entire village of Paraíso returned to their precontact area. By early 1976, the indigenous population at Culuene numbered five hundred and the Xavante stepped up pressure on FUNAI to create a new reserve.[22]

The Struggle over the Culuene Reserve

Mato Grosso elites bridled at the prospect of another indigenous reserve. Valdon Varjão, mayor of Barra do Garças, protested to Geisel that a new reserve would throttle investment in the region, given government disregard for "legal" titles.[23] The Barra do Garças town council warned that their county risked becoming one big "indigenous park."[24] Here, elites sought to play up the image of the Indian as latifundiário and to stoke fears of what has been referred to as the "Copacabana syndrome": honoring indigenous land claims risked descent down a slippery slope, for if Indians once controlled all of Brazil, what could stop them from demanding even Copacabana beach?[25] The image of the insatiably peripatetic and revanchist indigene made a mockery of Brazilian history as well as the legally grounded and territorially specific nature of Indian land claims—but it was, and is, an effective alarmist tactic.

As a final recourse, politicians and landowners in Mato Grosso challenged federal intervention on behalf of the Indians by casting themselves as populist defenders of the rural poor. Relocating eighty squatter families to an area in the Culuene region, many of whom had been expelled from local fazendas to begin with, elites sought to thwart creation of a new reserve. Like many of the landless in Legal Amazonia, a number of these families had been lured from the northeast by labor contractors (*gatos*) to clear pastureland for fazendas, only to be evicted thereafter. Others had squatted for years until title holders, backed by military security forces or extralegal violence, ran them off. Whereas in 1967 an estimated 6,640 squatters occupied 1,326 plots in Mato Grosso, by 1980 land conflicts multiplied as the squatter population soared to 200,000 occupying 31,933 plots.[26] Pitting squatter against Indian, elites sought to reap the spoils of a war of attrition. By June 1975, 350 squatters lived in the settlement of Novo Paraíso (New Paradise), whose squalor and impending doom belied its name.

The power of Mato Grosso influentials to dominate their "backyard" through violence and clientelism had been compromised somewhat with increased state intervention in Amazonia under military rule. In July, a joint commission of federal officials from FUNAI and INCRA visited the "atmosphere of great tension" and advised the squatters to withdraw.[27] To goad officials in Brasília, the Xavante, with the acquiescence of the post chief, destroyed a wooden bridge to Novo Paraíso, barring access to trucks transporting food, alcohol, and supplies. The showdown received widespread media coverage which, undoubtedly, the Indians relished as a means of pressuring the government. In a press interview, Chief Abraão played up the Indians' fearsome reputation, threatening to slaughter the squatters in a stealthy midnight attack.[28] The joint FUNAI-INCRA commission informed the squatters that the Xavante reserve under study would encompass Novo Paraíso and urged them to leave the area.[29]

In April 1976, the FUNAI-INCRA commission showed its final proposal for the Culuene reserve to the Xavante. Viewing the aerial photographs and the survey of the reserve, the Indians were "overcome with happiness at the opportunity to be able to identify all of the geographic contours, the former villages located there, the bush, etc." The Indians' alacrity, however, puzzled government officials. Although certain that the Xavante "would not demand the totality" of their former lands, the commission was stunned when the Indians accepted an area even smaller than expected, respecting "by their own initiative, a boundary fence of the Fazenda Xavantina, whose localization was for us questionable."[30]

The Xavante at Culuene, leery of a political tug-of-war with the powerful Fazenda Xavantina, had ceded rights to ancestral lands, swallowing their pride to secure territory. Still, given the initial opposition of FUNAI and local landowners to the Indians' return, the decree of the 51,000-hectare reserve in April 1976 was a significant accomplishment. Fazenda Xavantina now bordered on two Xavante reserves: on the east, Couto Magalhães; on the west, Culuene (see Map 6). The fazenda, however, continued to occupy close to 100,000 hectares of the Xavante's ancestral land, including the former village of Parabubu, site of the massacre two decades earlier.

Conflict at the Reservations

The Indians' challenges at Culuene and Couto Magalhães—the persistence of invaders inside the reservations, irregularities in demarcation, inadequate territory, government irresolution—confronted all Xavante communities. Environmental despoliation was another serious concern. On-site surveys and satellite images of the counties of Barra do Garças and Luciara from June 1975 and August 1976 found that 760,358 hectares had been deforested. Of the 85 SUDAM-backed projects in the region, the 57 visited by the team accounted for the deforestation of 289,840 hectares, or 38 percent of the total. Only approximately half of the lands cleared for pasture were used to potential.[31] Itamar Silveira do Amaral, a FUNAI official who visited three Xavante reserves in 1973, reported that landowners "graze cattle there, devastating the few existing forest reserves and destroying the fields and cerrados with their indiscriminate burnings."[32] In assessing environmental damage inflicted by cattle ranching in northern Mato Grosso, Hecht has persuasively argued that investors preoccupied with exchange rather than productive value showed slight interest in land management and ecological protection.[33]

Smallholders contributed their fair share to ecological destruction. Dispirited by the region's poor soils, many of the new colonists in Mato Grosso compensated by overhunting game. As one of the founders of the Coopercana colonization company recalled, "I wanted to preserve at least some examples of the extremely rich fauna that we found when we arrived. . . . Today it is difficult to find any kind of wild animal. Everything was slaughtered in only ten or fifteen years."[34] Squatters, lacking titles and harassed by large landowners and *grileiros* (land grabbers), engaged in reckless slash-and-burn cultivation as a means of establishing legal dominion.[35] A government report noted that improper care of cerrado soil resulted in its degradation, leading many colonists of small and medium holdings to abandon their properties.[36]

Confronted by environmental ravage, Xavante communities resorted to direct action. With their well-honed hunting skills, indigenous men carried out pointed attacks on fazendas. At Sangradouro, where fazendeiros continued to graze cattle inside the reserve and FUNAI had failed to annex an adjoining trekking area, the Xavante raided two ranches.[37] Likewise, at Pimentel Barbosa, the Xavante looted food and other goods from fazendeiros who refused to vacate the newly created reserve.[38]

Xavante offensives, however, were far from indiscriminate acts of violent rage. Apoena instructed warriors at Pimentel Barbosa never to kill or harm any waradzu, but merely to inflict material damage.[39] Outnumbered and ill-equipped, the Xavante knew they stood little chance of victory in hand-to-hand combat. Mato Grosso's federal congressman, Gastão Müller, taunted that landowners in Barra do Garças could readily "resolve everything with violence."[40] A brutal attack at the Bororo reserve at Merure, abutting that of the Xavante at São Marcos, drove this point home.

As at the Xavante reserves, landowners entrenched within the newly delimited indigenous area at Merure resisted pressure from FUNAI, Salesians, and the Bororo Indians to vacate. In July 1976, a throng of landowners arrived in a caravan at Merure and murdered Father Rodolfo Lunkenbein, the German-born director of the mission, and one Bororo and wounded several Indians.[41] These slayings formed part of the alarming incidence of violent land conflicts in Brazil that claimed the lives of several Indians and hundreds of peasants and rural workers in a reign of terror between 1970 and 1983 sanctioned by legal impunity.[42] Though the Xavante at São Marcos vowed to avenge the attack at Merure, no reprisal ensued. The massive popular support in Barra do Garças for the assassins, ultimately acquitted in a local court on the grounds of "self-defense," undoubtedly gave the Xavante pause.

For the Xavante, violence per se was no longer the solution to defend their land. Rather, its stylized deployment served as a means to pressure the state. Assessing Xavante raids on fazendas and blustery threats to destroy bridges leading to Barra do Garças, Manuel Pereira Brito, head of the city council, told the state governor that the Indians "go around affirming that they are proceeding in this way, so that the foreign newspapers, through their headline news, pressure the Brazilian government to resolve the problem of their reservation lands."[43] At FUNAI headquarters and regional offices, Xavante leaders besieged authorities with demands to secure or enlarge their reserves, with the Indians from São Marcos, for example, spending a good deal of the money they had earned from harvest on travel expenses to Brasília.[44]

One problem, however, was that the Indians could not rely on their guardian's goodwill. At the time of the demarcation of the Pimentel Barbosa reserve in 1975, a FUNAI cartographer, Valdênio Lopes, in collusion with several top agency officials, cajoled the Xavante (with the support of one of their leaders, Surupredu) to relinquish claim to 65,000 hectares. The FUNAI officials demarcated a smaller area, substituting one river for another to serve as the reserve's southern border, and sold off the outlying region. In exchange, the Indians received a pickup truck, twenty-five head of cattle, and some sewing machines.[45] Although an internal FUNAI investigation corroborated the defrauding of federal territory and indigenous patrimony, none of the malefactors was prosecuted, nor even fired.[46] (Lopes soon after left the agency on his own accord to run his newly "acquired" fazenda.) Notwithstanding the military's moralizing crusade, corruption in the public service flourished, along with flagrant violation of tutela. The Xavante faced battles on many fronts.

Conflict in Barra do Garças county might not have been "equal that of Vietnam," in the words of Gastão Müller, but it certainly smoldered as Indians and fazendeiros exchanged death threats.[47] As one FUNAI official who visited three Xavante reserves in 1973 reported, "I was able to observe and perceive that the friction between the Indians and the 'so-called' civilizados is *constant* and the animosity is intense. Therefore, the situation might soon worsen, with great moral and material damage to the Nation."[48] Spiraling violence had since claimed lives at Merure, whose victims proved an international embarrassment to the government. Xavante men from various reserves halted traffic on nearby roadways to interdict invasion of their lands, dramatize their plight, and collect "tolls" from passengers.[49] Landowners engaged in ecological warfare, depleting game and natural resources.

For the military government, the strife in Barra do Garças not only threatened the region's dynamic economic growth—a showcase of government policy for Legal Amazonia—but heightened concern over "national security." In 1972, military intelligence discovered a small guerrilla operation led by the Maoist Partido Comunista do Brasil, based in the Araguaia region of southern Pará. In separate campaigns between 1972 and 1975, the military succeeded in squelching the movement.[50] Although nearly one thousand kilometers from the site of the *foco*, the counties of Barra do Garças and Luciara in northern Mato Grosso would be swept up in the military dragnet, which placed the entire Araguaia region under surveillance and strategic intervention.[51]

National security defense sparked increased state intervention in land conflicts and federalization of Amazonian territory, viewed as an Achilles' heel of national security.[52] Yet the military government relied on more than repression to consolidate support. Another strategy entailed the adoption of "populist" policies in resolving land and mining conflicts in Amazonia, as well as the extension of social welfare benefits to rural workers.[53] In this vein, FUNAI President Ismarth Araújo de Oliveira dispatched an agency anthropologist, Claudio Romero, to all of the Xavante reserves in 1976 to defuse interethnic tension, mend the agency's tattered image in the aftermath of the Pimentel Barbosa land grab, and prepare the groundwork for indigenous community development projects (see chapter 8).[54]

Xavante leaders basked in the newfound attentiveness of FUNAI officials to their community woes. For example, in June 1977, after the Xavante at Sangradouro painted themselves for war against fazendeiros unwilling to vacate the reserve, Claudio Romero and Odenir Pinto de Oliveira, a FUNAI indigenista with long-term experience among the Xavante, arrived chaperoned by two federal policemen. The state officials led intruders away in handcuffs.[55]

The dedication and resoluteness of Romero and Pinto de Oliveira cheered the Xavante at Sangradouro. Celestino Tsererob'o, chief of one village, noted that unlike other FUNAI officials, Claudio Romero "is very good for the Indians. He is helping all of the villages, and kicking out all of the ranchers. . . . He is entrusted, sent by the government, [by the] president of FUNAI."[56] Likewise, Babatti (João Evangelista), another Xavante leader from Sangradouro, recounted the community's satisfaction: "It is good that our help came. Our Odenir—who is the great friend of the Xavante Indians—came to fortify us, no? We alone have little strength."[57] Heartened by the support of such "great friends," Celestino and other exiles at the Salesian missions advanced a startling demand: the repossession of Parabubu and additional ancestral territory in the Couto Magalhães–Culuene region held by Fazenda Xavantina and other landowners.

The exiles' challenge was formidable. An economic powerhouse, Fazenda Xavantina by 1979 boasted ten thousand head of cattle on 6,750 hectares of pasture (with another thousand in formation) and an average of 16,000 sacks of rice per harvest. Where once only nature murmured and whooped, the sound of tractors, trucks, threshing machines, harvesters, and generators now clattered. Brush had been razed, replaced by administrative buildings, an employee dormitory and food hall, brickyards, silos, warehouses, sawmills, sheds, and an airstrip. Over three hundred kilometers of internal road were constructed and more than four hundred kilometers of wire fence erected. The ranch employed, depending on seasonal demand, between fifty and two hundred workers who lived on the premises with their families.[58] Indeed, the fazenda embodied the rural enterprise that state planners upheld for Legal Amazonia (but rarely saw), as its owners were quick to remind government officials in self-defense. The fazenda also had influential backers: one member of Xavantina's board of directors was allegedly Ney Braga, a former minister of agriculture under Castelo Branco and governor of Paraná.[59]

Nonetheless, in August 1977, Celestino publicly proclaimed intent to return to the area of Parabubu (referred to by its diminutive, Parabubure) now occupied by Fazenda Xavantina:

> April [1978] I will go to Parabubure to make a new village. When the rainy season is over, I will go to Parabubure again. There, Parabubure, is the village of my grandfather, my father. There I was also born. [North] American killed Xavante. Burned houses, sent measles. So a lot of Xavante died. The rest went away. I went to Sangradouro. My grandfather, my uncle, many Xavante remained and were buried in Parabubure. Then [the North] American passed a tractor [over the] Xavante cemetery and made the headquarters of the fazenda. Now I will return. April, I will go to Parabubure to make a new village near the cemetery (of) my grandfather. The fazenda is finished. Now, Parabubure once again.[60]

Likewise, Tserede (Cirilo), another exile at the Sangradouro mission, declared, "We remember the people shot in that same village there where the Fazenda Xavantina is. . . . So, for the fazendeiros who are there, it is dangerous. He must think about this: not to grow all of the things he can. . . . He will lose the things he is raising."[61]

Xavante historical narratives must be examined carefully, for they too served as political weapons in irredentist struggle. Celestino's repeated references to kin burial sites in his recollections of Parabubu convey mournful evocation of the past and inconsolable grief from such loss.[62] Moreover, his memorial tribute, in time-honored tradition, respected the Xavante taboo on referring to the deceased by name.[63]

Yet there is more to Celestino's narrative, for as Joanne Rappaport notes, native histories address both internal *and* external ideological needs.[64] Grave sites offered historical evidence of prior dominion by the Xavante, furnishing proof of original occupancy in accordance with guidelines of Brazilian law for delimitation of indigenous lands. For this very reason, Fazenda Xavantina intentionally sought to bulldoze them. For a seminomadic people whose structures—and villages—were impermanent, burial grounds were key evidentiary artifacts to authenticate land claims. For a historically nonliterate people confronting a society

that privileged the written word, burial grounds provided titles of possession. Thus, Brazilian law, like its counterparts throughout the Americas,
served to shape the content of indigenous narratives.[65] For a people who
honored ancestors in dream narratives, the adhesion of traditional forms
to contemporary struggle was a brilliant cultural adaptation.[66]

Celestino's attribution of the attack at Parabubu to "Americans" is also
intriguing. Archival records show that the initial title holders of the various plots composing the Fazenda Xavantina were all Brazilian; North
Americans would not acquire the land until more than a decade after the
massacre. Furthermore, though the North American owners may have
destroyed gravesites with bulldozers, it is curious that Celestino made no
mention of the property's present-day ownership by a Brazilian corpora-
tion engaged in a similiar practice. It is possible that Celestino had confused the order of events. It is also conceivable that, much like old-time
indigenistas, he sought to rouse nationalist outrage by blaming foreigners
for wronging Indians. In either case, dwelling on the massacre at Parabubu galvanized Xavante to action, as memories of primitive accumulation are often spurs to political mobilization.[67]

To be sure, over the course of the 1970s, Xavante leaders lay claim to
their communities' rights as Indians and Brazilian citizens. As Tserede
(Cirilo) proclaimed, the Xavante "speak the truth, that we are the true
owners of this Country. So we have the right to say (this) in the presence
of the authorities or whomever."[68] As Aniceto Tsudazawéré and twenty-
nine other Xavante representatives told Minister of the Interior Mário
Andreazza in protesting corruption in FUNAI: "We speak not only in the
name of our Xavante nation," but "in the name of all the Indians."[69] Or, as
Mario Juruna, a leader from São Marcos, affirmed to a leading Brazilian
magazine in clamoring for the removal of invaders from his reserve: "We
are truer Brazilians than the whites. . . . Our fathers, our grandfathers, tell
us exactly how everything happened, from the time Portugal discovered
Brazil."[70] Moreover, recognizing the political significance of indigenous
culture as a banner for mobilization and legal entitlement, Xavante leaders steadfastly affirmed their ethnic identity. One Xavante leader stated in
1975, "We must not let them interefere with our culture. . . . What is important is our life, our customs. We cannot give up these things to take on
the ways of the white man. We have everything. We must not lose it. If we
lose our customs, ruin and destruction will put an end to the Indian."[71]

Xavante "grandfathers" would have preened at such consecration of custom, ancestral reverence, and the ongoing struggle against subordination to dominant society. Yet they undoubtedly would have been bemused by their descendants' self-denomination as "the truer Brazilians" and emissaries of "all the Indians," given that the nation-state and pan-Indianism had held little or unseemly significance for them. Although oral tradition remained instrumental in the transmission of historical knowledge and the formation of Xavante identity, indigenous leaders had distilled as well Brazil's "official" historical narrative, imparted over the years by government officials, missionaries, and the media. In articulating elements of dominant indigenista discourse—reifying indigenous "culture," upholding pan-Indian unity, and exuding nationalist ethos—Xavante leaders sought to anchor their claims to the bedrock of Brazilian politics. Indigenous leaders selectively *had* "taken on the ways of the white man," but the indoctrination designed to breed acquiescence was now fired back in political protest.

Xavante political mobilization gradually began to bear fruit. In May 1978, FUNAI President Ismarth Araújo de Oliveira upbraided Fazenda Xavantina for destroying Indian burial sites and for refusing to cede additional land (approximately 15,000 hectares) to the Indians, when "[the Xavante] recount, with a wealth of details, the facts which occurred to their people. And they guide those interested to the places where their villages were located and their dead buried. And these places are, today, inside the Fazenda Xavantina."[72]

Celestino's Defiance and Its Political Context

In December 1978, with the assistance of FUNAI, Celestino and sixty others relocated to the Couto Magalhães reserve, where they would take up the struggle against Fazenda Xavantina. Celestino's insistence on unconditional surrender from the regional titan represented a break from previous patterns of accommodation and co-optation at Couto Magalhães.[73] In confronting ranchers and military officials, Celestino exhibited the valor prized by a warrior people in their leaders. Cultural primordialism, however, will not suffice to explain this militancy. Consider, after all, that neither Benedito Loazo nor the leaders at Culuene at the time of the creation of their reserve had dared to confront Fazenda Xavantina. Why had Xavante defiance emerge at this particular historical moment? To understand this dramatic turn more fully, we must return to the Brazilian political scene, which served to embolden and sustain the Indians' struggle against Fazenda Xavantina.

Indigenous mobilization in the late 1970s bloomed with the reinvigoration of civil society that took root under Geisel's *abertura*, or gradual and controlled political opening. In embarking on liberalization, the Geisel government had faced a crisis of political legitimation. The "economic miracle" that sustained middle-class support for the Médici regime slowed up as the trade deficit and foreign debt increased, inflation spiraled, and the international economic climate worsened with skyrocketing oil prices. Members of the national bourgeoisie challenged the military's centralization of power and demanded greater participation in policy making.[74] In 1978, Geisel would reinstitute habeas corpus; remove prior censorship of newspapers, television, and radio; purge several hardliners from the army; and foster more amicable relations with the Catholic Church.[75] These new politicial boundaries were tested and stretched by mounting elite opposition from Catholic Church officials, journalists, and members of the legal profession who had suffered harassment, arrest, and torture at the hands of security forces under the Médici regime and from hardliners under Geisel.[76] Geisel's successor, General João Batista Figueiredo (1979–1985), would follow through the process of political liberalization that would lead to transition to democratic rule.

Not all of Gesiel's measures redounded to the Xavantes' favor. For example, a 1977 military decree-law subdivided the southern region of Mato Grosso into an independent state, Mato Grosso do Sul. The creation of new states where the military believed it held political advantage was one of various electoral manipulations, in light of the official party's poor showing in the 1974 congressional elections, to ensure control of the federal legislature without canceling its liberalization program.[77] With loss of the more developed southern region, Barra do Garças's star rose higher, providing 10 percent of the state's total tax revenues, and matogrossense elites would oppose even more fiercely the creation of another tax-exempt indigenous reserve.[78]

Nevertheless, the conquest of greater political space by elite sectors of civil society afforded more room to indigenous and other forms of popular opposition toward military rule.[79] The new social movements that erupted on the political scene in the 1970s—Christian base communities, rural labor and urban trade unions, grassroots and neighborhood organizations, women's groups—demanded social justice and democratic participation. Indeed, the indigenous struggle emerged in tandem with the dramatic growth of rural labor unions and popular political mobilization in the Brazilian countryside under military rule resulting from both state repression and concessions aimed at promoting agricultural modernization.[80] Furthermore, the new social movements of the late 1970s cultivated intricate and creative horizontal relations with each other to exert greater influence over the democratizing process.[81]

Let us return, then, to Celestino's proclamation of his intent to reclaim Parabubu. This call was issued at the Tenth Assembly of Indigenous Chiefs, which was held at a Tapirapé village in Mato Grosso and attended by Kaingang, Bororo, Pareci, Tapirapé, and Xavante delegates, as well as missionaries, journalists, and FUNAI officials. Between 1974 and 1978, eleven such pan-Indian congresses took place. The Catholic Church, the single largest opposition force to military rule in the late 1960s and early 1970s, played a pivotal role in organizing and promoting pan-Indian congresses, carving a political space for indigenous leaders to dialogue, articulate demands, and achieve national renown.[82] Indigenous leaders from throughout Brazil came together to share common problems—land invasion, environmental destruction, government repression and inaction—and to discuss strategies for mobilization. As Babatti (João Evangelista), a leader from Sangradouro, noted of the assembly of indigenous chiefs:

If we made this alone . . . it would not have helped at all. Nobody would have listened, nobody would have known what we were dealing with. Now the journalist came—from far away too, from São Paulo; he too listens. Afterwards, he takes down our words, what each one of us says he publishes in the newspaper and it goes everywhere, throughout the city. So whoever is there in the city sees the newspaper, reads something, until it arrives to the president. . . . The president of the Nation, the president of FUNAI sees our words here, so he thinks about us. He thinks about all of the Indians, he thinks about all of the villages.[83]

Pan-Indianism, of course, was another cultural legacy of conquest for the Xavante, who, prior to (twentieth-century) contact, had often combated rival communities, not to mention other indigenous groups.

With their newfound common language (Portuguese) and organizational framework and identity ("Indians"), Xavante leaders sought to rework dominant cultural interventions to their advantage. Even within Xavante society identity could be remolded for the sake of political expediency: David Maybury-Lewis noted that an individual might change lineage affiliation in associating with a particular village faction.[84] The Xavante, however, expanded considerably their political repertoire.

The Catholic Church and Civil Society

With its international links, nationwide infrastructure, and humanitarian stance, the Catholic Church emerged as a critical ally of indigenous people in pressuring the military government. Church designs for Indians were long-standing, but changes at the local, national, and international levels provoked tactical and attitudinal shifts. Vatican Council II (1962–1965) had urged greater commitment to social welfare as well as respect for non-Christian religions, and delegates to the Latin American Bishops Conference (CELAM) in 1968 endorsed a "preferential option for the poor." Catholic missionaries in Latin America, jarred by the Barbados Declaration of 1971, a manifesto by anthropologists for the immediate suspension of all missionary activity among native populations, would atone for past sins and vow greater respect for indigenous peoples.[85] At the grassroots level, missionaries encountered indigenous demands for territorial control and greater autonomy.

Within Brazil, Catholic missionaries were alarmed by the onslaught of frontier expansion on indigenous and peasant communities and suffered personal harassment from security forces under the Médici regime.[86] In 1972, Church officials formed Conselho Indigenista Missionário (Indigenist Missionary Council, CIMI), which endorsed indigenous peoples' right to land and self-determination.[87] In a manifesto entitled "Y-Juca-Pirama: The Indian, the One Who Is Supposed to Die," issued in 1973, Church officials assailed the military's development project and its acculturational bent. Enshrining indigenous culture as "a living denial of the capitalist system as well as the 'values' of a so-called Christian civilization," Church officials likened its purported simplicity, spirituality, and cooperativism to primitive Christianity.[88] The Médici regime, implicating the Church in indigenous mobilization, had attempted in 1974 to assert a veto over all Catholic missionaries working with Indians.[89]

It should be noted that the ideological positions of the progressive wing of the Catholic Church were never accepted uniformly by all missionary groups; the Salesians, in particular, were often criticized by CIMI for retaining heavy-handed methods. Moreover, "progressive" notions about Indians perpetuated an age-old and damaging tradition of typecasting and homogenizing indigenous peoples. Xavante families struggling to commercialize crops, men working on fazendas, and chiefs pocketing rancher "incentives" would probably have chuckled at their depiction as precapitalist fossils.[90]

There were, however, different implications when missionaries conceived of Indians as disciples in need of clerical solidarity rather than deviants worthy of reprobation. Indeed, pressure from colleagues, indigenous leaders, and internal dissent (the slain missionary Rodolfo Lunkenbein, for example, had been a board member of CIMI) led the Salesian mission of Mato Grosso in 1977 to draw up new guidelines for missionaries endorsing ethnographic training, an end to paternalistic practices, and the defense of Indian lands.[91] Furthermore, indigenous people, who long played one sector of dominant society against another to exercise greater political leverage, could profit from the Church offensive against the military government. In 1979, CIMI issued a press statement reiterating "unconditional solidarity" with the Xavante in their struggle against Fazenda Xavantina.[92]

The Xavante found "great friends" as well in anthropologists, journalists, health care officials, academics, students, and lawyers.[93] In the 1970s, a number of indigenous advocacy groups, such as the Associação Nacional de Apoio ao Índio (ANAI), the Commisão Pro-Índio (CPI), and the Centro de Trabalho Indigenista (CTI), emerged in response to a proposal by Minister of the Interior Rangel Reis in 1978 to "emancipate" Indians from government tutela.[94] The measure would have served to strip indigenous people of their constitutional land rights because according to Brazilian law, "emancipated" Indians were, by definition, no longer entitled to state protection as Indians.[95] Indigenous land rights, which derived from primordial possession and not from Indians' dependent status as tutelados, in theory would not have been compromised; yet interested parties would have attempted undoubtedly to obscure or repudiate such legal distinctions to usurp indigenous territory. In December 1978, twenty-three indigenous leaders, including four Xavante, traveled to Brasília with a petition to Geisel opposing "emancipation."[96] The military government ultimately shelved the project, but the indigenous support network remained in place. In December 1979, thirteen advocacy groups from São Paulo—including women's, environmental, indigenous, academic, and human rights organizations—signed a petition published in a leading São Paulo newspaper that called on the government to create a new reservation for the Xavante at Couto Magalhães.[97] Indeed, the press, enjoying newfound freedom from government censors, publicized Indian struggles, rediscovering the brave Xavante who had arisen phoenixlike in the aftermath of "pacification." This was the modified political arena, then, in which Celestino and other Xavante leaders would mobilize to reclaim land that had been usurped by fazendeiros and legitimized by state power.

The Showdown

Over the course of 1979, Xavante leaders and Fazenda Xavantina engaged in a war of nerves as each side tested the other's resolve while jockeying for state backing. Xavantina reported that the Indians "constantly solicited [us] to furnish meals and in some cases even with threats in the shacks of our employees. We are victims of a permanent slaughtering of animals by the Indians, obliging us to maintain our cattle under supervision and far from the borders of the reserves."[98] Miffed by such provocation, Hélio Stersa, a ranch administrator, threatened to drop a bomb on the Indians.[99] Meanwhile, Celestino traveled to FUNAI headquarters in Brasília together with another indigenous leader from Couto Magalhães, Martinho, to press for territorial annexation as well as assistance in relocating additional Indians from Sangradouro.[100]

When Fazenda Xavantina reactivated a sawmill located approximately one thousand meters from one Xavante village at Couto Magalhães, the Indians vowed to burn down the mill to halt deforestation. In February, after Stersa lodged a complaint that twenty-eight Indians had "invaded" ranch territory, fifteen military police officers were deployed to Fazenda Xavantina armed for combat. Before embarking from the local airport, the police officers allegedly received from one fazendeiro the promise of a bounty for every Xavante ear severed.[101] Rushed to the area by FUNAI, Claudio Romero found the police officers, armed with machine guns and hunkered behind a makeshift barricade of rice sacks at ranch headquarters, poised for attack. Romero warned the police of the worldwide repercussions for the Brazilian government of a violent confrontation and remained in close contact with superiors in Brasília who promised reinforcements. The following day, the military police withdrew from the ranch.[102]

For the state, the standoff underscored threats to regional stability and international reputation. For the Indians and the ranch, the dénouement signified deferral to the state in resolving the conflict. The Indians understood their vulnerability in hand-to-hand combat, and Xavantina's strategy, favoring bureaucratic lobbying over force, was not atypical for corporate landowners. In his study of land conflict in the Amazon region between 1965 and 1989, Alfredo Wagner Berno de Almeida found that industrial and financial capital in the region often opposed the use of extralegal force as potentially volatile and antithetical to "economic rationalism," favoring instead legal channels and bureaucratic lobbying to resolve conflicts.[103] To be sure, neither Xavante nor Xavantina relaxed their pressure on government officials.

Fazenda Xavantina decried FUNAI's laxity in curbing indigenous aggression. In April, forty Xavante from Couto Magalhães, primarily women and children, "invaded" the ranch to "gather rice from our plantings" without authorization.[104] The following month, the Indians returned to seize construction material from the sawmill (since shut down by the ranch), "grabbing doors, windows, boards, screens, and other materials, destroying houses, shacks, and installations . . . causing great damages to the fazenda."[105] A hunting expedition, led by Chief Martinho, "burned practically all of our native pasture there, placing in serious risk the cattle confined there, and obliging us to mobilize various cowhands to help remove the cattle. The area was rendered impossible to use, seriously damaged by the extemporaneous fire."[106] In July, Celestino's group began constructing huts near the ranch's airstrip and vowed to slaughter cattle.[107]

Regional FUNAI officials, barraged by Xavantina's protest, deemed many of the accusations overblown. So-called invasions were nothing more than treks for hunting and foraging, and the predatory depiction of Xavante a crude attempt to stoke fears of indigenous savagery.[108] Nevertheless, even local indigenistas confided to superiors their failure to

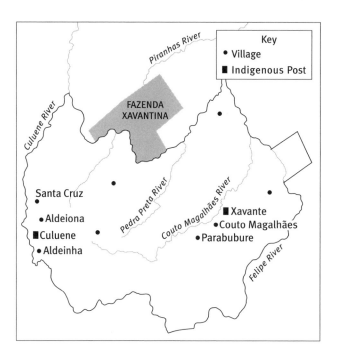

Map 7. Parabubure Reserve, 1980

convince Celestino to vacate land inside the Fazenda Xavantina where his group had begun to plant crops.[109] Indeed, throughout 1979, various ranchers in the Couto Magalhães region accused the Xavante of invading their land, threatening employees, burning down shacks, setting pasture ablaze, and raiding livestock—an indication that the situation was not as benign nor as controlled as local FUNAI officials suggested.[110] Strife engulfed other Xavante areas as well, as warriors at the Pimentel Barbosa reserve sacked four ranches (some belonging to former employers) established on the lands defrauded by FUNAI officials.[111]

The tension in the Xavante region alarmed upper echelons of the military government. In July 1979, FUNAI President Adhemar Ribeiro da Silva sent a letter to Minister of the Interior Andreazza requesting the collaboration of the CSN in resolving the dispute at Couto Magalhães. The involvement of the CSN would complement similar measures under Figueiredo to defuse rural violence in eastern Amazonia, most notably in southern Pará.[112]

As yet another troop of state officials trudged through their villages promising solutions, hope undoubtedly jostled with cynicism for the Indians. The Xavante, nevertheless, spoke firmly with the team, composed of a member of the CSN and two FUNAI officials, Romero and Pinto de Oliveira. Government officials noted that the Xavante community was "plainly conscious of its legal rights and of the struggle taking place to recover, at least partially, their former territories." Furthermore, if in the past the chiefs of the different communities had conflicting claims, they now jointly insisted that the new reserve encompass Fazenda Xavantina, including its headquarters.[113]

The government commission concluded that frequent conflicts between the Xavante and the surrounding population had led to the "discredit" of FUNAI and other state bureaus. The combined population of 1,220 at the two reserves—792 at Culuene and 428 at Couto Magalhães—along with the prospect of future returnees warranted additional territory. Prodded by the Xavante, the team endorsed the unification of the reserves of Couto Magalhães and Culuene.[114] When the presidential decree for the new reserve, promised by mid-November, still had not been issued in early December, the Indians vowed to carry out an attack on the ranch and hundreds of Xavante men painted themselves for war.[115] It is questionable if a violent attack would indeed have been carried out. Lured by its specter, however, journalists descended on Barra do Garças, thereby increasing pressure on the government.[116]

On December 21, 1979, President João Figueiredo signed a decree creating a new reserve named Parabubure. Although the Indians had called for a larger area, the new reserve extended much further than the 23,000 hectares decreed for the Indians at Couto Magalhães in 1972. Uniting the reserves of Couto Magalhães and Culuene, Parabubure encompassed 89,920 acres of Fazenda Xavantina (including its headquarters) as well as other ranches and squatter plots; it measured a total of 224,447 hectares. From "the minimum necessary" originally decreed by the military government for the Xavante at Couto Magalhães, the Indians had succeeded in increasing their reserved area nearly tenfold[117] (see Map 7).

Reconstruction

Now came the task of reconstruction at Parabubure. Within the newly decreed reserve, sixty-five property holders were affected: thirty-five possessed plots under 600 hectares; twenty-one had between 600 and

3,000; and six had over 3,000 hectares.[118] Although title holders were denied indemnification for their plots, they were eligible for compensation for all improvements made on the land. Federal officials estimated the value of the buildings, warehouses, and infrastructure on these properties at CR$250,200,000.[119] Fazenda Xavantina's investments alone were appraised at CR$141,377,440.[120]

Over the course of the next year, families were removed, with some relocated to a colonization project elsewhere in Mato Grosso. Banks restructured debt payment for stunned and embittered agriculturists; FUNAI annuled certidões negativas issued to title holders in the reserve and undertook its physical demarcation. The state of Mato Grosso and some aggrieved landowners filed lawsuits against the federal government for territorial indemnification.

The Xavante participated fully in the recovery of their ancestral territory, assisting in physical demarcation and the removal of recalcitrant landowners. Abandoned buildings were ransacked for housing material, with architectural ruins standing as markers of a historical past stolen and corrected, an inspiration for future struggle.[121] Approximately half of the exiles ultimately came back. Carlos Dumhiwe, who returned to Parabubure from Sangradouro in 1980, remarked of those who stayed behind at the Salesian missions, "We asked them to come, but our brothers didn't want to come. Because there's no car, no pharmacy here. There's nothing." Indeed, now that the "fazendeiros had destroyed the land," those who came back worried how they would reconstruct their lives when "there was no more game, no way to plant crops."[122] Like seafarers battered by storm, the returnees had stumbled to port having overcome a force far more powerful than they—exultant, yet mournful of the wreckage.

Of Frontier Accumulation, State Formation,
and Indigenous History

Increased settlement and investment in the Xavante region over the course of the 1970s, spurred by the military's developmental project, intensified social conflict. If we compare the reserved—and deforested—territory at Parabubure with extensive precontact domain, the Xavante "victory" rings hollow. Yet, although framed by a political economy that has favored capital accumulation, the historical experience of Brazilian indigenous groups must not be impoverished by reductionism. Xavante mobilized to roll back frontier accumulation, pressuring the military government to delimit larger reserves. In part, the Xavante triumph can be explained by the nature of the conflict in the Couto Magalhães–Culuene region, which arrayed Indians against large and small landowners, as opposed to "megaprojects" marked by more heavy-handed governmental response. In addition, the success owed to the political culture of the Xavante, who, like the Kayapó, melded traditional martial prowess with skillful manipulation of dominant cultural practices to influence state policy.[123] Indigenous groups such as the Xavante recognized both the importance and the shortcomings of FUNAI in community defense and sought to reinforce yet redefine state power on the frontier.

Indeed, as this chapter has shown, the Xavante resorted to both legal and extralegal measures to stretch the territorial and political boundaries imposed by authoritarian rule. Assisted by FUNAI officials, church leaders, and sectors of civil society, the Indians seized on the political liberalization orchestrated by the Geisel government to press for additional land. Xavante appeals, adapted from dominant discourse and law while drawing as well on the group's specific historical experience, upheld the constitutional rights and cultural sanctity of "Indians." Yet, through direct action, the Indians returned to the Culuene region, raided fazendas, slaughtered cattle, intimidated opponents, and sought to raise domestic and international awareness.

The Xavante case suggests, then, reassessment of the role of violence and its relation to conflict resolution on the frontier. Foweraker correctly notes that on the Brazilian frontier, the state has employed violence (along with bureaucratic and legal administration, or its absence) to replicate the capitalist social system. Repression against peasants, expulsion of squatters, and other forms of rural violence are condoned by and closely linked with the legal and administrative apparatuses of the state.[124] The Xavante land struggle, however, demonstrates how subaltern groups have used the spectacle of force—raiding ranches, interdicting road traffic, daubing war paint—to secure state backing against invaders.[125]

The interplay between state policy and Xavante mobilization illustrates Alves's contention that the Brazilian military state, engaged in a dialectic relationship with resilient and protean oppositional movements, was impelled to incorporate some of these demands.[126] Xavante pressure, heaped on a government preoccupied with Amazonian land conflicts in the aftermath of the Araguaia guerrilla movement, would help force a compromise. The recovery of a larger swath of land in the Couto Magalhães–Culuene region, from where the entire population had been exiled decades earlier, dramatically symbolized this strategic negotiation between Indians and the state. As a result of Xavante mobilization, the course of indigenous policy as well as indigenous politics was significantly altered.

The Xavante at Parabubure cherish their achievement. Carlos Dumhiwe, living a stone's throw from Xavantina's former headquarters, remembers how indomitable the ranch once was as he gazes on its abandoned buildings across low rolling hills of dry underbrush: "It had everything. Like a city that has things. A fortune, the fazenda . . . No one in the mission thought of returning to our land."[127] Renato Tsiwaradza, another villager, recounts the humiliation his people endured prior to creation of the Parabubure reserve: "In those days, the people from Culuene didn't pass there in the middle of the [ranch] headquarters if they were going to the Couto Magalhães reserve. No one passed through there, they went around the side like a dog." With pride, he adds, "Today it is Parabubure. It has no other name."[128]

8

The Xavante Project, 1978–1988

Although Xavante at various reserves celebrated their political triumph in securing territory, the future of their communities remained unclear. José Tsorompré of São Marcos lamented that, whereas his father had raised him on wild game and roots, he could not guarantee the same security to his son.[1] Indeed, given environmental degradation and a high birthrate, how would the Indians feed their families? How would the Xavante weather the shift to intensive agriculture? How would the Indians ensure proper education and health care for their communities? How would they satisfy their growing reliance on consumer goods? How would relations with fazendeiros be mended?

The Xavante had won the legal battle to recover territory, but a rupture with their neighbors was one of the casualties of war (see Table 3). With the string of indigenous victories, the fazendeiros disbanded the paternalistic "good neighbor policy" that had helped sustain needy communities, and moved to retaliate against the Xavante and FUNAI. In Barra do Garças, FUNAI officials were jeered and threatened, and local radio programs, newspaper articles, and placards protested the creation of the reserves. Merchants and white-collar professionals in Barra do Garças, who thrived on landowner patronage, closed ranks against the Xavante. Hospitals denied care to Indians and schools and commercial establishments turned them away. The Indians were denounced as vagabonds, vandals, and cattle rustlers.[2]

In a conciliatory appeal, fifteen Xavante chiefs signed a manifesto declaring that they merely sought "progress in production" on their reserves (see Map 8). Although they did recriminate:

These councilmen, fazendeiros and politicians want to do away with the Indians by taking all of the land of the Brazilian Indians. Is it not enough that our ancestors were killed the way animals are killed in the wild? Leaving from Barra do Garças, white men went armed to hunt the Indian and destroy the people of this Xavante nation. We have survivors of those skirmishes who can appear in Court to testify against those white bandits. In ninety years has justice been done? No one finds those people, they are hidden. The fazendeiros want to do the same with us.[3]

The camaradarie between Indian and white propagandized by Estado Novo ideologues in the March to the West eluded Barra do Garças, as in most of the Brazilian countryside.

Marooned in a sea of hostility, the Indians looked to FUNAI for rescue. In turn, FUNAI staked much on "productive" use of resources by the Xavante to deflect charges that too much land had been reserved for too few Indians.[4] Mutual suspicions, however, made for leery bedfellows. The Indians had bitter memories of the agency's previous infidelities; FUNAI cringed at the strong-minded Xavante's next stunt. Furthermore, neither side was entirely convinced of the soundness of the union. Some Xavante leaders denounced FUNAI intervention in indigenous affairs. And as local FUNAI agents in Barra do Garças prodded indigenous communities to exercise greater autonomy, officials in Brasília fretted over the loss of control.

Small wonder that at such crossroads all eyes turned anxiously to the Plano de Desenvolvimento para a Nação Xavante (Development Plan for the Xavante Nation), more commonly referred to as the Projeto Xavante. Drawn up in 1978 by two FUNAI anthropologists, Claudio Romero and José Claudinei Lombardi, the community development project aimed at generating self-sufficiency through mechanized rice production and cattle grazing and through educational and health programs at the Xavante reserves. FUNAI deployed a team of technicians, agronomists, educators, and health care officials to the area to train the Xavante as agriculturists, machinery operators, health care attendants, and bilingual teaching monitors. The agency, under the administration of General Ismarth Araújo de Oliveira, initially earmarked CR$8,635,207 for the Xavante Project and established a special coordinating unit in Barra do Garças, the Ajudância Autônoma de Barra do Garças, (Autonomous Adjutancy of Barra do Garças, AJABAG).[5]

The Xavante Project appealed to government planners as a recipe for agricultural modernization and indigenous self-sufficiency, as well as a means to consolidate state power in Legal Amazonia. Rooted in what James Scott has termed a "high-modernist ideology," the mechanized rice growing venture preached uncritical and unskeptical faith in science,

Table 3. Xavante Reserves by Area and Population, 1990

Reserve	Area (hectares)	Population
Areões	218,515	594
Marechal Rondon	98,500	245
Parabubure	224,447	2,697
Pimentel Barbosa	328,966	694
Sangradouro	100,260	635
São Marcos	188,478	1,368

Source: Centro Ecumênico de Documentação e Informação, *Povos indígenas no Brasil 1987/88/89/90* (São Paulo: CEDI, 1991), 503.

technical progress, and comprehensive planning to regiment production and nature (including human nature).[6] The Project privileged large-scale, commercial, mechanized monoculture, excluded Xavante input and know-how, and made cursory allowances for the functioning indigenous social order and local landscape. Devised under authoritarian rule, the project was implanted among communities with limited legal, economic, and political capacity to challenge state power.

The project was also calculated to defuse indigenous militancy, appease landed interests, and boost the regime's legitimacy under the liberalizing climate of abertura.[7] As Romero stated in 1978: "FUNAI only thought of elaborating a Project for the Xavante Community [of São Marcos] because those Indians were problems, and serious problems. The principal objective of that Project was political, because it sought to appease the Indians who always gave interviews criticizing this Agency."[8] Indeed, following its disappointing showing in the 1974 elections, the military government engaged in patronage politics on a massive scale at all state levels to secure electoral support and to counter the growing perception that the official party of the military, ARENA, represented only the rich.[9] While repression and electoral manipulation would continue to be employed during abertura, the military relied on patronage and clientelism both to reward traditional elites as well as to court underprivileged sectors. As the military government leaned on the Xavante Project to co-opt indigenous leadership and defuse territorial claims, state officials and Xavante chiefs became interlocked in a patron-client relationship.

This chapter probes the origins and evolution of the state-sponsored development program among Xavante communities. In examining the Xavante Project in the context of Brazilian state policy, I seek to bridge political analysis of military rule and democratic transition with the ethnographic work of Laura Graham that underscores the role of Xavante agency in mediating tumultuous socioeconomic change.[10] The objectives are twofold: to broaden understanding of mechanisms of rule employed by the military to consolidate power in the countryside and to control the process of democratic transition; and to highlight patterns of Xavante accommodation and resistance, dependency and defiance, that have constituted their complex engagement with state power. A dualist model of state versus subaltern, prominent in the literature on the "new social movements" under military rule, is problematized, and the enduring legacy of patronage in postauthoritarian Brazil highlighted.[11]

A Community Development Project Is Born

"Development by project," whether high-profile road building or community-based programs, conformed to the centralized economic planning of the military governments of Médici, Geisel, and Figueiredo.[12] Basic to this model was the very conceptualization of "development" as technological innovation and market participation rather than structural change, and the subordination of local initiative and know-how to state planning.[13] Rural community development projects would serve primarily as mechanisms to streamline agricultural production, promote capitalist growth, and expand state power in the countryside by ensuring the adhesion of local populations.

In the quest to modernize agricultural production, with special attention to the "problems" of Amazonia, military development planners targeted indigenous peoples. As Minister of the Interior Rangel Reis asserted in 1974, "The Indian is not a different being, to live segregated on reserves, but must participate in the effort of national development." Nurtured by the natives' putatively "cooperative system," community development projects would only strengthen the moral fiber and economic muscle of indigenous villages.[14] As a result of developmental planning, the "better Indian" that Brazilian policy makers long dreamed of crafting—small farmer, regimented laborer, and loyal citizen—would ideally emerge.

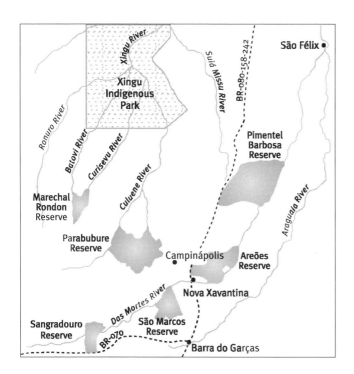

Map 8. Xavante Reserves, 1986

The FUNAI community development projects during Araújo de Oliveira's administration in fact passed through two distinct phases. Initial programs, more modest in scope, were devised by both Brazilian and foreign anthropologists with expertise among their respective indigenous groups. For the Xavante, a proposal for one community was drawn up by Aracy Lopes da Silva, who was carrying out her doctoral fieldwork at the time. George Zarur, director of FUNAI's Departamento Geral de Planejamento Comunitário, noted in 1975 that the economic success of the projects should not be measured solely by market performance but in the creation of "better human beings whose humanity is recognized in the society in which they live."[15] But, in a rapid about-face, FUNAI officials wrested control from these academics, who stood accused of being subversives or spies and often were expelled from the area, and redefined the community development projects.[16]

The Xavante Project, much grander in scope, presented a Sisyphean task for both the Indians and FUNAI. Even under optimal conditions, large-scale mechanized farming in the Mato Grosso cerrado contended with a regiment of foes: highly acidic soils demanded extensive liming and fertilization; erratic rainfall sowed ruin; floods, collapsed bridges, and potholed roads bedeviled hauls to economic markets; machinery required fuel, upkeep, and repair.[17] Indeed, such factors spelled disaster for many colonists and small producers in the region.[18] For the Xavante, the emphasis on monoculture, historically eschewed as environmental insurance, represented a dramatic and risky shift in subsistence patterns. Moreover, Xavante inexperience with high-input agriculture and overreliance on government investment and technical support boded ill for a project touted as a panacea for self-sufficiency. In fact, from an earlier debacle, the project's drafters were fully cognizant of the pitfalls of large-scale mechanized agriculture in Xavante communities.

Between 1975 and 1977, FUNAI implemented a pilot project at the Areões reservation for mechanized cultivation of rice that demonstrated that neither technological wonder nor indigenous virtue were impeccable, and that their union could spawn mutant results. Technical instruction promised by FUNAI was never given, and the Xavante were relegated to the sidelines as post officials carried out most tasks.[19] When FUNAI employees urged manual cultivation of plots the Indians scoffed: Why should they bother to hoe if the encarregado could plow with a tractor? Dispirited and idle, community members roamed about the town of Xavantina. Areões earned the dubious distinction as the only Xavante reservation with a serious problem of alcoholism.[20] In fact, many of the ills afflicting Areões pervaded the other thirty-six indigenous areas where FUNAI implemented community development projects at the time. In 1977, a Brazilian congressional inquest criticized the projects for excluding Indians from all aspects of decision making and production, provoking "disastrous alterations" in the division of labor and distribution of goods.[21]

The drafters of the Xavante Project, which would encompass all of the reserves, sought to rectify these problems. To curtail marginalization, Romero and Lombardi proposed indigenous cooperatives to ensure broad participation and decision making based on collective consultation. They explicitly warned the agency of the dangers of compacting with chiefs, noting that because "leadership among the Xavante is transitory," any clientelistic policy "could cause unforeseeable consequences." To stem village rivalries and cries of favoritism, the project should benefit all communities equally.[22] In practice, however, these guidelines would be difficult to follow and, ultimately, flouted.

A Community Development Project Is Adapted

Xavante responded to the project with both cynicism and excitement. Indeed, the implantation of the project highlighted the tenuous and ambiguous position of the Indians as legal wards of the state. Although the state guaranteed Indians permanent usufructuary rights to their land, FUNAI dictated the course of economic development and the management of natural resources. The Xavante had no say in preparing the project, devised in Brasília by planners concerned more with the schematic and orderly transformation of local communities than their day-to-day realities, struggles, aspirations, and limitations. Thus, for example, in areas where land conflicts continued to rage, some Xavante balked at the project when their territories were invaded or inappropriately demarcated.

Others, however, welcomed the project for both its promise and symbolism. For decades the state had neglected to provide adequate technical assistance, health care, and education, leaving the Indians to their own devices, until this sudden change of heart. For years, as they slashed and burned vegetation and manually cultivated, Indians had envied landowners equipped with labor-saving machinery.[23] Now the Indians would prove to detractors that they too could excel given a fair chance.[24] As a Xavante leader from São Marcos proclaimed in 1980, "We want our children and grandchildren to learn all they can to have professions, to become lawyers, to be officials in their own right."[25] Hope glimmered for hungry communities whose lands had been despoiled. Perseverance had earned the Xavante their time in the sun. Small wonder that many Indians viewed the project—as many had "pacification"—as *their* conquest.[26]

The Xavante struggled to adhere to the project's guidelines, which required reshuffling of traditional means of subsistence. Until recently, hunting and gathering dwarfed agricultural production, which had been carried out at the household rather than the community level. Moreover, the cultivation and distribution of subsistence crops had been traditionally the responsibility of Xavante women. Nevertheless, Xavante communities sought to adapt their gendered and age-based division of labor to the project. At São Marcos, for example, women worked on clearing the rice plantation of roots and branches and gathering the harvest. Furthermore, each male age set cultivated a designated area of rice. The yield from each tract was divided among the corresponding age set, with some consumed by the household and the remainder commercialized. Younger men tended to receive more profit, as the plots that they cultivated were twice the size of the elders'. When only several sacks of rice were produced, the Indians traveled unaccompanied to town to market their goods. Officials of FUNAI oversaw larger transactions to ensure fair distribution of earnings.[27]

The project revealed both productive potential and disruptive force. The São Marcos reserve produced 10,494 sacks of rice in the 1979–1980 harvest.[28] From 1981 to 1982, according to FUNAI statistics, 2,762 hectares of rice were harvested at the Xavante reservations, and 3,161 hectares in 1982–1983.[29] In 1982, nearly the entire village of Pimentel Barbosa would relocate approximately sixty kilometers from their base to work on the rice harvest.[30]

Nevertheless, with its monocrop emphasis and heavy infusion of capital, the mechanized rice growing project introduced new problems. With efforts devoted to rice cultivation, the Indians lost interest in their swidden plots and trekking. Meals—once a variety of animal game, tubers, wild fruits, and nuts—often consisted of a plateful of rice. Indeed, nutritionists warned that the excess of starch and the lack of protein in the Xavante diet could contribute to diabetes, goiter, vitamin deficiency, and other ailments.[31] Intensive agriculture degraded soil quality, poor by nature in the cerrado. Highly dependent on FUNAI for inputs and marketing, the Indians suffered from the agency's dereliction. Because FUNAI failed to provide fuel for machinery, 50 percent of the rice harvest in the Xavante areas in 1980 (roughly 2,400 hectares) was lost.[32]

For their part, state planners found that when Xavante communities were outfitted with a centrally planned development project, the material sagged and frayed when worn by their body politic. Indeed, the very notion of a community development project engineered by outsiders took on new meaning in an indigenous society where "community" orbited around factional rivalries, "development" assumed different permutations, and "project" had an immediate rather than forward-looking scope. Engaging and offsetting indigenous modes of production, exchange, and power dynamics, the project would lead to the reconfiguration of both Xavante politics and state policy.

In line with their long-standing pursuit of autonomy and territorial dominion, Xavante communities wrangled incessantly with FUNAI, as well as with each other, over the control of machinery. Although the equipment belonged to FUNAI, the Xavante viewed it as their own—except when it came time for repair. The Indians seized tractors for hunting expeditions and transportation to town; when reprimanded by post officials, they retorted that the equipment had been "given by his Excellency, the Minister of the Interior, and that they, as their owners, could do with these machines as they wished."[33] Villages prized "their" equipment as a status symbol. As one post chief noted, "Every time it is necessary to send the agricultural equipment to a determined area they nearly start a war."[34] Thus, when encarregado Francisco Magalhães urged communities in the Parabubure reserve to store machinery at the post shed to avoid rust, he encountered opposition to such symbolic "surrender." When the encarregado contravened the will of Benedito Loazo, he was tied up and beaten.[35]

In Xavante villages, the project contended with local power dynamics. Efforts by FUNAI to train indigenous bilingual school monitors, health care attendants, and skilled laborers to serve as future administrators of the project foundered as Xavante chiefs designated male members of their factions to these remunerated positions, regardless of qualification. Educators employed by FUNAI were dismayed to learn that many of the bilingual education monitors, for example, lacked basic Portuguese skills.[36] Moreover, the Indians placed on agency payroll viewed themselves, first and foremost, as FUNAI employees rather than guarantors of community welfare. When payment arrived late (as it often did) the tractors might lie idle or the infirmary inoperative as Xavante walked off the job.[37] (Then again, FUNAI infirmaries were often understocked and the medications out of date.)[38] Corruption surfaced, with the "secretary" from Pimentel Barbosa, Surupredu, accused of diverting earnings from community rice sales to personal bank accounts in Barra do Garças and Goiânia.[39] On a more mundane level, FUNAI vehicles and resources were often appropriated by chiefs for personal use.

Age and gender dynamics within villages were reconfigured as well. In the rush to FUNAI's door, many older leaders less adept in Portuguese or in mining agency riches were left behind or upstaged by their "secretaries." At the Salesian missions, in particular, younger Xavante leaders emerged, less well-versed in traditional customs because of their age and upbringing among the missionaries. Indeed, the staff at AJABAG noted the marginalization of members of the warã, or council of elders, from decision making.[40] Gender roles rigidified along new lines, as Xavante men gained access to government patronage, amplified political networks, and operated in urban arenas with increased social contacts, while women remained confined largely to the household.[41]

In general, many Xavante eyed the project's resources, rather than the promise of self-sufficiency, as the ultimate prize. In 1979, every day an average of sixty to eighty Xavante would descend on AJABAG (the FUNAI regional office in Barra do Garças) in search of food, clothes, shoes, and other handouts, perpetuating the very cycle of dependency that the project aimed to eradicate.[42] In freely disposing of state resources and machinery, many Indians undoubtedly believed that they *were* being self-sufficient.

Odenir Pinto de Oliveira, the head of AJABAG, convened meetings of Xavante leaders to resolve these problems. In one meeting, held at Merure in June 1979 and attended by FUNAI President Adhemar Ribeiro da Silva, agency officials and indigenous leaders from various reserves agreed that to stanch waste each post would hereafter administer its own funds.[43] Moreover, to discourage frequent trips to Barra do Garças, the office suspended all Xavante requests for goods, lodging, and transportation and informed local hoteliers and merchants that FUNAI would no longer pick up the Indians' tab.

During the next several months, according to the FUNAI post chief at Culuene, indigenous participation in the Project proceeded more smoothly: tasks were performed, Xavante left the reserves infrequently, and by early 1980, 2,000 sacks of rice had been harvested. Moreover, the Indians agreed to use half of the profits to acquire consumer goods, one quarter for ongoing funding of the project, and the remainder for the future harvest.[44] Predicting the future of the project, another post chief ventured, "The project can be a double-edged sword. If well oriented, the indigenista aspect [policy] might come to fruition. On the other hand, it might lead more speedily to individualization, dependency, 'white' vices, uncontrolled and futile consumption and tribal disintegration."[45]

Over the course of 1980 it became increasingly clear that the project would be a tool not for self-sufficiency but for dissection. The pact at Merure was torn asunder by indigenous competitiveness and mistrust. When Xavante from São Marcos and Sangradouro resumed their trips to Barra do Garças and Brasília, the others despaired that their unscrupulous competitors would dry up all of the project's funds. The agreement to hold posts responsible for financial expenses fell by the wayside as FUNAI officials reallocated funds for the project away from the local administration.[46] But the final blow to the project's integrity came about as the military government manipulated distributional policies to stifle indigenous protest, and Xavante leaders colluded in the share-out.

Multilevel Opposition to the Military's Indigenous Policy

The degeneration of the project into an insidious patronage racket ensued in the aftermath of a dramatic showdown in April–May 1980 between Xavante and FUNAI over the future of the Pimentel Barbosa reserve in particular, and the exercise of state power toward indigenous communities in general. Xavante at Pimentel Barbosa were embroiled in a dispute with FUNAI over the reserve's boundary, charging that the agency sought to exclude from demarcation 60,000 hectares occupied by several large fazendas. Two months earlier, shortly after the creation of the Parabubure reserve, Xavante men from Pimentel Barbosa had carried out a series of raids on the fazendas, drawing national attention.[47] In April 1980, at a momentous meeting at Pimentel Barbosa that brought together Xavante leaders from various reserves, an ultimatum was issued: If FUNAI failed to demarcate the appropriate boundaries, the Indians would do so themselves. When FUNAI stalled, the Xavante proceeded to demarcate a twenty-five-kilometer strip. Federal police stormed Pimentel Barbosa to halt the Indians, and Pinto de Oliveira was threatened with arrest for allegedly inciting and arming Xavante.[48]

The Xavante leaders demanded an immediate meeting with FUNAI President João Carlos Nobre da Veiga at the reserve. His consent was unlikely. Nobre da Veiga, a retired air force colonel, had been instated in 1979 after his predecessor, Adhemar Ribeiro da Silva, was removed by the Minister of the Interior; the Ministry allegedly had been under intense pressure from landowners and state officials in Mato Grosso who denounced Xavante "expansionism" and the creation of other indigenous reserves (constituting roughly 12 percent of the state's territory) and clamored for stronger institutional backing.[49] Nobre da Veiga had no background in indigenous affairs, little sympathy for Xavante territorial claims, and much disdain for ethnic politics. During his tenure (1979–1981), FUNAI would embark on a racist exercise to devise "criteria of Indianness," based on a perverse mishmash of cultural, biological, psychological, and social characteristics; those who failed this ethnic litmus test would be stripped of tutela and, ostensibly, their rights to land. (Bombarded by protest from indigenous people, missionaries, journalists, academics, and lawyers, FUNAI would shelve the initiative.)[50]

Snubbed by the FUNAI president, thirty-one Xavante "chiefs" headed in early May for agency headquarters in Brasília, accompanied by three federal congressmen from the opposition party. Elbowing their way through the FUNAI building (with reporters at their side), the Indians presented their list of demands: proper demarcation of the Pimentel Barbosa reserve; the removal of Nobre da Veiga (whom they threatened to defenestrate) and other high-level agency officials; and continued support for Pinto de Oliveira and the staff at AJABAG.[51]

The FUNAI officials responded by summoning the police, who promptly surrounded the building. Outraged, the Indians threatened bloodshed if the security forces were not withdrawn. Nobre da Veiga acceded.[52] The Xavante leaders' sense of entitlement and betrayal is captured in a subsequent letter from nine chiefs to the Minister of the Interior:

> We were very sad and revolted because we came here not to fight but to look out for our rights and we were received by the President of FUNAI like BANDITS.
>
> We never received in our villages any President of FUNAI, not even Colonel Veiga, with armed warriors.
>
> In this way, he violated our rights. He did not respect our condition as the Chiefs of a Village, nor our customs, as is written in the Estatuto [do Índio].[53]

Xavante demands roiled officials in Brasília. At a meeting held subsequent to the standoff at Pimentel Barbosa and agency headquarters, one government official told Romero, "From their perspective as hunters and gatherers, the land is not sufficient to maintain their lifestyle. Our worry is this: we know that the Xavante are a proud, warrior nation with an expansionist tendency."[54] The fruits of the project were supposed to sate Indian hunger for additional land, but in light of Xavante initiatives at Parabubure and Pimentel Barbosa, would they suffice? Moreover, Xavante publicity stunts embarrassed the agency. In launching the project, one of FUNAI's goals (publicly undisclosed) had been to silence blistering denunciations to the press. Now, in response to the duel at agency headquarters, newspapers of all political persuasions blasted FUNAI for its misguided response.[55]

Indeed, over the course of 1980, FUNAI was an embattled agency. Indigenous oppositional movements and their supporters vociferously lambasted heavy-handedness and corruption under Nobre da Veiga and the abuse of tutela to cudgel indigenous initiative. In April, a group of Terena, Xavante, Bororo, Pataxó, and Tuxá students studying in Brasília formed the Unĩao das Nações Indígenas (Union of Indigenous Nations), Brazil's first pan-Indian organization. Shortly after, another pan-Indian group with the same name was founded in Mato Grosso do Sul to promote indigenous self-determination, advance territorial claims, and defend legal rights. The two organizations soon merged. Military intelligence agents were particularly rankled by the use of the term "indigenous nations," with its connotation of political sovereignty.[56]

In November 1980, tutela came under international fire in an incident involving Mario Juruna, a Xavante leader from the São Marcos reserve. Juruna had been invited by the Fourth International Russell Tribunal in Holland, a worldwide body symbolically judging human rights abuses against Native Americans, to hear accusations against the Brazilian government.[57] Juruna, illiterate and semiconversant in Portuguese, had first risen to fame in the early 1970s in the struggle over land demarcation by using a hidden tape recorder to expose the double-talk of government officials. Along with the press, FUNAI interestingly had played a part in promoting Juruna, marveling at his masterful leap from a nonliterate "primitive" culture to electronic wizardry in defending his community.[58] The message was clear: the Indian could use technology like anyone else, and for nobler causes. (Juruna's antipathy toward the Salesians at São Marcos undoubtedly endeared him to some government officials as well.) But when Juruna's whimsical antics turned into potentially nasty denunciations in the worldwide arena, state officials scrambled to pull the plug. The Ministry of the Interior denied travel authorization, deeming Juruna, a ward of the state, unqualified to deliberate on behalf of other Indian groups before a tribunal unrecognized by the Brazilian goverment.

The controversy sparked domestic outcry. In Brazil, Juruna emerged as an icon of resistance to authoritarian rule, and his supporters vowed to challenge the travel ban in court.[59] Ultimately, the Federal Court of Appeals ruled that Juruna had the right to travel to the Netherlands. In November 1980, in a symbolic inversion of the colonial paradigm, a Xavante Indian took his seat in Europe as honorary president of a tribunal judging the misdeeds of the Brazilian government. (Two years later, under the wing of Brazil's inveterate populist politician, Leonel Brizola, Juruna would be elected as a federal deputy from Rio de Janeiro in another symbolic rebuff to military rule.)

Post officials and other indigenistas censured state violation of tutela and indigenous rights. In February 1980, eighty FUNAI employees critical of agency policy founded the Sociedade Brasileira de Indigenistas (Brazilian Society of Indigenists, SBI), with Pinto de Oliveira serving as vice president.[60] Following the confrontation at Pimentel Barbosa and at FUNAI headquarters, the SBI (together with other Indian advocacy groups) signed a manifesto decrying the directorate's ironfisted response to Xavante demands.[61]

FUNAI's Carrot and Stick

The leadership of FUNAI countered oppositional movements with a mixed dose of patronage and repression. Following the siege of agency headquarters, Nobre da Veiga met with Xavante leaders and insisted that he, rather than local officials, had their best interests at heart, and vowed to funnel funds directly to the indigenous leaders. To demonstrate his goodwill, he sent the chiefs to FUNAI's planning division to put in their requests. Warodi, the chief at Pimentel Barbosa, publicly denounced the president's offer as tantamount to bribery.[62] Yet, other leaders opened the floodgates: Joãozinho requested a Toyota pickup, a tractor, and blankets; Zacarias also wanted a tractor and a Toyota; and Celestino asked for a tractor, a truck, a Toyota, and even an airplane.[63] In return for FUNAI's offer of a tractor and a Banco do Brasil loan, João Evangelista (Babatti) retracted land claims at Sangradouro.[64] For the FUNAI directorate, the importance of defusing indigenous land claims and securing state power far outweighed eliminating dependency.[65] For indigenous leaders, privileged access to agency largesse was a signal opportunity not to be squandered. What mattered most to Xavante leaders was whether officials could deliver state and personal services rather than their ideological wholesomeness or partisan label—a political demand that of course is not restricted to the Xavante.[66]

Post officials who had watched the Xavante enter the ring pugnaciously in Brasília were surprised by the knockout dealt to them instead. For example, the Xavante harangued the encarregado at Culuene, Izanoel Sodré, "that the post chiefs do nothing but steal from the Indian, taking advantage of the trust they place in them. . . . That as proof that he, the President, is on their side, he would deal with all problems, directly with the Indians, without any interference by the post chief or the Adjutancy [AJABAG], and that at the moment, FUNAI is disposed to spend 30 (thirty) million cruzeiros in the Xavante area and the leaders themselves should make the Project and the demands that they believe necessary."[67]

With the green light from Brasília, Xavante leaders at Culuene informed the post chief that they would no longer store rice reserves for future harvests as the project prescribed, but instead planned to market them and count on FUNAI in case of shortage.[68] Meanwhile, the post chief at Couto Magalhães complained that the Xavante demanded "complete autonomy to use the machinery and the fuel destined for the implantation of the agricultural project for constant hunts and fishing trips, without accountability to the [post] chief, to the employees, or even the agricultural technician."[69] Likewise, a report from São Marcos noted that the indigenous leaders "see fit to proceed as they wish with the financial resources and implantation of the cattle-agricultural Project," notwithstanding their inability to repair machinery or oversee accounting matters.[70]

Yet, Xavante leaders engaged in the free-for-all were also clearly attuned to Nobre da Veiga's machinations. When questioned by encarregado Sodré as to whether they had faith in the president's word, the Xavante at Culuene said that "they were going to make the President believe that they believed everything and when the money ran out in Brasília, they would unite representatives from the 22 villages and would kick out the President of FUNAI, because he did not understand anything about Indians."[71]

In a further offensive, the FUNAI directorate, under Nobre da Veiga, moved aggressively against troublesome subordinates. After twelve years of working with the Xavante, Pinto de Oliveira was forcibly transferred to a new division. To signal his protest, he quit. He would be one of forty-three seasoned indigenistas and anthropologists who resigned or were pushed out in 1980 during the shakeup in the agency. Others ousted—in what has been termed the "symbolic castration" of FUNAI—included José Porfírio de Carvalho, the SBI president; Claudio Romero, coordinator of the Xavante Project; and several post chiefs and educators working among the Xavante.[72] Nobre da Veiga most likely worked with intelligence agents from the Serviço Nacional de Informações (National Information Service, SNI), placed by the military government in all major state enterprises and agencies to collect dossiers on officials, maintain surveillance, and formally review appointments.[73]

With key members of the original project purged, Nobre da Veiga appointed Colonel Anael Gonçalves as intervenor in AJABAG to strengthen ties between FUNAI and local elites. At a meeting with Xavante leaders at Pimentel Barbosa, Gonçalves threatened prison sentences for Indians leaving their reservations, raiding nearby ranches, or besieging FUNAI. When several Xavante sought to manhandle Gonçalves, the colonel had two Indians arrested.[74]

Between 1979 and 1984, FUNAI underwent a period of institutional instability and growing militarization. Four of the six presidents who headed FUNAI during this period were military colonels, and the agency worked closely with the CSN and the SNI.[75] The Indians would relish victory with a presidential decree in August 1980 delimiting the boundaries of the Pimentel Barbosa reservation along the lines they had demanded. And the following year, Nobre da Veiga was removed from office amid allegations of personal kickbacks and administrative graft.[76] Yet, amid such turbulence, state officials retained the clientelistic policy toward the Xavante as a means of political anchorage.

The Xavante's Gamble

In playing FUNAI's game, Xavante leaders had sought to profit from their privileged position within the agency to extract assistance until "the money ran out." But by the time the project's "money ran out" the Xavante reserves would become balkanized. Whereas in 1980 there were twenty-two villages, by 1987 there were over fifty. A population boom accounted partly for this transformation: between 1980 and 1984, FUNAI officials estimated, the Xavante population rose from 3,405 to 4,834. Nevertheless, neither demographic growth, nor long-standing factional disputes, nor strategies of village dispersal aimed at safeguarding newly demarcated reserves can explain this fragmentation. As Laura Graham has shown, FUNAI clientelism conjoined with Xavante political jockeying to fracture communities in furious crosscuts.[77]

Post officials had denounced Nobre da Veiga's distributional policy, admonishing that communities would fission to allow leaders of weaker factions to gain direct access to state resources.[78] Though the directorate may not have initially schemed to fracture Xavante communities, the consequences of patronage were certainly unmistakable. Indeed, the growing implication of FUNAI in factional rivalries was apparent at the reserves.

At the principal village of São Marcos, FUNAI became entangled in a power struggle involving Orestes, the son of the elder leader, Apoena (not the leader of Pimentel Barbosa), and Aniceto, Apoena's brother-in-law. In the struggle over land demarcation and project implementation, Aniceto, like other younger, mission-educated Indians, had gained local and national prominence due to his command of Portuguese, greater familiarity with the Brazilian political system, and backing by the Salesians. In a surprise move Apoena threw his support behind Aniceto rather than his son, who had left São Marcos for nearly four years to live in Brasília and São Paulo.

By the end of 1980, however, Apoena came to reconsider his decision. Aniceto had proven his adeptness in obtaining a tractor, a pickup truck, a thresher, and a harvester from FUNAI, but project resources had been unequally distributed.[79] Aniceto had awarded his kin with remunerated positions such as cowhand and tractor driver and excluded Apoena's. The elder Xavante accused Aniceto's brother, Fernando, of selling cattle belonging to the community.[80] Apoena began to oppose Aniceto, most likely in an effort to promote Orestes, who had returned to São Marcos. Both sides in the dispute turned to AJABAG for backing.

The trend was increasingly common. At a smaller village in the São Marcos reserve, São José, two contenders for leadership, João Nunes Xavante and Eduardo Xavante, would each appeal to FUNAI for support. There was much at stake: FUNAI provided chiefs and their "secretraries" with salaries as well as the cachet of official identification cards.[81] Another political aspirant, one Josué Gericó Xavante, offered to resolve the conflict—albeit not just by offering corn cakes as a peace offering. In a letter to state officials, Josué asked to be issued an ID card with his self-appointed title "peacekeeping counselor of the Xavante tribe." He also took the opportunity to request a personal loan from FUNAI.[82]

To mediate the power stuggle between Apoena and Aniceto, the new staff at AJABAG, instated after the administrative purge, organized a meeting in September 1980. Rodolfo Valentini, director of AJABAG, expressed his distaste for Aniceto, who "needs to confront FUNAI to obtain prestige among his community."[83] In fact, other agency officials alleged, AJABAG actively fomented the feud to dislodge Aniceto.[84] Under pressure, Aniceto agreed to step down and left the reservation for several months. In a sudden reversal, however, Aniceto, with the encouragement of many younger Xavante and the Salesians, struggled to recoup power. In a highly unorthodox procedure, the community resolved to hold an "election," which Aniceto won.[85] As a peace concession, the community gave nearly sixty head of cattle to Orestes, who relocated to another area of the reserve with his wife and child.

Orestes vowed to go to Brasília for backing to "participate in the [Xavante] Project."[86] Although he had shown no competence in leadership, or, for that matter, in tending to cattle (in a little over a year, fewer than half of his original herd remained), FUNAI persisted in underwriting his career. In early 1982, the head of AJABAG, on the recommendation of the president of FUNAI, approved the acquisition of a herd of cattle for Orestes, who presented himself as chief of the village of Buriti Alegre. In fact, the "village" consisted solely of Orestes and his nuclear family. Nevertheless, FUNAI provisioned twenty head of cattle. One year later, all of them had been sold.

On other reserves, FUNAI abetted the creation of breakaway (and often phantom) villages as well. In 1983, in the Culuene region of Parabubure, members of several communities resolved to split off under the leadership of one Honorato to form a new village. A FUNAI anthropologist working in the area, Luiz Otávio Pinheiro da Cunha, reported to Brasília that the falling out originated in a dispute over the distribution of project resources and appeared inevitable. Pinheiro da Cunha cautioned FUNAI headquarters to refrain from intervening in Xavante affairs: if Honorato and his group wished to found a new village, FUNAI should provide merely basic medical assistance. He noted that several years earlier, two Xavante villages that broke off in the Culuene region successfully weathered the transition because FUNAI, on the advice of the local post chief, limited its assistance to health care. Nonintervention had achieved two important results: communities were more self-sufficient (planting their own crops and constructing their own school), and legitimacy of political leadership devolved from village decision making rather than FUNAI backing.[87] The FUNAI directorate disregarded the anthropologist's suggestions, lavishing resources on Honorato. Shortly thereafter, officials learned that the money Honorato had requested for diesel fuel for his future "village" had been spent on clothes for himself and his family.[88]

The Logic of the Project

The FUNAI directorate and Xavante leaders had become locked in a patron-client relationship, a liaison fraught with suspicion and danger in the tense and inequitable share of power. Indigenous leaders exploited their aggressive reputation, media flash, relative proximity to Brasília, and political weight to ensure privileged status within FUNAI, squeeze resources from the agency, and jockey for power within their communities. Xavante "lobbying" of FUNAI, first mastered in the 1970s to demarcate reserves, retained time-tested strategies: the symbolic show of force or cliental deference, "traditional" pageantry, and shrewd usage of the press. Indeed, of the total CR$176 million earmarked in 1981 for indigenous community development projects throughout Brazil, the Xavante received the largest chunk, CR$57 million, whereas FUNAI allocated CR$50 million to be distributed among eighteen FUNAI posts and only CR$9.9 million to seven posts in Rio Grande do Sul.[89]

As Sherry Ortner has noted, in a relationship of power, subordinate peoples often display ambivalence toward dominant groups because the latter often have "something to offer, and sometimes a great deal (though always of course at the price of continuing in power)."[90] For the Xavante, such gains were substantial if gauged by the state's previous record, its policies toward other indigenous peoples or even, for that matter, most indigent people. Xavante privilege vis-à-vis other indigenous groups reflects "segmentary ethnicity," or nested hierarchy of ethnic identities, produced by the articulation between dominant society and diverse local social orders, which results in multilevel structures of inequality.[91] Political engagement allowed Xavante to climb within the lower ranks of the division of labor at the expense of other indigenous groups, notwithstanding the maintenance of larger structural inequalities.

If FUNAI meddled in communal disputes, Xavante leaders sought to influence agency affairs.[92] Like other interest groups in authoritarian Brazil, the Indians endeavored to secure advocates in state agencies and enterprise management.[93] For example, when charges of corruption dogged the administration of FUNAI President Colonel Paulo Leal, Nobre da Veiga's successor and ideological heir, Celestino and his "secretary," Carlos Dumhiwe, traveled from Parabubure to Brasília to defend their benefactor. In a statement to the press, Celestino declared, "No one can tell the President of FUNAI to leave."[94]

In 1985, with a succession crisis in the agency, Xavante burst forth onto the scene to endorse Gerson Alves, a FUNAI official who had served in Mato Grosso. During negotiations at FUNAI headquarters over the presidential appointment, the Xavante showed up armed with clubs and daubed with war paint, bullying functionaries.[95] When Alves assumed office, Xavante leaders ceremonially bedecked him with a feathered headdress at his inauguration, but soon after demanded due payback. A group of chiefs told the press that they would not leave Brasília until the new president delivered promised resources. The cacique of Santa Cruz village, Juvêncio Xavante, wrote to Alves that in return for his support he expected a Toyota pickup and ninety head of cattle for his community.[96]

Nor did Xavante "extortion" of FUNAI abate with the return to civilian rule in Brazil in 1985. In March 1986, FUNAI officials in Barra do Garças felt compelled to meet with eighty Xavante chiefs and "secretaries" at a nearby army barracks, rather than at AJABAG, for the payoff because "there were indications of tumult due to certain Caciques demanding more resources than FUNAI was providing."[97] Over the final months of 1986, nearly the entire Xavante male population flooded Barra do Garças searching for handouts from FUNAI.[98] With the transition to democratic rule, distributionist policies toward the Xavante persisted, as both the state and indigenous leaders relied on clientelism as a linchpin of political legitimacy.

For its part, FUNAI achieved several objectives through patronage politics: the agency muffled Xavante demands for additional territory, consolidated its position within indigenous communities, and sheathed an administrative apparatus benefiting bureaucrats and the larger class interests they served. An investigation by the federal auditing bureau, the

Tribunal das Contas da União (TCU), into FUNAI's budgetary expenditures between 1983 and 1985 sheds light on these trends.

The TCU, probing FUNAI's failure to demarcate all indigenous territory as mandated by the Estatuto do Índio notwithstanding ample funding, set out to locate fiscal black holes. The auditors found that of FUNAI's CR$12.28 billion budget in 1983, over CR$4.2 billion (more than 34 percent of the funds) had not been earmarked for specific ends. A prime offender was the Suprimento de Fundos, an agency slush fund that between January and November 1985, for example, disbursed billions of cruzeiros with "innumerable irregularities," of which roughly one-third were entirely unaccounted for. The "supplements" generally benefited individual Indians transiting through Brasília in search of handouts—ranging from food, utensils, medicine, and clothes to electronic and agricultural equipment—to the detriment of communities. Indeed, between June and December 1985, approximately 1,755 Indians lodged at hotels in Brasília, in addition to the estimated 100 who stayed daily at the agency's official residence, the Casa do Índio.[99] In 1987, FUNAI paid "supplements" to thirty-three Xavante leaders in amounts that averaged CR$60,000, essentially to induce the Indians to return home.[100] The TCU urged a restructuring of FUNAI, including immediate suspension of indiscriminate disbursement of the Suprimento de Fundos, to ensure proper application of public monies.

Yet, notwithstanding such "irregularities," Indians still received a small piece of the financial pie, for the TCU investigation revealed such concessions as pittances in overall agency expenditures. In 1983, for example, although FUNAI's budget totaled over CR$12 billion, only approximately CR$1.8 billion went to assist indigenous people. Furthermore, in that year FUNAI spent only CR$531 million for direct assistance to Indian communities: CR$420 million for demarcation of reserves; CR$100 million for community development; CR$11 million for improvement of indigenous posts. On the other hand, FUNAI expended approximately CR$6.2 billion on "general administration." In other words, for every one cruzeiro earmarked for Indians, three supported FUNAI staff. Although a fairly remunerated public service is essential for the functioning of good government, the administrative structure and functioning of FUNAI suggested the misuse of agency revenues. In Brasília alone, the agency had close to five hundred permanent employees on the payroll, a sign that the top-heavy behemoth from the days of the SPI lived on. Moreover, the TCU found that over CR$25 million of FUNAI's funds had been embezzled, deviated, or inappropriately handled in 1983. The FUNAI handouts to Xavante, then, formed but a link in the chain of state policy: a chain designed to restrain indigenous land claims while strengthening the presence of the state in the countryside as agent of capital accumulation and mediator of social conflict; a chain of patronage and corruption anchored in Brasília and stretching to the field.

The Project Collapses

By the mid-1980s crippling foreign debt, sluggish growth of the GDP, spiraling inflation, and economic austerity measures had brought the heady days of state-led "development by project" and debt-led growth to a crawl. After a second oil crisis in 1979 and the increase in interest rates in 1980–1981 triggered by the U.S. Federal Reserve Board, Brazil's foreign debt grew exponentially and foreign banks refused to continue financing the deficits of its balance of payments. Payments on account of foreign debt interests, which amounted to less than 0.5 percent of GDP in the 1970s, reached 3.5 percent of GDP in 1989. Brazil switched from being an importer to an exporter of capital.[101]

Economic crisis placed increasing constraints on state services under newly democratic rule. In 1986, FUNAI President Apoena Meireles (son of Chico), disavowed responsibility for the Indians' food and lodging expenses in Brasília and proposed closing the besieged regional office in Barra do Garças.[102] The Xavante did not appreciate FUNAI's unilateral dissolution of the partnership. In April 1986, they tramped angrily to Brasília, demanding more funding, vehicles, tractors, and clothing, but received nothing but promises. On their way home, the Indians took the driver and a FUNAI employee hostage. As ransom, they called for the resignation of the FUNAI president. The captives were ultimately released, without the trade-off.[103]

The situation at the Xavante reserves was a shambles. With machinery idled from disrepair or lack of fuel, rice production stalled. Because FUNAI neglected to fix the harvester at Pimentel Barbosa, the Indians were forced in 1986 to contract a local rancher, paying over half of their crop in exchange. In the October–November planting season, with FUNAI disbursing only half of the funds for diesel fuel, the area under cultivation at the reserve was reduced from 110 to 35 hectares. The following harvest, the Xavante of Pimentel Barbosa had to trade their cattle for outside assistance. At Sangradouro, where 600 hectares of rice had been planted, the entire village hand-cut the crop.[104]

Like a nasty divorce, the Xavante's tumultuous relationship with FUNAI unraveled amid damning accusations. In 1987, when FUNAI President Romero Jucá feared that Xavante were engineering his ouster, he publicly charged their leadership with contrabanding government resources and leasing out reservation lands. In Brasília, Jucá asserted, Xavante chiefs strong-armed officials for trucks, bicycles, sewing machines, tape recorders, and rifles; frequented shopping centers and pornographic movie theaters in their free time; and extorted money from FUNAI to return home.[105] Xavante chiefs from all six reserves repudiated Jucá's charges in a letter to President José Sarney as smear tactics aimed at covering up agency corruption.[106] (Jucá was ultimately removed, implicated in the illegal sale of lumber from indigenous reserves. As governor of Roraima, he would preside over a massive gold rush in Yanomami territory.) For the Xavante the era of "plenty" was clearly coming to an end. In July 1987, FUNAI allocated cz$300,000 to each chief for miscellaneous goods such as clothing, soap, and cooking oil. On the recommendation of a special administrator appointed by FUNAI to evaluate the Xavante Project, there would be no further investment in 1988.[107]

On Xavante reserves lay disabled machinery, a despondent reminder of how things continued to fall apart since contact. But their very resting place, territory reconstructed through suffering and struggle, also bore witness to Xavante resourcefulness. Many families returned to their subsistence plots. The community at Pimentel Barbosa looked to nongovernmental organizations and foreign governments to fund projects for sustainable development.[108] Yet others kept up appeals to FUNAI, missionaries, and outsiders for pickup trucks, agricultural machinery, and consumer goods or, in the Xavante shorthand, for a new *projeto*.

State Mediation of Rural Socioeconomic Change:
The Case of the Xavante Project

As Partha Chatterjee notes, postcolonial state planning sought to promote national development by harnessing within a single interconnected whole discrete subjects of power, subjects that planners reduced to objects of a single body of knowledge. Moreover, in locating planning outside the political process, state officials sought to resolve social conflict while ensuring accumulation. Yet, such has been an exercise in self-deception, for the state in actuality serves as a locus of social interaction, alliance, and contention among the subjects of power in the political process. Planning authorities themselves have become the objects for a configuration of power in which others are subjects. As Chatterjee concludes, "Even the best efforts to secure 'adequate information' leave behind an unestimated residue, which works imperceptibly and often perversely to upset the implementation of plans. This residue, as the irreducible, negative, and ever-present 'beyond' of planning, is what we may call, in its most general sense, politics."[109]

The Xavante Project, devised by state planners in Brasília, aimed at promoting agricultural modernization and self-sufficiency as well as muffling indigenous protest. It sought to establish the primacy of the state in the Mato Grosso countryside as social arbiter and economic allocator. For Xavante communities coping with reduced and deforested territory, growing demand for consumer goods, and enmity from their neighbors, state support offered a ray of hope. Indigenous adhesion to the project signified recognition of the state in its self-defined role of economic distributor.

Rather than fostering Xavante self-sufficiency, however, state distributional policies engendered a pernicious dependency. In the best of circumstances, the large-scale, fast-paced mechanized rice-growing project was a chancy venture in an inhospitable region among a socially complex and technologically unskilled population. Authoritarian high-mindedness and operational unreliability certainly helped little. But the problem was more far-reaching. In an effort to defuse indigenous land claims, silence political protest, and stanch rural-to-urban "migration," state planners strategically redeployed public monies to co-opt leaders and to foster a loyal (if rambunctious) clientele. Critics within FUNAI were purged by the military government.

Xavante leaders, seduced by state largesse and empowered by its obtainment, rose to the occasion. Employing political strategies mastered in the crucible of land struggles, the Indians achieved and exploited a privileged position in the corridors of state power. Communities subdivided as leaders of factions endeavored to procure state resources, engaging in shrewd "lobbying" of FUNAI and usage of the media to advance their interests. Moreover, the Indians sought to circumvent the control of post officials and missionaries in community affairs, contesting the use of machinery and tapping directly into agency resources. The distributional policies and patience of FUNAI officials wore thin as Xavante leaders aggressively engaged state planners. A centralized, orderly, and "rational" project for agricultural modernization and community development devolved into a diffuse, tumultuous, improvisational patron-client relationship.

As clients, however, the Xavante depended ultimately on the goodwill of their patron. Even during the heyday of the project, community development and "supplemental" assistance to indigenous groups represented a fraction of FUNAI expenditures. When economic austerity measures, political realignments, and grassroots disorder led the state to scrap the project, the Indians were left in the lurch. All polities contain a mix of both co-optation and representation, but where co-optation predominates, social groups will be disorganized, dependent, and hierarchically controlled.[110]

Reflecting over a half century, Brazilian state officials could assay the legacy of frontier expansion and indigenous policy since the March to the West. Capital accumulation thrived in the central west, national integration had been achieved, and the Xavante had been "pacified," confined to reserves, transformed more fully into agriculturalists, and subordinated to state power. Yet a triumphalist narrative ignores the multiple sites of contestation, negotiation, and compromise that in fact colored the process and contoured the shape of frontier expansion. It also overlooks that a different Xavante had indeed emerged—politically savvy, ethnically distinct, and economically dependent—to confound, tax, and complement state planners. The choreography of western expansion, consistently subjected to indigenous rhythms, has never been quite in step with the state's beat.

Conclusion

In 1987, Aniceto Tsudazawéré and Cosme Constantino Waioré, Xavante leaders from São Marcos, sent a letter to the Brazilian Constituent Assembly, which had convened to draft a new charter for democratic rule. Decrying the historic injustice suffered by the Xavante, the letter affirmed rights of citizenship and social entitlement:

> We are not invaders of Brazilian territory, nor strangers, because we are of Brazilian origin. Nevertheless, even being of origin, or better said, roots of the Brazilian earth, we do not have the resources nor even the inheritance of our grandparents who were killed by whites. . . . We are dying without anything and without leaving an inheritance or even resources for our grandchildren and children; dying with our poverty, because we didn't learn about survival as the white did to improve our Country. Also, I want to ask the congressmen and senators for more education for the Indians. We have to follow the others to learn to walk together.[1]

Frontier expansion had robbed the Xavante of much of their landed "inheritance," yet the indigenous appeal revealed the acquisition of another "resource": the wherewithal to engage dominant society on its own terrain in the hope of "walking together."

Indigenous peoples scored significant legal victories with the Constitution of 1988, which signaled a creditable repudiation of state heavy-handedness and evolutionist posture. Whereas earlier constitutions, informed by civil concepts of landholding, defined indigenous land in terms of physical occupation, the new charter stipulated all ecological areas indispensable for physical and cultural reproduction. Indians were guaranteed instruction in Portuguese as well as the right to bilingual education. The state no longer upheld legal jurisdiction for the "incorporation of the Indian into the national community," but merely the right to "legislate" on their behalf. The charter officially recognized the "manifestations of popular, indigenous, and Afro-Brazilian cultures and other participant groups" in contributing to the nation's historical patrimony. Finally, in an erosion of tutela, indigenous peoples gained the right to self-representation in civil disputes, with recourse to the office of the Attorney General.[2]

Constitutional change, hammered out in the spatial and temporal confines of the congressional forum, had far murkier origins. Advances in indigenous rights resulted from new ways in which legislators considered—or had been made to reconsider—the world around them. These modifications issued from shifting relations between state and society precipitated by the political transition to democratic rule and economic crisis of the 1980s. The "lost decade" of the 1980s—blighted by onerous debt service, dismal economic growth rates, high inflation, decline in foreign resource flow, and capital flight—placed a heavy strain on the Brazilian developmentalist state and the ties that bound it to society since the Vargas era. Constitutional innovations derived as well from the collision and intermingling of new and old ideas, both domestic and foreign, and elite and popular negotiation in the project of nation building.

International politics played no small part in the redesign of Brazilian indigenous policy. Brazil's sensitivity, in the face of acute economic crisis, to worldwide environmental politics triggered a newfound valorization—and reincarnation—of indigenous peoples as ecological wardens. As the national economy deteriorated over the course of the 1980s, Brazilian leaders increasingly recognized the importance of placating foreign lenders such as the World Bank and InterAmerican Development Bank who conditioned loans to environmental protection and demarcation of indigenous reserves. To demonstrate commitment to these goals as collateral for foreign finance, trade, and technology, President José Sarney successfully bid to host the United Nations Conference on the Environment and Development (the "Earth Summit") in Rio de Janeiro in 1992.[3] Indians would feature prominently in the media as caretakers of the forest and defenders of earth patrimony, although a virulent conservative backlash would decry foreign efforts to influence environmental and indigenous politics as a ploy to stunt national development and to "internationalize" the Amazon.[4]

Neither cultural trope was new. As this work has shown, Brazilians had long waxed ecstatic in historic narratives and civic commemorations over the indigenous contribution to the nation's moral regeneration, while lamenting their drag on national development. The recasting of Indians as innate ecologists, however, signified a creative ideological grafting by a host of interested actors: Brazilian political leaders endeavoring to rehabilitate the nation's worldwide reputation; international environmental groups procuring symbolic local partners; and indigenous peoples seeking allies in their quest for self-determination and resource control.[5]

The constitution's disavowal of an acculturationist model for indigenous integration reflected other international trends. The International Labor Organization's Convention 107 of 1957, under fire for a number of years for its ethnocentrism, would be replaced in 1989 by a charter emphasizing respect for indigenous socioeconomic organization, culture, and identity.[6] The worldwide tide of ethnic politics and "multiculturalism" had washed up on Brazil's shores.

Reform in indigenous legislation flowed not only from foreign exertions and elite self-interest, but from the historical struggles of native peoples, such as the Xavante, to shape Brazilian politics. As this study has demonstrated, from the outset of contact, the Xavante skillfully negotiated the intricacies of state power. The Indians challenged policies aimed at socioeconomic reorganization and subordination, even as they accepted Brazilian commodities, social welfare, and political intervention. While upholding the legitimacy of the Brazilian state, they pushed for the reconceptualization of indigenous territory, tested distributional capacities, and clamored for cultural respect. Through day-to-day or sensational acts of defiance, and compliance, Xavante served to shape Indian-state relations.

Indeed, as part of their ongoing struggle for greater power, indigenous groups had mobilized to influence directly the outcome of the Constituent Assembly. Indians from throughout Brazil flooded the nation's capital to lobby members of the Assembly. In public performances, television interviews, and the spectator gallery of the Assembly, Indians arrived bedecked in "traditional" garb to pressure delegates to protect indigenous lands, ensure social entitlements, and honor ethnic differences.[7] Eight Indian candidates, including two Xavante, even ran for election to the Assembly, although all were defeated.[8]

Political culture serves not only as the cradle of national legislation and reform but as its graveyard. Legislative nonenforcement, violence, judicial impunity, political corruption, and racial discrimination threaten constitutional advances as they historically have vitiated principles of Brazilian law. The institution of democratic government and political decentralization, after decades of authoritarian rule, does not per se safeguard indigenous rights, as the analysis of Mato Grosso politics during the postwar period compellingly illustrates. Indeed, the democratic transition has been marked by the persistence of traditional elites, patronage politics, an unstable party system, and bureaucratic rent seeking.[9] Thus, although the Constitution of 1988 stipulated a five-year deadline for the demarcation of all indigenous territory, at its expiration over one third still awaited demarcation. (As of 1993, FUNAI had not reserved territory for the Xavante in the Marãiwatsede region, from where they had been expelled nearly three decades earlier.)[10] Moreover, invasion of indigenous land often persists de facto after legal demarcation: perhaps 80 percent of the recognized indigenous areas in Brazil suffer some form of invasion by loggers, ranchers, miners, and squatters, or is infringed upon by roads, dams, power lines, and railroads.[11] Nor does democratization guarantee access to education and social welfare, as evinced by the Xavante leaders' appeal. In sum, the Constitution of 1988 did not concretize indigenous realities but rather set new terms for indigenous negotiation and struggle.

Reflections on Indian-State Relations in Brazil

Brazilian indigenous policy emerged out of the tug-of-war among various social groups to determine the mooring of state power, capital accumulation, and indigenous autonomy, a tug-of-war whose participants pulled in various directions and with unequal force. Political and ideological disunity within the state (both horizontal and vertical), pressure from private capital, the Church, sectors of civil society, the international community, and indigenous mobilization would constantly redraw the outlines of state policy. State efforts to consolidate power and centralize decision making over indigenous affairs would proceed falteringly as the Indian bureau remained enfeebled or embattled by competing interests. While recognizing the ongoing role of the Brazilian capitalist state in underpinning forms of appropriation and surplus transfer from the frontier, this study has explored the importance of changes in both the capacity of political regimes and the organization of classes (as well as ethnic groups) in understanding twentieth-century indigenous policy.[12]

If this book decenters analysis of Brazilian political history by exploring the contingent and contested, it recenters indigenous political engagement and representation within the scope of Brazilian state formation and nation building. Particular attention has been paid to the role of indigenous people in embracing, contesting, and reshaping policies with far-reaching impact over their lives. In the context of western frontier expansion and surplus appropriation, state efforts to confine the Xavante to minuscule plots, groom market-oriented agriculturists, and forge docile citizens had only mixed success. The Xavante were subordinated to state power but failed to metamorphose into the generic citizens, merry farmers, and disciplined laborers that government planners heralded. They became a politically mobilized ethnic group among Brazil's sprawling underclass, well informed of their rights, entitlements, and cultural symbolism. They remained A'uwē *and* became indigenous Brazilians.

Historical evidence, then, does not substantiate the irreconcilable dichotomy posited between Indians and the nation-state, rehashed in a highly publicized statement by political scientist Hélio Jaguaribe in 1994 that "national unity can be threatened if Brazilian underdevelopment is to persist, that is, if the Indians remain Indians."[13] As this book and archival research elsewhere in Latin America has revealed, indigenous peoples have sought to negotiate the terms of social incorporation and to adapt elite projects for nation building—only to be typecast as folkloric relics and exotic "others" or, alternatively, as "inauthentic" Indians.[14] Brazilian national unity and development are "threatened" by grossly inequitable distribution of land and wealth and by social discrimination—patterns that were replicated rather than rectified by frontier expansion.

Brazilian Indians *have* deployed "exotic" images, along with other forms of behavior and communication mandated by dominant society, as weapons to secure greater power within the nation's socioeconomic hierarchy. Comparative historical research ideally will shed light on the relationship between other indigenous groups and the Brazilian state.[15] What is known is that concomitant with the startling invasion and environmental devastation of indigenous areas over the past three decades was the rapid growth of Indian reserves: if in 1967, under the SPI, not more than 10 percent of indigenous lands, even by a generous estimate, had been delimited, by 1996, 205 indigenous areas, covering 106 million acres of land, had been officially registered (representing roughly 12 percent of national territory).[16] The political struggles surrounding the invasion and reservation of other indigenous territories—which redefined boundaries of federal jurisdiction in the countryside, configurations of indigenous power, and the nature of ethnic politics in twentieth-century Brazil— await their historian.

Looking forward, one of the greatest challenges facing Brazil's indigenous (and nonindigenous) populations in the struggle for social justice looms in redefining the relationship of the state to civil society. Since the 1980s, the Latin American state has come under assault from international financial agencies and neoclassical economists for stunting economic growth through excessive market intervention and regulatory mechanisms. A historic lack of democratic governance and unresponsiveness to public needs has further tarnished state legitimacy. In a turn of the tables, the Latin American state now confronts breakdown, fragmentation, and identity crisis whose void raises ponderous implications for indigenous people—implications oddly unappreciated (or perhaps overappreciated) by some observers.

The dark history of state heavy-handedness and patronage toward indigenous communities, amply chronicled in this study, cries out for change. Yet the evisceration of the Brazilian state, substitution by NGOS or free market initiatives, and knee-jerk political decentralization do not promise solutions in their own right. Nongovernmental organizations are not bound by democratic mechanisms nor accountable to their constituency; they are answerable to their directorate and contributors. Although perceived as more efficient, even-handed, and client-friendly than the state, NGOS have ridden roughshod over indigenous concerns, packaged essentialized images of Indians as noble savages, and relied on select individuals as mediators between their communities and the outside world.[17] The interaction of NGOS with the state, perpetuating long-standing patterns in Brazilian politics, has consisted primarily in alliance with sympathetic government officials rather than targeting political parties or the legislature. Although NGOS excel in disseminating information, empowering civic society, and pressuring the state through the internationalization of political struggle, the privatization of accountability for social welfare runs counter to democratic decision making and long-term sustainability of successful indigenous policy.[18] Civil society plays an important role in improving government, but good civil society is no more an innate guarantee than is good government. Indeed, though critical of bureaucratic inefficiency and corruption, public opinion in Latin America continues to value the importance of the state as a redistributive agent, principle of national unity, and motor of economic growth.[19]

Decentralization, another mantra invoked by pundits of political reform, likewise provides no cure-all for responsible and responsive state policy.[20] Centralization of power and resources in the SPI and FUNAI certainly had a deleterious effect on policy making and execution, as has the historic disregard for indigenous aspirations, initiatives, and capabilities. Nevertheless, this study has also highlighted the casualties indigenous communities have suffered from the absence of effective central leadership and sabotage by regional interests. Neither the track record of local governments nor of regional Indian bureau officials validates the hypothesis that a grassroots or "bottom-up" policy in itself ensures the social welfare of indigenous communities. Nor, for that matter, does the devolution of decision making to indigenous leaders resolve questions of representativeness, resource allocation, and accountability. Rather, improvement of indigenous policy is contingent on a dynamic, interactive relationship between civil society and a restructured state, a relationship built on a coalition of interests and a shared vision of the future.

Numerous analysts recognize that the capacity of the state rather than its size and the quality rather than the quantity of intervention are critical in ensuring economic growth and social welfare.[21] Reform of the tax system to strengthen state capability and of the judiciary to restore public legitimacy is indispensable. Administrative streamlining of FUNAI and other branches of the civil service must be bested by merit hiring, improved training, and incentives to bolster public employee commitment and productivity as well as efficient organizational structure. Indeed, Judith Tendler notes the lopsided attention that the development community has paid to users as opposed to workers in resolving difficulties with delivery of state services. She found that "good government" in rural (and historically patronage-ridden) Ceará owed, in part, to a dynamic state sector that energized employees through inspirational publicity campaigns and orientation programs, managerial attentiveness, and job performance rewards, and that educated the public as to their right to better government.[22]

A redefinition of state distributional policies toward indigenous peoples is in order as well. States must exercise adequate autonomy from distributional pressures to implement policy effectively, but this does not mean that they must sequester policy making from democratic deliberation and local input.[23] In consulting with indigenous leaders, state officals must, however, display sensitivity to internal power struggles, factionalism, and questions of representativeness. Indigenous communities, like other underprivileged sectors of civil society, must focus on quality rather than quantity of service to ensure equity—such as the demarcation of land, education, and health care.[24] Such reforms are necessary to forge a political culture based on citizens' rights and obligations and the rule of law rather than clientelism and dependency.[25] As with any movement for political change, opposition will inevitably surface from entrenched interests.

History matters, not because it repeats itself (which it never does), but because its narration can rid demons that torment the oppressed, shock the complacent and intransigent into self-reflection, and inspire feats of human perseverance and will. The racial democracy celebrated in Brazilian lore crumbles before the record of indigenous territorial usurpation, socioeconomic subordination, and enduring prejudice. "Indianness," rather than an essentialist quality, emerges as a historically constructed tool of domination as well as compromised empowerment to situate aboriginal peoples within the nation's sharply skewed field of wealth and power. The triumphs and ignominies of the state in upholding legal order and social justice surface, as well as the evanescence of patronage politics for indigenous peoples. Indigenous initiatives reveal victims as well as agents, resistors as well as collaborators. The acknowledgment of past rights and wrongs—of a history of coercion, contestation, collaboration, and compromise—can help lay the foundation to rebuild indigenous-state relations. The challenge to restructure this relationship may appear quixotic, but so did the March to the West.

Notes

Introduction

1 Aracy Lopes da Silva, "Dois séculos e meio de história Xavante," in *História dos índios no Brasil*, ed. Manuela Carneiro da Cunha (São Paulo: Companhia das Letras, Secretaria Municipal de Cultura, Fundação de Amparo à Pesquisa no Estado de São Paulo, 1992), 362.

2 For a more detailed examination of the bandeirantes, see Richard M. Morse, ed., *The Bandeirantes* (New York: Knopf, 1965), and John Hemming, *Red Gold: The Conquest of the Brazilian Indians* (Cambridge, MA: Harvard University Press, 1978), 238–53. For an overview of frontier expansion in eighteenth-century Goiás and Mato Grosso, see Hemming, *Red Gold*, 377–408; João Capistrano de Abreu, *Chapters of Brazil's Colonial History, 1500–1800*, trans. Arthur Brakel (New York: Oxford University Press, 1997), 128–36; and David M. Davidson, "How the Brazilian West Was Won: Freelance and State on the Mato Grosso Frontier, 1737–1752," in *Colonial Roots of Modern Brazil*, ed. Dauril Alden (Berkeley: University of California Press, 1973), 61–106.

3 Mary Karasch, "Interethnic Conflict and Resistance on the Brazilian Frontier of Goiás, 1750–1890," in *Contested Ground: Comparative Frontiers on the Northern and Southern Edges of the Spanish Empire*, ed. Donna J. Guy and Thomas E. Sheridan (Tucson: University of Arizona Press, 1998), 118–23.

4 See John Hemming, "Indians and the Frontier," in *Colonial Brazil*, ed. Leslie Bethell (Cambridge, England: Cambridge University Press, 1991), 176–79, and Colin M. Maclachlan, "The Indian Labor Structure in the Portuguese Amazon," in Alden, *Colonial Roots of Modern Brazil*, 199–230.

5 Karasch, "Interethnic Conflict and Resistance," 121–22.

6 Lopes da Silva, "Dois séculos e meio de história Xavante," 363, and Karasch, "Interethnic Conflict and Resistance," 131.

7 Laura R. Graham, *Performing Dreams: Discourses of Immortality among the Xavante of Central Brazil* (Austin: University of Texas Press, 1995), 28.

8 Cunha Mattos, quoted in Lopes da Silva, "Dois séculos e meio de história Xavante," 364.

9 Ibid. On the failure of the aldeiamentos in nineteenth-century Goiás, see also Mary Karasch, "Catequese e cativeiro, política indigenista em Goiás: 1780–1889," in *História dos índios no Brasil*, ed. M. Cunha, 409–10.

10 Karasch, "Interethnic Conflict and Resistance," 131.

11 Hemming, "Indians and the Frontier," 189.

12 Lopes da Silva, "Dois séculos e meio de história Xavante," 364.

13 Karasch, "Catequese e cativeiro," 408.

14 David Maybury-Lewis speculates that the split took place in the 1840s, although other scholars have argued that it occurred earlier in the century. See the discussion in Laura Graham, *Performing Dreams*, 25–26.

15 Karasch, "Interethnic Conflict and Resistance," 117–21.

16 See David Maybury-Lewis, *Akwẽ-Shavante Society*, 2d ed. (New York: Oxford University Press, 1974), 2.

17 See Emilio F. Moran, *Through Amazonian Eyes: The Human Ecology of Amazonian Population* (Iowa City: University of Iowa Press, 1993), 124–25; Nancy Flowers, "Subsistence Strategy, Social Organization, and Warfare in Central Brazil in the Context of European Penetration," in *Amazonian Indians from Prehistory to the Present*, ed. Anna Roosevelt (Tucson: University of Arizona Press, 1994), 260–61.

18 Marta Maria Lopes, "A resistência do índio ao extermínio: O caso dos Akwẽ-Xavante, 1967–1980" (Master's thesis, Universidade Estadual Paulista, 1988), 33.

19 See, for example, Darcy Ribeiro, *Os índios e a civilização* (Rio de Janeiro: Civilização Brasileira, 1970); Shelton H. Davis, *Victims of the Miracle* (Cambridge, England: Cambridge University Pres, 1986); Alcida Rita Ramos, *Indigenism: Ethnic Politics in Brazil* (Madison: University of Wisconsin Press, 1998); Antonio Carlos de Souza Lima, *Um grande cerco de paz: Poder tutelar, indianidade e formação do Estado no Brasil* (Petrópolis: Vozes, 1995); Jean Hébette, ed., *O cerco está se fechando* (Petrópolis: Vozes, 1991); João Pacheco de Oliveira Filho, *"O nosso governo": Os Ticuna e o regime tutelar* (São Paulo: Marco Zero, 1988).

20 See Robert F. Berkhofer Jr., *The White Man's Indian: Images of the American Indian from Columbus to the Present* (New York: Knopf, 1978). As one of Brazil's most renowned historians stated about the nation's indigenous peoples: "The same lack of cooperation, the same incapacity to act in a wise and single-minded fashion, with division of labor and its consequences, seem to be the legacies these forebears passed on to their descendants." See Abreu, *Chapters of Brazil's Colonial History, 1500–1800*, 13.

21 The myth of racial democracy in Brazil as applied to indigenous peoples is debunked in D. Ribeiro, *Os índios e a civilização*, 200.

22 Statistics are from Centro Ecumênico de Documentação e Informação, *Povos indígenas no Brasil, 1987/88/89/90* (São Paulo: CEDI, 1991), 64.

23 See, for example, John Manuel Monteiro, *Negros da terra: Índios e bandeirantes nas origens de São Paulo* (São Paulo: Companhia das Letras, 1994); Nádia Farage, *As muralhas dos sertões: Os povos indígenas no Rio Branco e colonização* (Rio de Janeiro: Paz e Terra and Anpocs, 1991); John Hemming, *Amazon Frontier: The Defeat of the Brazilian Indians* (Lon-

don: Macmillan, 1987); Alida C. Metcalf, "Millenarian Slaves? The Santidade de Jaguaripe and Slave Resistance in the Americas," *American Historical Review* 104 (1999): 1531–59; Ronaldo Vainfas, *A heresia dos índios: Catolicismo e rebeldia no Brasil colonial* (São Paulo: Companhia das Letras, 1995); B. J. Barickman, "'Tame Indians,' 'Wild Heathens,' and Settlers in Southern Bahia in the Late Eighteenth and Early Nineteenth Centuries," *The Americas* 51 (1995): 325–68. On the national period, see Hal Langfur, "Myths of Pacification: Brazilian Frontier Settlement and the Subjugation of the Bororo Indians," *Journal of Social History* 32 (1999): 879–905.

24 See, for example, Florencia E. Mallon, *Peasant and Nation: The Making of Postcolonial Mexico and Peru* (Berkeley: University of California Press, 1995); Mark Thurner, *From Two Republics to One Divided* (Durham, NC: Duke University Press, 1997); Jeffrey L. Gould, *To Die in This Way: Nicaraguan Indians and the Myth of Mestizaje, 1880–1965* (Durham, NC: Duke University Press, 1998); Charles R. Hale, *Resistance and Contradiction: Miskitu Indians and the Nicaraguan State, 1894–1987* (Stanford: Stanford University Press, 1994); Joanne Rappaport: *Cumbe Reborn: An Andean Ethnography of History* (Chicago: University of Chicago Press, 1994); Thomas A. Abercrombie, *Pathways of Memory and Power: Ethnography and History among an Andean People* (Madison: University of Wisconsin Press, 1998); Greg Grandin, *The Blood of Guatemala: The Making of Race and Nation, 1750–1954.* (Durham, NC: Duke University Press, 2000).

25 On frontiers as "contact zones," see Mary Louise Pratt, *Imperial Eyes: Travel Writing and Transculturation* (New York: Routledge, 1992). For further conceptualizations of the frontier in Brazil and Latin America, see Morse, *The Bandeirantes,* 30–31; Donna J. Guy and Thomas E. Sheridan, eds., *Contested Ground: Comparative Frontiers on the Northern and Southern Edges of the Spanish Empire* (Tucson: University of Arizona Press, 1998), 3–15; David J. Weber and Jane M. Rausch, eds., *Where Cultures Meet: Frontiers in Latin American History* (Wilmington, DE: Scholarly Resources, 1994), xiii–xli; Silvio R. Duncan Baretta and John Markoff, "Civilization and Barbarism: Cattle Frontiers in Latin America," *Comparative Studies in Society and History* 20 (1978): 587–620; Ana María Alonso, *Thread of Blood: Colonialism, Revolution, and Gender on Mexico's Northern Frontier* (Tucson: University of Arizona Press, 1995), 15–20; Mary Lombardi, "The Frontier in Brazilian History: An Historiographical Essay," *Pacific Historical Review* 44 (1975): 441–42.

26 Doreen Massey, *Space, Place, and Gender* (Minneapolis: University of Minnesota Press, 1994), 154.

27 Joe Foweraker, *The Struggle for Land: A Political Economy of the Pioneer Frontier in Brazil from 1930 to the Present Day* (Cambridge, England: Cambridge University Press, 1981), 3–12.

28 On the export-oriented frontier, see Martin T. Katzman, "The Brazilian

Frontier in Comparative Perspective," *Comparative Studies in Society and History* 17 (1975): 266–85; J. F. Normano, *Brazil: A Study of Economic Types* (Chapel Hill: University of North Carolina Press, 1935), 1–17.

29   Foweraker, *The Struggle for Land*, 3–12, 58–69.

30   See Philip Corrigan and Derek Sayer, *The Great Arch: English State Formation as Cultural Revolution* (Oxford: Basil Blackwell, 1985), 1–13.

31   On the interlocking material and cultural processes embedded in state formation, see John Comaroff and Jean Comaroff, *Ethnography and the Historical Imagination* (Boulder, CO: Westview Press, 1992); for the Latin American context, see Gilbert M. Joseph and Daniel Nugent, eds., *Everyday Forms of State Formation: Revolution and the Negotiation of Rule in Modern Mexico* (Durham, NC: Duke University Press, 1994), 3–23.

32   See Werner Baer, *The Brazilian Economy: Growth and Development*, 3d ed. (New York: Praeger, 1989); Celso Furtado, *Economic Development of Latin America*, 2d ed., trans. Suzette Macedo (Cambridge, England: Cambridge University Press, 1976), 242–50; Albert Fishlow, "Origins and Consequences of Import Substitution in Brazil," in *International Economics and Development: Essays in Honor of Raul Prebisch*, ed. L. Di Marco (New York: Academic Press, 1972); Ludwig Lauerhass Jr., *Getúlio Vargas e o triunfo do nacionalismo brasileiro* (Belo Horizonte: Itatiaia and São Paulo: Editora da Universidade de São Paulo, 1986).

33   Theda Skocpol, "Bringing the State Back In," in *Bringing the State Back In*, ed. Peter Evans, Dietrich Rueschmeyer, and Theda Skocpol (Cambridge, England: Cambridge University Press, 1985), 22–23.

34   Partha Chatterjee, *The Nation and Its Fragments: Colonial and Postcolonial Histories* (Princeton, NJ: Princeton University Press, 1993), 204–14.

35   See Simon Schwartzman, Helena Maria Bousquet Bomeny, and Vanda Maria Ribeiro Costa, *Tempos de Capanema* (Rio de Janeiro: Paz e Terra, 1984), 146.

36   E. J. Hobsbawm, *Nations and Nationalism since 1780: Programme, Myth, Reality* (Cambridge, England: Cambridge University Press, 1990), 10. On the nation as "imagined community," see Benedict Anderson, *Imagined Communities: Reflections on the Origin and Spread of Nationalism* (London: Verso, 1991).

37   On the disjuncture between image and reality of social reform under Vargas, see Robert M. Levine, *Father of the Poor? Vargas and His Era* (Cambridge, England: Cambridge University Press, 1998).

38   Philip Abrams, "Notes on the Difficulty of Studying the State," *Journal of Historical Sociology* 1 (1988): 81.

39   Chatterjee, *The Nation and Its Fragments*, 207.

40   See James C. Scott, *Seeing Like a State: How Certain Schemes to Improve the Human Condition Have Failed* (New Haven: Yale University Press, 1998), 2–3.

41 See Alan Knight, "Racism, Revolution and Indigenismo: Mexico, 1910–1940," in *The Idea of Race in Latin America, 1870–1940*, ed. Richard Graham (Austin: University of Texas Press, 1990), 72–73; Peter Wade, *Blackness and Race Mixture: The Dynamics of Racial Identity in Colombia* (Baltimore: Johns Hopkins University Press, 1995), 3–4.

42 John L. Comaroff, "Of Totemism and Ethnicity," in Comaroff and Comaroff, *Ethnography and the Historical Imagination*, 52–62.

43 Hobsbawm, *Nations and Nationalism since 1780*, 46.

44 See Corrigan and Sayer, *The Great Arch*, 3.

45 Gerald Sider, "When Parrots Learn to Talk, and Why They Can't: Domination, Deception, and Self-Deception in Indian-White Relations," *Comparative Studies in Society and History* 29 (1987): 3.

46 Wade, *Blackness and Race Mixture*, 19; see also J. Jorge Klor de Alva, "The Postcolonialization of the (Latin) American Experience: A Reconsideration of 'Colonialism,' 'Postcolonialism' and 'Mestizaje,' " in *After Colonialism: Imperial Histories and Postcolonial Displacements*, ed. Gyan Prakash (Princeton, NJ: Princeton University Press, 1995), 241–75.

47 Skocpol, "Bringing the State Back In," 16–17.

48 Antonio Gramsci noted that hegemony entailed both "spontaneous" consent given by the mass of the population to dominant ideals as well as the coercive power of the state to enforce discipline on those groups who fail to "consent." See Gramsci, *Selections from the Prison Notebooks*, ed. and trans. Quintin Hoare and Geoffrey Nowell-Smith (New York: International Publishers, 1971), 12.

49 Comaroff and Comaroff, *Ethnography and the Historical Imagination*, 28–30.

50 For celebratory accounts of the origins and ideals of the Brazilian Indian Service, see José M. Gagliardi, *O indígena e a República* (São Paulo: Hucitec, 1989); D. Ribeiro, *Os índios e a civilização*. For revisionist accounts critical of state domination, see A. C. Lima, *Um grande cerco de paz*; Ramos, *Indigenism*.

51 Marshall Sahlins, "Goodbye to *Tristes Tropes*: Ethnography in the Context of Modern World History," *Journal of Modern History* 65 (1993): 13.

52 For a critique of cultural change as a "billiards game," see William Roseberry, *Anthropologies and Histories: Essays in Culture, History, and Political Economy* (New Brunswick, NJ: Rutgers University Press, 1989), 84. For an analysis of Brazilian Indians employing such a framework, see D. Ribeiro, *Os índios e a civilização*.

53 D. Ribeiro, *Os índios e a civilização*, 434–35.

54 For a fine bibliographic review of recent literature on indigenous peoples, see Les W. Field, "Who Are the Indians? Reconceptualizing Indigenous Identity, Resistance, and the Role of Social Science in Latin America," *Latin American Research Review* 29, no. 3 (1994): 237–56.

55 Ranajit Guha, ed., *A Subaltern Studies Reader, 1986–1995* (Minneapolis: University of Minnesota Press, 1997), ix–xxi.

56 For a trenchant critique, see Thurner, *From Two Republics to One Divided*, 13–15.

57 A similar argument is set forth for analyzing popular culture in Joseph and Nugent, *Everyday Forms of State Formation*, 21–22.

58 See Kay B. Warren, "Transforming Memories and Histories: The Meanings of Ethnic Resurgence for Mayan Indians," in *Americas: New Interpretive Essays*, ed. Alfred Stepan (New York: Oxford University Press, 1992), 205.

59 As John Comaroff notes, "It is the *marking* of relations—of identities in opposition to one another—that is 'primordial,' not the substance of those identities" ("Of Totemism and Ethnicity," 51).

60 Corrigan and Sayer, *The Great Arch*, 4, 205.

61 Thomas Abercrombie, "To Be Indian, To Be Bolivian: 'Ethnic' and 'National' Discourses of Identity," in *Nation-States and Indians in Latin America*, ed. Greg Urban and Joel Sherzer (Austin: University of Texas Press, 1991), 105.

62 Sahlins, "Goodbye to *Tristes Tropes*," 18–19.

63 The term "hidden transcripts" is borrowed from James C. Scott, *Domination and the Arts of Resistance: Hidden Transcripts* (New Haven: Yale University Press, 1990).

64 For an institutional history of the Brazilian Indian Service, see David Hall Stauffer, "The Origin and Establishment of Brazil's Indian Service, 1889–1910" (Ph.D. diss., University of Texas at Austin, 1955).

65 Scott, *Seeing Like a State*, 1–8.

66 For an ethnographic study of the Xavante in the early postcontact period, see D. Maybury-Lewis, *Akwẽ-Shavante Society*. For an approach that emphasizes Xavante understandings of their historical experience, see Laura Graham, *Performing Dreams*; Sereburã et al., *Wamrêmé za'ra-Nossa palavra: Mito e história do povo Xavante*, trans. Paulo Supretaprã Xavante and Jurandir Siridiwẽ Xavante (São Paulo: Editora senac, 1998); Aracy Lopes da Silva, *Nomes e amigos: Da prática Xavante a uma reflexão sobre os Jê* (São Paulo: Universidade de São Paulo, 1986); Bartolomeu Giaccaria and Adalberto Heide, *Jerônimo Xavante conta* (Campo Grande: Casa da Cultura, 1975). For a methodological approach stressing an indigenous-centered understanding of history, see Jonathan D. Hill, ed., *Rethinking History and Myth: Indigenous South American Perspectives on the Past* (Urbana: University of Illinois Press, 1988).

67 Ramos, *Indigenism*, 3–4.

68 Stephen Greenblatt notes that since conquest Europeans defined indigenous people in such contradictory terms. See Greenblatt, *Marvelous Possessions: The Wonder of the New World* (Oxford: Oxford University Press, 1991), 109.

69   William Roseberry, "Hegemony and the Language of Contention," in Joseph and Nugent, eds., *Everyday Forms of State Formation*, 361.

1 "The Base of Our National Character": Indians and the Estado Novo, 1937–1945

1   Brasil, Departamento de Imprensa e Propaganda, *Rumo ao Oeste*, no. 134 (n.d.), unpaginated. On Vargas's self-styled image as benevolent patriarch, see Alcir Lenharo, *Sacralização da política* (Campinas: Papirus, 1986), 48–50.

2   Getúlio Vargas, *Diário* (São Paulo: Siciliano; Rio de Janeiro: Fundação Getúlio Vargas, 1995), 2:330.

3   Departamento de Imprensa e Propaganda, *Rumo ao Oeste*.

4   For further discussion of the origins of tutela, see Manuela Carneiro da Cunha, *Os direitos do índio* (São Paulo: Brasiliense, 1987), 28–30, 103–17.

5   Departamento de Imprensa e Propaganda, *Rumo ao Oeste*.

6   Here Vargas propagated the image of the forlorn backlander awaiting social welfare programs that had been popularized by writer Monteiro Lobato's well-known character, Jeca Tatu. See Nísia Trindade Lima and Gilberto Hochman, "Condenado pela raça, absolvido pela medicina: O Brasil descoberto pelo movimento sanitarista da Primeira República," in *Raça, ciência, sociedade*, ed. Marcos Chor Maio and Ricardo Ventura Santos (Rio de Janeiro: FIOCRUZ, 1996), 23–40.

7   On the Estado Novo, see Edgard Carone, *O Estado Novo (1937–1945)* (Rio de Janeiro: DIFEL, 1977); Thomas E. Skidmore, *Politics in Brazil, 1930–1964* (New York: Oxford University Press, 1986), 30–47; Robert M. Levine, *The Vargas Regime: The Critical Years, 1934–1938* (New York: Columbia University Press, 1970); Levine, *Father of the Poor? Vargas and His Era*; Kurt Loewenstein, *Brazil under Vargas* (New York: Macmillan, 1942).

8   On the DASP, see Lawrence S. Graham, *Civil Service Reform in Brazil: Principles versus Practice* (Austin: University of Texas Press, 1968), 28–30.

9   On the DIP, see Carone, *O Estado Novo*, 169–72.

10 On cordiality as a marker of so-called Brazilian national character, see Sérgio Buarque de Holanda, *Raízes do Brasil* (1936; Rio de Janeiro: José Olympio, 1989), 106–7.

11 See João Pacheco de Oliveira Filho, "Pardos, mestiços ou caboclos: Os índios nos censos nacionais no Brasil (1872–1980)," *Horizontes Antropológicos* 3, no. 6 (Oct. 1997): 60–83. The 1940 census did not include uncontacted indigenous populations nor Indians unassisted by the SPI. Nor can we assume that language is the sole marker of ethnic identity. In 1957, Darcy Ribeiro estimated the indigenous population between 68,000 and 99,000.

12 Getúlio Vargas, *A nova política do Brasil* (Rio de Janeiro: J. Olympio, 1938), 5:124.

13 William Summerhill, "Transport Improvements and Economic Growth in Brazil and Mexico," in *How Latin America Fell Behind*, ed. Stephen Haber (Stanford: Stanford University Press, 1997), 96–97.

14 Ibid., 96.

15 Emilia Viotti da Costa, *The Brazilian Empire: Myths and Histories* (Chicago: University of Chicago Press, 1985), 173–74.

16 Ibid., 78–93.

17 Steven Topik, *The Political Economy of the Brazilian State, 1889–1930* (Austin: University of Texas Press, 1987), 15–16.

18 On the Revolution of 1930, see Boris Fausto, *A revolução de 1930: Historiografia e história*, 13th ed. (São Paulo, Brasiliense, 1991); Thomas E. Skidmore, *Brazil: Five Centuries of Change* (New York: Oxford University Press, 1999), 99–108.

19 See Aspasia Camargo et al., *O golpe silencioso: As origens da república corporativa* (Rio de Janeiro: Rio Fundo, 1989).

20 Foweraker, *The Struggle for Land*, 223–24.

21 Geraldo Ireneo Joffily, *Brasília e sua ideologia* (Brasília: Thesaurus, 1977), 22–31.

22 Edilberto Coutinho, *Rondon, o civilizador da última fronteira* (Rio de Janeiro: Olive, 1969), 51–87.

23 See Thomas E. Skidmore, *Black into White: Race and Nationality in Brazilian Thought* (Durham, NC: Duke University Press, 1993), 157–59.

24 See Angela de Castro Gomes, *A invenção do trabalhismo*, 2d ed. (Rio de Janeiro: Relume Dumará, 1994), 224–25.

25 See Jeffrey Lesser, *Welcoming the Undesirables: Brazil and the Jewish Question* (Berkeley: University of California Press, 1995), 66–67.

26 Vargas, *A nova política do Brasil*, 5:124.

27 Brasil, Ministério da Agricultura, *Marcha para Oeste* (Conferências Culturais, 1939–1943), 237. See also Alcir Lenharo, "A civilização vai ao campo," *Anais do Museu Paulista* 34 (1985): 7–19.

28 Lenharo, *Sacralização da política*, 14.

29 See A. Gomes, *A invenção do trabalhismo*, 182–94.

30 Alcir Lenharo, *Colonização e trabalho no Brasil: Amazônia, Nordeste, e Centro-Oeste—Os anos 30* (Campinas: UNICAMP, 1986), 34–57. In Spanish America, indigenismo often served as a weapon in the central government's struggle against local boss rule. See Knight, "Racism, Revolution and *Indigenismo*," 83.

31 Vargas, *Diário*, 2:330, 418.

32 Maria Esperança Fernandes Carneiro, *A revolta camponesa de Formoso e Trombas* (Goiânia: Editora de Universidade Federal de Goiás, 1986), 80.

33 Brasil, Ministério da Agricultura, *Decreto-Lei no. 6155*, 30 December 1943.

On other federal institutes created by Vargas, see Skidmore, *Politics in Brazil*, 34.

34 José Murilo de Carvalho, "Armed Forces and Politics in Brazil, 1930–45," *Hispanic American Historical Review* 62 (1982): 203.

35 Stanley E. Hilton, "Military Influence on Brazilian Economic Policy, 1930–1945: A Different View," *Hispanic American Historical Review* 53 (1973): 74.

36 General José Pessoa to Vargas, 29 August 1938. Arquivo Nacional (AN), Rio de Janeiro, Fundo Secretaria da Presidência da República (SPE) 025, Lata 98. See also Nelson Werneck Sodré, "Oeste," *Revista Militar Brasileira* 41, nos. 1–2 (1944): 83–98.

37 Mario Travassos, *Projeção continental do Brasil* (São Paulo: Companhia Editora Nacional, 1938).

38 Ken Conca, *Manufacturing Insecurity: The Rise and Fall of Brazil's Military-Industrial Complex* (Boulder, CO: Westview, 1997), 25–28.

39 Lenharo, *Sacralização da política*, 73–74.

40 See Cliff Welch, *The Seed Was Planted: The São Paulo Roots of Brazil's Rural Labor Movement, 1924–1964* (University Park: The Pennsylvania State University Press, 1999), 84–98; Frances Hagopian, *Traditional Politics and Regime Change in Brazil* (New York: Cambridge University Press, 1996), 90; and Marta Cehelsky, *Land Reform in Brazil: The Management of Social Change* (Boulder, CO: Westview, 1979), 26–28.

41 For a penetrating critique of the March to the West, see Otávio Guilherme Velho, *Capitalismo autoritário e campesinato*, (Rio de Janeiro: DIFEL, 1976); Lenharo, *Colonização e trabalho no Brasil*; Neide Esterci, "O Mito da Democracia no Pais das Bandeiras" (Master's thesis, Universidade Federal do Rio de Janeiro, 1972).

42 The lyrics to songs are reprinted in Lenharo, *Sacralização da política*, 53, 73.

43 Cassiano Ricardo, *Marcha para Oeste* (1940; Rio de Janeiro: José Olympio, 1959), 2:278–79. Gilberto Freyre, echoing Ricardo, advanced the same argument in *New World in the Tropics: The Culture of Modern Brazil* (New York: Knopf, 1971), 72–73.

44 See the chapter "O índio na sociedade bandeirante" in Ricardo, *Marcha para Oeste*, 1:95–126.

45 Ibid., 2:50–51. For an enlightening comparison of Brazilian and American frontier myths, see Velho, *Capitalismo autoritário e campesinato*, 143.

46 Ricardo, *Marcha para Oeste*, 2:50–51, 277.

47 On the origins of the SPI, see Souza Lima, *Um grande cerco de paz*, 95–153.

48 On the CNPI, see Carlos Augusto da Rocha Freire, "Indigenismo e antropologia: O Conselho Nacional de Proteção aos Índios na gestão Rondon, 1939–1955" (Master's thesis, Universidade Federal do Rio de Janeiro, 1990).

49 Cândido Mariano da Silva Rondon, *Rumo ao Oeste* (Rio de Janeiro: Laemmert, 1942), 21–22.

50 See Hemming, *Red Gold: The Conquest of the Brazilian Indians*, 292–311.

51 For a more nuanced analysis of Indian-white relations in colonial Brazil exposing the tensions and violence as well as other forms of unequal exchange governing interethnic relations, see Sérgio Buarque de Holanda, *Caminhos e fronteiras*, 3d ed. (São Paulo: Companhia das Letras, 1994); Monteiro, *Negros da terra*; Alida C. Metcalf, *Family and Frontier in Colonial Brazil: Santana de Parnaíba* (Berkeley: University of California Press, 1992).

52 Ricardo, *Marcha para Oeste*, 1:108–10.

53 Ricardo, for example, contrasted the supposed goodwill of the Portuguese men in their sexual relations with indigenes with the cruelty of the Cossack treatment of peasant women. See *Marcha para Oeste*, 1:124.

54 Eric J. Hobsbawm, "Introduction: Inventing Traditions," in *The Invention of Tradition*, ed. Eric J. Hobsbawm and Terence Ranger (Cambridge, England: Cambridge University Press, 1983), 1–4.

55 On the Vargas regime's efforts to define and preserve Brazilian "historical patrimony," see Daryle Williams, "*Ad perpetuam rei memoriam*: The Vargas Regime and Brazil's National Historical Patrimony, 1930–1945," *Luso-Brazilian Review* 31 (1994): 45–75.

56 See Conselho Nacional de Proteção aos Índios, *19 de Abril: O Dia do Índio as comemorações realizadas em 1944 e 45* (Rio de Janeiro: Imprensa Nacional, 1946).

57 See Freire, "Indigenismo e antropologia," 209; Nilo Oliveira Velloso, *Rumo ao desconhecido* (Rio de Janeiro: n.d.), 5.

58 See Hemming, "Indians and the Frontier," 189.

59 See Lilia Moritz Schwarcz, *The Spectacle of the Races: Scientists, Institutions, and the Race Question in Brazil, 1870–1930*, trans. Leland Guyer (New York: Hill and Wang, 1999), 75–84; and John Manuel Monteiro, "As 'raças' indígenas no pensamento brasileiro do Império" in *Raça, ciência e sociedade*, ed. Marcos Chor Maio and Ricardo Ventura Santos (Rio de Janeiro: FIOCRUZ, 1996), 15–21.

60 On the cultural and institutional links between Mexican and Brazilian indigenismo, see Freire, "Indigenismo e antropologia," 57–68.

61 See Sergio Miceli, *Intelectuais e classe dirigente no Brasil (1920–45)* (São Paulo: DIFEL, 1979), 77; and Randal Johnson, "The Dynamics of the Brazilian Literary Field, 1930–1945," *Luso-Brazilian Review* 31 (1994): 11–13.

62 Angyone Costa, *Indiologia* (Rio de Janeiro: Zenio Valverde, 1943), 13.

63 For an overview of intellectuals' search for the "real Brazil" in the 1930s, see A. Camargo et al., *O golpe silencioso*, 253–54.

64 Zoroastro Artiaga, *Dos índios do Brasil Central* (Uberaba: Departamento Estadual de Cultura do Estado, n.d.), 13–26.

65 Affonso Arinos de Mello Franco, *O índio brasileiro e a revolução francesa* (Rio de Janeiro: José Olympio, 1937).

66 For additional texts published on Indians and the west during the Vargas era, see Seth Garfield, "'The Roots of a Plant That Today Is Brazil': Indians and the Nation-State under the Brazilian Estado Novo," *Journal of Latin American Studies* 29 (1997): 747–68. On Spanish America, see Efraín Kristal, *The Andes Viewed from the City: Literary and Political Discourse on the Indian in Peru, 1848–1930* (New York: Peter Lang, 1987); and Cynthia Hewitt de Alcántara, *Anthropological Perspectives on Rural Mexico* (London: Routledge and Kegan Paul, 1984).

67 David Brookshaw, *Paradise Betrayed: Brazilian Literature of the Indian* (Amsterdam: CEDLA, 1988), 75.

68 See Monteiro, "As 'raças' indígenas no pensamento brasileiro do Império," 16.

69 Mike Gonzalez and David Treece, *The Gathering of Voices: The Twentieth-Century Poetry of Latin America* (London: Verso, 1992), 96–101. For a discussion of the embrace of "primitivism" during the Week of Modern Art by Brazilian intellectuals—and their European influences—see K. David Jackson, *A prosa vanguardista na literatura brasileira: Oswald de Andrade* (São Paulo: Perspectiva, 1978), 9–18.

70 The symbol of the Verdeamarela movement was the *curupira*, the Tupi-Guarani mythical protector of the hinterland. See Gilberto Vasconcellos, *A ideologia Curupira: Análise do discurso integralista* (São Paulo: Editora Brasiliense, 1979), 20.

71 See Gilberto Freyre, *The Masters and the Slaves*, 2d rev. ed., trans. Samuel Putnam (Berkeley: University of California Press, 1986), 81–184.

72 See Lúcia Lippi Oliveira, Mônica Pimenta Velloso, and Angela Castro Gomes, *Estado Novo: Ideologia e poder* (Rio de Janeiro: Fundação Getúlio Vargas, 1982), 10–11.

73 Hobsbawm, *Nations and Nationalism since 1780*, 92.

74 See Miceli, *Intelectuais e classe dirigente no Brasil*, 129–87; Lúcia Lippi Oliveira, *Elite intelectual e debate político nos anos 30* (Rio de Janeiro: Fundação Getúlio Vargas, 1980); and Johnson, "The Dynamics of the Brazilian Literary Field, 1930–1945," 7–11.

75 For a discussion of the Romantic poets and the ideological message of their Indianist literature, see Dante Moreira Leite, *O caráter nacional brasileiro: História de uma ideologia* (São Paulo: Editora Ática, 1992), 171–73.

76 On scientific racism in Brazil, see Skidmore, *Black into White*, 48–77.

77 One prominent intellectual who had espoused white supremacist ideas in his writings in the 1920s, Francisco José Oliveira Viana, headed Vargas's Ministry of Accounts during the Estado Novo. I am not arguing here that racism disappeared from the Brazilian state under Vargas. Rather, I am

suggesting that its propagation had been muted or recast. It is telling, for example, that after 1938 Oliveira Viana published no book-length study dealing with race despite his announcement several years earlier of intention to do so. On the legacy of Oliveira Viana, see Jeffrey D. Needell, "History, Race, and the State in the Thought of Oliveira Viana," *Hispanic American Historical Review* 75 (1995): 1–30. For an overview of Brazilian social thought in the 1930s, see Dain Borges, "Brazilian Social Thought of the 1930s," *Luso-Brazilian Review* 31 (1994): 137–49.

78 See Skidmore, *Black into White*, 205–7.

79 A. Costa, *Indiologia*, 11.

80 Serviço de Proteção aos Índios (SPI), "Memória sobre as causas determinantes da diminuição das populações indígenas do Brasil," paper presented at the 9th Congresso Brasileiro de Geografia, 29 July 1940. Fundação Nacional do Índio (FUNAI), Brasília, Documentação (DOC), SPI/ Documentos Diversos, 1–2.

81 Olegário Moreira de Barros, "Rondon e o índio," *Revista do Instituto Histórico de Mato Grosso* 22, nos. 43–44 (1940): 15–26. For a discussion of the Estado Novo's efforts to forge robust citizens through physical education, see Maria Luiza Tucci Carneiro, *O anti-semitismo na era Vargas: Fantasmas de uma geração (1930–1945)* (São Paulo: Brasiliense, 1988), 139–42.

82 Edgar Roquette-Pinto, "Contribuição a antropologia do Brasil," *Revista de Imigração e Colonização* 1, no. 3 (July 1940): 440.

83 Paulo de Figueiredo, "O Estado Novo e o Homem Novo," *Cultura Política* 1, no. 1 (Mar. 1941), reprinted in Paulo de Figueiredo, *Aspectos ideológicos do Estado Novo* (Brasília: Senado Federal Centro Gráfico, 1983), 20.

84 For a discussion of nineteenth-century Brazilian elites' selective adherence to European liberal ideas, see Viotti da Costa, *The Brazilian Empire*, 53–77; and Roberto Schwarz, *Misplaced Ideas: Essays on Brazilian Culture* (London: Verso, 1992), 19–31. On the Brazilian manipulation of European racial doctrines, see Skidmore, *Black into White*, 77.

85 José de Oliveira Marques, "Colonização e povoamento," *Revista de Imigração e Colonização* 1, no. 2 (Apr. 1940): 207. The journal was the official publication of the government's Council on Immigration and Colonization. For a sample of the nativist attacks on immigrant "cysts" embedded in the Brazilian body politic, see Leão Padilha, *O Brasil na posse de si mesmo* (Rio de Janeiro: Olímpica, 1941), 63–67. For a discussion of the Vargas regime's crackdown on German schools and cultural organizations in Brazil as part of its nationalization drive, see Schwartzman, Bomeny, and Costa, *Tempos de Capanema*, 142–48; Loewenstein, *Brazil under Vargas*, 187–204. On anti-Semitic immigration policy under Vargas, see Lesser, *Welcoming the Undesirables*; and Carneiro, *O anti-semitismo na era Vargas*.

86   Marques, "Colonização e povoamento," 205.

87   SPI, "Memória sobre as causas," 9.

88   Rondon, quoted in *O Radical*, 30 March 1940; see also Juarez Távora to Senhor Chefe do Gov. Provisório, 30 October 1933, Museu do Índio (MI), Setor de Documentação (SEDOC), Film 380, Fot 864–68.

89   Report by SPI Director Colonel Vicente de Paula Teixeira da Fonseca Vasconcelos (1940?), MI, Rio de Janeiro, SEDOC, Film 337, Fot 1237–73.

90   João Lyra, "Raça, educação, e desporto," *Estudos e Conferências* 14 (Dec. 1941): 32.

91   Brasil, Departamento Administrativo do Serviço Público, *Revista do Serviço Público* 3, nos. 1–2 (July–Aug. 1939): 35.

92   SPI, "Memória sobre as causas," 2.

93   See Scott, *Seeing Like a State*, 3.

94   On the conflictual relationship between Indians and the nation-state, see Greg Urban and Joel Sherzer, eds., *Nation-States and Indians in Latin America* (Austin: University of Texas Press, 1991), 1–18; and Eunice Ribeiro Durham, "O lugar do índio," in *O índio e a cidadania*, ed. Comissão Pró-Índio/SP (São Paulo: Brasiliense, 1983), 11–19.

95   Themístocles Paes de Souza Brazil, *Íncolas selvícolas* (Rio de Janeiro: Ministério de Relações Exteriores, 1937), 65–69.

96   For further discussion of military concern with the nationalization of the Indian and the defense of Brazil's borders, see A. C. Lima, *Um grande cerco de paz*, 54–57.

97   Ildefonso Escobar, *A Marcha para o Oeste: Couto Magalhães e Getúlio Vargas* (Rio de Janeiro: A Noite, 1941), 116.

98   A. Gomes, *A invenção do trabalhismo*, 228–29.

99   SPI, *Relatório* (1939), Annex Doc. 14, p. 3.

100 See SETH [Álvaro Marins], *O Brasil pela imagem: Quadros expressivos da formação e do progresso da pátria brasileira* (Rio de Janeiro: Indústria do Livro, 1943); and Renato Sêneca Fleury, *Pátria brasileira* (São Paulo: Melhoramentos, 1944), 8.

101 On positivism in Brazil, see João Cruz Costa, *A History of Ideas in Brazil* (Berkeley: University of California Press, 1964), 82–175; José Murilo de Carvalho, *A formação das almas: O imaginário da República no Brasil* (São Paulo: Companhia das Letras, 1990).

102 Cândido Rondon, "José Bonifácio e o problema indígena," *Instituto Histórico e Geográfico Brasileiro* 174 (1939): 882.

103 See Antonio Carlos de Souza Lima, "A identificação como categoria histórica," in *Os poderes e as terras dos Índios*, ed. João Pacheco de Oliveira Filho (Rio de Janeiro: PPGAS, 1989), 139–97.

104 C. Rondon, *Rumo ao Oeste*, 30–31.

105 Boaventura Ribeiro da Cunha, *Educação para os selvícolas* (Rio de Janeiro: Ministério da Agricultura, 1946), 102. See also the plan to transform Indi-

ans into colonists and defenders of the hinterland in Joaquim Rondon, *O índio como sentinela das nossas fronteiras* (Rio de Janeiro: Departamento de Imprensa Nacional 1946), 37–39.

106 Ribeiro da Cunha, *Educação para os selvícolas*, 53–61. On this same theme of Indian villages as models of communitarianism, see also SPI, *Boletim* 14 (Jan. 1943): 5.

107 Ribeiro da Cunha, *Educação para os selvícolas*, 102.

108 Brasil, Ministério da Agricultura, *Marcha para Oeste* (Conferências Culturais 1939–43), 47, 90.

109 Joaquim Rondon, *O índio como sentinela das nossas fronteiras*, 34.

110 José Maria de Paula, *Terras dos índios* (Rio de Janeiro Ministério da Agricultura/SPI 1944), 90–91.

111 SPI, *Boletim* 20 (July 1943): 196.

112 On the Vargas regime's courtship of the urban working class and symbolic promotion of popular culture, see A. Gomes, *A invenção do trabalhismo*, 159–248; and John D. French, *The Brazilian Workers' ABC: Class Conflict and Alliance in Modern São Paulo* (Chapel Hill: University of North Carolina Press, 1992). On rural labor, see Welch, *The Seed Was Planted*, 63–98.

113 Excerpt from Article 6 of the Civil Code, reprinted in Ramos, *Indigenism*, 18.

114 On a comparative note, see Knight's penetrating analysis of indigenismo in postrevolutionary Mexico in "Racism, Revolution, and *Indigenismo*," 71–113.

115 Sider, "When Parrots Learn to Talk, and Why they Can't," 17.

2 "Pacifying" the Xavante, 1941–1966

1 See Acary de Passos Oliveira, *Roncador-Xingu: Roteiro de uma expedição* (Goiânia, 1976), 175–77.

2 Silo Meireles, *Brasil Central* (Rio de Janeiro: Biblioteca do Exército, 1960), 29–30.

3 For first-hand accounts of the Roncador-Xingu Expedition, see A. Oliveira, *Roncador-Xingu*, and Orlando Villas Bôas and Cláudio Villas Bôas, *A Marcha para o Oeste* (São Paulo: Globo, 1994).

4 John H. Galey, "The Politics of Development in the Brazilian Amazon, 1940–1950" (Ph.D. diss., Stanford University, 1977), 100–101.

5 See Maria Lúcia Pires Menezes, "Parque Indígena do Xingu: A construção de um território estatal" (Master's thesis, Universidade Federal de Rio de Janeiro, 1990), 15–21. For an indictment of corruption in the FBC, see Carlos Telles, *História secreta da Fundação Brasil Central* (Rio de Janeiro: Editora Chavantes, 1946).

6   On the tenente revolts and their ramifications, see John D. Wirth, "Te-
    nentismo in the Brazilian Revolution of 1930," *Hispanic American Histor-
    ical Review* 44 (1964): 161–79, and Neill Macaulay, *The Prestes Column:
    Revolution in Brazil* (New York: New Viewpoints, 1974).

7   João Alberto Lins de Barros, *Memórias de um revolucionário* (Rio de Ja-
    neiro: Civilização Brasileira, 1953), 101–6.

8   Jorge Ferreira, quoted in Villas Bôas and Villas Bôas, *A Marcha para o
    Oeste*, 24.

9   Ibid., 25, and A. Oliveira, *Roncador-Xingu*, 14. On European ceremonial
    possessions of the New World, see Patricia Seed, *Ceremonies of Possession
    in Europe's Conquest of the New World, 1492–1640* (Cambridge, England:
    Cambridge University Press, 1995).

10 Villas Bôas and Villas Bôas, *A Marcha para o Oeste*, 34.

11 A. Oliveira, *Roncador-Xingu*, 137.

12 Excerpt from "Nas margens do Araguaia," in Valdon Varjão, *Aragarças:
    Portal da Marcha para o Oeste* (Brasília: Senado Federal Centro Gráfico,
    1989), 78.

13 M. Menezes, "Parque Indígena do Xingu," 11.

14 D. Maybury-Lewis, *Akwẽ-Shavante Society*, 3.

15 Archie MacIntyre, *Down the Araguaya: Travels in the Heart of Brazil* (Lon-
    don: Religious Tract Society, 1924?).

16 Alencarliense Fernandes da Costa, Ministério do Trabalho e Comércio,
    *Relatório do Serviço de Proteção aos Índios no Estado de Goyaz Relativo ao
    Ano de 1930*, 1a volume, 5 January 1931, MI, SEDOC, Film 342, Fot 1–109.

17 Report by João Alberto Lins de Barros, President of the FBC, 1944, MI,
    SEDOC, Film 389, Fot 598.

18 For a triumphal account of the origins and goals of the SPI—if not neces-
    sarily its achievements—see D. Ribeiro, *Os índios e a civilização*. A cele-
    bratory account of Rondon and the SPI can also be found in John J. John-
    son, *The Military and Society in Latin America* (Stanford, CA: Stanford
    University Press, 1964), 198–99. For a revisionist analysis, see A. C. Lima,
    Um grande cerco de paz, and Ramos, *Indigenism*, 147–67.

19 Vicente de Paula Teixeira da Fonseca Vasconcelos, Director of the SPI, to
    the Minister of Agriculture, Rio de Janeiro, 9 February 1943, FUNAI, DOC,
    FUNAI/Of. 014/SPI.

20 Vicente de Paula Teixeira da Fonseca Vasconcelos to Ciro Goes, SPI Direc-
    tor in Goiás, Rio de Janeiro, 22 November 1941, MI, SEDOC, Film 263, Fot
    934–39.

21 See James R. Scobie, *Argentina: A City and a Nation* (New York: Oxford
    University Press, 1971), 115.

22 See Evelyn Hu-DeHart, *Yaqui Resistance and Survival: The Struggle for
    Land and Autonomy, 1821–1910* (Madison: University of Wisconsin Press,
    1984), 155–200.

23   See Foweraker, *The Struggle for Land*, 65–66.

24   Instituto Brasileiro de Geografia e Estatística, *Enciclopédia dos municípios brasileiros* (Rio de Janeiro: IBGE, 1958), 35:84.

25   Valdon Varjão, *Barra do Garças no passado* (Brasília: Senado Federal Centro Gráfico, 1980), 22.

26   Armando de Arruda Pereira, *Diário de viagem de São Paulo a Belém do Pará descendo o Araguaya* (São Paulo: Gráfica Paulista, 1935), 7–8.

27   Valdon Varjão, *Barra do Garças: Migalhas de sua história* (Brasília: Senado Federal Centro Gráfico, 1985), 194–96.

28   Hipólito Chovelon, Francisco Fernandes, and Pedro Sbardelotto, *Do primeiro encontro com os Xavante à demarcação de suas reservas* (Campo Grande: Editorial Dom Bosco, 1996), 48–49.

29   Oswaldo Martins Ravagnani, "A experiência Xavante com o mundo dos brancos" (Ph.D. diss., Fundação Escola de Sociologia e Política de São Paulo, 1978), 172–73.

30   A. Estigarríbia to SPI Director Vasconcelos, 1 April 1942, MI, SEDOC, Film 263, Fot 1437–38.

31   Ibid.; Vasconcelos to the Minister of Agriculture, Rio de Janeiro, 9 February 1943, FUNAI, DOC, FUNAI/Of. 014/SPI.

32   SPI, *Relatório-Referente ao ano de 1934* (1934).

33   See A. C. Lima, *Um grande cerco de paz*, 166–77.

34   SPI, *Relatório* (1939): 9.

35   See Antonio Carlos de Souza Lima, "On Indigenism and Nationality in Brazil," in *Nation-States and Indians in Latin America*, ed. Urban and Sherzer, 253; Mathias C. Kiemen, *The Indian Policy of Portugal in the Amazon Region, 1614–1693* (New York: Farrar, Straus and Giroux, 1973), 45, 68; Regina Maria de Carvalho Erthal, "Atrair e pacificar: A estratégia da conquista" (Master's thesis, Universidade Federal do Rio de Janeiro, 1992).

36   When a 1954 congressional bill called for the abolition of the SPI, the agency reminded the public of ten "spectacular pacifications" (including the Xavante) carried out over the previous forty years. SPI, *Relatório* (1954): 23–24. The congressional bill was never passed.

37   On "symbolic capital" see Pierre Bourdieu, *Outline of a Theory of Practice*, trans. Richard Nice (Cambridge, England: Cambridge University Press, 1977), 171–83.

38   On gender as a principal site for the militarization of subjects, the production of relations of power, and the achievement of status honor on the frontier, see Alonso, *Thread of Blood*, 73–111.

39   See SPI, *Relatório* (1954): 117.

40   By design of regional oligarchies under the Old Republic, the central government's share of public revenues had fallen from 65.8 percent to 51.2 percent and the central government ran budget deficits every year from 1910 to 1926. See Hagopian, *Traditional Politics and Regime Change in Brazil*, 142.

41 See Hermano Ribeiro da Silva, *Nos sertões do Araguaia* (São Paulo: J. Fagundes, 1936); and Willy Aureli, *Roncador* (Rio de Janeiro: Edições Cultura Brasileira, 1939). They followed in the footsteps of Percy Fawcett, a British adventurer who set out in 1925 to find a "lost civilization" in central Brazil and never returned. On the Fawcett expedition, see Georges Miller Dyott, *Man Hunting in the Jungle, Being the Story of a Search for Three Explorers Lost in the Brazilian Wilds* (Indianapolis: Bobbs-Merrill, 1930).

42 *Boletim Salesiano* 1 (1935): 55–56; SPI, *Relatório* (1939): Annexo.

43 D. Maybury-Lewis, *Akwē-Shavante Society*, 3.

44 "A vocação do missionário," *Suplemento do Boletim Salesiano* 8, no. 9 (1947): 1.

45 *Boletim Salesiano* 1 (1935): 57–59.

46 SPI, *Relatório* (1939): Annex doc. 6, 6.

47 Chovelon to Minister of Education and Health, Rio de Janeiro, 25 April 1941, MI, SEDOC, Film 263, Fot 1444.

48 See Freire, "Indigenismo e antropologia," 146–55.

49 Thomas C. Bruneau, *The Political Transformation of the Brazilian Catholic Church* (Cambridge, England: Cambridge University Press, 1974), 30–51.

50 For a discussion of the rivalry between the SPI and missionaries, see Mércio Pereira Gomes, *Os índios e o Brasil* (Petrópolis: Vozes, 1988), 191–93; and Freire, "Indigenismo e antropologia," 123–30.

51 SPI, *Relatório* (1939): 8.

52 SPI, *Relatório-Referente ao Ano de 1934*.

53 SPI, *Relatório* (1939): 11.

54 According to Freire, in the 1940s nearly one-third of the Catholic clergy in Brazil was foreign-born ("Indigenismo e antropologia," 183). For further discussion of the Estado Novo's policies toward European-born clergy in southern Brazil, see Schwartzman, Bomeny, and Costa, *Tempos de Capanema*, 154–70.

55 Malan, quoted in Sylvia Caiuby Novaes, *Jogo de espelhos: Imagens da representação de si através dos outros* (São Paulo: Editora da Universidade de São Paulo, 1993), 171.

56 A Estigarríbia to Vasconcelos, 27 January 1942, MI, SEDOC, Film 263, Fot 1507–11.

57 A Estigarríbia to Alvaro Duarte Monteiro, Rio de Janeiro, 20 April 1942, MI, SEDOC, Film 263, Fot 1441; see also Vasconcelos to Minister of Agriculture, 9 February 1943, FUNAI, DOC, FUNAI/Of. 014/SPI.

58 D. Maybury-Lewis, *Akwē-Shavante Society*, 4.

59 SPI, *Boletim* 2 (Dec. 1941): 1.

60 Ibid.

61 On the colonial period, see Beatriz Perrone-Moisés, "Índios livres e índios escravos: Os princípios da legislação indigenista do período colo-

nial (séculos xvi–xviii)," in *História dos índios no Brasil*, ed. M. Cunha, 115–32. In the late nineteenth century, Brazilians likewise classified indigenous groups in binary terms: the "Tupi," the noble, heroic Indian of the past who had contributed to the nation's social and cultural formation; and the "Tapuia," the violent marauder, impeding settler advance (Monteiro, "As 'raças' indígenas no pensamento brasileiro do Império," 15–17). On the nineteenth-century dichotomy between "Tupi" and "Tapuia," see also Manuela Carneiro da Cunha, ed., *Legislação indigenista no século xix: Uma compilação: 1808–1889* (São Paulo: Comissão Pro-Índio de São Paulo, Editora da Universidade de São Paulo, 1992), 7–8.

62 See Berkhofer, *The White Man's Indian*; on the construction of the Noble Savage as a challenge to European social privilege, see Hayden White, *Tropics of Discourse: Essays in Cultural Criticism* (Baltimore: Johns Hopkins University Press, 1985), 183–95.

63 D. Ribeiro, *Os índios e a civilização*, 128–29. Ribeiro notes that one of the motivations behind the creation of the Museu do Índio in the 1950s was the elimination of the stereotype of the sanguinary Indian held by many Brazilians. See Darcy Ribeiro, *Confissões* (São Paulo: Companhia das Letras, 1997), 196.

64 Rondon, quoted in *A Noite*, 16 November 1941.

65 On the theme of the Indian corrupted by white evil, see Heitor Marçal, *Moral ameríndia* (Rio de Janeiro: Ministério de Educação e Saúde, 1946).

66 On Meireles's biography, see "Vida e idéias de Meireles," *Revista de atualidade indígena* 21 (July–Aug. 1981): 54–59.

67 A. Oliveira, *Roncador-Xingu*, 105.

68 Instruções ao inspetor especializado Francisco F. Soares de Meireles, para os trabalhos de pacificação dos índios chavantes, memorandum, 6 October 1944, mi, sedoc, Film 381, Fot 277–79.

69 Vargas, quoted in Varjão, *Aragarças*, 118.

70 Meireles, *Brasil Central*, 29.

71 Villas Bôas and Villas Bôas, *A Marcha para o Oeste*, 75–77.

72 Ibid., 34; Orlando Villas Bôas and Cláudio Villas Bôas, *Almanaque do sertão: Histórias e visitantes, sertanejos e índios* (São Paulo: Globo, 1997), 286.

73 On the origins of the Correio Aéreo Nacional, see Deoclécio Lima de Siqueira, *Caminhada com Eduardo Gomes* (Rio de Janeiro: Novas Direções, 1989), 51–53. On aircraft assembly plants, see Conca, *Manufacturing Insecurity*, 28.

74 Nelson Freire Lavenére-Wanderley, *História da Força Aérea Brasileira* (Rio de Janeiro: np. 1975), 220–23.

75 Manoel Rodrigues Ferreira, a paulista reporter, published a series of articles focusing on the landscape and inhabitants of Central Brazil, including "the ferocious Xavantes." See, for example, *A Gazeta de São Paulo*, 14 September 1945.

76 David Nasser and Jean Manzon, *Mergulho na aventura* (Rio de Janeiro: O Cruzeiro, 1945), 312–13.

77 David Nasser and Jean Mazon, "Voando a 8 metros, em pique, sobre os Chavantes!", reprinted in Varjão, *Aragarças*, 296–98.

78 Sereburã et al., *Wamrêmé za'ra-Nossa palavra*, 144.

79 Francisco Meireles, Relatório dos trabalhos das turmas de atração dos índios chavantes durante o ano de 1945, MI, SEDOC, Film 381, Fot 308.

80 SPI, "Nota da Seção de Estudos do SPI," January 1947, FUNAI, DOC, FUNAI/Of. 014/SPI.

81 On Meireles's historic exchange with the Xavante, see Lincoln de Souza, *Os Xavantes e a civilização* (Rio de Janeiro: Instituto Brasileiro de Geografia e Estatística, 1953), 40–42.

82 See ibid.; Lincoln de Souza, *Entre os Xavantes do Roncador* (Rio de Janeiro: Ministério de Educação e Saúde, 1952); and Sylvio da Fonseca, *Frente a frente com os Xavantes* (Rio de Janeiro: Pongetti, 1948). On documentary films, see two movies made by Genil Vasconcelos: *Sertão: Entre os índios do Brasil Central* (1949), and *Frente a frente com os Xavantes* (1948).

83 *Time*, 2 September 1946.

84 Amilcar A. Botelho de Magalhães, "A pacificação dos índios chavante," *América Indígena* 7, no. 3 (Jan. 1947): 333–39.

85 Herbert Serpa, "A pacificação dos xavantes," SPI, Seção de Estudos do Serviço de Proteção aos Índios, August 1947(?), FUNAI, DOC, FUNAI/Of. 014/SPI.

86 Lopes da Silva, "Dois séculos e meio de história Xavante," 68–69; and Laura Graham, *Performing Dreams*, 33–35.

87 See Laura Graham, *Performing Dreams*, 33–34; Sereburã et al., *Wamrêmé za'ra-Nossa palavra*, 137–38; and D. Ribeiro, *Os índios e a civilização*, 184–86.

88 Sereburã et al., *Wamrêmé za'ra-Nossa palavra*, 104.

89 See Lopes da Silva, "Dois séculos e meio de história Xavante," 367–71; Laura Graham, *Performing Dreams*, 29–31. Both authors note divergent accounts among the Xavante regarding the history of these various communities—a logical extension of the rivalries among them.

90 Chovelon, Fernandes, and Sbardelotto, *Do primeiro encontro com os xavante à demarcação de suas reservas*, 94.

91 Newspaper responses to the massacre of Pimentel Barbosa are found in MI, SEDOC, Film 325, Fot 672–743.

92 See, for example, *A Notícia*, 24 June 1947. See also Fonseca, *Frente a frente com os Xavantes*, 123, 132.

93 Bueno's appeal to the minister of agriculture appeared in the newspaper *Folha da Manhã*, 7 May 1949 and is excerpted in Herbert Baldus, "É belicoso o Xavante?," *Revista do Arquivo Municipal* 142 (1951): 131–32.

94 Baldus, "Tribos da bacia do Araguaia e o Serviço de Proteção aos Índios," *Revista do Museu Paulista* 2 (1948): 154.

95 Baldus, "É belicoso o Xavante?", 125–26.

96 Baldus, "Tribos da bacia do Araguaia," 162–68.

97 Vasconcelos Costa, "Problemas do Brasil Central," 1949, MI, SEDOC, Film 389, Fot 759–60.

98 The epithets were given by Assis Chateaubriand in *O Jornal*, 29 May 1949.

99 Renato Rosaldo, *Culture and Truth* (Boston: Beacon Press, 1993), 69.

100 For a discussion of the evolution of the project for the Xingu National Park, see Freire, "Indigenismo e antropologia," 223–46, and Davis, *Victims of the Miracle*, 47–52. For an examination of the territorial dispute between the central government and the state of Mato Grosso, see Gilmar Ferreira Mendes, *Domínio da União sobre as Terras Indígenas: O Parque Nacional do Xingu* (Brasília: Ministério Público Federal, 1988).

101 See the Ante-Projeto de Lei-Cria o Parque Indígena e dispõe sobre sua organização, reprinted in Vanessa R. Lea, *Parque Indígena do Xingu: Laudo antropológico* (Campinas: UNICAMP, Instituto de Filosofia e Ciências Humanas, 1997), 153.

102 Leandro Mendes Rocha, "A Marcha para o Oeste e os índios do Xingu," in FUNAI, *Índios do Brasil* 2 (June 1992): 21–23.

103 For a comparative look at the range of positions within Mexican indigenismo, see Knight, "Racism, Revolution, and *Indigenismo*," 80–81.

104 M. Menezes suggests that Meireles's reticence may have stemmed from his fear of alienating matogrossense elites by denouncing their actions in Congress ("Parque Indígena do Xingu," 182).

105 "Vida e idéias de Meireles," 57.

106 Davis, *Victims of the Miracle*, 50–52; and D. Maybury-Lewis, *Akwẽ-Shavante Society*, 8.

107 A. Estigarríbia to SPI Director Vasconcelos, 1 April 1942, MI, SEDOC, Film 263, Fot 474–75; and Vasconcelos to Minister of Agriculture, 9 February 1943, FUNAI, DOC, FUNAI/Of. 014/SPI.

108 SPI, "Nota de Seção de Estudos do SPI."

3 "The Father of the Family Provoking Opposition":
State Efforts to Remake the Xavante, 1946–1961

1 Meireles, *Brasil Central*, 99.

2 *O Globo*, 11 January 1954.

3 Conselho Nacional de Proteção aos Índios, "Com relação a vinda de índios Xavante a este Capital declarou-nos o Diretor do SPI . . . ," 1954, MI, SEDOC, Film 356, Fot 49–50.

4 Meireles, *Brasil Central*, 95–98.

5   SPI official quoted in *Tribuna da Imprensa*, 4 January 1958. Similar inter-
      est among the Yanomami in one of their compatriots' descriptions of Ca-
      racas is recounted in Napoleon A. Chagnon, *Yanomamö: The Fierce Peo-
      ple*, 3d ed. (New York: Holt, Rinehart and Winston, 1983), 196.

6   *O Globo*, 11 January 1954.

7   SPI, *Boletim*, no. 1 (Mar. 1961): 5–6.

8   SPI, *Boletim*, no. 5 (July 1957): 3.

9   D. Maybury-Lewis, *Akwẽ-Shavante Society*, 23–24.

10   Richard White, *The Middle Ground: Indians, Empires, and Republics in
      the Great Lakes Region, 1650–1815* (New York: Cambridge University Press,
      1995), x.

11   Sherry B. Ortner, "Resistance and the Problem of Ethnographic Refusal,"
      Comparative Studies in Society and History 37 (1995): 176.

12   On the ecology of the cerrado, see Nancy Flowers, "Forager-Farmers: The
      Xavante Indians of Central Brazil" (Ph.D. diss., City University of New
      York, 1983); Moran, *Through Amazonian Eyes*, 118–39; Daniel Gross et al.,
      "Ecology and Acculturation among Native Peoples of Central Brazil," *Sci-
      ence* 206 (Sept. 1979): 234.

13   D. Maybury-Lewis, *Akwẽ-Shavante Society*, 48.

14   Ibid.

15   Ibid., 43–47.

16   Ibid., 41–42.

17   Ibid., 35–43.

18   Moran, *Through Amazonian Eyes*, 118.

19   Indeed, as Nancy Flowers asserts, such was the case of Apoena's base vil-
      lage, which had been occupied in the 1930s, 1950s, and 1970s—each time
      for about five years—and left fallow for stretches of roughly fifteen years
      to allow the soil to regenerate ("Forager-Farmers: The Xavante Indians of
      Central Brazil," 295).

20   Ibid., 289.

21   Indigenous mobility is often demonized as vagrancy. For a perceptive
      analysis, see Ramos, *Indigenism*, 33–40.

22   D. Maybury-Lewis, *Akwẽ-Shavante Society*, 53.

23   For a discussion of Amazonian Indians as environmental stewards, see
      Darrell A. Posey and William Balée, eds., *Resource Management in Ama-
      zonia: Indigenous and Folk Strategies* (Bronx: New York Botanical Garden,
      1989). On the negative impact of the Tupi population on the Atlantic for-
      est in Brazil, see Warren Dean, *With Broadax and Firebrand: The Destruc-
      tion of the Brazilian Atlantic Forest* (Berkeley: University of California
      Press, 1995), 20–40. For a critique of the essentialist image of the Native
      American as ecologist, see Shepard Krech III, *The Ecological Indian: Myth
      and History* (New York: Norton, 1999).

24   José de Lima Figueiredo, *Índios do Brasil* (São Paulo: Nacional, 1939), 184.

Since the Conquest, Europeans had pointed to indigenes' "unsavory" eating habits as evidence of their "barbarism." See Anthony Pagden, *The Fall of Natural Man* (Cambridge, England: Cambridge University Press, 1986), 87–89.

25 Rodrigo Otávio, *Os selvagens americanos perante o direito* (São Paulo: Nacional, 1946), 159.

26 Immigration policy during the Estado Novo barred "vagabonds" and "gypsies" from entering the country. See Tucci Carneiro, *O anti-semitismo na era Vargas*, 180.

27 Lopes da Silva, *Nomes e amigos*, 47.

28 On the political economy of other food-collecting "bands," see Eric Wolf, *Europe and the People without History* (Berkeley: University of California Press, 1982), 91–92.

29 D. Maybury-Lewis, *Akwẽ-Shavante Society*, 104–5, 143.

30 Laura Graham, *Performing Dreams*, 147.

31 Bartolomeu Giaccaria and Adalberto Heide, *Xavante (Auwẽ Uptabi: Povo Autêntico)*, 2d ed. (São Paulo: Dom Bosco, 1984), 62–64.

32 See Terence Turner, "The Gê and Bororo Societies as Dialectical Systems: A General Model," in *Dialectical Societies: The Gê and Bororo of Central Brazil*, ed. David Maybury-Lewis (Cambridge, MA: Harvard University Press, 1979), 168.

33 See Lopes da Silva, *Nomes e amigos*, 47–48.

34 Giaccaria and Heide, *Xavante (Auwẽ Uptabi)*, 66–71.

35 See Teodor Shanin, "Peasantry as a Political Factor," in *Peasants and Peasant Societies* (Hammondsworth, England: Penguin, 1971), 246–47.

36 See R. Brian Ferguson, "Explaining War," in *The Anthropology of War*, ed. Jonathan Haas (Cambridge, England: Cambridge University Press, 1990), 26–55.

37 On the comparative study of precapitalist and capitalist societies, see Roseberry, *Anthropologies and Histories*, 55–58; Jay O'Brien and William Roseberry, eds., *Golden Ages, Dark Ages: Imagining the Past in Anthropology and History* (Berkeley: University of California Press, 1991).

38 See Laura Graham, *Performing Dreams*, 67.

39 D. Maybury-Lewis, *Akwẽ-Shavante Society*, 167–70.

40 Lopes da Silva, "Dois séculos e meio de história Xavante," 365–67; Giaccaria and Heide, *Xavante (Auwẽ Uptabi)*, 36–43.

41 D. Maybury-Lewis, *Akwẽ-Shavante Society*, 275

42 Sereburã et al., *Wamrêmé za'ra-Nossa palavra*, 97–101.

43 D. Maybury-Lewis, *Akwẽ-Shavante Society*, 147–48.

44 Giaccaria and Heide, *Xavante (Auwẽ Uptabi)*, 69.

45 D. Maybury-Lewis, *Akwẽ-Shavante Society*, 189, 205.

46 Ibid., 212–13.

47 Ibid., 205–6.

48 Ferguson, "Explaining War," 45.

49 See Flowers, "Subsistence Strategy, Social Organization, and Warfare in Central Brazil," 261; Ferguson, "Explaining War," 53–54.

50 On indigenous leadership in Central Brazil, see Claude Lévi-Strauss, "The Social and Psychological Aspects of Chieftainship in a Primitive Tribe: The Nambikwara of Northwestern Mato Grosso," in *Comparative Political Systems: Studies in the Politics of Pre-Industrial Societies*, ed. Ronald Cohen and John Middleton (Garden City, NY: National History Press, 1967), 52.

51 D. Maybury-Lewis, *Akwẽ-Shavante Society*, 190.

52 Ibid., 200.

53 Ibid., 190–204.

54 Wolf, *Europe and the People without History*, 99.

55 See Charles Wagley, *Welcome of Tears: The Tapirapé Indians of Central Brazil* (New York: Oxford University Press, 1977), 48; Oliveira Filho, "O nosso governo," 31.

56 Wolf, *Europe and the People without History*, 96.

57 Chovelon, Fernandes, and Sbardelotto, *Do primeiro encontro com os Xavantes*, 96–99.

58 Serebura et al., *Wamrêmé za'ra-Nossa palavra*, 105.

59 David Maybury-Lewis, *The Savage and the Innocent*, 2d ed. (Boston: Beacon Press, 1988), 170.

60 Rolf Blomberg, *Chavante: An Expedition to the Tribes of the Mato Grosso* (New York: Taplinger, 1961), 22, 79.

61 D. Maybury-Lewis, *The Savage and the Innocent*, 266.

62 Lopes da Silva, "Dois séculos e meio de história Xavante," 370–1.

63 Chovelon, Fernandes, and Sbardelotto, *Do primeiro encontro com os Xavantes*, 81, 98.

64 Interview with João Gomes, Nova Xavantina, July 1994.

65 D. Maybury-Lewis, *Akwẽ-Shavante Society*, 22.

66 Ibid., 185.

67 Chovelon, Fernandes, and Sbardelotto, *Do primeiro encontro com os Xavantes*, 80, 97–98.

68 SPI, *Boletim* 22 (Sept. 1943): 3.

69 Benjamin Duarte Monteiro, Chief of the SPI 6th Inspectorate, to Indian Post Agents, Cuiabá, 24 August 1951, MI, SEDOC, Film 233, Fot 1391.

70 D. Maybury-Lewis, *Akwẽ-Shavante Society*, 24.

71 Nobue Miazaki, Relatório sobre os Índios do P.I. Chavante Capitariquara, Rio das Mortes, MT, October 1957, MI, SEDOC, Film 381, Fot 428–41.

72 Walter Velloso to Lincoln Pope, Chief of the Secção de Orientação e Assistência, Posto Indígena Xavante, 18 October 1957, MI, SEDOC, Film 381, Fot 411–15. The documents are silent regarding the extent to which the post overrode the Xavante's sexual division of labor as well.

73 Miazaki, Relatório sobre os Índios, MI, SEDOC, Film 381, Fot 428–41.

74 SPI, *Boletim* 11 (Oct. 1942): 27.

75 SPI, *Boletim* 10 (Sept. 1942): 2.

76 For a discussion of ILO Convention 107, officially ratified by the Brazilian government in 1966, see M. Cunha, *Os direitos do índio*, 127–32.

77 SPI, *Relatório* (1953): 16–17.

78 SPI Director Colonel José Luis Guedes, Da Renda Indígena (Circular no. 808), Rio de Janeiro, November 1957, MI, SEDOC, Film 265, Fot 1185. For further discussion of renda indígena, see Roberto Cardoso de Oliveira, *A sociologia do Brasil indígena* (Rio de Janeiro: Tempo Brasileiro, 1972), 63–64, 136–37.

79 SPI, *Boletim* 10 (Sept. 1942): 2.

80 Velloso to Pope, MI, SEDOC, Film 381, Fot 411–15.

81 Marinoni Almiro Gutenberg, Chief of the SPI 8th Inspectorate, Ordem de Serviço No. 8: Determina ao encarregado do Posto Pimentel Barbosa atrair os Xavantes, que se encontram perambulando, a voltarem as suas aldeias, Goiânia, 21 December 1958, MI, SEDOC, Film 273, Fot 1598.

82 Ismael Leitão to the Chief of the SPI 8th Inspectorate of the SPI, 15 October 1959, personal archive of Ismael Leitão (Goiânia).

83 Amaury Sadock de Freitas Filho, "Inquérito médico-sanitário entre os índios Xavante," in SPI, *Relatório* (1954): 145–71.

84 D. Maybury-Lewis, *Akwẽ-Shavante Society*, 48–49.

85 Ibid., 27–28.

86 Ibid., 169–77.

87 L. Souza, *Os Xavantes e a civilização*, 44.

88 D. Maybury-Lewis, *Akwẽ-Shavante Society*, 187–89.

89 SPI, *Relatório* (1939): 9.

90 Miazaki, Relatório sobre os Índios, MI, SEDOC, Film 381, Fot 428–41.

91 Interview with João Gomes, Nova Xavantina, July 1994.

92 Miazaki, Relatório sobre os Índios, MI, SEDOC, Film 381, Fot 428–41.

93 Ibid.

94 Velloso to Pope, MI, SEDOC, Film 381, Fot 411–15.

95 D. Maybury-Lewis, *Akwẽ-Shavante Society*, 24–25.

96 Eduardo Barros Prado, *Mato Grosso: El infierno junto al paraíso* (Buenos Aires: Ediciones Peuser, 1968), 23.

97 D. Maybury-Lewis, *Akwẽ-Shavante Society*, 209–10.

98 Walter Velloso, "A integração dos índios dentro da economia regional," SPI, *Boletim* 33 (Oct. 1959): 17–23.

99 SPI, *Boletim* 21 (Oct. 1958): 18.

100 Miazaki, Relatório sobre os Índios, MI, SEDOC, Film 381, Fot 428–41.

101 Interview with João Gomes, Nova Xavantina, July 1994. Gomes noted that Butler had made several trips to the United States and returned with supplies for the Indians.

102 Terence Turner, "Representing, Resisting, Rethinking: Historical Trans-

formations of Kayapo Culture and Anthropological Consciousness," in *Colonial Situations: Essays on the Contextualization of Ethnographic Knowledge*, ed. George W. Stocking Jr. (Madison: University of Wisconsin Press, 1991), 292.

103   D. Maybury-Lewis, *Akwē-Shavante Society*, 209–10.

104   Chovelon, Fernandes, and Sbardelotto, *Do primeiro encontro com os Xavantes*, 99.

105   Ibid., 98–100; D. Maybury-Lewis, *Akwē-Shavante Society*, 22–27, 209–13.

106   Guedes, quoted in *O Jornal*, 23 May 1958.

107   *Última Hora*, 26 May 1958.

108   D. Maybury-Lewis, *Akwē-Shavante Society*, 23.

109   Orlando Villas Bôas, quoted in SPI, *Boletim* 47 (Jan. 1961): 6–7.

4   "Noble Gestures of Independence and Pride":
Land Policies in Mato Grosso, 1946–1964

1   Tasso Villas de Aquino, "Plano Diretor de Trabalho do SPI, 1961/65," 10 June 1961, MI, SEDOC.

2   Ismael Leitão to Chief of the SPI 8th Inspectorate, 19 December 1960, personal archive of Ismael Leitão.

3   SPI, *Boletim* 39 (Apr. 1960): 18.

4   See M. Cunha, *Os direitos do índio*, 74–78.

5   José Maria de Paula, *Terras dos índios*, 78.

6   See Aurélio Wander Bastos, "As terras indígenas no direito constitucional brasileiro e na jurisprudência do STF," in *Sociedades indígenas e o direito: Uma questão de direitos humanos*, ed. Sílvio Coelho dos Santos et al. (Florianópolis: Universidade Federal de Santa Catarina, 1985), 87–90; and Fernando da Costa Tourinho Neto, "Os direitos originários dos índios sobre as terras que ocupam e suas conseqüências jurídicas," in *Os direitos indígenas e a constituição*, ed. Juliana Santilli (Porto Alegre: Núcleo de Direitos Indígenas/Sergio Antonio Fabris Editor, 1993), 18–19.

7   See Expedito Aranud, *Aspectos da legislação sobre os índios do Brasil* (Belém: Museu Goeldi, 1973), 28–29.

8   For a penetrating analysis of the Brazilian legal system as an "instrument of calculated disorder," see James Holston, "The Misrule of Law: Land and Usurpation in Brazil," *Comparative Studies in Society and History* 33 (1991): 695–725.

9   Arquimedes Pereira Lima, *Problemas matogrossenses* (Cuiabá: n.p., 1941), 21.

10   Ibid., 72.

11   Secretaria da Presidência da República, "Informações sobre Mato Grosso, 1941," AN, SPE, 025, Lata 325. By 1950, the state's population was estimated

at 522,044, only 1 percent of the national population, according to Campanha Nacional de Aperfeiçoamento Pessoal de Nível Superior (CAPES), *Estudos de Desenvolvimento Regional (Mato Grosso)* (Rio de Janeiro: ED-CAPES, 1958), 25.

12   Lima, *Problemas matogrossenses*, 142.

13   On the precariousness of road networks in Mato Grosso, see Virgílio Correa Filho, *Mato Grosso* (Rio de Janeiro: Editora Brasílica, 1939), 232–33.

14   *Brasil-Oeste* 5, no. 47 (Apr. 1960): 24; Marília Galvão and Roberto Galvão, *Áreas amazônicas de Mato Grosso, Goiás, e Maranhão* (Belém: Superintêndencia do Plano de Valorização Econômica da Amazônia, 1955), 52–53.

15   CAPES, *Estudos de Desenvolvimento Regional*, 28, 59–60.

16   Raymundo Santos, mayor of the county of Mato Grosso, to Vargas, 11 April 1942, AN, SPE, 025, Lata 390.

17   Secretaria da Presidência da República, Informações Sobre Mato Grosso, 1941, AN, SPE, 025, Lata 325.

18   Galvão and Galvão, *Áreas amazônicas de Mato Grosso*, 49–50.

19   Ibid., 50–52.

20   See Fausto Vieira de Campos, *Retrato de Mato Grosso* (São Paulo: Brasil-Oeste, 1969), 268.

21   See CAPES, *Estudos de Desenvolvimento Regional*, 27, 64.

22   José de Mesquita's speech, delivered to the Instituto Histórico e Geográfico Brasileiro in 1939, is reprinted in *Revista do Instituto Histórico de Mato Grosso* 11, nos. 41–42 (1939): 17–18.

23   Ponta Porã was restored to Mato Grosso in 1946; Guaporé remained a federal territory until becoming the state of Rondônia.

24   José de Mesquita, "Espírito matogrossense," *Cultura Política* 3, no. 28 (June 1943): 90.

25   The historiography of late-nineteenth- and twentieth-century Mato Grosso, celebrating the accomplishments of elites (and often written by them), is woefully lacking in social history and theoretical analysis. For more methodologically rigorous studies, see Valmir Batista Correa, "Coronéis e bandidos em Mato Grosso (1889–1943)" (Ph.D. diss., Universidade de São Paulo, 1981); and Elizabeth Madureira Siqueira, Lourença Alves da Costa, and Cathia Maria Coelho Carvalho, *O processo histórico de Mato Grosso* (Cuiabá: Universidade Federal de Mato Grosso, 1990).

26   Correa Filho, *Mato Grosso*, 97.

27   On coronelismo, see Victor Nunes Leal, *Coronelismo: The Municipality and Representative Government in Brazil*, trans. June Henfrey (New York: Cambridge University Press, 1977).

28   Correa Filho, *Mato Grosso*, 141–43.

29   Ibid., 129–31.

30 On the origins of separatist movements in southern Mato Grosso, see Maria Manuela Renha de Novis Neves, *Elites políticas: Competição e dinâmica patridário-eleitoral (Caso de Mato Grosso)* (Rio de Janeiro: IUPERJ, 1988), 92–127.

31 Correa Filho, *Mato Grosso*, 97, 150.

32 See, for example, the discourse of the governor of Mato Grosso, Arnaldo Estevão de Figueiredo (1946–1951), in Lélia Rita E. de Figueiredo Ribeiro, *O homem e a terra* (n.p., n.d.), 357–58.

33 Speech by Júlio Müller published in *Revista do Instituto Histórico de Mato Grosso* 20, nos. 39–40 (1938): 69.

34 On Vargas's use of interventors as a means of consolidating federal power, see Skidmore, *Politics in Brazil, 1930–1964*, 37.

35 See M. Menezes, "Parque Indígena do Xingu," 144.

36 Skidmore, *Politics in Brazil, 1930–1964*, 69.

37 M. Menezes, "Parque Indígena do Xingu," 146.

38 Barry Ames notes that some states, such as Maranhão, historically opposed federal programs because they might eventually lead to greater social diversity and political competition that could escape elite control. Although he does not discuss the case of Mato Grosso specifically, it would appear to follow this pattern in terms of land policies during the postwar period. See Barry Ames, *Political Survival: Politicians and Public Policy in Latin America* (Berkeley: University of California Press, 1987), 135.

39 Diário Oficial do Estado de Mato Grosso, *Ato do Poder Legislativo-Lei No. 336*, December 1949, MI, SEDOC, Film 245.

40 Benjamin Duarte Monteiro, SPI Inspector, to the SPI Director, Cuiabá, 23 and 29 December 1950, MI, SEDOC, Film 265, Fot 17–18, 09–10.

41 Chovelon, Fernandes, and Sbardelotto, *Do primeiro encontro com os Xavantes*, 95.

42 See M. Menezes, "Parque Indígena do Xingu," 121–26.

43 F. Campos, *Retrato de Mato Grosso*, 192.

44 M. Menezes, "Parque Indígena do Xingu," 137–38.

45 See Roberto Cardoso de Oliveira, "Relatório de uma investigação sobre terras em Mato Grosso," in SPI, *Relatório* (1954): 173–84; and Mendes, *Domínio da União sobre as terras indígenas: O Parque Nacional do Xingu*, 42.

46 M. Menezes, "Parque Indígena do Xingu," 156–57.

47 *Última Hora*, 21 October 1952.

48 See F. Campos, *Retrato de Mato Grosso*, 197–98, 245.

49 A 1954 study found that of Mato Grosso's 1,244 industrial establishments, primarily involved in food production, only 275 (22 percent) employed more than five people. The insignificance of industry was further highlighted by its minimal annual contribution—4 percent—to state revenues (CAPES, *Estudos de Desenvolvimento Regional*, 80–81).

50 Alcir Lenharo, "A terra para quem nela não trabalha," *Revista Brasileira de História* 6, no. 12 (1986): 55.
51 Hagopian, *Traditional Politics and Regime Change in Brazil*, 57.
52 See Paul Cammack, "Clientelism and Military Government in Brazil," in *Private Patronage and Public Power*, ed. Christopher Clapham (New York: St. Martin's Press, 1982), 58–72.
53 José Maria da Gama Malcher, *Por que fracassa a Proteção aos Índios?* (Unpublished manuscript, 1963).
54 F. Campos, *Retrato de Mato Grosso*, 201–2.
55 "Desaconselhável a segregação de contingentes silvícolas," *Brasil-Oeste* 1, no. 2 (Feb. 1956): 22.
56 "Practicamente fora do cartaz o Parque Indígena do Xingu," *Brasil-Oeste* 1, no. 6 (Oct. 1956): 31.
57 Galvão and Galvão, *Áreas amazônicas*, 28.
58 "Practicamente fora do cartaz," 30–31.
59 See Cardoso de Oliveira, "Relatório de uma investigação sobre terras en Mato Grosso," 173–84.
60 M. Menezes, "Parque Indígena do Xingu," 117.
61 See F. Campos, *Retrato de Mato Grosso*, 198.
62 Ponce de Arruda, quoted in Lenharo, "A terra para quem nela não trabalha," 52.
63 D. Maybury-Lewis, *Akwẽ-Shavante Society*, 9.
64 Ismael Leitão to Chief of the SPI 8th Inspectorate, 19 December 1960, personal archive of Ismael Leitao.
65 "Febre imobiliária atinge Cuiabá," *Brasil-Oeste* 4, no. 47 (Apr. 1960): 22–24.
66 Ministério do Interior, Divisão de Segurança e Informações, "Venda Ilegal de Terras em Mato Grosso," Anexo do Processo 4483/68, vol. 16, August 1964, FUNAI, DOC.
67 F. Campos, *Retrato de Mato Grosso*, 198.
68 On the use of state land policies for electoral purposes, see Foweraker, *The Struggle for Land*, 133; and M. Menezes, "Parque Indígena do Xingu," 115.
69 Ministério do Interior, Divisão de Segurança e Informações, "Venda ilegal de terras em Mato Grosso," FUNAI, DOC. On the repeated closure of the DTC, see Foweraker, *The Struggle for Land*, 119–20.
70 M. Menezes, "Parque Indígena do Xingu," 133–34.
71 Benjamin Duarte Monteiro, Chief of the SPI Sixth Inspectorate, "Portaria No. 12," Cuiabá, 6 September 1952, MI, SEDOC, Film 234, Fot 1354; and Chief of the Sixth Inspectorate to SPI headquarters, Cuiabá, 8 August 1956, MI, SEDOC, Film 235, Fot 960.
72 For a comparative study of land grabbing in Maranhão during this period, see Victor Asselin, *Grilagem: Corrupção e violência em terras do Carajás* (Petrópolis: Vozes, 1982).

73 FUNAI, "Relato sobre a ocupação Xavante de Couto Magalhães," Brasília, June 1979, Projeto Estudo sobre Terras Indígenas no Brasil (PETI), Rio de Janeiro, FNF 0228.

74 Giaccaria and Heide, *Xavante (Auwẽ Uptabi)*, 40.

75 Benjamin Duarte Monteiro to SPI Director, 23 April 1952, MI, SEDOC, Film 245, Fot 2177–78.

76 The FUNAI historical archive in Brasília has extensive documentation on the transaction of Xavante land compiled from the Mato Grosso state archives and local *cartórios*.

77 FUNAI, "Relato sobre a Ocupação Xavante de Couto Magalhães," June 1979.

78 Cláudio Martins to Benjamin Duarte Monteiro, Cuiabá, 16 February 1953, MI, SEDOC, Film 234, Fot 1758–61.

79 Severiano Nunes to Mato Grosso Governor Arnaldo Estevam de Figueiredo, São Félix, 7 May 1950, MI, SEDOC, Film 265, Fot 135.

80 Benjamin Duarte Monteiro to SPI Director José Maria da Gama Malcher, Cuiabá, 25 January 1952, MI, SEDOC, Film 245, Fot 2189.

81 Ismael Silva Leitão to Director of the SPI, 28 November 1951, MI, SEDOC, Film 245, Fot 2030–36. An account of the Xavante raid on São Félix can also be found in Leolídio di Ramos Caiado, *Dramas do Oeste: História de uma excursão nas regiões da Ilha do Bananal em 1950* (São Paulo: Edigraf, 1961), 113–17.

82 Antônio Cardoso de Melo to Cândido Mariano da Silva Rondon, Araguacema, 26 December 1953, MI, SEDOC, Film 251, Fot 2121.

83 Antônio Cardoso de Melo to SPI Director José Maria da Gama Malcher, Araguacema, 26 December 1953, MI, SEDOC, Film 251, Fot 2125.

84 Iara Ferraz and Mariano Mampieri, "Suiá-Missu: Um mito refeito," in *Carta': Falas, reflexões, memórias/informe de distribuição restrita do Senador Darcy Ribeiro* 4, no. 9 (1993): 76.

85 José Luiz Guedes to Ponce de Arruda, Rio de Janeiro, 28 November 1958, MI, SEDOC, Film 265, Fot 1321.

86 See Merilee S. Grindle, *State and Countryside* (Baltimore: Johns Hopkins University Press, 1986), 48–75; and Charles H. Wood and José Alberto Magno de Carvalho, *The Demography of Inequality in Brazil* (Cambridge, England: Cambridge University Press, 1988), 60.

87 SPI, *Boletim* 40 (May 1960): 9.

88 Almeida Netto, "Relatório," in SPI, *Relatório* (1959): 42.

89 A. C. Lima, *Um grande cerco de paz*, 235.

90 Benjamin Monteiro Duarte to SPI Director, Cuiabá, 2 March 1953, MI, SEDOC, Film 245, Fot 2330.

91 SPI, *Boletim* 15 (Mar. 1966): 4–5.

92 Benjamin Monteiro Duarte to SPI Director, Cuiabá, 2 March 1953, MI, SEDOC, Film 245, Fot 2330.

93 Octaviano Calmon to the Director of the DTC, 21 August 1956, MI, SEDOC, Film 247, Fot 1281–84.

94 José Maria da Gama Malcher to Deputy Jânio da Silva Quadros, October 1960, MI, SEDOC.

95 See "O inquérito sobre as concessões de terras em Mato Grosso," *Correio da Manhã*, 5 August 1955.

96 Brasil, Congresso Nacional, Camâra dos Deputados, "Projeto de Resolução No 65–1964, Aprova as Conclusões da Comissão Parlamentar de Inquérito para Apurar Irregularidades no Serviço de Proteção aos Índios."

97 See, for example, Aprígio Alves de Almeida Netto, "Relatório," Goiânia, 29 July 1964, MI, SEDOC.

98 See the SPI directorate's concerns regarding the *procuradoria* system in "Plano Diretor de Trabalho do SPI, 1961/65," MI, SEDOC.

99 See, for example, Christopher J. Tavener, "The Karajá and the Brazilian Frontier," in *Peoples and Cultures of Native South America*, ed. Daniel R. Gross (Garden City, NY: Doubleday, 1973), 450–56.

100 Malcher to Quadros, October 1960. Several years later, Malcher denounced the SPI in an unpublished manuscript entitled *Por que fracassa a Proteção aos Índios?* (1963).

101 Hagopian, *Traditional Politics and Regime Change in Brazil*, 58.

102 Lawrence Graham, *Civil Service Reform in Brazil*, 92.

103 Philippe C. Schmitter, *Interest Conflict and Political Change in Brazil* (Stanford: Stanford University Press, 1971), 33.

104 See Barbara Geddes, *Politician's Dilemma: Building State Capacity in Latin America* (Berkeley: University of California Press, 1994), 53.

105 Ibid., 32.

106 Ibid., 55, 123, 187.

107 Lawrence Graham, *Civil Service Reform in Brazil*, 129.

108 Geddes, *Politician's Dilemma*, 57–8.

109 See D. Ribeiro, *Confissões*, 197.

110 Brasil, Congresso Nacional, Câmara dos Deputados, "Relatório da CPI— Resoluções 1963 Ns 01–10," 1963.

111 Brasil, Congresso Nacional, Câmara dos Deputados, Projeto de Resolução No 65–1964, "Aprova as conclusões da Comissão Parlamentar do Inquérito para apurar irregularidades no Serviço de Proteção aos Índios."

112 D. Ribeiro, *Os índios e a civilização*, 128.

113 For a discussion of political dynamics during Brazil's postwar democracy, see Schmitter, *Interest Conflict and Political Change in Brazil*, 249.

5 "Brazilindians": Accomodation with Waradzu, 1950–1964

1 Skidmore, *Politics in Brazil*, 167–68.

2 Joffily, *Brasília e sua ideologia*, 59.

3   *Brasil-Oeste* 4, no. 41 (Oct. 1959): 6.

4   Anthony Smith, *Mato Grosso: The Last Virgin Land* (New York: Dutton, 1971), 102.

5   For Spanish American ethnography, see Robert Redfield, *The Primitive World and Its Transformations* (Ithaca, NY: Cornell University Press, 1953). For a fine critique of ethnographic essentialism, see Warren, "Transforming Memories and Histories."

6   Claude Lévi-Strauss, *Tristes Tropiques* (New York: Atheneum, 1967), 374.

7   See Fredrik Barth, ed., *Ethnic Groups and Boundaries: The Social Organization of Cultural Difference* (Boston: Little, Brown, 1969), 9–38.

8   Sahlins, "Goodbye to *Tristes Tropes*," 3, 13.

9   For a comparative examination, see Turner, "Representing, Resisting, Rethinking," 294.

10 See Lopes da Silva, *Nomes e amigos*, 31–44.

11 J. V. Neel et al., "Studies on the Xavante Indians of the Brazilian Mato Grosso," *American Journal of Human Genetics* 16 (Mar. 1964): 57.

12 D. Maybury-Lewis, *Akwẽ-Shavante Society*, 18.

13 J. R. do Amaral Lapa, *Missão do Sangradouro* (São Paulo: Colecão Saraiva, 1963), 83.

14 Giaccaria and Heide, *Xavante (Auwẽ Uptabi)*, 276.

15 See Neel et al., "Studies on the Xavante Indians," 110, 124; and E. David Weinstein, James V. Neel, and F. M. Salzano, "Further Studies on the Xavante Indians: The Physical Status of the Xavantes of Simões Lopes," *American Journal of Human Genetics* 19 (July 1967): 540.

16 Indeed, geneticists have asserted that South American Indians living today may represent remnants of former populations that survived early epidemics on the basis of hereditary ability to respond to infectious challenge. See Francisco M. Salzano and Sidia M. Callegari-Jacques, *South American Indians: A Case Study in Evolution* (Oxford: Clarendon Press, 1988), 104.

17 Francisco M. Salzano, James V. Neel, and David Maybury-Lewis, "Further Studies on the Xavante Indians—Demographic Data on Two Additional Villages: Genetic Structure of the Tribe," *American Journal of Human Genetics* 19 (July 1967): 485.

18 Ibid.

19 Nancy M. Flowers, "Crise e recuperação demográfica: Os Xavante de Pimentel Barbosa, Mato Grosso," in *Saúde e povos indígenas*, ed. Ricardo V. Santos and Carlos E. A. Coimbra Jr. (Rio de Janeiro: Editora FIOCRUZ, 1994), 213–42.

20 *O índio do Brasil* 97 (Jan.–Mar. 1959): 11. The magazine was published in Belém by the Brazilian affiliate of the World Evangelical Crusade.

21 Lopes, "A resistência do índio ao extermínio," 65–68.

22 Lapa, *Missão do Sangradouro*, 121.

23 James V. Neel, *Physician to the Gene Pool* (New York: Wiley, 1994), 127.

24 I have borrowed here from Turner, "Representing, Resisting, Rethinking," 287.

25 Thomas Young, "Avante ao Chavante," *O índio do Brasil* 90 (Apr.–June 1957): 7.

26 On the Summer Institute of Linguistics, see David Stoll, *Fishers of Men or Founders of Empire? The Wycliffe Bible Translators in Latin America* (London: Zed Press, 1982); and Gerard Colby with Charlotte Dennett, *Thy Will Be Done—The Conquest of the Amazon: Nelson Rockefeller and Evangelism in the Age of Oil* (New York: Harper Collins, 1995).

27 D. Ribeiro, *Confissões*, 241.

28 Colby with Dennett, *Thy Will Be Done*, 318–19.

29 Lopes da Silva, *Nomes e amigos*, 54.

30 *O índio do Brasil* 97 (Jan.–Mar. 1959): 11.

31 D. Maybury-Lewis, *Akwẽ-Shavante Society*, 26.

32 Laura Graham, *Performing Dreams*, 92.

33 Lopes da Silva, *Nomes e amigos*, 54.

34 *Boletim Salesiano* 29, no. 5 (Sept.–Oct. 1979): 3.

35 On Salesian policies toward the Bororo and the mission's activities in Mato Grosso, see Novaes, *Jogo de espelhos*, 137–86.

36 See Bartolomeu Meliá, *Educação indígena e alfabetização* (São Paulo: Loyola, 1979).

37 Lapa, *Missão do Sangradouro*, 98.

38 D. Maybury-Lewis, *Akwẽ-Shavante Society*, 19; Salzano et al., "Further Studies on the Xavante Indians," 472.

39 Claudia Menezes, "Missionários e índios em Mato Grosso: Os Xavante da Reserva de São Marcos" (Ph.D. diss., Universidade de São Paulo, 1984), 277.

40 See D. Maybury-Lewis, *Akwẽ-Shavante Society*, 19; and *O Jornal*, 1 July 1962.

41 C. Menezes, "Missionários e índios em Mato Grosso," 382–83. (The internato was discontinued in Sangradouro at the end of the 1970s and subsequently at São Marcos as well.)

42 D. Maybury-Lewis, *Akwẽ-Shavante Society*, 20.

43 Interview with Renato Tsiwaradza, Parabubure Indigenous Reserve, August 1994.

44 Ismael da Silva Leitão, "Relatório da viagem de inspeção feita a Missão Salesiana São Marcos," Goiânia, 21 September 1966, MI, SEDOC, Film 273, Fot 837–39.

45 D. Maybury-Lewis, *Akwẽ-Shavante Society*, 19.

46 Giaccaria to FUNAI, 10 July 1971, MI, SEDOC, Film 237, Fot 1294–308.

47 C. Menezes, "Missionários e índios em Mato Grosso," 359–60.

48 D. Maybury-Lewis, *The Savage and the Innocent*, 234–36.

49 Ibid., 205.

50 George Huestis, SIL Director in Cuiabá, "Relatório: Os missionários-linguísticos de Summer Institute of Linguistics que trabalham nas tribos sob a jurisdição de SPI," 29 November 1967, MI, SEDOC, Film 252, Fot 1006–7.

51 Robert Crump, "Relatório Conciso (June 1, 1966–June 30, 1967)," Rio Batovi, 18 July 1967, MI, SEDOC, Film 252, Fot 1016.

52 See Oswaldo Martins Ravagnani and Zélia Maria Presotto, "Processo aculturativo dos índios Xavante," *Logos* 3, no. 3 (1971): 71–82.

53 Darcy Ribeiro, *A política indigenista brasileira* (Rio de Janeiro: Ministério da Agricultura, 1962), 157.

54 Ibid., 155–56.

55 SPI, *Relatório* (1939): 19.

56 SPI, *Relatório* (1954): 26.

57 Agapto Silva, post chief P. I. Xavante (Couto Magalhães), to FUNAI 7a Delegacia Regional, 30 July 1973, MI, SEDOC, Film 294, Fot 1360–61.

58 D. Ribiero, *A política indigenista brasileira*, 156.

59 SPI, *Relatório* (1954): 27–28.

60 For the colonial period, Schwartz has highlighted the degree to which both Jesuits and colonists shared in their basic goal to Europeanize the native American. See Stuart B. Schwartz, "Indian Labor and New World Plantations: European Demands and Indian Responses in Northeastern Brazil," *American Historical Review* 83 (1978): 50.

61 On the condescension of SPI educators toward indigenous pupils, see Sílvio Coelho dos Santos, "A escola em duas populações tribais," *Revista de antropologia* 14 (1966): 31–35.

62 Judith Friedlander advances a similar argument in *Being Indian in Hueyapan: A Study of Forced Identity in Contemporary Mexico* (New York: St. Martin's Press, 1975), 128–64.

63 On indigenous education, see Eneida Corrêa de Assis, "Escola indígena: Uma 'frente ideológica'" (Master's thesis, Universidade de Brasília, 1981); and Mariana Kawall Leal Ferreira, "Da origem dos homens à conquista da escrita: Um estudo sobre povos indígenas e educação escolar no Brasil" (Master's thesis, Universidade de São Paulo, 1992).

64 Agapto Silva, post chief P. I. Xavante (Couto Magalhães), to FUNAI 7a Delegacia Regional, 30 July 1973, MI, SEDOC, Film 294, Fot 1360–61.

65 Eurides Radunz to Chief of the Eighth Inspectorate, P. I. Pimentel Barbosa, 30 January 1965, MI, SEDOC, Film 270, Fot 1892.

66 José de Souza Martins, *A chegada do estranho* (São Paulo: Editora Hucitec, 1993), 31.

67 See Turner, "Representing, Resisting, Rethinking," 293.

68 Ibid., 287.

69 See Laura Graham, *Performing Dreams*, 5–9.

70 D. Maybury-Lewis, *Akwẽ-Shavante Society*, 240.

71 Laura Graham, *Performing Dreams*, 8–9.

72 Rappaport, *Cumbe Reborn*, 152.

73 See James C. Scott, *Weapons of the Weak: Everyday Forms of Peasant Resistance* (New Haven: Yale University Press, 1985).

74 On diet as a marker of "civilized man," see Pagden, *The Fall of Natual Man*, 87–89.

75 D. Ribeiro, *Confissões*, 158.

76 Salzano, Neel, and Maybury-Lewis, "Further Studies on the Xavante Indians," 473.

77 Lapa, *Missão do Sangradouro*, 102–3.

78 Lopes, "A resistência do índio ao extermínio," 74.

79 SPI Eighth Inspectorate to Ismael da Silva Leitão, 20 September 1962, MI, SEDOC, Film 273, Fot 511.

80 SPI, *Boletim* 48 (Aug. 1961): 14.

81 See Guha, *A Subaltern Studies Reader*, xiv–xv.

82 See D. Ribeiro, *Os índios e a civilização*, 212–13. For a trenchant analysis of the ambiguity of subaltern response to domination, see Ortner, "Resistance and the Problem of Ethnographic Refusal."

83 For comparative studies of shame and indigenous self-censorship, see Turner, "Representing, Resisting, Rethinking," 289; and Gould, *To Die in This Way*, 205–6.

84 D. Maybury-Lewis, *Akwẽ-Shavante Society*, 18–23. On Xavante enthusiasm for soccer, see Vivian Flanzer, "Índios Xavante são loucos por futebol," *A Bola* (Oct. 1994): 64–67.

85 Lapa, *Missão do Sangradouro*, 94.

86 For a comparative exploration of segmentation by generation and gender within indigenous communties, see Mallon, *Peasant and Nation*, 63–88; Jan Rus, "The 'Comunidad Revolucionaria Institucional': The Subversion of Native Government in Highland Chiapas, 1936–1968," in *Everyday Forms of State Formation*, ed. Joseph and Nugent, 265–300; and Loretta Fowler, *Shared Symbols, Contested Meanings: Gros-Ventre Culture and History, 1778–1984* (Ithaca, NY: Cornell University Press, 1987), 185–91.

87 D. Maybury-Lewis, *Akwẽ-Shavante Society*, 26, 255–69.

88 See the discussion in Eneida Assis, "Educação indígena no Brasil," *Cadernos do Centro de Filosofia e Ciências Humanas, UFPA* 1 (1980): 35–52.

89 Report by Marta Maria Lopes, 30 August 1979, quoted in "Atuação da FUNAI na Área Xavante," FUNAI, DOC, Relatórios de Avaliação RO/MT.

90 Escobar, *A Marcha para o Oeste*, 117–18; emphasis in original.

91 Arthur Neiva, *Estudos da língua nacional* (São Paulo: Editora Nacional, 1940), 368.

92 Francisco Campos, *Educação e cultura* (Rio de Janeiro: José Olympio, 1941), 143–45.

93 CNPI, "Relatório Apresentado pelo General Cândido Mariano da Silva Rondon, Presidente do Conselho Nacional de Proteção aos Índios ao

Exmo. Sr. Ministro da Agricultura Correspondente ao Ano de 1944," 1944, MI, SEDOC.

94 Escobar, *A March para o Oeste*, 117; D. Ribeiro, *A política indigenista brasileira*, 156.

95 Giaccaria and Heide, *Xavante (Auwẽ Uptabi)*, 16.

96 See Hobsbawm, *Nations and Nationalism since 1780*, 115–16.

97 For a discussion of the subversion of European language by African intellectuals, see Kwame Anthony Appiah, *In My Father's House: Africa in the Philosophy of Culture* (New York: Oxford University Press, 1992), 55–56.

98 On national language as cultural artifact rather than primordial basis of national consciousness, see Hobsbawm, *Nations and Nationalism since 1780*, 110–20.

99 For discussion of Xavante linguistic range and its relationship to political oratory, see Laura Graham, "Three Modes of Shavante Vocal Expression: Wailing, Collective Singing, and Political Oratory," in *Native South American Discourse*, ed. Greg Urban and Joel Sherzer (Berlin: Mouton de Gruyter, 1986), 83–118.

100 Giaccaria and Heide, *Xavante (Auwẽ Uptabi)*, 110; and D. Maybury-Lewis, *Akwẽ-Shavante Society*, 39.

101 Lopes da Silva, *Nomes e amigos*, 51.

102 Lucy Soares da Silva, "Relatório das Atividades da Escola Mixta de Posto Colisêvu," 30 June 1960, MI, SEDOC, Film 269, Fot 1345–47.

103 Violeta Ribeiro Tocantins, "Plano de Ensino para a Escola do PI Simões Lopes Estabelecido para 1° Semestre de 1965," 5 March 1965, MI, SEDOC, Film 215, Fot 1670–81.

104 M. Cunha, *Os direitos do índio*, 30.

105 Tocantins, "Plano de Ensino para a Escola do PI Simões Lopes Estabelecido para 10 Semestre de 1965."

106 Interview with Ismael Leitão, Goiânia, August 1994.

107 See also Fleury, *Série Pátria Brasileira*, 8. On efforts to rectify the representation of indigenous history in school curricula, see Aracy Lopes da Silva and Luís Donisete Benzi Grupioni, *A temática indígena na escola: Novos subsídios para professores de 1° e 2° graus* (Brasília: MEC/MARI/UNESCO, 1995).

108 SPI, *Boletim* 26 (Mar. 1959): 4.

109 Camilo Corrêia, "Relação das Manifestações em Comemoração do dia do Índio, 19 de abril com as seguintes serimonias (sic)," Posto Indígena Colizevu, 30 April 1960, MI, SEDOC, Film 269, Fot 1353–54.

110 SPI, *Boletim* 1 (May 1965): 12.

111 Laura Graham, *Performing Dreams*, 24.

112 For a comparative study, see Turner, "Representing, Resisting, Rethinking," 304–5.

113 Sahlins, "Goodbye to *Tristes Tropes*," 19.

6 "Where the Earth Touches the Sky": New Horizons for Indigenous Policy under Early Military Rule, 1964–1973

1 For a succinct review of the literature on the breakdown of democracy in Brazil in 1964, see Hagopian, *Traditional Politics and Regime Change in Brazil*, 66.

2 Wood and Carvalho, *The Demography of Inequality in Brazil*, 61–62.

3 See Hagopian, *Traditional Politics and Regime Change in Brazil*, 104–11.

4 On the doctrine of national security, see Maria Helena Moreira Alves, *State and Opposition in Military Brazil* (Austin: University of Texas Press, 1988), 13–28.

5 General Golbery Couto e Silva, quoted in ibid., 26.

6 On the military project for agricultural modernization, see Grindle, *State and Countryside*; Bernardo Sorj, *Estado e classes sociais na agricultura* (Rio de Janeiro: Zahar, 1980); Biorn Maybury-Lewis, *The Politics of the Possible: The Brazilian Rural Workers Trade Union Movement, 1964–1985* (Philadelphia: Temple University Press, 1994); Anthony Pereira, *The End of the Peasantry: The Rural Labor Movement in Northeast Brazil, 1961–1988* (Pittsburgh: University of Pittsburgh Press, 1997); Peter Houtzager, "State and Unions in the Transformation of the Brazilian Countryside, 1964–1979," *Latin American Research Review* 33, no. 2 (1998): 103–42.

7 Dennis J. Mahar, *Frontier Development in Brazil: A Study of Amazonia* (New York: Praeger, 1979), 7.

8 Ibid., 6–13.

9 See Davis, *Victims of the Miracle*.

10 Mahar, *Frontier Development in Brazil*, 52; Susanna B. Hecht, "Cattle Ranching in the Eastern Amazon: Evaluation of a Development Policy" (Ph.D. diss., University of California, Berkeley, 1982), 93–94.

11 See Alves, *State and Opposition in Military Brazil*, 27; and Hagopian, *Traditional Politics and Regime Change in Brazil*, 73. For a broader analysis of the alliance among state, domestic, and multinational capital, see Peter Evans, *Dependent Development: The Alliance of Multinational, State, and Local Capital in Brazil* (Princeton, NJ: Princeton University Press, 1979).

12 See Davis, *Victims of the Miracle*, 38.

13 On the Brazilian government's fiscal incentives in Legal Amazonia, see Mahar, *Frontier Development Policy in Brazil*, 88–92; and Fernando Henrique Cardoso and Geraldo Müller, *Amazônia: Expansão do capitalismo* (São Paulo: Brasiliense, 1977), 117–18.

14 For a discussion of the importance of regularizing land titles in the Amazon under military rule, see Alfredo Wagner Berno de Almeida, "O intransitivo da transição: O Estado, os conflitos agrários e violência na Amazônia (1965–1989)," in *Amazônia: A fronteira agrícola 20 anos depois*, ed. Philippe Lena and Adélia Engracia de Oliveira (Bélem: Museu Paraense Emilio Goeldi, 1991), 259–90.

15 See Lucy Paixão Linhares, "A ação discriminatória: terras indígenas como terras públicas," in *Os poderes e as terras dos índios*, ed. João Pacheco de Oliveira Filho (Rio de Janeiro: PPGAS/UFRJ-MN, 1989), 104.

16 José de Souza Martins, "The State and the Militarization of the Agrarian Question in Brazil," in *Frontier Expansion in Amazonia*, ed. Marianne Schmink and Charles H. Wood (Gainesville: University of Florida Press, 1991), 474.

17 See Wendy Hunter, *Eroding Military Influence in Brazil: Politicians against Soldiers* (Chapel Hill: University of North Carolina Press, 1997), 33, 121.

18 The sole exception was the Marechal Rondon reservation decreed for the Xavante in May 1965 by the government of Mato Grosso. An area of 50,000 hectares, the reservation comprised poor land. See Lopes, "A resistência do índio ao extermínio," 64.

19 Davis, *Victims of the Miracle*, 10–13.

20 "Inquérito Administrativo Referente a Apuração de Iregularidades no Extinto SPI," vol. 20, FUNAI, DOC, Processo 4483–68.

21 Davis, *Victims of the Miracle*, 11; *Jornal do Brasil* (Rio de Janeiro), 13 September 1969.

22 See Hagopian, *Traditional Politics and Regime Change in Brazil*, 106–7; and Alves, *State and Opposition in Military Brazil*, 35–36.

23 *Jornal do Brasil*, 10 April 1968.

24 See, for example, *Correio de Manhã*, 17 September 1967; *Jornal do Brasil*, 24 April 1968.

25 *Jornal do Brasil*, 20 April 1968.

26 Perhaps the most notable was Norman Lewis's "Genocide: From Fire and Sword to Arsenic and Bullets, Civilization Has Sent Six Million Indians to Extinction," *Sunday Times* (London), 23 February 1969. In France, Lucien Bodard published a book on atrocities against Brazilian Indians that was translated into English as *Massacre on the Amazon* (London: Tom Stacey, 1971). The FUNAI archive contains newspaper clips from Europe and the United States, suggesting the Brazilian government's sensitivity to foreign criticism.

27 See *O Globo*, 2 May 1968; *Jornal do Brasil*, 13 September 1969.

28 Aborigines Protection Society of London, *The Tribes of the Amazon Basin in Brazil, 1972* (London: C. Knight, 1973).

29 See *Estado de São Paulo*, 25 April 1969; *O Globo*, 30 July 1968; *Jornal do Brasil*, 13 November 1969.

30 *Estado de São Paulo*, 20 June 1969.

31 Quoted in *Estado de São Paulo*, 25 April 1969, and reprinted in Pedro Casaldáliga, *Uma igreja da Amazônia em conflito com o latifúndio e a marginalização social* (Mato Grosso: 1971), 100.

32 *O Globo*, 30 July 1968, and *Estado de São Paulo*, 25 April 1969, reprinted in Casaldáliga, *Uma igreja da Amazônia*, 100.

33 José de Queirós Campos to Oscar Gerônimo Bandeira de Mello, Brasília,

20 June 1969, PETI, FNH0099. See the vociferous attack on FUNAI and its defense of indigenous "privilege" leveled by the *Estado de Mato Grosso*, 15 December 1968.

34 On the federal bureaus and projects created by the military that encompassed the Amazon, see Cardoso and Müller, *Amazônia*, 115–28. On bureaucracy as arbiter of political and class conflict, see Foweraker, *The Struggle for Land*, 82.

35 See Hagopian, *Traditional Politics and Regime Change in Brazil*, 142.

36 On the legal history of indigenous land rights in the twentieth century, see Bastos, "As terras indígenas no direito constitucional brasileiro e na jurisprudência do STF," 90–95.

37 See Brasil, Ministério do Interior, Fundação Nacional do Índio, Legislação (Brasília, 1974): 5–16.

38 See Cardoso and Müller, *Amazônia*, 161.

39 Mahar, *Frontier Development Policy in Brazil*, 92.

40 Malori José Pompermayer, "Strategies of Private Capital in the Brazilian Amazon," in *Frontier Expansion in Amazonia*, ed. Schmink and Wood, 423–25.

41 Fernando Henrique Cardoso, *Autoritarismo e democratização* (Rio de Janeiro: Paz e Terra, 1975), 206.

42 For a more detailed description of the Suiá-Missu ranch in the late 1960s, see Smith, *Mato Grosso*, 251–72.

43 Pompermayer, "Strategies of Private Capital," 419–29.

44 Cardoso and Müller, *Amazônia*, 156.

45 See Susanna B. Hecht, "Cattle Ranching in Amazonia: Political and Ecological Considerations," in *Frontier Expansion in Amazonia*, ed. Schmink and Wood, 366–98; and Hecht, "Environment, Development and Politics: Capital Accumulation and the Livestock Sector in Eastern Amazonia," *World Development* 13 (1985): 663–84.

46 Davis, *Victims of the Miracle*, 114.

47 Mahar, *Frontier Development Policy in Brazil*, 100–103. For comparative study of another Amazonian region, Conceição do Araguaia, Pará, see Octavio Ianni, *A luta pela terra* (Petrópolis: Vozes, 1978).

48 Brasil, Ministerio do Interior, Secretaria Geral. *Relatório de Atividades 69/73* (Brasília, n.d.), 65–66; Davis, *Victims of the Miracle*, 64–65. For an "insider's" critique of the World Bank, exploring its decision to fund Polonoroeste, an Amazonian road-building project with profoundly deleterious effects on local indigenous populations, see David Price, *Before the Bulldozer: The Nambiquara Indians and the World Bank* (Cabin John, MD: Seven Locks Press, 1989).

49 Davis, *Victims of the Miracle*, 39–41; Alves, *State and Opposition in Military Brazil*, 106.

50 Davis, *Victims of the Miracle*, 114. For further discussion of the spectacular

growth of Barra do Garças county resulting from SUDAM fiscal incentives, see Luis R. Cardoso de Oliveira, "Colonização e diferenciação: Os colonos de Canarana" (Master's thesis, Universidade Federal de Rio de Janeiro–Museu Nacional, 1981), 38–44.

51 Smith, *Mato Grosso*, 60.

52 Varjão, *Barra do Garças no passado*, 62–63.

53 See Hagopian, *Traditional Politics and Regime Change in Brazil*, 147.

54 See Casaldáliga, *Uma igreja da Amazônia*, 28–35. For denouncing violence and fraud in the region, Bishop Casaldáliga, whose prelacy was based in the town of São Félix, received repeated death threats and calls for his deportation to his native Spain.

55 Mato Grosso, Secretaria de Planejamento e Coordenação Geral, *Mato Grosso é assim* (Rio de Janeiro: Secretaria de Planejamento e Coordenação Geral, n.d.), 6.

56 Hecht, "Environment, Development and Politics," 678.

57 See Davis, *Victims of the Miracle*, 115–17.

58 Hecht, "Environment, Development and Politics," 680.

59 Mahar, *Frontier Development Policy in Brazil*, 124–26.

60 Antônio Tebaldi Tardin et al., "Projetos agropecuários da Amazônia: Desmatamento e fiscalização—Relatório," *A Amazônia Brasileira em Foco* 12 (1978): 37.

61 FUNAI, "11 Titulos que Compõem a Fazenda Xavantina e 2 Mapas," (n.d.), FUNAI, DOC.

62 See Eudson de Castro Ferreira, *Posse e propriedade territorial: A luta pela terra em Mato Grosso* (Campinas: UNICAMP, 1986), 75.

63 A notorious case was that of the Codeara ranch, which gained title to an entire town, Santa Terezinha, occupied by long-term peasants and squatters. See Neide Esterci, *Conflito no Araguaia: Peões e posseiros contra a grande empresa* (Petrópolis: Vozes, 1987).

64 Governor Garcia Neto, quoted in E. Ferreira, *Posse e propriedade territorial*, 71.

65 Ibid., 69–78.

66 Marianne Schmink and Charles H. Wood, *Contested Frontiers in Amazonia* (New York: Columbia University Press, 1992), 64–65.

67 Post Chief at P. I. Areões to Eighth Inspectorate of the SPI, 28 February 1966, MI, SEDOC, Film 272, Fot 857–60.

68 José de Souza Martins, *Não há terra para plantar neste verão* (Petrópolis: Vozes, 1986), 16.

69 Agapto Silva, encarregado of P. I. Xavante, Couto Magalhães, to 7th Delegacia Regional of FUNAI, 6 May 1973, MI, SEDOC, Film 294, Fot 1348–50; Silva to 7th Delegacia Regional, 30 July 1973, MI, SEDOC, Film 294, Fot 1363.

70 See Casaldáliga, *Uma igreja da Amazônia*, 22.

71 See the memo from Agapto Silva to 7th Delegacia Regional of FUNAI, 9 March 1973, MI, SEDOC, Film 294, Fot 1351–53.

72 Telegraphs from P. I. Chief Pedro V. de Oliveira, encarregado of P. I. Paraíso (Batovi), to 6th Regional Inspectorate of FUNAI, 29 June, 31 July, 28 October 1968, MI, SEDOC, Film 217, Fot 553.

73 José Aparecido da Costa to Minister of the Interior General Costa Cavalcanti, Batatais, São Paulo, 10 April 1970, FUNAI, DOC.

74 José de Queiros Campos, President of FUNAI, to General José Costa Cavalcanti, Minister of the Interior, Rio de Janeiro, 20 June 1969, Instituto Socioambiental (ISA), São Paulo, XVD30.

75 Costa Cavalcanti, quoted in Cardoso and Müller, *Amazônia*, 154.

76 Paulo Dias Veloso, Secretário-Geral Adjunto Ministério do Interior, to Sílvio Caetano, president of the Sindicato Rural of Barra do Garças, 10 December 1969 (Terra MI/NIA/No. 077/73), FUNAI, DOC.

77 On varied meanings of "traditional" lands for indigenous peoples, see Oliveira Filho, *Os poderes e as terras dos índios*, 7.

78 See Foweraker, *The Struggle for Land*, 124.

79 José Jaime Mancin, FUNAI engineer/surveyor, "Certidões Negativas Expedidas Na Área Indígena Parabubure," Brasília, 6 February 1980, FUNAI, DOC.

80 FUNAI, *Relatório das Atividades da FUNAI durante o exercício de 1970* (Brasília, 1971).

81 Testimony of Ismarth Araújo de Oliveira in Brasil, Congresso Nacional, Câmara dos Deputados, *Projeto de Resolução No. 172 de 1978* (CPI– Reservas Indígenas).

82 FUNAI, *FUNAI em números* (July 1972).

83 FUNAI, *Relatório das atividades da FUNAI durante o exercício de 1970.*

84 Mahar, *Frontier Development Policy in Brazil*, 18.

85 For a discussion of repression under Médici, see Skidmore, *The Politics of Military Rule in Brazil, 1964–85* (New York: Oxford University Press, 1988), 105–59.

86 Alves, *State and Opposition in Military Brazil*, 109.

87 Mahar, *Frontier Development Policy in Brazil*, 18.

88 Davis, *Victims of the Miracle*, 59–88.

89 FUNAI President Oscar Jerônimo Bandeira de Mello, quoted in Shelton Davis and Patrick Menget, "Povos primitivos e ideologia civilizada no Brasil," in *Antropologia e indigenismo na América Latina*, ed. Carmen Junqueira and Edgard de A. Carvalho (São Paulo: Cortez, 1981), 49–50.

90 FUNAI, *Relatório das atividades da FUNAI durante o exercício de 1970.* During General Bandeira de Mello's administration, FUNAI issued various publications to boost the agency's public image, such as *FUNAI em números* (1972) and *O que é a FUNAI* (1973).

91 See "The Politics of Genocide against the Indians of Brazil," report by a group of Brazilian anthropologists presented at the 41st International

Congress of Americanists, Mexico City, September 1974, reprinted in *Supysáua: A Documentary Report of the Conditions of Indian Peoples in Brazil* (Berkeley: Indígena and American Friends of Brazil, 1974).

92 See Ricardo Arnt, Lúcio Flávio Pinto, and Raimundo Pinto, *Panará: A volta dos índios gigantes* (São Paulo: Instituto Socioambiental, 1998); Jean Hébette, ed., *O cerco está se fechando* (Petrópolis: Vozes, 1991); Shelton H. Davis and Robert O. Matthews, *The Geological Imperative: Anthropology and Development in the Amazon Basin of South America* (Cambridge, MA: Anthropology Resource Center, 1976), 25–49; Ramos, *Indigenism*, 201–15.

93 D. Ribeiro, *Os índios e a civilização*, 35–144.

94 Ismael Leitão, "Relatório do Sr. Ismael da Silva Leitão referente a incidentes ocorridos no PI Xavantes," 1970, FUNAI, DOC.

95 Aparecido da Costa to Costa Cavalcanti, 10 April 1970, FUNAI, DOC.

96 See Ranajit Guha, "The Prose of Counter-Insurgency," in *Subaltern Studies 2*, ed. Guha (New Delhi: Oxford University Press, 1983), 1–42.

97 Manoel dos Santos Pinheiro, Chefe da Ajudância Minas-Bahia, to President of FUNAI, Belo Horizonte, 1 June 1970, FUNAI, DOC.

98 See Claudio Romero, "Relatório de Viagem," February 1979, FUNAI, DOC.

99 Costa Cavalcanti, quoted in *Diário de Brasília*, 9 August 1972.

100 José Carlos Alves, encarregado of P. I. Xavante (Couto Magalhães), to the Chief of the 7th Regional Delegacy, Xavantina, 10 October 1971, FUNAI, DOC.

101 On land as a mnemonic device for indigenous historical memory and narrative, see Joanne Rappaport, *The Politics of Memory: Native Historical Interpretation in the Colombian Andes* (Durham, NC: Duke University Press, 1998), 163–67.

102 Agapto Silva to Seventh Regional Delegacy of FUNAI, 6 May 1973, MI, SEDOC, Film 294, Fot 1348–50.

103 Report from post chief at P. I. Xavante (Couto Magalhães) to 7th Delegacia Regional of FUNAI, 20 December 1972, MI, SEDOC, Film 294, Fot 1878–80.

7 The Exiles Return, 1972–1980

1 José Jaime Mancin, FUNAI engineer/surveyor, "Certidões Negativas Expedidas Na Área Indígena Parabubure," Brasília, 6 February 1980, FUNAI, DOC.

2 Clovis Ribeiro Cintra to Orlando de Almeida Albuquerque, chief of staff of the Minister of the Interior, August (?) 1974, FUNAI, DOC.

3 See Flávio Pinto Soares to FUNAI, Barra do Garças, 11 April 1973, FUNAI, DOC.

4 On his trip to the Couto Magalhães post in 1977, FUNAI Regional

Delegate Ivan Baiochi was told by Xavantina's manager, Hélio Stersa, that Loazo received monthly "protection" money from the ranch and had recently requested an increase. See Baiochi, "Relatório de viagem ao Posto Indígena Couto Magalhães," 7 April 1977, FUNAI, DOC. See also A. C. Moura, "Parabubure, a nova reserva Xavante, nasceu do sangue dos índios massacrados," *Boletim do CIMI* 9, no. 61 (Jan.–Feb. 1980): 8.

5   On the Geisel regime, see Alves, *State and Opposition in Military Brazil*, 141–72; and Skidmore, *The Politics of Military Rule in Brazil*, 160–209.

6   For further discussion of POLAMAZÔNIA, see Davis, *Victims of the Miracle*, 112–13.

7   See Hélio Ponce de Arruda, *Os problemas fundiários na estratégia do desenvolvimento e de segurança* (Brasília: Ministério da Agricultura, 1977); and Hecht, "Environment, Development and Politics," 672–73.

8   E. Ferreira, *Posse e propriedade territorial*, 66–68.

9   L. Oliveira, "Colonização e diferenciação," 39.

10   On the modernization of agriculture in the south, the displacement of small farmers and tenants, and the migratory outflow, see Grindle, *State and Countryside*, 73–74. According to INCRA officials, approximately 120,000 people from Rio Grande do Sul left the countryside annually. See Arruda, *Os problemas fundiários*, 12.

11   Norberto Schwantes, *Uma cruz em Terranova* (São Paulo: Scritta Oficina Editorial, 1989), 8–10.

12   Ibid., 43, 87. See also Siqueira, Costa, and Carvalho, *O processo histórico de Mato Grosso*, 133–34.

13   Lopes, "A resistência do índio a extermínio," 57–62.

14   Alceu Mariz, FUNAI anthropologist, "Relatório Sobre Couto Magalhães," Brasília, 14 April 1978, FUNAI, DOC.

15   L. Oliveira, "Colonização e diferenciação," 83, 133.

16   Sereburã et al., *Wamrêmé za'ra-Nossa palavra*, 154.

17   Agapto Silva, post chief of P. I. Xavante, to 7a Delegacia Regional of FUNAI, Xavantina, 6 May 1973, MI, SEDOC, Film 294, Fot 1348–50.

18   Agapto Silva, "Ref. Invasões Terras Situadas entre os rios Couto Magalhães e Culuene," P. I. Xavante, 15 December 1973, FUNAI, DOC.

19   Jamiro Arantes, chief of the Culuene Post, to the 5a Delegacia Regional, 11 February 1976, FUNAI, DOC; José Carlos Alves, post chief at Areões, "Sobre movimento entre fazendeiros em Barra do Garças, visando eliminar funcionários, ex-funcionário e empreiteiro desta fundação," P. I. Areões, 8 November 1975, FUNAI, DOC.

20   5a Delegacia Regional to the Director of the DGO, FUNAI, Cuiabá, 20 December 1973, FUNAI, DOC.

21   Ibid.

22   Arantes to the 5a Delegacia Regional, 11 February 1976, FUNAI, DOC.

23   Valdon Varjão to Ernesto Geisel, Barra do Garças, 28 May 1975, FUNAI, DOC.

24 Senator Saldanha Derzi to FUNAI, 28 April 1975, FUNAI, DOC.

25 On the "Copacabana syndrome," see Stephan Schwartzman, Ana Valéria Araújo, and Paulo Pankarurú, "Brazil: The Legal Battle over Indigenous Land Rights," *NACLA Report on the Americas* 29, no. 5 (Mar.–Apr. 1996): 40.

26 Statistics are from INCRA and the Comissão Pastoral da Terra and cited in E. Ferreira, *Posse e propriedade territorial*, 88.

27 Romildo Carvalho, Luiz Cezar Barrata, and João Oliveira Ribeiro, "Relatório de Viagem da Comissão Mista FUNAI/INCRA, Período de 06 a 16/7/75—Locais: Reserva de São Marcos, Área Xavante de Culuene," Brasília, 18 July 1975, FUNAI, DOC.

28 *O Estado de São Paulo*, 14 October 1975.

29 President of the FUNAI/INCRA Mixed Commission to the FUNAI President, Brasília, 3 November 1975 (Ofício No. 17/Com. FUNAI/INCRA), FUNAI, DOC.

30 Romildo Carvalho et al., "Relatório Final da Comissão Mista FUNAI/INCRA, Relativo aos Seus Trabalhos, Objetivando a Delimitação da Área Indígena dos Xavante do PI Culuene," Brasília, 22 April 1976, FUNAI, DOC.

31 Tardin et al., "Projetos agropecuários da Amazônia," 38–42.

32 Itamar Silveira do Amaral to Seventh Regional Delegacy of FUNAI, 26 June 1973, MI, SEDOC, Film 296, Fot 0057–63.

33 Hecht, "Environment, Development and Politics," 679–80.

34 Schwantes, *Uma cruz em Terranova*, 198–99.

35 Hecht, "Environment, Development and Politics," 679–80.

36 See Brasil, Ministério do Interior, Projeto de Desenvolvimento Integrado da Bacia do Araguaia–Tocantins (PRODIAT), *Diagnóstico da Bacia do Araguaia–Tocantins-I* (Brasília, 1982), 43.

37 Conselho Indigenista Missionário, "A luta dos Xavante em defesa de seus territórios," n.d., Conselho Indigenista Missionário (CIMI), Brasília, BR.MT.XV. 4b/26.

38 Flávio Pinto Soares to FUNAI, Barra do Garças, 11 April 1973, FUNAI, DOC.

39 Sereburã et al., *Wamrêmé za'ra-Nossa palavra*, 157.

40 Müller, quoted in *Veja*, 5 September 1973.

41 For more detailed analysis of the impact of the murders on the Bororo and the Salesian missionaries, see Novaes, *Jogo de espelhos*, 195–96, 221–54. To place Lunkenbein's murder in the context of escalating violence toward Church officials in the mid-1970s, see Scott Mainwaring, *The Catholic Church and Politics in Brazil, 1916–1985* (Stanford: Stanford University Press, 1986), 155. For the landowners' rendition, see José Mario Guedes Miguez, *Chacina do Meruri: A Verdade dos Fatos* (São Paulo: Editora A Gazeta Maçônica, 1980).

42 A. Almeida, "O intransitivo da transição," 272. See also Maria Cristina

Vannuchi Leme and Vânia Mara de Araújo Pietrafesa, *Assassinatos no campo: Crime e impunidade, 1964–86* (São Paulo: Global Ed., 1987).

43 Manuel Pereira Brito, president of city council of Barra do Garças, to José Fragelli, governor of Mato Grosso, October 1973, FUNAI, DOC.

44 7a Delegacia Regional to FUNAI Director of General Operations (DGO), Goiânia, 16 October 1973, FUNAI, DOC; *Folha de São Paulo*, 27 June 1975.

45 See Flowers, "Forager-Farmers: The Xavante Indians of Central Brazil," 259, 306–9; and Laura Graham, *Performing Dreams*, 37.

46 CIMI, "Pimentel Barbosa," Brasília, 17 January 1979, CIMI, BR.MT.XV. 4b/27.

47 *Jornal do Brasil*, 30 August 1973.

48 Amaral to 7a Delegacia Regional, 26 June 1973, MI, SEDOC, Film 296, Fot 0057–63; emphasis in original.

49 Claudio Romero, FUNAI anthropologist, "Relatório sobre a situação das reservas indígenas xavante," Brasília, n.d., PETI, FNA 0211.

50 Skidmore, *The Politics of Military Rule in Brazil*, 122–23.

51 See Palmério Dória, Sérgio Buarque, Vicente Carelli, and Jaime Sautchuk, *A guerrilha do Araguaia* (São Paulo: Alfa-Omega, 1979), 18; and Alves, *State and Opposition in Military Brazil*, 122.

52 J. Martins, "The State and the Militarization of the Agrarian Question in Brazil," 480–81.

53 See Schmink and Wood, *Contested Frontiers in Amazonia*, 72–73; and Houtzager, "State and Unions in the Transformation of the Brazilian Countryside," 117–18.

54 Fernando Schiavini de Castro et al., "Enfoque Situacional da Fundação Nacional do Índio no Município de Barra do Garças-MT," Barra do Garças, n.d., ISA, COD XVD04.

55 Romero, "Relatório sobre a Situação das Reservas Indígenas Xavante," Brasília, n.d., PETI, FNA 0211.

56 Celestino Tsererob'o (translated by Werehite), quoted in *Boletim do CIMI* 6, no. 43 (Dec. 1977): 75.

57 Babatti, quoted in ibid., 31.

58 Letter from Mario Seara, administrator of Fazenda Xavantina, to Moacir Couto, Polícia Militar, Barra do Garças, 23 January 1979, FUNAI, DOC; Daniel Macedo et al., "Relação das Benfeitorias Existentes na Área das 03 Empresas Rurais: Fazenda Xavantina S/A, Fazenda Estrela D'Oeste S/A e Fazenda Capim Branco," Barra do Garças, 16 March 1980 (FUNAI/BSB/ 3816/81-vol. 15), FUNAI, DOC.

59 Murilo Carvalho, *Sangue da terra* (São Paulo: Ed. Brasil Debates, 1980), 100.

60 Celestino Tsererob'o, quoted in Moura, "Parabubure, a nova reserva Xavante," 5.

61 Tserede (Cirilo), quoted in *Boletim do CIMI* 6 no. 43 (Dec. 1977): 79.

62 D. Maybury-Lewis found that Xavante were provoked to vociferous demonstrations of grief even years after the death of a relative. See *Akwē-Shavante Society*, 281–82.

63 See Laura Graham, *Performing Dreams*, 164.

64 Rappaport, *The Politics of Memory*, 9.

65 Rappaport, *Cumbe Reborn*, 125.

66 See Laura Graham, *Performing Dreams*, 9.

67 See Gould, *To Die This Way*, 228–66; Rappaport, *Cumbe Reborn*, 143–44.

68 Cirilo, quoted in *Boletim do CIMI* 6, no. 43 (Dec. 1977): 19.

69 Aniceto Tsudzawéré, chief of the village of São Marcos, "Palavra que nós xavante vai (sic) falar para Ministro Andreazza," Brasília, 16 March 1979, CIMI, BR.MT.XV. 1e/9. See also *Estado de São Paulo*, 17 March 1979.

70 Álvaro Pereira and Armando Rollemberg, "Entrevista: Dzururan (Mario), Cacique/Em Busca da Sobrevivência," *Veja*, 20 November 1974.

71 Quoted in Sue Branford and Oriel Glock, *The Last Frontier: Fighting over Land in the Amazon* (London: Zed Books, 1985), 196.

72 Ismarth de Araújo Oliveira to Clovis Ribeiro Cintra, Brasília, 31 May 1978, FUNAI, DOC.

73 Landowners provided "incentives" to various indigenous leaders according to Francisco de Campos Figueiredo, chief of the Couto Magalhães Post, "Relatório enfocando as atividades de Francisco de Campos Figueiredo do Projeto Xavante," 30 May 1980, FUNAI, DOC.

74 Alves, *State and Opposition in Military Brazil*, 254.

75 Skidmore, *The Politics of Military Rule in Brazil*, 160–209.

76 See Alves, *State and Opposition in Military Brazil*, 153–72.

77 Hagopian, *Traditional Politics and Regime Change in Brazil*, 150.

78 Schwantes, *Uma cruz em Terranova*, 143–44; L. Oliveira, "Colonização e diferenciação," 46.

79 Alves, *State and Opposition in Military Brazil*, 174.

80 On rural unionization under the military, see B. Maybury-Lewis, *The Politics of the Possible*.

81 Alfred Stepan, ed., *Democratizing Brazil: Problems of Transition and Consolidation* (New York: Oxford University Press, 1989), xii.

82 For a more comprehensive analysis of the Church's evolving role in the Brazilian Amazon and on behalf of indigenous rights, see Mainwaring, *The Catholic Church and Politics in Brazil*, 84–94; M. Gomes, *Os índios e o Brasil*, 195; Paulo Suess, *A causa indígena na caminhada e a proposta do CIMI: 1972–1989* (Petrópolis: Vozes, 1989); Ralph Della Cava, "The 'People's' Church, the Vatican, and *Abertura*," in *Democratizing Brazil*, ed. A. Stepan, 147.

83 Babatti, quoted in *Boletim do CIMI* 6, no. 43 (Dec. 1977): 24.

84 D. Maybury-Lewis, *Akwē-Shavante Society*, 169–73.

85 The Declaration of Barbados for the Liberation of the Indian is reprinted in W. Dostal, ed., *The Situation of the Indian in South America* (Geneva, Switzerland: World Council of Churches, 1972), 376–81.

86 See Suess, *A causa indígena na caminhada*, 11–16.

87 Ibid., 31.

88 "Y-Juca-Pirama" is reprinted in *Supysáua: A Documentary Report on the Conditions of Indian Peoples in Brazil.*

89 See Skidmore, *The Politics of Military Rule*, 181.

90 See Flowers, "Forager-Farmers," 256–57.

91 For a reprinting of the "Diretório da Missão Salesiana de Mato Grosso para a Atividade Missionária Junto as Populações Indígenas," see C. Menezes, "Missionários e índios em Mato Grosso," 630–36. For further discussion of cleavages within CIMI, see Mário Fioravanti, "Índio-CIMI ou CIMI-Índio?: A razão crítica de uma 'nova' perspectiva interétnica e missionária" (Master's thesis, Pontifícia Universidade Católica, São Paulo, 1990).

92 CIMI, "Nota do CIMI a Opinião Pública," Brasília, 21 December 1979, CIMI, BR.MT.XV. 6a/8.

93 For a discussion of Brazilian Church-based and nongovernmental organizations that have emerged as advocates of indigenous rights over the past two and a half decades, see Operação Anchieta, *Ação indigenista como ação política* (Cuiabá: OPAN, 1987).

94 For further discussion, see Greg Urban, "Developments in the Situation of Brazilian Tribal Populations from 1976 to 1982," *Latin American Research Review* 20, no. 1 (1985): 7–25.

95 See Ramos, *Indigenism*, 243–48, and Cunha, *Os direitos do índio*, 93. Recent research suggests that the military's call for indigenous emancipation entailed more bark than bite. Throughout the controversy, FUNAI displayed concerted interest in the reservation of Indian lands: in 1976, the agency instituted a Permanent Work Group for Land Affairs, and in 1978, FUNAI issued norms for delimiting indigenous areas. See João Pacheco de Oliveira Filho and Alfredo Wagner Berno de Almeida, "Demarcação e reafirmação étnica: Um ensaio sobre a FUNAI," in *Os poderes e as terras dos índios*, ed. Oliveira Filho, 51–52.

96 See *Jornal do Brasil*, 20 December 1978.

97 Petition excerpted in *Folha de São Paulo*, 21 December 1979.

98 Seara to Couto, 23 January 1979, FUNAI, DOC.

99 Romero, "Relatório de Viagem," February 1979, FUNAI, DOC.

100 Claudio Romero, "Relatório de Viagem," Brasília, February 1979, FUNAI, DOC.

101 Ibid.

102 Taped testimony of Claudio Romero, Brasília, 1980. Copy in author's possession.

103 See A. Almeida, "O intransitivo da transição," 262.

104 Mario Seara to Odenir Pinto de Oliveira, Barra do Garças, 10 April 1979, FUNAI, DOC.

105 Seara to Oliveira, Barra do Garças, 10 May 1979, FUNAI, DOC.

106 Seara to FUNAI Ajudância Autônoma de Barra do Garças (AJABAG), Barra do Garças, 7 June 1979, FUNAI, DOC.

107 Seara to AJABAG, Barra do Garças, 15 June 1979, FUNAI, DOC.

108 Odenir Pinto de Oliveira to Seara, Barra do Garças, 30 July 1979, FUNAI, DOC.

109 Pinto de Oliveira to President of FUNAI, 15 June 1979, FUNAI, DOC.

110 Francisco de Campos Figueiredo, head of P. I. Couto Magalhães, to Chief of AJABAG, Couto Magalhães, 2 July 1979, FUNAI, DOC.

111 *Estado de São Paulo*, 7 January 1979.

112 Schmink and Wood, *Contested Frontiers in Amazonia*, 80.

113 Valter Ferreira Mendes to the Director of the Departamento Geral de Patrimônio Indígena of FUNAI, Brasília, 13 June 1979, FUNAI, DOC.

114 "Regularização Fundiária das Terras da Reserva Indígena Parabubure nos Termos das Orientações Aprovadas pela Exposição de Motivos No. MINTER-MA-MF-SG-CSN/002 de 16/06/80," vol. 1, folhas 40–46, FUNAI, DOC.

115 *Folha de São Paulo*, 20 December 1979.

116 Seara to AJABAG, Barra do Garças, 20 December 1979, FUNAI, DOC.

117 "Regularização Fundiária das Terras da Reserva Indígena Parabubure," FUNAI, DOC.

118 D. Cabrera, Executor of the PF of Vale do Araguaia to Claudio José Ribeiro, INCRA, Barra do Garças, 22 August 1980, FUNAI, DOC; INCRA, "Relação dos Posseiros da Reserva Indígena Parabubure—Área Aproximada de Culturas," Barra do Garças, 23 April 1980, FUNAI, DOC.

119 *Jornal de Brasília*, 1 July 1980.

120 Macedo et al., "Relação das Benfeitorias Existentes na Área Das 03 Empresas Rurais," Barra do Garças, 16 March 1980 (FUNAI/BSB/3816/81-vol. 15), FUNAI, DOC. (The three properties had at one time all been part of Fazenda Xavantina and remained under the same ownership.)

121 I have borrowed here from Rappaport, *Cumbe Reborn*, 83.

122 Interview with Carlos Dumhiwe, Parabubure village, Parabubure Indigenous Reserve, July 1994.

123 On the Kayapó, see Turner, "Representing, Resisting, Rethinking," 285–313; Schmink and Wood, *Contested Frontiers in Amazonia*, 253–75.

124 Foweraker, *The Struggle for Land*, 24–25.

125 For a similar case, see Anthony Hall's brief discussion of the direct action taken by the Gavião and Apinayé Indians in the 1980s—obstruction of rail and road traffic, occupation of FUNAI offices—to pressure the state to remove invaders: *Developing Amazonia: Deforestation and Social Con-*

flict in Brazil's Carajás Programme (Manchester, England: Manchester University Press, 1989), 222–25.

126 Alves, *State and Opposition in Military Brazil*, 255.

127 Interview with Carlos Dumhiwe, Parabubure village, Parabubure Indigenous Reserve, July 1994.

128 Interview with Renato Tsiwaradza, Parabubure village, Parabubure Indigenous Reserve, July 1994.

8 The Xavante Project, 1978–1988

1 The comments made by Tsorompré were recalled by Claudio Romero in a discussion with FUNAI officials. Taped meeting of FUNAI officials, Brasília, 9 May 1980 in the possession of Arthur Wollman, INCRA, Brasília.

2 *Folha de São Paulo*, 17 March 1980.

3 "A respeito do jornal *O pioneiro*, da Nova Xavantina . . . ", manifesto signed by fifteen Xavante caciques and delivered to Colonel João Nobre da Veiga, President of FUNAI, São Marcos, 6 March 1980, ISA, XVD03. See also *Jornal de Brasília*, 13 March 1980.

4 Fernando Schiavini de Castro, "Relatório Geral Referente ao Projeto Xavante Posto Indígena Pimentel Barbosa—AJABAG," P. I. Pimentel Barbosa, 28 May 1980, FUNAI, DOC.

5 FUNAI, Assessoria de Planejamento e Coordenação, "Programa de Desenvolvimento para a Nação Xavante," 1978, FUNAI, DOC.

6 See Scott, *Seeing Like a State*, 3–6, 262–306.

7 See Hagopian, *Traditional Politics and Regime Change in Brazil*, 151–61.

8 Claudio Romero to the Director of the DGO, Brasília, November 1978, FUNAI, DOC.

9 See Hagopian, *Traditional Politics and Regime Change in Brazil*, 140–77.

10 On military rule and democratic transition, see ibid; Juan J. Linz and Alfred Stepan, *Problems of Democratic Transition and Consolidation* (Baltimore: Johns Hopkins University Press, 1996), 150–230; Stepan, *Democratizing Brazil*. For Laura Graham's discussion of the Xavante Project, see *Performing Dreams*, 44–63.

11 See, for example, Alves, *State and Opposition in Military Brazil*; Sonia Alvarez, *Engendering Democracy in Brazil* (Princeton, NJ: Princeton University Press, 1990); and Juan E. Corradi, Patricia Weiss Fagen, and Manuel Antonio Garretón, eds., *Fear at the Edge: State Terror and Resistance in Latin America* (Berkeley: University of California Press, 1992). On the "new social movements" as but one contender in a contested field of political projects and ideological alternatives, see John Burdick, "Rethinking the Study of Social Movements: The Case of Christian Base Commu-

nities in Urban Brazil," in *The Making of Social Movements in Latin America*, ed. Arturo Escobar and Sonia E. Alvarez (Boulder, CO: Westview Press, 1992), 171–84. On the varied responses of rural workers to military government initiatives, see B. Maybury-Lewis, *The Politics of the Possible.*

12   On the military's big development projects, see Ben Ross Schneider, *Politics within the State: Elite Bureaucrats and Industrial Policy in Brazil* (Pittsburgh: University of Pittsburgh Press, 1991).

13   See Safira Bezerra Ammann, *Ideologia do desenvolvimento de comunidade no Brasil* (São Paulo: Cortez Ed., 1987).

14   Speech by Maurício Rangel Reis, reprinted in Brasil, Ministério do Interior, *Política indigenista—Governo do Presidente Ernesto Geisel* (Brasília, 1974).

15   George de Carqueira Leite Zarur, "Ação indigenista e antropologia aplicada," in FUNAI, *Política e ação indigenista brasileira* (Brasília, 1975), 26.

16   Personal communication from Aracy Lopes da Silva, July 1993.

17   On the difficulty of transporting goods to market, see David da Rocha, "Relatório," P. I. Areões, 11 October 1976, FUNAI, DOC.

18   L. Oliveira, "Colonização e diferenciação," 278–79.

19   Ivan Baiochi, "Relatório final sobre o projeto Areões que Ivan Baiochi, Delegado da 7a DR submete ao superior julgamento do DGO," 25 October 1977, FUNAI, DOC; João Carlos Alves, Post Chief at Areões, "Relatório," 29 October 1975, FUNAI, DOC.

20   Claudio Romero to Director of the DGO of FUNAI, Brasília, November 1978, FUNAI, DOC.

21   Brasil, Congresso Nacional, Câmara dos Deputados, *Diário do Congresso Nacional: Projeto de Resolução No. 172, de 1978* (Comissão Parlamentar de Inquérito—Reservas Indígenas), Brasília, 17 June 1978, 15.

22   FUNAI, Assessoria de Planejamento e Coordenação (ASPLAN), "Plano de desenvolvimento para a Nação Xavante," 1978, FUNAI, DOC.

23   See Flowers, "Forager-Farmers," 312.

24   See Fernando Schiavini de Castro, "Relatório Geral de Atividades—Exercício de 1979—Pimentel Barbosa—AJABAG," n.d., FUNAI, DOC.

25   Aniceto, quoted in *O Estado de Mato Grosso*, 20 April 1980.

26   Lopes da Silva, "Dois séculos e meio de história Xavante," 377.

27   Claudia Menezes, "Os Xavante e o movimento de fronteira no leste mato-grossense," *Revista de antropologia* 25 (1982): 81–82.

28   *Jornal do Comércio*, 2 April 1981.

29   FUNAI, Diretoria de Assistência (DAI), "Projeto Integrado da Área Xavante-MT," n.d., FUNAI, DOC; FUNAI, ASPLAN, "Atuação da FUNAI na Área Xavante," 1986, FUNAI, DOC.

30   For more detail, see Laura Graham, *Performing Dreams*, 44–47.

31   João Paulo Botelho Vieira Filho, "Problemas da aculturação alimentar dos Xavantes e Bororo," *Revista de antropologia* 24 (1981): 37–39.

32 *Correio Braziliense*, 6 May 1980.

33 Alves, "Relatório," February 1976, FUNAI, DOC.

34 See Francisco dos Santos Magalhães, "Relatório de Ocorrência em 17-10-81," n.d., FUNAI, DOC; and Luis Carlos Mattos Rodrigues, "Relatório Analítico do 3° e 4° Trimestre/82, Referente Implantação do Projeto Agrícola Xavante/Bororo," n.d., FUNAI, DOC. For further discussion of intervillage rivalry, see Seth Garfield, "'Civilized' but Discontent: The Xavante Indians and Government Policy in Brazil, 1937–1988" (Ph.D. diss., Yale University, 1996), chap. 9.

35 Magalhães, "Relatório de Ocorrência em 17–10–81," n.d. FUNAI, DOC.

36 FUNAI Departamento Geral de Operações (DGO), "Projeto de Idelva Nadir Kern e Lucia Magaly Ramos Sendeski referente ao curso de treinamento de monitores bilíngües xavante para o ano de 1982," n.d., FUNAI, DOC.

37 Luiz Otávio Pinheiro da Cunha, "Criação de Nova Aldeia Xavante na Reserva Parabubure," Aragarças, 24 May 1983, FUNAI, DOC.

38 Laura Graham, *Performing Dreams*, 9.

39 José Carlos Alves, 7a Delegacia Regional of FUNAI, to Director of DGO, "Relatório de viagem de Emi de Paula e Souza," 16 March 1983, FUNAI, DOC.

40 Castro, "Relatório Geral de Atividades—Exercício de 1979," FUNAI, DOC.

41 I have borrowed here from Marisol de la Cadena, "Women Are More Indian: Gender and Ethnicity in Cuzco," in *Ethnicity, Markets and Migration in the Andes: At the Crossroads of History and Anthropology*, ed. Brooke Larson, Olivia Harris, and Enrique Tandeter (Durham, NC: Duke University Press, 1995), 329–48.

42 Odenir Pinto de Oliveira to Diretor do DGO, Barra do Garças, 16 April 1979, FUNAI, DOC.

43 Castro, "Relatório Geral de Atividades—Exercício de 1979," FUNAI, DOC.

44 Izanoel Sodré, "Relatório sobre a situação do Projeto Xavante na Área do P. I. Culuene," Barra do Garças, 26 May 1980, FUNAI, DOC.

45 Castro, "Relatório Geral de Atividades—Exercício de 1979," FUNAI, DOC.

46 Personal Communication from Odenir Pinto de Oliveira, May 1994.

47 Centro Ecumênico de Documentação e Informação (CEDI), *Aconteceu Especial: Povos Indígenas no Brasil 1980* (São Paulo: Ed. Sagarana, 1981), 18.

48 Ibid., 19.

49 Suzanne Williams, "Land Rights and the Manipulation of Identity: Official Indian Policy in Brazil" *Journal of Latin American Studies* 15 (1983): 154–55. See also the scathing attack on FUNAI by Mato Grosso's Secretary of Justice Domingos Sávio Brandão, quoted in *Correio Braziliense*, 1 May 1980.

50 See Ramos, *Indigenism*, 249–52.

51 *Jornal do Brasil*, 6 May 1960.

52 Ibid.

53 "Nós, CACIQUES e representantes da TRIBO XAVANTE, queremos apresentar ao Senhor o seguinte," letter to Minister of the Interior Mario David Andreazza signed by nine Xavante caciques, Brasília, 6 May 1980, ISA, XVD11; emphasis in original. See also *Correio Braziliense*, 8 May 1980.

54 Statement by unnamed government official from taped meeting involving FUNAI leadership, Brasília, 9 May 1980, in the possession of Arturo Wollman, INCRA, Brasília.

55 See *Jornal de Brasília*, 9 May 1980; and *O Estado de São Paulo*, 11 May 1980.

56 CEDI, *Aconteceu especial: Povos indígenas no Brasil*, 1980, 38–39; for further analysis, see Ramos, *Indigenism*, 168–94.

57 For a penetrating analysis of the Juruna controversy, see Ramos, *Indigenism*, 104–18.

58 Afonso Ligório Pires de Carvalho, "Juruna, o índio que aprisiona a memória dos brancos," *Revista da atualidade indígena* 2, no. 9 (Mar.–Apr. 1978): 9–11.

59 For further background on the Juruna contoroversy, with a highly romanticized portrayal of the Xavante leader, see Mario Juruna, Antônio Hohlfeldt, and Assis Hoffmann, *O gravador do Juruna* (Porto Alegre: Mercado Alberto, 1982). On the symbolism of Juruna, see Beth A. Conklin and Laura R. Graham, "The Shifting Middle Ground: Amazonian Indians and Eco-Politics," *American Anthropologist* 97 (1995): 699.

60 *Jornal de Brasília*, 12 April 1980.

61 "Os últimos conflitos entre os Xavante e a direção da Fundação Nacional do Índio . . . ", manifesto signed by the Sociedade Brasileira de Indigenistas (SBI), Conselho Indigenista Missionário (CIMI), Centro de Trabalho Indigenista (CTI), Associação Nacional de Apoio ao Índio (ANAI), Comissão Pro-Índio-São Paulo, n.d., CIMI, BR.MT.XV.6b/7.

62 *Correio Braziliense*, 9 May 1980.

63 Francisco de Campos Figueiredo, "Relatório enfocando as atividades do indigenista Francisco de Campos Figueiredo no Projeto Xavante," P. I. Couto Magalhães, 30 May 1980, FUNAI, DOC.

64 S. Williams, "Land Rights and the Manipulation of Identity," 158.

65 The Xavante case was far from isolated. Nobre da Veiga, for example, would pay off the Tupiniquim in Espírito Santo to silence their demand for land seized by a cellulose company. See S. Williams, "Land Rights and the Manipulation of Identity," 153.

66 See Hagopian, *Traditional Politics and Regime Change in Brazil*, 152–55.

67 Izanoél dos Santos Sodré, "Relatório sobre a Atuação do Projeto Xavante na Área do P. I. Culuene," Barra do Garças, 26 May 1980, FUNAI, DOC.

68 Ibid.

69 Magalhães, "Relatório de Ocorrência em 17–10–81," n.d., FUNAI, DOC.

70   Antônio Vicente et al., "Da Comissão de Serviço Comunicação No. 114/81 de 09/04/81 ao Senhor Chefe da Ajudância Autônoma de Barra do Garças, MT," Barra do Garças, 27 April 1981, FUNAI, DOC.

71   Sodré, "Relatório sobre a Atuação do Projeto Xavante," 26 May 1980, FUNAI, DOC.

72   Letter from the Sociedade Brasileira de Indigenistas to Minister of the Interior, Brasília, 16 June 1980, personal archive of Odenir Pinto de Oliveira, Brasília. For further discussion on the shakeup in FUNAI, see M. Gomes, *Os índios e o Brasil*, 200–202.

73   See Schneider, *Politics within the State*, 89.

74   CEDI, *Aconteceu Especial: Povos Indígenas no Brasil, 1980*, 20.

75   CEDI, *Povos Indígenas no Brasil-1985/1986* (São Paulo: CEDI, 1987), 27–28.

76   CEDI, *Aconteceu* (1981), 14.

77   For discussion of the fissioning of Xavante villages over the course of the 1980s, see Laura Graham, *Performing Dreams*, 50–55.

78   Sodré, "Relatório sobre a Atuação do Projeto Xavante," FUNAI, DOC.

79   Izanoél Sodré, "Relatório de indigenista Izanoél Sodré sobre a viagem a São Marcos em cumprimento a comunicação de serviço No. 182/80/AJABAG, 13/10/80," Barra do Garças, 20 October 1980, FUNAI, DOC.

80   Ibid.

81   Dilce Claudino da Silva, "Relatório da Reunião," Barra do Garças, 14 August 1980, FUNAI, DOC. In August 1983, under the administration of Octávio Ferreira Lima, FUNAI canceled the practice of issuing formal credentials to indigenous leaders, stating that this was an internal matter for indigenous communities. See FUNAI, Atos da Presidência, "Portaria no 835," 1 August 1983, FUNAI, DOC.

82   Rodolfo Valentini, head of AJABAG, to José Antônio Silveira, Barra do Garças, 13 April 1981, FUNAI, DOC.

83   Rodolpho Valentini to Director of DGO/FUNAI, Barra do Garças, 29 October 1980, FUNAI, DOC.

84   Luiz Otávio Pinheiro da Cunha, "Sobre a 'Aldeia' Buriti Alegre," Aragarças, 2 September 1983, FUNAI, DOC.

85   Anael Gonçalves, "Ajudância de Barra do Garças Situação Geral, período de 08 a 17/out/80," Brasília, 20 October 1980, FUNAI, DOC.

86   Dilce Claudino da Silva Lisowski, "Relatório de reunião"; and Father Gino Favaro, Director of Colônia Indígena S. Marcos, to Otávio Ferreira Lima, FUNAI President, São Marcos, 11 July 1983, FUNAI, DOC.

87   Cunha, "Criação de Nova Aldeia Xavante na Reserva Parabubure," Aragarças, 24 May 1983, FUNAI, DOC.

88   José Carlos Alves to Director of DGO, Aragarças, 6 October 1983, FUNAI, DOC.

89   S. Williams, "Land Rights and the Manipulation of Identity," 157.

90   Ortner, "Resistance and the Problem of Ethnographic Refusal," 175.

91 See Comaroff and Comaroff, *Ethnography and the Historical Imagination*, 58.

92 "Xavantaço ou Funailaço?," in CEDI, *Povos Indígenas do Brasil–1985/1986*, 344–45.

93 On the jockeying by interest groups to secure loyal appointees to state enterprise management, see Schneider, *Politics within the State*, 85.

94 Celestino, quoted in Carlos Dumhiwe, "Nota para Imprensa," n.d., CIMI, BR.MT.XV.1e/44.

95 "Xavantaço ou Funailaço?" 344–45.

96 *Jornal de Brasília*, 23 May 1985.

97 José Carlos Barbosa, Delegado da 7a DR, "Declaração do Delegado—Ministério do Interior, Fundação Nacional do Índio, 7a DR," reprinted in "Xavantaço ou Funailaço?" 347.

98 Laura Graham, "Uma aldeia por um 'projeto,'" in CEDI, *Povos Indígenas no Brasil—1985/1986*, 348–50; and Laura Graham, *Performing Dreams*, 57–58.

99 Tribunal das Contas da União, "Relatório e voto do Ministro Adhemar Ghisi, cujas conclusões form acolhidas pelo Tribunal, na Sessão Extraordinária realizada em 30 de julho de 1987, ao deliberar, conforme figura no contexto desta Ata, sobre as contas da Fundação Nacional do Índio-FUNAI, exercícios de 1983 (Proc. no. 020 276/84-2), 1984 (Proc. no. 016 950/85-2) e 1985 (Proc. no. 010 028/86-2), examinadas em conjunto com processos de denúncia (Procs. nos. 006 262/84-9 e 013 437/84-4) e com os resultados de Inspeção Extraordinária *in loco* (Proc. 018 683/85-1)," *Diário Oficial*, Seção 1 (20 August 1987): 13273–78.

100 Laura Graham, *Performing Dreams*, 57.

101 Gilberto Dupas, "Competitive Integration and Recovery of Growth," in *Brazil and the Challenge of Economic Reform*, ed. Werner Baer and Joseph C. Tulchin (Washington, DC: Woodrow Wilson Center, 1993), 9–30.

102 Laura Graham, "Uma aldeia por um 'projeto,'" 348–50.

103 *Correio Braziliense*, 15 April 1986.

104 Laura Graham, *Performing Dreams*, 59–61.

105 FUNAI, "Xavantes: Os Índios privilegiados têm 'lobby' para presidir a FUNAI," n.d., FUNAI, DOC.

106 "Ao Excelentíssimo Senhor Presidente da Republica Fed. do Brasil, Dr. José Sarney," letter signed by Xavante chiefs from various reservations, Brasília, 7 September 1987, CEDI, BR.MT.XV.6b10.

107 Laura Graham, *Performing Dreams*, 61.

108 Ibid., 61–63.

109 Chatterjee, *The Nation and Its Fragments*, 207–8.

110 See Simon Schwartzman, *Bases do autoritarismo brasileiro*, 2d ed. (Rio de Janeiro: Editora Campus, 1982), 23.

Conclusion

1   "Aos Excelentíssimos Deputados e Senadores," letter from Cosme Constantino Waioré and Aniceto Tsudazawéré to members of the Constituent Assembly, Brasília, 26 January 1987, CEDI, BR.MT.XV.1e/11.

2   On indigenous rights in the 1988 Constitution, see Sílvio Coelho dos Santos, *Os povos indígenas e a Constituinte* (Florianópolis: Universidade Federal de Santa Catarina/Movimento, 1989), 69–71; and Elizabeth Allen, "Brazil: Indians and the New Constitution," *Third World Quarterly* 10, no. 4 (1989): 148–65.

3   See Hunter, *Eroding Military Influence in Brazil*, 126–27.

4   See the discussion in Geoffrey O'Connor, *Amazon Journal: Dispatches from a Vanishing Frontier* (New York: Penguin, 1998), 297–306.

5   On the strategic, and problematic, alliance between Brazilian Indians and environmentalists, see Conklin and Graham, "The Shifting Middle Ground," 695–710; and Alison Brysk, "Acting Globally: Indian Rights and International Politics in Latin America," in *Indigenous Peoples and Democracy in Latin America*, ed. Donna Lee Van Cott (New York: St. Martin's Press, 1994), 29–54.

6   Organização Internacional do Trabalho, *Convenção (169) sobre Povos Indígenas e Tribais em Países Independentes e Resolução sobre a Ação da OIT concernante aos Povos Indígenas e Tribais* (Brasília: n.p., 1992). Brazil abstained from voting on Convention 169, objecting to its concession to Indians the rights to ownership rather than permanent possession of their lands. For further discussion, see Enio Cordeiro, "Política indigenista brasileira e promoção internacional dos direitos das populações indígenas," manuscript (Brasília: Ministério das Relações Exteriores, 1993), 100–19.

7   See Ramos, *Indigenism*, 257.

8   Santos, *Os povos indígenas e a constituinte*, 46–47.

9   See Hagopian, *Traditional Politics and Regime Change in Brazil*, 211–52.

10 See Ferraz and Mampieri, "Suiá-Missu: Um mito refeito," 75–84.

11 Schwartzman, Araújo, and Pankararú, "Brazil: The Legal Battle over Indigenous Land Rights," 40.

12 For an argument stressing the relative unimportance of regime change, see Foweraker, *The Struggle for Land*, 12. For a critique of Marxist reductionism, see Skocpol, "Bringing the State Back In," 25.

13 Jaguaribe, quoted in Ramos, *Indigenism*, 189.

14 See, among others, Mallon, *Peasant and Nation*; Thurner, *From Two Republics to One Divided*; Rappaport, *Cumbe Reborn*; and Cecilia Méndez, "Incas Sí, Indios No: Notes on Peruvian Creole Nationalism and Its Contemporary Crisis," *Journal of Latin American Studies* 28 (1996): 197–225.

15 The literature on the Kayapó is already rather abundant. See, among oth-

ers, Turner, "Representing, Resisting, Rethinking"; Schmink and Wood, *Contested Frontiers in Amazonia*; and Linda Rabben, *Unnatural Selection: The Yanomami, the Kayapó and the Onslaught of Civilisation* (Seattle: University of Washington Press, 1998).

16 Schwartzman, Araújo, and Pankararú, "Brazil: The Legal Battle over Indigenous Rights," 39.

17 See Conklin and Graham, "The Shifting Middle Ground," and Ramos, *Indigenism*, 267–83.

18 See Margaret E. Keck, "Sustainable Development and Environmental Politics in Latin America," in *Redefining the State in Latin America*, ed. Colin I. Bradford Jr. (Paris: OECD, 1994), 91–107.

19 Manuel Antonio Garretón, "New State-Society Relations in Latin America," in *Redefining the State in Latin America*, ed. Bradford, 244.

20 For a penetrating critique of political decentralization as the panacea for improved social services, see Judith Tendler, *Good Government in the Tropics* (Baltimore: Johns Hopkins University Press, 1997), 142–50.

21 Merilee S. Grindle, *Challenging the State: Crisis and Innovation in Latin America and Africa* (Cambridge, England: Cambridge University Press, 1996), 5.

22 Tendler, *Good Government in the Tropics*, 13–20; 42–45.

23 Keck, "Sustainable Development and Environmental Politics in Latin America," 106.

24 Garretón, "New State-Society Relations in Latin America," 247.

25 Grindle, *Challenging the State*, 7.

Bibliography

Archives

Public Archives

Arquivo Nacional (AN), Rio de Janeiro. Fundo Secretaria da Presidência da República (SPE).
Fundação Nacional do Índio (FUNAI), Brasília. Departamento de Documentação (DOC).
Museu do Índio (MI), Rio de Janeiro. Setor de Documentação (SEDOC).

Nongovernmental Organization Archives

Instituto Socioambiental (ISA), São Paulo.
Conselho Indigenista Missionário (CIMI), Brasília.
Projeto Estudo sobre Terras Indígenas no Brasil (PETI), Rio de Janeiro.

Private Archives

Archive of Ismael Leitão, Goiânia.
Archive of Odenir Pinto de Oliveira, Brasília.

Interviews

Cunha, Luis Otávio Pinheiro da. Brasília, D.F., May 1994.
Dumhiwe, Carlos. Parabubure Indigenous Reserve, Mato Grosso, July, 1994.
Gomes, João. Nova Xavantina, Mato Grosso, July 1994.
Leitão, Ismael. Goiânia, Goiás, August 1994.
Mattos, Jaime. Brasília, D.F., May 1994.
Oliveira, Odenir Pinto de. Brasília, D.F., May 1994.
Romero, Claudio. Brasília, D.F., May 1994.
Tsiwaradza, Renato. Parabubure Indigenous Reserve, Mato Grosso, July 1994.

Periodicals

Amazônia (São Paulo); *Boletim do CIMI* (Brasília); *Boletim Salesiano* (São
Paulo); *Brasil-Oeste* (São Paulo); *Correio Braziliense* (Brasília); *Correio da
Fronteira* (Barra do Garças); *Correio da Manhã* (Rio de Janeiro); *O Dia* (Rio
de Janeiro); *Diário Carioca* (Rio de Janeiro); *Diário de Brasília* (Brasília);
Diário de Cuiabá (Cuiabá); *Diário de São Paulo* (São Paulo); *O Estado de
Mato Grosso* (Cuiabá); *O Estado de São Paulo* (São Paulo); *A Folha da
Manhã* (São Paulo); *A Folha de Goiás* (Goiânia); *A Folha de São Paulo* (São
Paulo); *Gazeta* (Barra do Garças); *Gazeta de Notícias* (Rio de Janeiro); *A
Gazeta de São Paulo* (São Paulo); *O Globo* (Rio de Janeiro); *O Índio do Brasil*
(Belém); *O Jornal* (Rio de Janeiro); *Jornal de Brasília* (Brasília); *A Manhã*
(Rio de Janeiro); *A Noite* (Rio de Janeiro); *A Notícia* (Rio de Janeiro); *O Radi-
cal* (Rio de Janeiro); *Revista Agroeste* (Barra do Garças); *Tribuna da Imprensa*
(Rio de Janeiro); *Última Hora* (Rio de Janeiro); *Veja* (Rio de Janeiro)

Public Documents

Brasil. Congresso Nacional. Câmara dos Deputados. *Diário do Congresso
Nacional: Projeto de Resolução No. 172, de 1978 (CPI–Reservas Indígenas)*.
Brasília, 17 June 1978.
———. Congresso Nacional. Câmara dos Deputados. *Relatório da CPI-
Resoluções 1–10*. Brasília, 1963.
———. Departamento Administrativo do Serviço Público. *Revista do Serviço
Publico*. 1939–1943.
———. Departamento de Imprensa e Propaganda. *Rumo ao Oeste*. Casa
Almeida Marques, n.d.
———. Instituto Nacional de Colonização e Reforma Agrária. Sistema de Cad-
astro Rural. *Recadastramento, 1972*.
———. Ministério da Agricultura. Conselho Nacional de Proteção aos Índios.
19 de Abril: O Dia do Índio—As comemorações realizadas em 1944 e 45. 1946.
———. Ministério da Agricultura. Conselho Nacional de Proteção aos Índios.
Relatório. 1944.
———. Ministério da Agricultura. *Decreto Lei no. 6155*. 30 December 1943.
———. Ministério da Agricultura. *Marcha para Oeste* (Conferências Cultu-
rais 1939–1943).
———. Ministério da Agricultura. *Relatório: As atividades da agricultura*.
1942–1943.
———. Ministério da Agricultura. Serviço de Proteção aos Índios. *Boletim*.
1939–1966.
———. Ministério da Agricultura. Serviço de Proteção aos Índios. *Relatório*,
1939–1960.

————. Ministério da Guerra. Serviço de Proteção aos Índios. *Relatório Refer-*
ente ao ano de 1934, 1934.

————. Ministério do Interior. Fundação Nacional do Índio. *Boletim Informa-*
tivo FUNAI. Brasília: FUNAI, 1972–1974.

————. Ministério do Interior. Fundação Nacional do Índio. *Legislação.* Brasília, 1974.

————. Ministério do Interior. Fundação Nacional do Índio. *Política e ação*
indigenista brasileira. Brasília, 1975.

————. Ministério do Interior. Fundação Nacional do Índio. *Políticas e pro-*
gramas de Ação da FUNAI. Brasília, 1988.

————. Ministério do Interior. Fundação Nacional do Índio. *O que é a Funai?*
Brasília, 1973.

————. Ministério do Interior. Fundação Nacional do Índio. *Relatório de ativi-*
dades da FUNAI durante o exercício de 1970. Brasília, 1971.

————. Ministério do Interior. Fundação Nacional do Índio. *Revista da atuali-*
dade indígena. Brasília, 1976–1979.

————. Ministério do Interior. *Linhas de ação do Ministério do Interior no*
Governo do Presidente Ernesto Geisel. Brasília, 1974.

————. Ministério do Interior. *Política indigenista—Governo do Presidente*
Ernesto Geisel. Brasília, 1974.

————. Ministério do Interior. Projeto de Desenvolvimento Integrado da
Bacia do Araguaia–Tocantins. *Diagnóstico da Bacia do Araguaia-Tocantins.*
Brasília, 1982.

————. Ministério do Interior. *Relatório de atividades.* 1969–1973.

————. Ministério do Interior. Secretaria Geral. *Relatório de atividades 69/73.*
Brasília, n.d.

————. Presidência da República. Secretaria de Imprensa e Divulgação. *Esta-*
tuto do Índio. Brasília, 1982.

————. Superintendência de Desenvolvimento da Amazônia [SUDAM].
A Amazônia e o novo Brasil. Belém, 1972.

————. Superintendência de Desenvolvimento da Amazônia. *Biblioteca da*
SUDAM informa. Belém, 1969.

————. Superintendência de Desenvolvimento da Amazônia. *Isto é Amazônia.*
Belém, 1972.

————. Superintendência de Desenvolvimento do Centro-Oeste. *The Brazil-*
ian Center-West. Brasília, 1981.

————. Superintendência de Desenvolvimento do Centro-Oeste. *Diagnóstico*
geo-socio-econômico da região Centro-Oeste do Brasil. Brasília, 1978.

Abercrombie, Thomas A. *Pathways of Memory and Power: Ethnography and History among an Andean People*. Madison: University of Wisconsin Press, 1998.

———. "To Be Indian, to Be Bolivian: 'Ethnic' and 'National' Discourses of Identity." In *Nation-States and Indians in Latin America*, ed. Greg Urban and Joel Sherzer, 95–130. Austin: University of Texas Press, 1991.

Aborigines Protection Society of London. *The Tribes of the Amazon Basin in Brazil, 1972*. London: C. Knight, 1973.

Abrams, Philip. "Notes on the Difficulty of Studying the State," *Journal of Historical Sociology* 1 (1988): 58–89.

Abreu, João Capistrano de. *Chapters of Brazil's Colonial History, 1500–1800*. Trans. Arthur Brakel. New York: Oxford University Press, 1997.

Allen, Elizabeth. "Brazil: Indians and the New Constitution." *Third World Quarterly*, 10 no. 4 (1989): 148–65.

Almeida, Alfredo Wagner Berno de. "O intransitivo da transição: O Estado, os conflitos agrários e violência na Amazônia (1965–1989)." In *Amazônia: A fronteira agrícola 20 anos depois*, ed. Philippe Lena and Adélia Engracia de Oliveira. Bélem: Museu Paraense Emilio Goeldi, 1991.

Almeida, Geraldo Gustavo de. *Heróis indígenas do Brasil*. Rio de Janeiro: Catedra, 1988.

Alonso, Ana María. *Thread of Blood: Colonialism, Revolution, and Gender on Mexico's Northern Frontier*. Tucson: University of Arizona Press, 1995.

Alvarez, Sonia. *Engendering Democracy in Brazil*. Princeton, NJ: Princeton University Press, 1990.

Alves, Maria Helena Moreira. *State and Opposition in Military Brazil*. Austin: University of Texas Press, 1988.

Amarante, Elizabeth Aracy Rondon, ed. *Precisamos um chão: Depoimentos indígenas*. São Paulo: Ed. Loyola, 1981.

Ames, Barry. *Political Survival: Politicians and Public Policy in Latin America*. Berkeley: University of California Press, 1987.

Ammann, Safira Bezerra. *Ideologia do desenvolvimento de comunidade no Brasil*. São Paulo: Cortez Ed., 1987.

Anderson, Benedict. *Imagined Communities: Reflections on the Origin and Spread of Nationalism*. London: Verso, 1991.

Appiah, Kwame Anthony. *In My Father's House: Africa in the Philosophy of Culture*. New York: Oxford University Press, 1992.

Arnaud, Expedito. *Aspectos da legislação sobre os índios do Brasil*. Belém: Museu Goeldi, 1973.

Arnt, Ricardo, Lúcio Flávio Pinto, and Raimundo Pinto. *Panará: A volta dos índios gigantes*. São Paulo: Instituto Socioambiental, 1998.

Arruda, Hélio Ponce de. *Os problemas fundiários na estratégia do desenvolvimento e de segurança*. Brasília: Ministério da Agricultura, 1977.

Artiaga, Zoroastro. *Dos índios do Brasil Central.* Uberaba: Departamento Estadual de Cultura do Estado, n.d.

Asselin, Victor. *Grilagem: Corrupção e violência em terras do Carajás.* Petrópolis: Vozes, 1982.

Assis, Eneida Corrêa de. "Educação indígena no Brasil." *Cadernos do Centro de Filosofia e Ciências Humanas, UFPA* 1 (1980): 35–52.

———. "Escola indígena: Uma 'frente ideológica.'" Master's thesis, Universidade de Brasília, 1981.

Audrim, José M. *Entre sertanejos e índios do Norte.* Instituto Histórico e Geográfico de Belém do Pará, n.d.

Aureli, Willy. *Roncador.* São Paulo: Edições Cultura Brasileira, 1939.

Baer, Werner. *The Brazilian Economy: Growth and Development,* 3d ed. New York: Praeger, 1989.

Baldus, Herbert. "É belicoso o xavante?" *Revista do Arquivo Municipal* 142 (1951): 125–29.

———. *Ensaios de etnologia brasileira.* São Paulo: Editora Nacional, 1937.

———. "Tribos da bacia do Araguaia e o Serviço de Proteção aos Índios." *Revista do Museu Paulista* 2 (1948): 154–68.

Banco da Amazônia, S.A. *Investimentos privilegiados na Amazônia,* n.d.

Baretta, Silvio R. Duncan, and John Markoff. "Civilization and Barbarism: Cattle Frontiers in Latin America." *Comparative Studies in Society and History* 20 (1978): 587–620.

Barickman, B. J. "'Tame Indians,' 'Wild Heathens,' and Settlers in Southern Bahia in the Late Eighteenth and Early Nineteenth Centuries." *The Americas* 51 (1995): 325–68.

Barros, Olegário Moreira de. "Rondon e o índio." *Revista do Instituto Histórico de Mato Grosso* 22, nos. 43–44 (1940): 15–26.

Barros, Paula. "A contribuição do índio a civilização." *Instituto Histórico e Geográfico do Brasil,* no. 4 (1949): 529–40.

Barth, Fredrik, ed. *Ethnic Groups and Boundaries: The Social Organization of Cultural Difference.* Boston: Little, Brown, 1969.

Bastos, Aurélio Wander. "As terras indígenas no direito constitucional brasileiro e na jurisprudência do STF." In *Sociedades indígenas e o direito: Uma questão de direitos humanos,* ed. Sílvio Coelho dos Santos et al. Florianópolis: Universidade de Santa Catarina, 1985.

Beltrão, Luiz. *O índio, um mito brasileiro.* Petrópolis: Vozes, 1977.

Bennett, Gordon. "Aboriginal Rights in International Law." *Survival International.* Occasional Paper 37. London: Royal Anthropological Institute for Great Britain and Ireland, 1978.

Berkhofer, Robert F., Jr. *The White Man's Indian: Images of the American Indian from Columbus to the Present.* New York: Knopf, 1978.

Blomberg, Rolf. *Chavante: An Expedition to the Tribes of the Mato Grosso.* New York: Taplinger, 1961.

Bodard, Lucien. *Massacre on the Amazon*. London: Tom Stacey, 1971.

Bodley, John H. *Victims of Progress*. Menlo Park: Benjamin/Cummings, 1982.

Bonfil Batalla, Guillermo, ed. *América Latina, etnodesarrollo y etnocidio*. San José: FLACSO, 1982.

————. *Utopia y revolución: El pensamiento político contemporaneo de los índios en América Latina*. Mexico: Editorial Nueva Imagen, 1981.

Borges, Dain. "Brazilian Social Thought of the 1930s." *Luso-Brazilian Review* 31 (1994): 137–49.

Borges, Durval Rosa Sarmento. *Rio Araguaia, corpo e alma*. São Paulo: USP, 1987.

Bourdieu, Pierre. *Outline of a Theory of Practice*. Trans. Richard Nice. Cambridge, England: Cambridge University Press, 1977.

Bradford, Colin, Jr., ed. *Redefining the State in Latin America*. Paris: OECD, 1994.

Branford, Sue, and Oriel Glock. *The Last Frontier: Fighting over Land in the Amazon*. London: Zed Books, 1985.

Brasileiro, Francisco. *Na Serra do Roncador*. São Paulo: Nacional, 1938.

Brazil, Themístocles Paes de Souza. *Íncolas selvícolas*. Rio de Janeiro: Ministério de Relações Exteriores, 1937.

Brooks, Edwin, and others. *Tribes of the Amazon Basin in Brazil 1972*. London: Charles Knight & Co., 1973.

Brookshaw, David. *Paradise Betrayed: Brazilian Literature of the Indian*. Amsterdam: CEDLA, 1988.

Bruneau, Thomas C. *The Political Transformation of the Brazilian Catholic Church*. Cambridge, England: Cambridge University Press, 1974.

Brysk, Alison. "Acting Globally: Indian Rights and International Politics in Latin America." In *Indigenous Peoples and Democracy in Latin America*, ed. Donna Lee Van Cott. New York: St. Martin's Press, 1994.

Buarque de Holanda, Sérgio. *Raízes do Brasil*. 1936. Rio de Janeiro: José Olympio, 1989.

Bunker, Stephen. *Underdeveloping the Amazon: Extraction, Unequal Exchange and the Failure of the Modern State*. Urbana: University of Illinois Press, 1985.

Burdick, John. "Rethinking the Study of Social Movements: The Case of Christian Base Communities in Urban Brazil." In *The Making of Social Movements in Latin America*, ed. Arturo Escobar and Sonia E. Alvarez. Boulder, CO: Westview Press, 1992.

Caiado, Leolídio di Ramos. *Dramas do Oeste: História de uma excursão nas regiões da Ilha do Bananal em 1950*. São Paulo: Edigraf, 1961.

Camargo, Aspasia, et al. *O golpe silencioso: As origens da república corporativa*. Rio de Janeiro: Rio Fundo, 1989.

Camargo, S. P., Jr. *Problemas do Oeste*. Rio de Janeiro: A Noite, 1948.

Cammack, Paul. "Clientelism and Military Government in Brazil." In *Private Patronage and Public Power*, ed. Christopher Clapham. New York: St. Martin's Press, 1982.

Campanha Nacional de Aperfeiçoamento Pessoal de Nivel Superior [CAPES]. *Estudos de Desenvolvimento Regional (Mato Grosso)*. Rio de Janeiro: EDCAPES, 1958.

Campos, Fausto Vieira de. *Retrato de Mato Grosso*. São Paulo: Brasil-Oeste, 1969.

Campos, Francisco. *Educação e cultura*. Rio de Janeiro: José Olympio, 1941.

Cardoso, Fernando Henrique. *Autoritarismo e democratização*. Rio de Janeiro: Paz e Terra, 1975.

Cardoso, Fernando Henrique, and Geraldo Müller. *Amazônia: Expansão do capitalismo*. São Paulo: Brasiliense, 1977.

Carletti, Ernesto. *Lembrança dos Missionários Salesianos Pe. Pedro Sacilotti e Pe. João Fuchs Trucidados pelos Índios Chavantes no Rio das Mortes*. São Paulo: Escolas Profissionais Salesianas, 1935.

Carneiro, Maria Esperança Fernandes. *A revolta camponesa de Formoso e Trombas*. Goiânia: Editora da Univesidade Federal de Goiás, 1986.

Carone, Edgard. *O Estado Novo (1937–1945)*. Rio de Janeiro: DIFEL, 1977.

Carvalho, Afonso Ligório Pires de. "Juruna, o índio que aprisiona a memória dos brancos." *Revista da atualidade indígena* 2, no. 9 (Mar.–Apr. 1978): 9–11.

Carvalho, José Murilo de. "Armed Forces and Politics in Brazil, 1930–45." *Hispanic American Historical Review* 62 (1982): 193–223.

———. *A formação das almas: O imaginário da República no Brasil*. São Paulo: Companhia das Letras, 1990.

Carvalho, J. R. de Sá. *Brazilian El Dorado*. London: Blackie and Son, 1938.

Carvalho, Murilo. *Sangue da terra*. São Paulo: Ed. Brasil Debates, 1980.

Casaldáliga, Pedro. *Uma igreja da Amazônia em conflito com o latifúndio e a marginalização Social*. Mato Grosso: n.p., 1971.

———. *I Believe in Justice and Hope*. Notre Dame, IN: Fides/Claretian, 1978.

Cascudo, Luiz da Câmara. *Montaigne e o índio brasileiro*. São Paulo: Cadernos da Hora Presente, 1940.

Cavalcanti, Mário de Barros. *Da SPVEA a SUDAM (1964–1967)*. Belém: 1967.

Cehelsky, Marta. *Land Reform in Brazil: The Management of Social Change*. Boulder, CO: Westview, 1979.

Celso, Conde de Affonso. *Direito de Goyaz no litígio contra Matto-Grosso*. Rio de Janeiro: Imprensa Nacional, 1921.

Centro Ecumênico de Documentação e Informação [CEDI]. *Aconteceu especial: Povos indígenas no Brasil/80, 83 e 84*. São Paulo: Ed. Sagarana, 1981–85.

———. *Povos indígenas no Brasil 1985/1986*. São Paulo: CEDI, 1987.

———. *Povos indígenas no Brasil 1987/88/89/90*. São Paulo: CEDI, 1991.

———. *Terras indígenas no Brasil*. CEDI/Museu Nacional, 1987.

Chagnon, Napoleon A. *Yanomamö: The Fierce People*, 3d ed. New York: Holt, Rinehart and Winston, 1983.

Chatterjee, Partha. *The Nation and Its Fragments: Colonial and Postcolonial Histories*. Princeton: Princeton University Press, 1993.

Chovelon, Hipólito, Francisco Fernandes, and Pedro Sbardelotto. *Do primeiro encontro com os Xavante à demarcação de suas reservas.* Campo Grande: Editorial Dom Bosco, 1996.

Clifford, James. *The Predicament of Culture.* Cambridge, MA: Harvard University Press, 1988.

Colbacchini, R. Antônio. *A luz do Cruzeiro do Sul.* São Paulo: Escolas Profissionais Salesianas, 1939.

Colby, Gerard, with Charlotte Dennett. *Thy Will Be Done—The Conquest of the Amazon: Nelson Rockefeller and Evangelism in the Age of Oil.* New York: Harper Collins, 1995.

Comaroff, John, and Jean Comaroff. *Ethnography and the Historical Imagination.* Boulder, CO: Westview Press, 1992.

Comissão Pró-Índio/sp. *O índio e a cidadania.* São Paulo: Brasiliense, 1983.

———. *Índios: direitos históricos.* São Paulo: Comissão Pró-Índio, 1982.

———. *A questão da educação indígena.* São Paulo: Brasiliense, 1981.

———. *A questão da emancipação.* São Paulo: Global, 1979.

———. *A questão da mineração em terra indígena.* São Paulo: Comissão Pró-Índio, 1985.

———. *A questão da terra indígena.* São Paulo: Global, 1981.

Comité International de la Croix Rouge. *Report of the International Red Cross Committee Medical Mission to the Brazilian Amazon Region.* Geneva, 1970.

Conca, Ken. *Manufacturing Insecurity: The Rise and Fall of Brazil's Military-Industrial Complex.* Boulder, CO: Westview, 1997.

Conklin, Beth A., and Laura R. Graham. "The Shifting Middle Ground: Amazonian Indians and Eco-Politics." *American Anthropologist* 97 (1995): 695–710.

Conselho Indigenista Missionário. *Os povos indígenas e a Nova República.* São Paulo: Edições Paulinas, 1986.

Conselho Nacional de Proteção aos Índios. *19 de Abril: O Dia do Índio as comemorações realizadas em 1944 e 45.* Rio de Janeiro: Imprensa Nacional, 1946.

Cordeiro, Enio. "Política indigenista brasileira e promoção internacional dos direitos das populações indígenas." Manuscript. Brasília: Ministério das Relações Exteriores, 1993.

Corradi, Juan E., Patricia Weiss Fagen, and Manuel Antonio Garretón, eds. *Fear at the Edge: State Terror and Resistance in Latin America.* Berkeley: University of California Press, 1992.

Correa, Valmir Batista. "Coronéis e bandidos em Mato Grosso (1889–1943)." Ph.D. diss., Universidade de São Paulo, 1981.

Correa Filho, Virgílio. *História de Mato Grosso.* Rio de Janeiro: Instituto Nacional do Livro, Ministério da Educação, 1969.

———. *Mato Grosso.* Rio de Janeiro: Editora Brasílica, 1939.

Corrigan, Philip, and Derek Sayer. *The Great Arch: English State Formation as Cultural Revolution.* Oxford: Basil Blackwell, 1985.

Costa, Angyone. *Indiologia.* Rio de Janeiro: Zenio Valverde Editora, 1943.

Costa, Emilia Viotti da. *The Brazilian Empire: Myths and Histories.* Chicago: University of Chicago Press, 1985.

Costa, João Cruz. *A History of Ideas in Brazil.* Berkeley: University of California Press, 1964.

Courteville, Roger. *Mato Grosso: Terre inconnue.* Paris: La Colombe, 1954.

Coutinho, Edilberto. *Rondon e a integração amazônica.* São Paulo: Arquimedes, 1968.

——. *Rondon e a política indigenista brasileira no século vinte.* Rio de Janeiro: PUC, 1978.

——. *Rondon, o civilizador da última fronteira.* Rio de Janeiro: Olive, 1969.

Cowell, Adrian. *The Decade of Destruction.* New York: Anchor, 1990.

Cunha, Ayres Câmara. *Além de Mato Grosso.* São Paulo: Clube do Livro, 1974.

——. *Entre os índios do Xingu: a verdadeira história de Diacui.* São Paulo: Exposição do Livro, 1960.

Cunha, Boaventura Ribeiro da. *Educação para os selvícolas.* Rio de Janeiro: Ministério da Agricultura/CNPI, 1946(?).

Cunha, Manuela Carneiro da. *Antropologia do Brasil: Mito, história e etnicidade.* São Paulo: Brasiliense/EDUSP, 1986.

——. *Os direitos do índio.* São Paulo: Brasiliense, 1987.

——, ed. *História dos índios no Brasil.* São Paulo: Companhia da Letras Fundação de Amparo à Pesquisa no Estado de São Paulo, Secretaria Municipal de Cultura, 1992.

——, ed. *Legislação ingigenista no século XIX: Uma compilação, 1808–1889.* São Paulo: Comissão Pró-Índio de São Paulo, Editora da Universidade de São Paulo, 1992.

Davidson, David M. "How the Brazilian West Was Won: Freelance and State on the Mato Grosso Frontier, 1737–1752." In *Colonial Roots of Modern Brazil,* ed. Dauril Alden. 61–106. Berkeley: University of California Press, 1973.

Davis, Shelton H. *Victims of the Miracle: Development and the Indians of Brazil.* Cambridge, England: Cambridge University Press, 1986.

Davis, Shelton H., and Robert O. Matthews. *The Geological Imperative: Anthropology and Development in the Amazon Basin of South America.* Cambridge, MA: Anthropology Resource Center, 1976.

Davis, Shelton, and Patrick Menget. "Povos primitivos e ideologia civilizada no Brasil." In *Antropologia e indigenismo na América Latina,* ed. Carmen Junqueira and Edgard de A. Carvalho. São Paulo: Cortez, 1981.

Dean, Warren. *With Broadax and Firebrand: The Destruction of the Brazilian Atlantic Forest.* Berkeley: University of California Press, 1995.

de la Cadena, Marisol. "Women Are More Indian: Gender and Ethnicity in Cuzco." In *Ethnicity, Markets and Migration in the Andes: At the Crossroads of*

History and Anthropology, ed. Brooke Larson, Olivia Harris, and Enrique Tandeter. 319–28. Durham, NC: Duke University Press, 1995.

Demarquet, Sonia de Almeida. *A questão indígena.* Rio de Janeiro: Vigilia, 1986.

Dória, Palmério, Sérgio Buarque, Vincente Carelli, and Jaime Sautchuk. *A guerrilha do Araguaia.* São Paulo: Alfa-Omega, 1979.

Dostal, W., ed. *The Situation of the Indian in South America.* Geneva, Switzerland: World Council of Churches, 1972.

Duarte, Bandeira. *Rondon: O bandeirante do século XX.* Rio de Janeiro: N.S. de Fátima Editora, 1957.

Dupas, Gilberto. "Competitive Integration and Recovery of Growth." In *Brazil and the Challenge of Economic Reform,* ed. Werner Baer and Joseph C. Tulchin. Washington, DC: Woodrow Wilson Center, 1993.

Durham, Eunice Ribeiro. "O lugar do índio." In *O índio e a cidadania,* ed. Comissão Pró-Índio/sp. São Paulo: Brasiliense, 1983).

Dyott, Georges Miller. *Man Hunting in the Jungle, Being the Story of a Search for Three Explorers Lost in the Brazilian Wilds.* Indianapolis: Bobbs-Merrill, 1930.

Erthal, Regina Maria de Carvalho. "Atrair e pacificar: A estratégia da conquista." Master's thesis, Universidade Federal do Rio de Janeiro, 1992.

Escobar, Ildefonso. *A Marcha para o Oeste: Couto Magalhães e Getúlio Vargas.* Rio de Janeiro: A Noite, 1941.

Esterci, Neide. *Conflito no Araguaia.* Petrópolis: Vozes, 1987.

———. "O mito da democracia no pais das bandeiras." Master's thesis, Universidade Federal do Rio de Janeiro, 1972.

Evans, Peter. *Dependent Development: The Alliance of Multinational, State, and Local Capital in Brazil.* Princeton, NJ: Princeton University Press, 1979.

Fabre, D. G. *Beyond the River of the Dead.* London: R. Hall, 1963.

Farage, Nádia. *As muralhas dos sertões: Os povos indígenas no Rio Branco e colonização.* Rio de Janeiro: Paz e Terra and Anpocs, 1991.

Fausto, Boris. *A revolução de 1930: Historiografia e história,* 13th ed. São Paulo: Brasiliense, 1991.

Ferguson, R. Brian. "Explaining War." In *The Anthropology of War,* ed. Jonathan Haas. Cambridge, England: Cambridge University Press, 1990.

———. *Yanomami Warfare: A Political History.* Santa Fe, NM: School of American Research, 1995.

Ferraz, Iara, and Mariano Mampieri. "Suiá-Missu: Um mito refeito." *Carta': Falas, reflexões, memórias/informe de distribuição restrita do Senador Darcy Ribeiro* 4, no. 9 (1993): 75–84.

Ferreira, Eudson Castro de. *Posse e propriedade territorial: A luta pela terra em Mato Grosso.* Campinas: UNICAMP, 1986.

Ferreira, Manoel Rodrigues. *Nos sertões do lendário Rio das Mortes.* Rio de Janeiro: Editora do Brasil, 1946.

Ferreira, Mariana Kawall Leal. "Da origem dos homens à conquista da escrita: Um estudo sobre povos indígenas e educação escolar no Brasil." Master's thesis, Universidade de São Paulo, 1992.

Field, Les W. "Who Are the Indians? Reconceptualizing Indigenous Identity, Resistance, and the Role of Social Science in Latin America." *Latin American Research Review* 29, no. 3 (1994): 237–56.

Figueiredo, José de Lima. *Índios do Brasil.* São Paulo: Nacional, 1939.

———. *Terras de Matto-Grosso e da Amazônia.* Rio de Janeiro: A Noite, 1935.

Figueiredo, Paulo de. *Aspectos ideológicos do Estado Novo.* Brasília: Senado Federal Centro Gráfico, 1983.

Fioravanti, Mário. "Índio-CIMI ou CIMI-Índio? A razão crítica de una 'nova' perspectiva interétnica e missionária." Master's thesis, Pontifícia Universidade Católica, São Paulo, 1990.

Fishlow, Albert. "Origins and Consequences of Import Substitution in Brazil." In *International Economics and Development: Essays in Honor of Raul Prebisch*, ed. L. Di Marco. New York: Academic Press, 1972.

Flanzer, Vivian. "Índios Xavante são loucos por futebol." *A Bola* (Oct. 1994): 64–67.

Fleming, Peter. *Brazilian Adventure.* New York: The Press of the Reader Club, 1942.

Fleury, Renato Sêneca. *Pátria brasileira.* São Paulo: Melhoramentos, 1944.

Flowers, Nancy. "Crise e recuperação demográfica: Os Xavante de Pimentel Barbosa, Mato Grosso." In *Saúde e povos indígenas*, ed. Ricardo V. Santos and Carlos E. A. Coimbra Jr. 213–42. Rio de Janeiro: Editora FIOCRUZ, 1994.

———. "Forager-Farmers: The Xavante Indians of Central Brazil." Ph.D. diss., City University of New York, 1983.

———. "Subsistence Strategy, Social Organization, and Warfare in Central Brazil in the Context of European Penetration." In *Amazonian Indians from Prehistory to the Present*, ed. Anna Roosevelt. Tucson: University of Arizona Press, 1994.

Fonseca, Sylvio da. *Frente a frente com os Xavantes.* Rio de Janeiro: Pongetti, 1948.

Fontaine, Pierre-Michel, ed. *Race, Class and Power in Brazil.* Los Angeles: Center for Afro-American Studies, University of California–Los Angeles, 1985.

Foweraker, Joe. *The Struggle for Land: A Political Economy of the Pioneer Frontier in Brazil from 1930 to the Present Day.* Cambridge, England: Cambridge University Press, 1981.

Fowler, Loretta. *Shared Symbols, Contested Meanings: Gros Ventre Culture and History, 1778–1984.* Ithaca, NY: Cornell University Press, 1987.

Franco, Affonso Arinos de Mello. *O índio brasileiro e a revolução francesa.* Rio de Janeiro: José Olympio, 1937.

Freire, Carlos Augusto da Rocha. "Indigenismo e antropologia: O Conselho

Nacional de Proteção aos Índios na gestão Rondon, 1939–1955." Master's thesis, Universidade Federal do Rio de Janeiro, 1990.

French, John D. *The Brazilian Workers' ABC: Class Conflict and Alliance in Modern São Paulo.* Chapel Hill: University of North Carolina Press, 1992.

Freyre, Gilberto. *The Masters and the Slaves,* 2d rev. ed. Trans. Samuel Putnam. Berkeley: University of California Press, 1986.

———. *New World in the Tropics: The Culture of Modern Brazil.* New York: Knopf, 1971.

Friedlander, Judith. *Being Indian in Hueyapan: A Study of Forced Identity in Contemporary Mexico.* New York: St. Martin's Press, 1975.

Fuerst, Rene. *Bibliography of the Indigenous Problem and Policy of the Brazilian Amazon Region (1957–1972).* Geneva: AMAZIND, 1972.

Furtado, Celso. *Economic Development of Latin America,* 2d ed. Trans. Suzette Macedo. Cambridge, England: Cambridge University Press, 1976.

Gagliardi, José Mauro. *O indígena e a República.* São Paulo: Hucitec, 1989.

Gaiger, Julio M. G. *Direitos indígenas na Constituição Brasileira de 1988.* Brasília: CIMI, 1989.

Gaiger, Julio, Wilmar Alves, and Eduardo Leão. *A verdadeira conspiração contra os povos indígenas, a Igreja, e o Brasil.* Brasília: CNBB/CIMI, 1987.

Galey, John H. "The Politics of Development in the Brazilian Amazon, 1940–1950." Ph.D. diss., Stanford University, 1977.

Gallais, Etienne Marie. *Uma catequese entre os índios do Araguaia.* Salvador: Progresso, 1954.

Galvão, Eduardo. *Encontro de sociedades: Índios e brancos no Brasil.* Rio de Janeiro: Paz e Terra, 1979.

Galvão, Marília, and Roberto Galvão. *Áreas amazônicas de Mato Grosso, Goiás, e Maranhão.* Belém: Superintendência do Plano de Valorização Econômica da Amazônia, 1955.

Gamio, Manuel. *Actividades del Instituto Indigenista Interamericano.* Mexico City: Ediciones del Instituto Indigenista Interamericano, 1944.

Garfield, Seth. " 'Civilized' but Discontent: The Xavante Indians and Government Policy in Brazil, 1937–1988." Ph.D. diss., Yale University, 1996.

———. " 'The Roots of a Plant That Today Is Brazil': Indians and the Nation-State under the Brazilian Estado Novo." *Journal of Latin American Studies* 29 (1997): 747–68.

Garretón, Manuel Antonio. "New State-Society Relations in Latin America." In *Redefining the State in Latin America,* ed. Colin I. Bradford Jr. Paris: OECD, 1994.

Geddes, Barbara. *Politician's Dilemma: Building State Capacity in Latin America.* Berkeley: University of California Press, 1994.

Giaccaria, Bartolomeu. *Pe. João Fuchs, Pe. Pedro Sacilotti: Duas vidas em busca dos Xavante.* N.p., 1984.

———. *Xavante (Auwẽ Uptabi: Povo Autêntico),* 2d ed. São Paulo: Dom Bosco, 1972.

Giaccaria, Bartolomeu, and Adalberto Heide. *Jerônimo Xavante conta*. Campo Grande: Casa da Cultura, 1975.

——. *Xavante, reserva de brasilidade*. São Paulo: Dom Bosco, 1975.

Gita, Ana, ed. *Atas indigenistas*. Brasília: Oriente, 1988.

Gomes, Angela de Castro. *A invenção do trabalhismo*, 2d ed. Rio de Janeiro: Relume Dumará, 1994.

Gomes, Mércio Pereira. *Os índios e o Brasil*. Petrópolis: Vozes, 1988.

Gonçalves, José Reginaldo Santos. "A luta pela identidade social: o caso das relações entre índios e brancos no Brasil Central." Master's thesis, Universidade Federal do Rio de Janeiro, 1981.

Gonzalez, Mike, and David Treece. *The Gathering of Voices: The Twentieth-Century Poetry of Latin America*. London: Verso, 1992.

Gould, Jeffrey L. *To Die in This Way: Nicaraguan Indians and the Myth of Mestizaje, 1880–1965*. Durham, NC: Duke University Press, 1998.

Graham, Laura. "Uma aldeia por um 'projeto.'" In CEDI, *Povos indígenas no Brasil—1985/1986*. São Paulo: CEDI, 1987.

——. *Performing Dreams: Discourses of Immortality among the Xavante of Central Brazil*. Austin: University of Texas Press, 1995.

——. "Three Modes of Xavante Vocal Expression: Wailing, Collective Singing, and Public Oratory." In *Native South American Discourse*, ed. Joel Sherzer and Greg Urban. Berlin: Mouton de Gruyter, 1986.

Graham, Lawrence S. *Civil Service Reform in Brazil: Principles versus Practice*. Austin: University of Texas Press, 1968.

Gramsci, Antonio. *Selections from the Prison Notebooks*. Ed. and trans. Quintin Hoare and Geoffrey Nowell Smith. New York: International Publishers, 1971.

Grandin, Greg. *The Blood of Guatemala: The Making of Race and Nation, 1750–1954*. Durham, NC: Duke University Press, 2000.

Greenblatt, Stephen. *Marvelous Possessions: The Wonder of the New World*. Oxford: Oxford University Press, 1991.

Gregório, Irmão Jose. *Contribuição indígena ao Brasil*. 3 vols. Belo Horizonte: União Brasileira de Educação e Ensino, 1980.

Grindle, Merilee S. *Challenging the State: Crisis and Innovation in Latin America and Africa*. Cambridge, England: Cambridge University Press, 1996.

——. *State and Countryside*. Baltimore: Johns Hopkins University Press, 1986.

Gross, Daniel, et al. "Ecology and Acculturation among Native Peoples of Central Brazil." *Science* 206 (Sept. 1979): 234.

Guariglia, Guglielmo. *Gli Xavante in Fase Acculturativa*. Milan: Vita e Pensiero, 1973.

Guerra, Flávio. *Rondon o sertanista*. Rio de Janeiro: Record, n.d.

Guha, Ranajit. "The Prose of Counter-Insurgency." In *Subaltern Studies 2*, ed. Guha. (New Delhi: Oxford University Press, 1983): 1–42.

——, ed. *A Subaltern Studies Reader, 1986–1995*. Minneapolis: University of Minnesota Press, 1997.

Guy, Donna J., and Thomas E. Sheridan, eds. *Contested Ground: Comparative Frontiers on the Northern and Southern Edges of the Spanish Empire.* Tucson: University of Arizona Press, 1998.

Haberly, David. *Three Sad Races: Racial Identity and National Consciousness in Brazilian Literature.* Cambridge, England: Cambridge University Press, 1983.

Hagopian, Frances. *Traditional Politics and Regime Change in Brazil.* New York: Cambridge University Press, 1996.

Hale, Charles R. *Resistance and Contradiction: Miskitu Indians and the Nicaraguan State, 1894–1987.* Stanford: Stanford University Press, 1994.

Hall, Anthony L. *Developing Amazonia: Deforestation and Social Conflict in Brazil's Carajás Programme.* Manchester, England: Manchester University Press, 1989.

Hanbury-Tenison, Robin. *A Question of Survival for the Indians of Brazil.* New York: Scribner's, 1973.

Hay, Alex Rattray. *Saints and Savages: Brazil's Indian Problem.* London: Hodder and Sloughton, 1920.

Hébette, Jean, ed. *O cerco está se fechando.* Petrópolis: Vozes, 1991.

Hecht, Susanna B. "Cattle Ranching in Amazonia: Political and Ecological Considerations." In *Frontier Expansion in Amazonia,* ed. Marianne Schmink and Charles Wood. 366–98. Gainesville: University of Florida Press, 1991.

———. "Cattle Ranching in the Eastern Amazon: Evaluation of a Development Policy." Ph.D. diss., University of California, Berkeley, 1982.

———. "Environment, Development and Politics: Capital Accumulation and the Livestock Sector in Eastern Amazonia." *World Development* 13 (1985): 663–84.

Hecht, Susanna B., and Alexander Cockburn. *The Fate of the Forest: Developers, Destroyers, and Defenders of the Amazon.* London: Verso, 1989.

Hemming, John. *Amazon Frontier: The Defeat of the Brazilian Indians.* London: Macmillan, 1987.

———. "Indians and the Frontier." In *Colonial Brazil,* ed. Leslie Bethell. 145–89. Cambridge, England: Cambridge University Press, 1991.

———. *Red Gold: The Conquest of the Brazilian Indians.* Cambridge, MA: Harvard University Press, 1978.

Hertzberg, Hazel. *The Search for an American Indian Identity: Modern Pan-Indian Movements.* Syracuse, NY: Syracuse University Press, 1971.

Hewitt de Alcántara, Cynthia. *Anthropological Perspectives on Rural Mexico.* London: Routledge and Kegan Paul, 1984.

Hill, Jonathan D., ed. *Rethinking History and Myth: Indigenous South American Perspectives on the Past.* Urbana: University of Illinois Press, 1988.

Hilton, Stanley E. "Military Influence on Brazilian Economic Policy, 1930–1945: A Different View." *Hispanic American Historical Review* 53 (1973): 71–94.

Hindness, B., and Hirst, P. Q. *Pre-Capitalist Modes of Production.* London: Routledge and Kegan Paul, 1975.

Hobsbawm, E. J. *Nations and Nationalism since 1780: Programme, Myth, Reality.* Cambridge, England: Cambridge University Press, 1990.

Hobsbawm, Eric, and Terence Ranger, eds. *The Invention of Tradition.* Cambridge, England: Cambridge University Press, 1983.

Holanda, Sérgio Buarque de. *Caminhos e fronteiras.* São Paulo: Companhia das Letras, 1994.

———. *Raízes do Brasil.* 1936. Rio de Janeiro: José Olympio, 1989.

Holston, James. "The Misrule of Law: Land and Usurpation in Brazil." *Comparative Studies in Society and History* 33 (1991): 695–725.

Hopper, Janice H., ed. *Indians of Brazil in the Twentieth Century.* Washington, DC: Institute for Cross Cultural Research, 1967.

Horta Barbosa, Luiz Bueno. *O problema indígena do Brasil.* Rio de Janeiro: Imprensa Nacional, 1947.

Houtzager, Peter. "State and Unions in the Transformation of the Brazilian Countryside, 1964–1979." *Latin American Research Review* 33, no. 2 (1998): 103–42.

Hu-DeHart, Evelyn. *Yaqui Resistance and Survival: The Struggle for Land and Autonomy, 1821–1910.* Madison: University of Wisconsin Press, 1984.

Hunter, Wendy. *Eroding Military Influence in Brazil: Politicians against Soldiers.* Chapel Hill: University of North Carolina Press, 1997.

Ianni, Octavio. *Colonização e contra-reforma agrária na Amazônia.* Petrópolis: Vozes, 1979.

———. *A luta pela terra.* Petrópolis: Vozes, 1978.

Instituto Brasileiro de Geografia e Estatística. *Enciclopédia dos Municípios Brasileiros.* Rio de Janeiro: IBGE, 1958.

———. *Geografia do Brasil: Região Centro-Oeste.* Rio de Janeiro: IBGE, 1989.

———. *Goiânia.* Rio de Janeiro: IBGE, 1942.

———. *Sinopse Preliminar do Censo Demográfico: 1991.* Rio de Janeiro: IBGE, 1991.

Jackson, Jean E. "Being and Becoming an Indian in the Vaupés." In *Nation-States and Indians in Latin America,* ed. Greg Urban and Joel Sherzer. 131–55. Austin: University of Texas Press, 1991.

Jackson, K. David. *A prosa vanguardista na literatura brasileira: Oswald de Andrade.* São Paulo: Perspectiva, 1978.

Jobim, Danton. *O problema do índio e a acusação de genocídio.* Brasília: Ministério da Justiça, 1970.

Joffily, Geraldo Ireneo. *Brasília e sua ideologia.* Brasília: Thesaurus, 1977.

Johnson, John J. *The Military and Society in Latin America.* Stanford, CA: Stanford University Press, 1964.

Johnson, Randal. "The Dynamics of the Brazilian Literary Field, 1930–1945." *Luso-Brazilian Review* 31 (1994): 11–13.

Joseph, Gilbert M., and Daniel Nugent, eds. *Everyday Forms of State Formation: Revolution and the Negotiation of Rule in Modern Mexico.* Durham, NC: Duke University Press, 1994.

Junqueira, Carmen. *The Brazilian Indigenous Problem and Policy: The Example of the Xingu National Park*. AMAZIND/IWGIA Document No. 13. Copenhagen, Denmark, 1976.

Junqueira, Carmen, and E. de A. Carvalho, eds. *Antropologia e indigenismo na América Latina*. São Paulo: Cortez Editora, 1981.

Juruna, Mario. *Discursos de liberdade, 1983–86*. Brasília: Câmara dos Deputados, 1986.

Juruna, Mario, Antonio Hohlfeldt, and Assis Hoffmann. *O gravador do Juruna*. Porto Alegre: Mercado Aberto, 1982.

Kane, Joe. *Savages*. New York: Vintage, 1996.

Karasch, Mary. "Catequese e cativeiro, política indigenista em Goiás: 1780–1889." In *História dos índios no Brasil*, ed. Manuela Carneiro da Cunha. 397–412. São Paulo: Companhia das Letras/Fundação de Amparo à Pesquisa no Estado de São Paulo/Secretaria Municipal de Cultura, 1992.

———. "Interethnic Conflict and Resistance on the Brazilian Frontier of Goiás, 1750–1890." In *Contested Ground: Comparative Frontiers on the Northern and Southern Edges of the Spanish Empire*, ed. Donna J. Guy and Thomas E. Sheridan. 115–34. Tucson: University of Arizona Press, 1998.

Katzman, Martin T. "The Brazilian Frontier in Comparative Perspective." *Comparative Studies in Society and History* 17 (1975): 266–85.

Keck, Margaret E. "Sustainable Development and Environmental Politics in Latin America." In *Redefining the State in Latin America*, ed. Colin I. Bradford Jr. Paris: OECD, 1994.

Kiemen, Mathias C. *The Indian Policy of Portugal in the Amazon Region, 1614–1693*. New York: Farrar, Straus and Giroux, 1973.

Klor de Alva, J. Jorge. "The Postcolonialization of the (Latin) American Experience: A Reconsideration of 'Colonialism,' 'Postcolonialism' and 'Mestizaje.'" In *After Colonialism: Imperial Histories and Postcolonial Displacements*, ed. Gyan Prakash. 241–75. Princeton: Princeton University Press, 1995.

Knight, Alan. "Racism, Revolution and *Indigenismo*: Mexico, 1910–1940." In *The Idea of Race in Latin America, 1870–1940*, ed. Richard Graham. 71–113. Austin: University of Texas, 1990.

Krech III, Shepard. *The Ecological Indian: Myth and History*. New York: Norton, 1999.

Kristal, Efraín. *The Andes Viewed from the City: Literary and Political Discourse on the Indian in Peru, 1848–1930*. New York: Peter Lang, 1987.

Langfur, Hal. "Myths of Pacification: Brazilian Frontier Settlement and the Subjugation of the Bororo Indians." *Journal of Social History* 32 (1999): 879–905.

Lapa, J. R. do Amaral. *Missão do Sangradouro*. São Paulo: Coleção Saraiva, 1963.

Lauerhass, Ludwig, Jr. *Getúlio Vargas e o triunfo do nacionalismo brasileiro*. Belo Horizonte: Itatiaia and São Paulo: Editora da Universidade de São Paulo, 1986.

Lavenére-Wanderley, Nelson Freire. *História da Força Aérea Brasileira*. Rio de Janeiro: n.p., 1975.

Lea, Vanessa R. *Parque Indígena do Xingu: Laudo antropológico*. Campinas: UNICAMP/Instituto de Filosofia e Ciências Humanas, 1997.

Leal, Victor Nunes, *Coronelismo: The Municipality and Representative Government in Brazil*. Trans. June Henfrey. New York: Cambridge University Press, 1977.

Leite, Dante Moreira. *O caráter nacional brasileiro: História de uma ideologia*. São Paulo: Editora Ática, 1992.

Leme, Maria Cristina Vannuchi, and Vânia Maria de Araújo Pietrafesa. *Assassinatos no campo: Crime e impunidade, 1964–86*. São Paulo: Global Ed., 1987.

Lenharo, Alcir. "A civilização vai ao campo." *Anais do Museu Paulista* 34 (1985): 7–19.

———. *Colonização e trabalho no Brasil: Amazônia, Nordeste e Centro-Oeste—Os anos 30*. Campinas: UNICAMP, 1986.

———. *Sacralização da política*. Campinas: Papirus, 1986.

———. "A terra para quem nela não trabalha." *Revista Brasileira de História* 6, no. 12 (1986): 47–64.

Lesser, Jeffrey. *Welcoming the Undesirables: Brazil and the Jewish Question*. Berkeley: University of California Press, 1995.

Lévi-Strauss, Claude. "The Social and Psychological Aspects of Chieftainship in a Primitive Tribe: The Nambikuara of Northwestern Mato Grosso." In *Comparative Political Systems: Studies in the Politics of Pre-Industrial Societies*, ed. Ronald Cohen and John Middleton. Garden City, NY: Natural History Press, 1967.

———. *Tristes Tropiques*. New York: Atheneum, 1967.

Levine, Robert M. *Father of the Poor? Vargas and His Era*. Cambridge, England: Cambridge University Press, 1998.

———. *The Vargas Regime: The Critical Years, 1934–1938*. New York: Columbia University Press, 1970.

Lima, Antonio Carlos de Souza. "O governo dos índios sob a gestão do SPI." In *História dos índios no Brasil*, ed. Manuela Carneiro da Cunha. São Paulo: Companhia das Letras/Fundação de Amparo à Pesquisa no Estado de São Paulo/Secretaria Municipal de Cultura, 1992.

———. *Um grande cerco de paz: Poder tutelar, indianidade e formação do Estado no Brasil*. Petrópolis: Vozes, 1995.

———. "A identificação como categoria histórica." In *Os poderes e as terras dos índios*, ed. João Pacheco de Oliveira Filho. Rio de Janeiro: PPGAS, 1989.

Lima, Arquimedes Pereira. *Problemas matogrossenses*. Cuiabá: n.p., 1941.

Lima, Nísia Trindade, and Gilberto Hochman. "Condenado pela raça, absolvido pela medicina: O Brasil descoberto pelo movimento sanitarista da Primeira República." In *Raça, ciência, sociedade*, ed. Marcos Chor Maio and Ricardo Ventura Santos. 23–40. Rio de Janeiro: FIOCRUZ, 1996.

Lins de Barros, João Alberto. *Memórias de um revolucionário*. Rio de Janeiro: Civilização Brasileira, 1953.

Linz, Juan J., and Alfred Stepan. *Problems of Democratic Transition and Consolidation*. Baltimore: Johns Hopkins University Press, 1996.

Lippi Oliveira, Lúcia. *Elite intelectual e debate político nos anos 30*. Rio de Janeiro: Fundação Getúlio Vargas, 1980.

Lippi Oliveira, Lúcia, Mônica Pimenta Velloso, and Angela Castro Gomes. *Estado Novo: Ideologia e poder*. Rio de Janeiro: Fundação Getúlio Vargas, 1982.

Loewenstein, Kurt. *Brazil under Vargas*. New York: Macmillan, 1942.

Lombardi, J. C. "O Xavante e a política indigenista no Brasil nos séculos XVIII e XIX." Master's thesis, Universidade de São Paulo, 1985.

Lombardi, Mary. "The Frontier in Brazilian History: An Historiographical Essay." *Pacific Historical Review* 44 (1975): 437–57.

Lopes, Marta Maria. "A resistência do índio ao extermínio: O caso dos Akwẽ-Xavante, 1967–1980." Master's thesis, Universidade Estadual Paulista Julio de Mesquita Filho, 1988.

Lopes da Silva, Aracy. "Dois séculos e meio de história Xavante." In *História dos índios no Brasil*, ed. Manuela Carneiro da Cunha. São Paulo: Companhia das Letras, Fundação de Amparo à Pasquisa no Estado de São Paulo, Secretaria Municipal de Cultura, 1992.

———. *Nomes e amigos: Da prática Xavante a uma reflexão sobre os Jê*. São Paulo: Universidade de São Paulo, 1986.

———. "Social Practice and Ontology in Akwẽ-Xavante Naming and Myth." *Ethnology* 28, no. 4 (October 1989): 331–42.

Lopes da Silva, Aracy, and Luís Donisete Benzi Grupioni. *A temática indígena na escola: Novos subsídios para professores de 1° e 2° graus*. Brasília: MEC/MARI/NIVESCO, 1995.

Lorenz, Francisco Vladomiro. *A mentalidade ameríndia*. São Paulo: Editora O Pensamento, 1938.

Lyra, João. "Raça, educação e desporto." *Estudos e Conferências* 14 (Dec. 1941): 41–67.

Macaulay, Neill. *The Prestes Column: Revolution in Brazil*. New York: New Viewpoints, 1974.

Macedo, Agenor F., and Eduardo P. C. de Vasconcellos. *O índio brasileiro*. Rio de Janeiro: Ferreira de Mattos, 1935.

MacIntyre, Archie. *Down the Araguaya: Travels in the Heart of Brazil*. London: Religious Tract Society, 1924(?).

Maclachlan, Colin M. "The Indian Labor Structure in the Portuguese Amazon." In *Colonial Roots of Modern Brazil*, ed. Dauril Alden. 199–230. Berkeley: University of California Press, 1973.

Magalhães, Agenor Couto de. *Encantos do Oeste*. Rio de Janeiro: Imprensa Nacional, 1945.

Magalhães, Amilcar Botelho de. *Índios do Brasil*. Mexico City: Instituto Indigenista Interamericano, 1947.

———. *A obra ciclópica do General Rondon*. Rio de Janeiro: Biblioteca do Exército, 1956.

———. "A pacificação dos índios chavante." *América Indígena* 7, no. 3 (Jan. 1947): 333–39.

Magalhães, Basílio de. *Em defesa dos Brasilíndios*. Rio de Janeiro: Imprensa Nacional, 1946.

Mahar, Dennis J. *Frontier Development Policy in Brazil: A Study of Amazonia*. New York: Praeger, 1979.

Mainwaring, Scott. *The Catholic Church and Politics in Brazil, 1916–1985*. Stanford: Stanford University Press, 1986.

Maio, Marcos Chor, and Ricardo Ventura Santos, eds. *Raça, ciência, sociedade*. Rio de Janeiro: FIOCRUZ, 1996.

Malcher, José Maria da Gama. *Índios: Grau de integração na comunidade nacional*. Rio de Janeiro: CNPI, 1963.

———. *Por que fracassa a Proteção aos Índios?* Unpublished manuscript, 1963.

Mallon, Florencia E. *Peasant and Nation: The Making of Postcolonial Mexico and Peru*. Berkeley: University of California Press, 1995.

Marçal, Heitor. *Moral ameríndia*. Rio de Janeiro: Ministério de Educação e Saude, 1946.

Marcigaglia, Luiz. *Os Salesianos no Brasil*. São Paulo: Escolas Profissionais Salesianas, 1955.

Margolis, Maxine, and William E. Carter, eds. *Brazil: Anthropological Perspectives*. New York: Columbia University Press, 1979.

Marques, José de Oliveira. "Colonização e povoamento." *Revista de Imigração e Colonização* 1, no. 2 (Apr. 1940): 205–10.

Martins, Edilson. *Nós do Araguaia*. Rio de Janeiro: Graal, 1974.

Martins, José de Souza. *A chegada do estranho*. São Paulo: Editora Hucitec, 1993.

———. *Expropriação e violência: A questão política no campo*. São Paulo: Hucitec, 1980.

———. *Não há terra para plantar neste verão*. Petrópolis: Vozes, 1986.

———. "The State and the Militarization of the Agrarian Question in Brazil." In *Frontier Expansion in Amazonia*, ed. Marianne Schmink and Charles H. Wood. Gainesville: University of Florida Press, 1991.

Massey, Doreen. *Space, Place, and Gender*. Minneapolis: University of Minnesota Press, 1994.

Mato Grosso. Secretaria de Planejamento e Coordenação Geral. *Mato Grosso é assim*. Rio de Janeiro: Secretaria de Planejamento e Coordenação Geral, n.d.

Matthews, Kenneth. *Brazilian Interior*. London: Peter Davies, 1957.

Maufrais, Raymond. *Aventuras em Mato Grosso*. São Paulo: Edições Melhoramentos, 1960.

Maybury-Lewis, Biorn. *The Politics of the Possible: The Brazilian Rural Workers Trade Union Movement, 1964–1985*. Philadelphia: Temple University Press, 1994.

Maybury-Lewis, David. *Akwē-Shavante Society,* 2d ed. New York: Oxford University Press, 1974.

———. *The Savage and the Innocent,* 2d ed. Boston: Beacon Press, 1988.

———. "Some Crucial Distinctions in Central Brazilian Ethnology." *Anthropos* 60 (1965): 340–58.

———, ed. *Dialectical Societies: The Ge and Bororo of Central Brazil.* Cambridge, MA: Harvard University Press, 1979.

———, ed. *The Prospects for Plural Societies.* Washington, DC: American Ethnological Society, 1982.

Meireles, Silo. *Brasil Central: Notas e impressões.* Rio de Janeiro: Biblioteca do Exército, 1960.

Melatti, Julio Cezar. *Índios do Brasil.* São Paulo: Hucitec, 1987.

Meliá, Bartolomeu. *Educação indígena e alfabetização.* São Paulo: Loyola, 1979.

Mello, Darcy S. Bandeira de. *Entre Índios e revoluções.* São Paulo: Editora Soma Ltda., 1982.

Mello, Raul Silveira de. *Aos Guaicurus deve o Brasil o Sul de Mato Grosso.* Rio de Janeiro: Imprensa de Exército, 1957.

Mendes, Gilmar Ferreira. *Domínio da União sobre as terras indígenas: O Parque Nacional do Xingu.* Brasília: Ministério Público Federal, 1988.

Méndez, Cecilia. "Incas Sí, Indios No: Notes on Peruvian Creole Nationalism and Its Contemporary Crisis." *Journal of Latin American Studies* 28 (1996): 197–225.

Mendonça, Rubens de. *História de Mato Grosso.* São Paulo, 1970.

Menezes, Claudia. "Missionários e índios em Mato Grosso: Os Xavante da Reserva de São Marcos." Ph.D. diss., Universidade de São Paulo, 1984.

———. "Os Xavantes e o movimento de fronteira no leste matogrossense." *Revista de antropologia* 25 (1982): 63–87.

Menezes, Maria Lúcia Pires. "Parque Indígena do Xingu: A construção de um território estatal." Master's thesis, Universidade Federal do Rio de Janeiro, 1990.

Mesquita, José de. "Espírito matogrossense." *Cultura Política* 3, no. 28 (June 1943): 89–93.

Metcalf, Alida C. *Family and Frontier in Colonial Brazil: Santana de Parnaíba.* Berkeley: University of California Press, 1992.

———. "Millenarian Slaves? The Santidade de Jaguaripe and Slave Resistance in the Americas." *American Historical Review* 104 (1999): 1531–59.

Miceli, Sergio. *Intelectuais e classe dirigente no Brasil (1920–45).* São Paulo: DIFEL, 1979.

Miguez, José Maria Guedes. *Chacina do Meruri: A verdade dos fatos.* São Paulo: Editora Gazeta Maçônica, 1980.

Miracle, A. W., Jr., ed. *Bilingualism: Social Issues and Policy Implications.* Athens: University of Georgia Press, 1983.

Monteiro, John Manuel. *Negros da terra: Índios e bandeirantes nas origens de São Paulo.* São Paulo: Companhia das Letras, 1994.

————. "As 'raças' indígenas no pensamento brasileiro do Império." In *Raça, ciência e sociedade*, ed. Marcos Chor Maio and Ricardo Ventura Santos. 15–21. Rio de Janeiro: FIOCRUZ, 1996.

Moog, Clodomir Vianna. *Bandeirantes and Pioneers*. Trans. L. L. Barrett. New York: George Braziller, 1964.

Moran, Emilio F. *Through Amazonian Eyes: The Human Ecology of Amazonian Population*. Iowa City: University of Iowa Press, 1993.

Morse, Richard M., ed. *The Bandeirantes*. New York: Knopf, 1965.

Nasser, David, and Jean Manzon. *Mergulho na aventura*. Rio de Janeiro: O Cruzeiro, 1945.

Needell, Jeffrey D. "History, Race, and the State in the Thought of Oliveira Viana." *Hispanic American Historical Review* 75 (1995): 1–30.

Neel, James V. *Physician to the Gene Pool*. New York: Wiley, 1994.

Neel, J. V., et al. "Studies on the Xavante Indians of the Brazilian Mato Grosso." *American Journal of Human Genetics* 16 (Mar. 1964): 52–140.

Neiva, Arthur. *Estudos da língua nacional*. São Paulo: Editora Nacional, 1940.

Neves, Maria Manuela Renha de Novis. *Elites políticas: Competição e dinâmica patridário-eleitoral (caso de Mato Grosso)*. Rio de Janeiro: IUPERJ, 1988.

Normano, J. F. *Brazil: A Study of Economic Types*. Chapel Hill: University of North Carolina Press, 1935.

Novaes, Sylvia Caiuby. *Jogo de espelhos: Imagens da representação de si através dos outros*. São Paulo: Editora da Universidade de São Paulo, 1993.

O'Brien, Jay, and William Roseberry, eds. *Golden Ages, Dark Ages: Imagining the Past in Anthropology and History*. Berkeley: University of California Press, 1991.

O'Connor, Geoffrey. *Amazon Journal: Dispatches from a Vanishing Frontier*. New York: Penguin, 1998.

Oliveira, Acary de Passos. *Roncador-Xingu: Roteiro de uma Expedição*. Goiânia: n.p., 1976(?).

Oliveira, Haroldo Cândido de. *Índios e sertanejos do Araguaia*. São Paulo: Edições Melhoramentos, n.d.

Oliveira, Ismarth Araujo de. *FUNAI: Dez anos de política indigenista unificada*. Brasília: FUNAI, n.d.

Oliveira, Luis R. Cardoso de. "Colonização e diferenciação: Os colonos de Canarana." Master's thesis, Universidade Federal do Rio de Janeiro, 1981.

Oliveira, Plínio Correa. *Tribalismo indígena: Ideal comuno-missionário para o Brasil*. São Paulo: Vera Cruz, 1978.

Oliveira, Roberto Cardoso de. *Do índio ao bugre: O processo de assimilação dos Terena*. Rio de Janeiro: F. Alves, 1977.

————. "Relatório de uma investigação sobre terras em Mato Grosso." In SPI, *Relatório* (1954): 173–84.

————. *A sociologia do Brasil indígena*. Rio de Janeiro: Tempo Brasileiro, 1972.

Oliveira Filho, João Pacheco de. *"O nosso governo": Os Ticuna e o regime militar*. São Paulo: Marco Zero, 1988.

————. "Pardos, mestiços ou caboclos: Os índios nos censos nacionais no Brasil (1872–1980)." *Horizontes Antropológicos* 3, no. 6 (Oct. 1997): 60–83.

————, ed. *Os poderes e as terras dos índios*. Rio de Janeiro: PPGAS/UFRJ-MN, 1989.

————, ed. *Sociedades indígenas e indigenismo no Brasil*. Rio de Janeiro: Marco Zero, 1987.

Operação Anchieta. *Ação indigenista como ação política*. Cuiabá: OPAN, 1987.

Operação Anchieta and Conselho Indigenista Missionário. *Dossiê índios em Mato Grosso*. Cuiabá: CIMI, 1987.

Organização Internacional do Trabalho. *Convenção (169) sobre Povos Indígenas e Tribais em Países Independentes e Resolução sobre a Ação da OIT concernante aos Povos Indígenas e Tribais*. Brasília: n.p., 1992.

Ortner, Sherry B. "Resistance and the Problem of Ethnographic Refusal." *Comparative Studies in Society and History* 37 (1995): 173–93.

Otávio, Rodrigo. *Os selvagens americanos perante o direito*. São Paulo: Nacional, 1946.

Padilha, Leão. *O Brasil na posse de si mesmo*. Rio de Janeiro: Olímpica, 1941.

Padilla, Ezequiel. *O homem livre da América*. Trans. Fernando Tudé de Souza. Rio de Janeiro: O Cruzeiro, 1943.

Pagden, Anthony. *The Fall of Natural Man: The American Indian and the Origins of Comparative Ethnology*. Cambridge, England: Cambridge University Press, 1986.

Paula, José Maria de. *Terras dos índios*. Rio de Janeiro: Ministério da Agricultura/SPI, 1944.

Pereira, Anthony. *The End of the Peasantry: The Rural Labor Movement in Northeast Brazil, 1961–1988*. Pittsburgh: University of Pittsburgh Press, 1997.

Pereira, Armando de Arruda. *Diário de viagem de São Paulo a Belém do Pará Descendo o Araguaya*. São Paulo: Gráphica Paulista, 1935.

Pompermayer, Malori José. "The State and the Frontier in Brazil: A Case Study of the Amazon." Ph.D. diss., Stanford University, 1979.

Posey, Darrell A., and William Balée, eds. *Resource Management in Amazonia: Indigenous and Folk Strategies*. Bronx: New York Botanical Garden, 1989.

Povoas, Lenine. *História de Mato Grosso*. São Paulo: Resenha, 1992.

Prado, Eduardo Barros. *Matto Grosso: El infierno junto al paraíso*. Buenos Aires: Ediciones Peuser, 1968.

Pratt, Mary Louise. *Imperial Eyes: Travel Writing and Transculturation*. New York: Routledge, 1992.

Price, David. *Before the Bulldozer: The Nambiquara Indians and the World Bank*. Cabin John, MD: Seven Locks Press, 1989.

Price, Richard. *First Time: The Historical Vision of an Afro-American People*. Baltimore: Johns Hopkins University Press, 1983.

Primitive People's Fund/Survival International. *Report of a Visit to the Indians of Brazil*. London, 1971.

Rabben, Linda. *Unnatural Selection: The Yanomami, the Kayapó and the Onslaught of Civilisation.* Seattle: University of Washington Press, 1998.

Ramos, Alcida Rita. *Indigenism: Ethnic Politics in Brazil.* Madison: University of Wisconsin Press, 1998.

Rappaport, Joanne. *Cumbe Reborn: An Andean Ethnography of History.* Chicago: University of Chicago Press, 1994.

———. *The Politics of Memory.* Durham, NC: Duke University Press, 1998.

Ravagnani, Oswaldo Martins. "A experiência Xavante com o mundo dos brancos." Ph.D. diss., Fundação Escola de Sociologia e Política de São Paulo, 1978.

Ravagnani, Oswaldo Martins, and Zélia Maria Presotto. "Processo aculturativo dos índios Xavante." *Logos* 3, no. 3 (1971): 71–82.

Redfield, Robert. *The Primitive World and Its Transformations.* Ithaca, NY: Cornell University Press, 1953.

Ribeiro, Darcy. *Confissões.* São Paulo: Companhia das Letras, 1997.

———. *Os índios e a civilização.* Rio de Janeiro: Civilização Brasileira, 1970.

———. *A política indigenista brasileira.* Rio de Janeiro: Ministério da Agricultura, 1962.

Ribeiro, Lélia Rita E. de Figueiredo. *O homem e a terra.* N.p., n.d.

Ribeiro da Silva, Hermano. *Nos sertões do Araguaia.* São Paulo: J. Fagundes, 1936.

Ricardo, Cassiano. *Marcha para Oeste: A influência de "bandeira" na formação social e política do Brasil.* 1940. Rio de Janeiro: José Olympio, 1959.

———. *O indianismo de Gonçalves Dias.* São Paulo: Edição de Conselho Estadual de Cultura, 1964.

The Rights of Indigenous Peoples. Geneva, Switzerland: Centre for Human Rights, 1990.

Rocha, Leandro Mendes. "A Marcha para o Oeste e os índios do Xingu." FUNAI, *Índios do Brasil* 2 (June 1992): 3–25.

Rondon, Cândido Mariano da Silva. "José Bonifácio e o problema indígena." *Instituto Histórico e Geográfico Brasileiro* 174 (1939): 867–93.

———. *Matto-Grosso: O que ella nos offerece e o que espera de nós.* N.d.

———. *Rumo ao Oeste: Conferência realizada pelo General Rondon no D.I.P. em 3-XI-40 e discursos do Dr. Ivan Lins e do General Rondon, pronunciados na Associação Brasileira da Educação.* Rio de Janeiro: Laemmert, 1942.

Rondon, Cândido Mariano da Silva, and Esther de Viveiros. *Rondon conta sua vida.* Rio de Janeiro: São José, 1958.

Rondon, Frederico. *Colonização nacional, o magno problema brasileiro.* Rio de Janeiro: IBGE, 1948.

Rondon, Joaquim. *O índio como sentinela das nossas fronteiras.* Rio de Janeiro: Departamento de Imprensa Nacional, 1949.

Rondon, José Lucídio Nunes. *Geografia e história de Mato Grosso.* São Paulo: Gráfica Urupés, 1970.

———. *Recursos econômicos de Mato Grosso.* São Paulo: Gráfica Urupés, 1972.

Roquette-Pinto, Edgar. "Contribuição a antropologia do Brasil." *Revista de Imigração e Colonização* 1, no. 3 (July 1940): 437–54.

Rosaldo, Renato. *Culture and Truth.* Boston: Beacon Press, 1993.

Roseberry, William. *Anthropologies and Histories: Essays in Culture, History, and Political Economy.* New Brunswick, NJ: Rutgers University Press, 1989.

———. "Hegemony and the Language of Contention." In *Everyday Forms of State Formation: Revolution and the Negotiation of Rule in Modern Mexico*, ed. Gilbert M. Joseph and Daniel Nugent. 355–66. Durham, NC: Duke University Press, 1994.

Rubim, Rezende. *Reservas de brasilidade.* São Paulo: Editora Nacional, 1939.

Russell Tribunal IV on the Rights of the Indians of the Americas. *Report of the Fourth Russell Tribunal on the Rights of the Indians of the Americas.* Amsterdam: Workgroup Indian Project, 1980.

Sá, Cassio Veiga de. *Memórias de um cuiabano honorário, 1939–45.* São Paulo: Resenha Tributária, n.d.

Sá, Cristina. "Aldeia de São Marcos: Transformações na habitação de uma comunidade Xavante." Master's thesis, Universidade de São Paulo, 1982.

Sahlins, Marshall. "Goodbye to *Tristes Tropes*: Ethnography in the Context of Modern World History." *Journal of Modern History* 65 (1993): 1–25.

Salzano, Francisco M., James V. Neel, and David Maybury-Lewis. "Further Studies on the Xavante Indians—Demographic Data on Two Additional Villages: Genetic Structure of the Tribe." *American Journal of Human Genetics* 19 (July 1967): 463–89.

Salzano, Francisco M., and Sidia M. Callegari-Jacques. *South American Indians: A Case Study in Evolution.* Oxford: Clarendon Press, 1988.

Santilli, Juliana. *Os direitos indígenas e a constituição.* Porto Alegre: Núcleo de Direitos Indígenas/Sérgio Antonio Fabris Editor, 1993.

Santos, Sílvio Coelho dos. *Educação e Sociedades Tribais.* Porto Alegre: Movimento, 1975.

———. "A escola em duas populações tribais." *Revista de antropologia* 14 (1966): 31–35.

———. *Índios e brancos no Sul do Brasil: A dramática experiência dos Xokleng.* Florianópolis: Edeme, 1973.

———. *A integração do índio na sociedade regional: A função dos postos indígenas em Santa Catarina.* Florianópolis: Universidade Federal de Santa Catarina, 1970.

———. *Os povos indígenas e a Constituinte.* Florianópolis: UFSC/Movimento, 1989.

———, ed. *O índio perante o direito.* Florianópolis: Universidade Federal de Santa Catarina, 1982.

Santos, Sílvio Coelho dos, et al. *Sociedades indígenas e o direito: Uma questão de direitos humanos.* Florianópolis: Universidade Federal de Santa Catarina, 1985.

Schmink, Marianne, and Charles H. Wood, *Contested Frontiers in Amazonia.* New York: Columbia University Press, 1992.

———, eds. *Frontier Expansion in Amazonia.* Gainesville: University of Florida Press, 1984.

Schmitter, Philippe C. *Interest Conflict and Political Change in Brazil.* Stanford: Stanford University Press, 1971.

Schneider, Ben Ross. *Politics within the State: Elite Bureaucrats and Industrial Policy in Brazil.* Pittsburgh: University of Pittsburgh Press, 1991.

Schwantes, Norberto. *Uma cruz em Terranova.* São Paulo: Scritta Oficina Editorial, 1989.

Schwarcz, Lilia Moritz. *The Spectacle of the Races: Scientists, Institutions, and the Race Question in Brazil, 1870–1930.* Trans. Leland Guyer. New York: Hill and Wang, 1999.

Schwartz, Stuart B. "Indian Labor and New World Plantations: European Demands and Indian Responses in Northeastern Brazil." *American Historical Review* 83 (1978): 43–79.

Schwartzman, Simon. *Bases do Autoritarismo Brasileiro,* 2d ed. Rio de Janeiro: Editora Campus, 1982.

Schwartzman, Simon, Helena Maria Bousquet Bomeny, and Vanda Maria Ribeiro Costa. *Tempos de Capanema.* Rio de Janeiro: Paz e Terra, 1984.

Schwartzman, Stephan, Ana Valéria Araújo, and Paulo Pankararú. "Brazil: The Legal Battle over Indigenous Land Rights." *NACLA Report on the Americas* 29, no. 5 (Mar.–Apr. 1996): 36–43.

Schwarz, Roberto. *Misplaced Ideas: Essays on Brazilian Culture.* London: Verso, 1992.

Scobie, James R. *Argentina: A City and a Nation.* New York: Oxford University Press, 1971.

Scott, James C. *Domination and the Arts of Resistance: Hidden Transcripts.* New Haven: Yale University Press, 1990.

———. *Seeing Like a State: How Certain Schemes to Improve the Human Condition Have Failed.* New Haven: Yale University Press, 1998.

———. *Weapons of the Weak: Everyday Forms of Peasant Resistance.* New Haven: Yale University Press, 1985.

Seed, Patricia. *Ceremonies of Possession in Europe's Conquest of the New World, 1492–1640.* Cambridge, England: Cambridge University Press, 1995.

Seeger, Anthony. *Os índios e nós.* Rio de Janeiro: Campus, 1980.

Sereburã et al. *Wamrêmé za'ra-Nossa Palavra: Mito e história do povo Xavante.* Trans. Paulo Supretaprã Xavante and Jurandir Siridiwê Xavante. São Paulo: Editora SENAC, 1998.

Serviço de Proteção aos Índios [SPI]. "Memória sobre as causas determinantes da diminuição das populações indígenas do Brasil." Paper presented at the 9th Congresso Brasileiro de Geografia, 29 July 1940.

SETH (pseud. Álvaro Marins). *O Brasil pela imagem: Quadros expressivos da formação e do progresso da pátria brasileira.* Rio de Janeiro, Indústria do Livro 1943.

Shanin, Teodor, ed. *Peasants and Peasant Societies.* Hammondsworth, England: Penguin, 1971.

Sider, Gerald. "When Parrots Learn to Talk, and Why They Can't: Domination, Deception, and Self-Deception in Indian-White Relations." *Comparative Studies in Society and History* 29 (1987): 3–23.

Siqueira, Deoclécio Lima de. *Caminhada com Eduardo Gomes.* Rio de Janeiro: Novas Direções, 1989.

Siqueira, Elizabeth Madureira, Lourença Alves da Costa, and Cathia Maria Coelho Carvalho. *O processo histórico de Mato Grosso.* Cuiabá: Universidade Federal de Mato Grosso, 1990.

Simonian, Lígia. "'Terra de posseiros': Um estudo sobre as políticas de terras indígenas." Master's thesis, Universidade Federal do Rio de Janeiro, 1981.

Skidmore, Thomas E. *Black into White: Race and Nationality in Brazilian Thought.* Durham, NC: Duke University Press, 1993.

———. *Brazil: Five Centuries of Change.* New York: Oxford University Press, 1999.

———. *Politics in Brazil, 1930–1964.* New York: Oxford University Press, 1986.

———. *The Politics of Military Rule in Brazil, 1964–85.* New York: Oxford University Press, 1988.

Skocpol, Theda. "Bringing the State Back In: Strategies of Analysis in Current Research." In *Bringing the State Back In*, ed. Peter Evans, Dietrich Rueschmeyer, and Theda Skocpol. 3–37. Cambridge, England: Cambridge University Press, 1985.

Smith, Anthony. *Mato Grosso: The Last Virgin Land.* New York: Dutton, 1971.

Sodré, Nelson Werneck. "Oeste." *Revista Militar Brasileira* 41, nos. 1–2 (1944): 83–98.

Sorj, Bernardo. *Estado e classes sociais na agricultura.* Rio de Janeiro: Zahar, 1980.

Souza, Lincoln de. *Entre os Xavantes do Roncador.* Rio de Janeiro: Ministério da Educação e Saude, 1952.

———. *Os Xavantes e a civilização.* Rio de Janeiro: Instituto Brasileiro de Geografia e Estatística, 1953.

Souza, Márcio, and others. *Os índios vão a luta.* Rio de Janeiro: Marco Zero, 1981.

Spivak, Gayatri Chakravorty. "Can the Subaltern Speak?" In *Marxism and the Interpretation of Culture*, ed. Cary Nelson and Lawrence Grossberg. 271–313. Urbana: University of Illinois Press, 1988.

Stauffer, David Hall. "The Origin and Establishment of Brazil's Indian Service, 1889–1910." Ph.D. diss., University of Texas at Austin, 1955.

Stepan, Alfred, ed. *Democratizing Brazil: Problems of Transition and Consolidation.* New York: Oxford University Press, 1989.

Stepan, Nancy Leys. *"The Hour of Eugenics": Race, Gender and Nation in Latin America.* Ithaca, NY: Cornell University Press, 1991.

Steward, Julian, ed. *Handbook of South American Indians*. Washington, DC: Smithsonian Institution, 1946.

Stoll, David. *Fishers of Men or Founders of Empire? The Wycliffe Bible Translators in Latin America*. London: Zed Press, 1982.

Suess, Paulo. *A causa indígena na caminhada e a proposta do CIMI: 1972–1989*. Petrópolis: Vozes, 1989.

———. *Culturas indígenas e evangelização*. Petrópolis: Vozes, 1981.

———. *Em defesa dos povos indígenas: Documentos e legislação*. Petrópolis: Vozes, 1980.

Summerhill, William. "Transport Improvements and Economic Growth in Brazil and Mexico." In *How Latin America Fell Behind*, ed. Stephen Haber. 93–117. Stanford: Stanford University Press, 1997.

Supysáua: A Documentary Report on the Conditions of Indian Peoples in Brazil. Berkeley: Indígena and American Friends of Brazil, 1974.

Supysáua: O índio brasileiro. Rio de Janeiro: Editora Vecchi, 1970.

Tardin, Antônio Tebaldi, et al. "Projetos agropecuários da Amazônia: Desmatamento e fiscalização—Relatório." *A Amazônia Brasileira em Foco* 12 (1978): 7–45.

Tavener, Christopher J. "The Karajá and the Brazilian Frontier." In *Peoples and Cultures of Native South America*, ed. Daniel R. Gross. Garden City, NY: Doubleday, 1973.

Telles, Carlos. *História secreta da Fundação Brasil Central*. Rio de Janeiro: Editora Chavantes, 1946.

Tendler, Judith. *Good Government in the Tropics*. Baltimore: Johns Hopkins University Press, 1997.

Thompson, Paul. *The Voice of the Past: Oral History*. New York: Oxford University Press, 1988.

Thurner, Mark. *From Two Republics to One Divided*. Durham, NC: Duke University Press, 1997.

Topik, Steven. *The Political Economy of the Brazilian State, 1889–1930*. Austin: University of Texas Press, 1987.

Travassos, Mario. *Projeção continental do Brasil*. São Paulo: Companhia Editora Nacional, 1938.

Tucci Carneiro, Maria Luiza. *O anti-semitismo na era Vargas*. São Paulo: Brasiliense, 1988.

Turner, Terence. "The Gê and Bororo Societies as Dialectical Systems: A General Model." In *Dialectical Societies: The Gê and Bororo of Central Brazil*, ed. David Maybury-Lewis. Cambridge, MA: Harvard University Press, 1979.

———. "Representing, Resisting, Rethinking: Historical Transformations of Kayapo Culture and Anthropological Consciousness." In *Colonial Situations: Essays on the Contextualization of Ethnographic Knowledge*, ed. George W. Stocking Jr. 285–313. Madison: University of Wisconsin Press, 1991.

Tyler, S. Lyman. *The Indian Cause in Contemporary Brazilian Law*. Salt Lake City: University of Utah Press, 1981.

Urban, Greg. "Developments in the Situation of Brazilian Tribal Populations from 1976 to 1982." *Latin American Research Review* 20, no. 1 (1985): 7–25.

Urban, Greg, and Joel Sherzer, eds. *Nation-States and Indians in Latin America*. Austin: University of Texas Press, 1991.

Vainfas, Ronaldo. *A heresia dos índios: Catolicismo e rebeldia no Brasil colonial*. São Paulo: Companhia das Letras, 1995.

Varese, Stefano. *Indianidad y descolonización en América Latina: Documentos de la Segunda Reunión de Barbados*. Mexico: Editorial Nueva Imagen, 1979.

Vargas, Getúlio. *Diário*. São Paulo: Siciliano; Rio de Janeiro: Fundação Getúlio Vargas, 1995.

———. *A nova política do Brasil*. Rio de Janeiro: J. Olympio, 1938.

Varjão, Valdon. *Aragarças: Portal da Marcha para o Oeste*. Brasília: Senado Federal Centro Gráfico, 1989.

———. *Barra do Garças: Migalhas de sua história*. Brasília: Senado Federal Centro Gráfico, 1985.

———. *Barra do Garças no passado*. Brasília: Senado Federal Centro Gráfico, 1980.

Vasconcellos, Gilberto. *A ideologia Curupira: Análise do discurso integralista*. São Paulo: Editora Brasiliense, 1979.

Velho, Otávio Guilherme. *Capitalismo autoritário e campesinato*, Rio de Janeiro: DIFEL, 1976.

Velloso, Nilo Oliveira. *Rumo ao desconhecido*. Rio de Janeiro: n.p., n.d.

"Vida e idéias de Meireles." *Revista de atualidade indígena* 21 (July–Aug. 1981): 54–59.

Vieira Filho, J. P. B. "Problemas de aculturação alimentar dos Xavante e Bororo." *Revista de antropologia* 24 (1981): 37–40.

Villas Bôas, Orlando, and Cláudio Villas Bôas. *Almanaque do sertão: Histórias e visitantes, sertanejos e índios*. São Paulo: Globo, 1997.

———. *A Marcha para o Oeste*. São Paulo: Globo, 1994.

Wade, Peter. *Blackness and Race Mixture: The Dynamics of Racial Identity in Colombia*. Baltimore: Johns Hopkins University Press, 1995.

Wagley, Charles. *Welcome of Tears: The Tapirapé Indians of Central Brazil*. New York: Oxford University Press, 1977.

Warren, Kay B. "Transforming Memories and Histories: The Meanings of Ethnic Resurgence for Mayan Indians." In *Americas: New Interpretive Essays*, ed. Alfred Stepan. 189–219. New York: Oxford University Press, 1992.

Weber, David J., and Jane M. Rausch, eds. *Where Cultures Meet: Frontiers in Latin American History*. Wilmington, DE: Scholarly Resources, 1994.

Weinstein, E. David, James V. Neel, and F. M. Salzano. "Further Studies on the Xavante Indians: The Physical Status of the Xavantes of Simões Lopes." *American Journal of Human Genetics* 19 (July 1967): 532–42.

Welch, Cliff. *The Seed Was Planted: The São Paulo Roots of Brazil's Rural Labor Movement, 1924–1964*. University Park, PA: The Pennsylvania State University Press, 1999.

Weyer, Edward, Jr. *Jungle Quest*. New York: Harper and Brothers, 1955.

White, Hayden. *Tropics of Discourse: Essays in Cultural Criticism*. Baltimore: Johns Hopkins University Press, 1985.

White, Richard. "Frederick Jackson Turner and Buffalo Bill." In *The Frontier in American Culture*, ed. James R. Grossman. Berkeley: University of California, 1994.

———. *The Middle Ground: Indians, Empires, and Republics in the Great Lakes Region, 1650–1815*. New York: Cambridge University Press, 1995.

Williams, Daryle. "*Ad perpetuam rei memoriam*: The Vargas Regime and Brazil's National Historical Patrimony, 1930–1945." *Luso-Brazilian Review* 31 (1994): 45–75.

Williams, Suzanne. "Land Rights and the Manipulation of Identity: Official Indian Policy in Brazil." *Journal of Latin American Studies* 15 (1983): 137–61.

Wirth, John D. "Tenentismo in the Brazilian Revolution of 1930." *Hispanic American Historical Review* 44 (1964): 161–79.

Wolf, Eric. *Europe and the People without History*. Berkeley: University of California Press, 1982.

Wood, Charles H., and José Alberto Magno de Carvalho. *The Demography of Inequality in Brazil*. Cambridge, England: Cambridge University Press, 1988.

Wright, Robin, and Ismaelillo, eds. *Native Peoples in Struggle*. New York: E.R.I.N. Publications, 1982.

Young, Thomas. "Avante ao Chavante." *O índio do Brasil* 90 (Apr.–June 1957): 7–8.

Index

Abertura. *See* Military Rule: political liberalization

Abreu, João Capistrano de, 222 n.20

Aeronautics: and western expansion, 78, 83, 94–95, 102. *See also* Força Aérea Brasileira

Ajudância Autônoma de Barra do Garças (Autonomous Adjutancy of Barra do Garças, AJABAG), 188, 195–98, 201–4, 206–8

Aldeias, 4–5, 41, 253 n.60

Alencar, José de, 36

Amazonia. *See* Legal Amazonia

Andrade, Oswald de, 36

Aniceto, 174, 203–4, 212

Anthropologists, 7, 51, 118, 178, 188, 191, 202, 204–5, 261 n.91

Apoena (Chief of Pimentel Barbosa community), 59–60, 62, 77–78, 82–84, 86, 88, 102, 116, 127–28, 169, 241 n.19

Apoena (Chief of São Marcos community), 117, 203–4

Aragarças, 46, 57

Araguaia guerrillas, 171, 186

Araguaia River, 3–5, 23, 46, 48, 50, 60, 101–2; environs of, 50, 93, 14, 171

Araújo de Oliveira, Ismarth, 156, 171, 175, 188, 191

Areões. *See* Xavante communities: Areões

Associação dos Empresários da Amazônia (Association of Amazonian Entrepeneurs, AEA), 147–48, 150, 155

A'uwe, 67, 116, 216

Babatti (João Evangelista), 172, 177, 200

Backlands. *See* Frontier

Baldus, Herbert, 62

Bananal Island, 23, 30, 46, 50, 144

Banco da Amazônia (BASA), 141, 148

Bandeira de Mello, Oscar Jerônimo, 157, 162

Bandeirantes. *See* Bandeiras

Bandeiras: and enslavement of Indians, 3–4, 32; and symbolism for twentieth-century expansionism, 32–34, 59, 93

Barra do Garças: county of, 94–96, 108, 148, 150–51, 155, 168–71, 176, 188; map of county of, 92; migration of southerners to, 163–64; town of, 101, 150, 166, 183, 187, 195–96, 206

Batovi River, 117, 119–21, 165–66. *See also* Simões Lopes post

Bororo, 5, 53, 98, 117, 121, 133, 144, 169–70, 177

Brasília, 21, 113–14, 161, 140, 150, 170, 180, 193, 196, 198, 201, 203–7, 210

Brazilian law: and definition of indigenous peoples, 21, 24, 40, 52; indigenous engagement with, 16, 21, 23–24, 174, 214; and indigenous rights, 16, 89–90, 94–98, 107–8, 132, 145–46, 173, 179; and status of indigenous land, 16, 24, 89–90, 142–46, 153, 164, 212, 215. *See also* Civil Code of 1916; Constitution of 1988; Tutela

Butler, Robert, 79, 85–87

Caboclo, 24

Caciques. *See* Xavante leadership

Capitariquara post, 79, 81, 83–87

Casaldáliga, Pedro, 259 n.54

Castelo Branco, Humberto, 141, 173

Catholic Church: and defense of indigenous rights, 176–80; and promotion of pan-Indianism, 177; and relations with Brazilian state, 54, 176. *See also*

213; and cultural construction of Indian, 8, 11–13, 18, 25–26, 32–44, 48, 56–57, 63, 130, 188; and developmentalist nationalism, 8, 10, 18, 28, 114; and foreign immigrants, 29, 39, 50, 130, 232 n.85, 237 n.54; and political centralization, 8, 25, 28, 31, 34, 42, 48, 140; and racial discourse, 38–39, 43, 188, 231 n.77; and ramifications for indigenous peoples, 8, 11, 42–44, 65; and relations with Catholic Church, 54; and rights of rural workers, 31; and role of intellectuals, 35–37; state censorship and propaganda under, 25, 31–35, 38, 57; and western expansion, 8, 10, 12, 26, 28–31, 45–46, 57–58, 65. *See also* March to the West; Vargas, Getúlio

Estatuto do Índio (Indian Statute), 145–46, 198, 207

Ethnicity, 7, 72–74; and Brazilian state, 10, 13, 18, 26, 39, 43, 130, 205, 214, 217; conceptual definitions of, 12, 15–16, 115, 205, 226 n.59; as political marker, 16, 20, 130–36, 174, 216. *See also* Indianness

Evangelical Protestant missionaries, 55, 79, 85–87; and efforts to reorder Xavante lifestyles, 86, 117–21, 123–29. *See also* Missionaries; Summer Institute of Linguistics

Expedição Roncador-Xingu. *See* Roncador-Xingu Expedition

Fazenda Xavantina, 1, 152–54, 159–60, 162, 164–65, 168, 172–76, 180–84, 186

Fazendeiros, 78, 101, 117, 147–48, 151, 153–55, 158, 164–72, 180, 183–84, 187, 197, 208, 215

Figueiredo, Arnaldo de, 95–96

Figueiredo, João Batista, 176, 182–83, 190

Figueiredo Report, 142–44. *See also* Genocide

Firearms, 77, 83–85, 87, 158, 165, 181

Flowers, Nancy, 118, 241 n.19

Força Aérea Brasileira (Brazilian Air Force, FAB), 64, 77–78, 94, 102, 127

Foreign Debt: crisis of, 208, 213

Foweraker, Joe, 9

Freyre, Gilberto, 37

Frontier: Brazilian state developmental policy and, 6, 8–11, 44, 114, 138–42, 210, 215; and capital accumulation, 5, 7–10, 19, 40, 45, 55, 72, 74, 90, 96, 101, 107, 118, 136, 138–45, 211, 215; conceptualization of, 8–9; constructed as masculine domain, 52, 54, 236 n.38; migration to, 9–10, 19, 45, 50, 136, 148, 163–64, 167; myth of racial harmony on, 13, 25; and national security, 10–11, 26, 29–31, 39–40, 138; violence on, 5, 9, 34, 48, 51, 55, 62, 95, 100–102, 115–18, 142, 153, 156, 160, 165, 167, 169–71, 181–82, 185. *See also* Central Brazil; Legal Amazonia; March to the West; Military rule

Fundação Brasil Central (Central Brazil Foundation, FBC), 45–46, 57–58, 78, 94–95

Fundação Nacional do Índio (National Indian Foundation, FUNAI), 165–72, 177, 189, 191–99, 218; creation and jurisdiction of, 143–47; corruption in, 156, 170, 174, 206–9; and employment of Xavante, 2, 195–96; and initial efforts to reserve Xavante land, 154–61; and issuing of certidão negativa, 153, 155–56, 162, 184; landowners' rancor toward, 158, 165–67, 181, 187–88, 197, 202; and poor conditions at indigenous posts, 2, 154, 195, 209; post chiefs, 159, 192, 195–97, 200–205, 211; Xavante descend upon headquarters of, 113, 165, 180, 196, 198, 200–208. *See also* Ajudância Autônoma de Barra do Garças; Indigenous policy; Military rule: indigenous policy; Ministry of Interior

Garimpeiros, 50–51, 57, 80, 150, 215

Gathering. *See* Xavante political economy: hunting and gathering

Gê: languages, 1, 67; social structures, 5, 16, 71

Geisel, Ernesto, 162–63, 166, 176, 180, 185, 190
Genocide, 15, 143–44, 257 n.26, 260 n.91
Giaccaria, Bartolomeu, 123, 131
Goiás, 3, 5, 26–30, 36, 45–48, 50, 55, 62, 95, 114, 139
Goulart, João, 107, 137
Graham, Laura, 126, 190, 203
Grilagem, 89, 100, 169, 171, 248 n.72
Guardianship. *See* Tutela
Guha, Ranajit, 15, 158

Health. *See* Xavante communities: health
Hecht, Susanna, 169
Hegemony, 9, 13–15, 17, 22, 28, 49–50, 54, 125, 225 n.48
Hinterland. *See* Central Brazil; Frontier
Historical memory, 73, 101, 115, 134, 159, 173–74, 184. *See also* Xavante oral histories
Hobsbawm, Eric, 10, 34
Hunting. *See* Xavante political economy: hunting and gathering

Indianness, 16, 133–36, 178, 198, 219. *See also* Ethnicity
Indigenismo: in hemispheric context, 11, 35–36, 59–60, 228 n.30, 230 n.60, 231 n.66, 240 n.103
Indigenous land: Brazilian law and status of, 16, 24, 89–90, 142–46, 153, 164, 212, 215; and increase in reserves since 1970, 216–17; March to the West and appropriation of, 37, 41–43, 48, 51, 55, 62, 67; SPI and demarcation of, 14, 23–24, 51, 89–90, 95, 99–104, 153, 216; and violations by matogrossense state officials and elites, 90, 95–96, 98–108, 170, 249 n.76. *See also* Xavante land
Indigenous languages: as marker of indigenous identity, 25, 227 n.11; missionary approaches to, 120–21; state policy toward, 120–22, 124–25, 130–31, 212; and their symbolism for nationalists, 37, 130; variety of, 18, 125. *See also* Gê: languages
Indigenous peoples, images of: as Ama-

zonian, 18–19; as bloodthirsty, 23, 36, 44, 48, 56, 58, 123, 145, 181, 238 nn.61, 75; as brawny, 13, 18, 38–39, 58–59, 62; as childlike or deficient, 12, 19, 23, 40–41, 43, 124–25, 134–35, 216; as cooperativist, 13, 33, 42, 68, 80, 84, 178–79, 190; as disappearing, 7, 13, 39, 41, 98, 114–15, 120, 130, 134, 146; as ecologist, 71, 213–14; feminized, 52; as latifundiário, 167; as lazy, 12, 19, 43, 66, 97–98; as noble savage, 12, 13, 19, 33, 35, 38, 56–57, 63, 134, 217, 238 n.61; as proto-patriot in nationalist iconography, 7, 12–13, 18–19, 35–37, 39, 42, 48, 56, 63, 66, 133–36, 161, 174–75, 213. *See also* Indianness; Racial mixture
Indigenous policy: and arbitrary validation of indigenous traditions, 81, 134; and condemnation of indigenous dependency, 81–82, 196; and disregard of indigenous modes of production, 11, 17, 21, 73, 80, 189–210; and efforts to eliminate nomadism, 11, 19, 24, 41, 67–68, 71–72, 80–85, 134, 241 n.21, 242 n.26; and grooming of rural laborers and agriculturalists, 11, 19, 24, 65–68, 79–85, 124–25, 129, 188–92, 211, 216; and inculcation of notions of citizenship, 11, 24, 68, 116, 124–25, 132–36, 175, 190, 216; and limited state expenditures, 19, 43, 48, 50, 69, 78, 80–81, 85, 87, 103–8, 125; and March to the West, 24, 26, 30–35, 39, 41–44, 52, 56–59, 62, 65, 89, 102, 130, 188, 211; and military rule, 20, 137–44, 146, 157–58, 166, 190, 198; and position toward indigenous languages, 120–22, 124–25, 130–31, 212; and privileging of chiefs, 67–69, 74, 77, 84–88, 192, 195, 200, 272 n.81; and schism between integrationists and preservationists, 19, 49, 61–65, 87. *See also* Developmentalism: objectification; Fundação Nacional do Índio; Serviço de Proteção aos Índios; Xavante Project
Indigenous population: during colonial period, 4; as percentage of total Bra-

zilian population, 18; in twentieth century, 7, 11, 25

Industrialization, 9–10, 28–29, 31, 24, 103, 137–38

Instituto Nacional de Colonização e Reforma Agrária (National Institute for Colonization and Agrarian Reform, INCRA), 151, 153, 163, 167–68

International Labor Organization (United Nations), 81, 214, 274 n.6

Jucá, Romero, 209
Juruna, Mario, 174, 199, 200

Karajá, 3, 5, 23, 42, 48, 144–45
Kayapó, 3, 4, 86, 104, 144
Kubitschek, Juscelino, 8, 106–7, 114

Land grabbing. *See* Grilagem
Landowners. *See* Fazendeiros
Legal Amazonia, 8, 20, 25–26, 45, 138, 142, 145, 160, 163, 167, 171; corporate investment and influence in, 14, 141–42, 147–50, 155–56, 160–61, 172; delimitation of, 139–40; environmental degradation in, 136, 160, 163, 168–69, 180, 184, 187, 193, 210, 216; map of, 139; missionary penetration of, 120. *See also* Frontier; Military rule; Superintendência do Desenvolvimento da Amazônia

Leitão, Ismael, 81–83, 99
Lenharo, Alcir, 31
Lévi-Strauss, Claude, 115
Lins de Barros, João Alberto, 46, 48
Loazo, Benedito, 128, 153, 162, 175, 195
Lopes da Silva, Aracy, 78, 116, 191
Lunkenbein, Rodolfo, 170, 179
Luz, Lúcio da, 50–51, 65, 101

Malcher, José da Gama, 64, 102, 104–5, 250 n.100
Marãiwatsede. *See* Xavante communities: Marãiwatsede
March to the West, 53, 57, 62–63, 94, 109, 145, 157, 211, 219; and appropriation of indigenous land, 37, 41–43, 48, 51, 55, 62, 67; as counterbalance to oligarchy, 30, 94; and cultural propaganda, 23,

25, 30–34; historical antecedents of, 29; military support for, 30–31, 140; and incorporation of western territory, 28, 31, 39, 46, 94–95, 140; and policy for indigenous population, 24, 26, 30–35, 39, 41–44, 52, 56–59, 62, 65, 89, 102, 130, 188, 211; and policy for peasantry, 24, 29–31, 42, 94–95. *See also* Central Brazil; Estado Novo; Frontier

Mato Grosso, 1–6, 16, 18–30, 45–55, 58, 60, 66, 74–78, 81, 107, 114, 171, 177–79, 191, 206, 210, 215; clientelism in, 20, 97, 99, 100, 167; and economic investment under military rule, 148–53, 163; elite opposition to indigenous reserves in, 65, 88, 90, 95–108, 142, 145, 164–70, 176, 184, 187, 197, 249 n.76, 257 n.18; and inclusion of northern region in Legal Amazonia, 139–40; land policies in, 20, 89–90, 94–100, 104, 107–8, 247 n.38; map of, 92; obstacles to economic development of, 91–94, 247 n.49; political infighting among elites of, 98–100; and private colonization companies, 95–97, 99, 163–64, 169, 184, 192; regional identity in, 93; subdivision of southern region of, 176; violence and fraud in, 20, 89, 100–102, 107. *See also* Barra do Garças; Central Brazil; Departamento de Terras e Colonização; Frontier

Maybury-Lewis, David, 71, 79, 82–86, 123, 126, 178, 222 n.14

Media: and assistance in indigenous struggles, 14, 16, 21, 113, 143–44, 157, 161, 167, 170, 174–75, 177, 180, 183, 189, 198–99, 205, 210, 213; and censorship under Estado Novo, 25; and fascination with Xavante, 57–59, 66, 68, 78, 87, 205, 238 n.75

Médici, Emílio Garrastazu, 156–57, 176, 178, 190

Meireles, Francisco ("Chico"), 57, 59–60, 64, 66–67, 111, 208, 240 n.104

Merure, 51, 53, 117, 121, 169–71, 196. *See also* Salesian missionaries

Mestiçagem. *See* Racial mixture

Military rule: and colonization of Amazon, 8, 20, 138, 141–42, 148, 156–57, 160; and doctrine of national security, 20, 137–38, 142–43, 156–57, 166, 171, 186, 191; and environmental destruction in Amazonia, 136, 146, 160, 163, 168–69, 171, 177, 184, 216; and indigenous policy, 20, 137–44, 146, 157–58, 166, 190, 198; international criticism of, 7, 16, 142–45, 156–57, 171, 181, 199, 215, 257 n.26; and modernization of agriculture, 21, 137–38, 141–42, 145, 163, 177, 188, 190, 210, 262 n.10; and political liberalization, 21, 113, 162–64, 176–80, 185–86, 189–90; and repression, 137–38, 156, 189, 200–202; and roadbuilding in Amazonia, 8, 20, 138, 141, 146, 148, 150, 156–57, 160, 166, 190; and subsidies for corporate capital in Amazonia, 20, 136, 141, 146–50, 155–56, 172; and use of patronage, 189–90; 197–211

Miners. *See* Garimpeiros

Mining, 4, 26–27, 93, 146–47, 157, 163, 166, 171

Ministry of Agriculture, 40, 103, 106, 143

Ministry of Interior, 143, 146, 155–56, 162, 164–65, 197, 199

Missionaries, 6, 14, 21, 51, 55, 60, 67, 69, 116, 125–28, 132, 135, 145, 153, 175–79, 198, 211; in colonial period, 3–4; and competition with state over indigenous affairs, 19, 44, 49–50, 80, 87; and condemnation by Barbados Declaration, 178. *See also* Evangelical Protestant missionaries; Salesian missionaries; Summer Institute of Linguistics

Müller, Júlio, 94–95

Museu do Índio: origins of, 238 n.63

Nationalism. *See* Central Brazil: nationalist symbol; Developmentalism; Estado Novo; Indigenous peoples, images of: and nationalist iconography

Noble Savage. See Indigenous peoples, images of

Nobre da Veiga, João Carlos, 197–203, 206, 271 n.65

Nongovernmental Organizations (NGOS), 217–18

Oliveira, Odenir Pinto de, 172, 183, 196–202

Ortner, Sherry, 69, 205

Pacification, 19, 45, 48–51, 56, 77, 89, 110, 180, 193, 211; colonial precedents for, 52; compared with Mexican and Argentine campaigns, 49; critics' denunciation of, 62–63; industrial goods as tactic of, 49, 52, 56–59, 65, 68, 77–78, 82–87, 112; revisionists decry insidious motivations behind, 14, 48, 51; settlers' version of, 51, 117; state claims to exclusive capacity for, 52–57, 236 n.36; and Xavante communities, 56–61, 65, 77–79, 94, 101–2, 117, 135

Pan-Indianism, 131, 133, 145, 175, 177–78, 180, 191, 199

Parabubu. *See* Parabubure

Parabubure, 1, 101, 117, 152, 168, 172–73, 177, 183–86, 195–98, 204, 206; map of, 182

Paraíso. *See* Batovi River; Simões Lopes post

Paula, José Maria de, 42, 90

Pimentel Barbosa, Genésio, 56, 62

Pimentel Barbosa community. *See* Xavante communities: Pimentel Barbosa

Pimentel Barbosa post, 57, 77–79, 81–89, 102, 112

Plano de Desenvolvimento para a Nação Xavante (Development Plan for the Xavante Nation). *See* Xavante Project

Plano de Integração Nacional (National Integration Plan, PIN), 156, 163

Polamazônia, 163

Polonoroeste, 258 n.48

Ponce de Arruda, João, 99–100, 103

Portuguese: instruction of, 14, 116, 122–25, 130–32, 136, 212; as language of

123, 177, 192–97; Sangradouro, 53, 87, 117, 119–122, 127–28, 145, 155, 158, 165, 169–73, 177, 180, 184, 196, 200, 209; Santa Teresinha, 53, 79, 86–87; São Marcos, 87, 117, 119, 122, 127–28, 145, 155, 158–59, 165, 169–70, 174, 187–89, 193–96, 199–204; Simões Lopes, 117, 119–21, 124, 127, 132–33, 166; and state pacification efforts, 56–61, 65, 77–79, 94, 101–2. 117, 135. *See also* Parabubure

Xavante cultural traditions: arbitrary validation by state officials of, 81, 134; challenged by missionaries, 119–29; as matrix for political empowerment and mobilization, 16, 69, 113, 115, 126–27, 130, 134–36, 161, 174; wai'a, 121, 129. *See also* Xavante political economy; Xavante social structure

Xavante land: deforestation of, 1, 136, 146–47, 160, 163, 168–72, 180, 184, 187, 193, 210, 216; and efforts to include in Xingu National Park, 64–65, 96; and extensive precontact domain, 2, 71, 160; and inclusion in Legal Amazonia, 139–40; invasion and usurpation of, 11, 19–20, 89, 101–2, 107, 115–18, 123, 130, 135, 146–47, 154, 159, 164, 173–74, 177, 193, 210, 212, 215. *See also* Indigenous land; Xavante communities; Xavante reservations

Xavante language: missionary policy toward, 120–21; as reflective of unimportance of acquisitiveness, 73, 131. *See also* Gê: languages

Xavante leadership: 16, 21, 116, 129–32, 162, 175, 183, 187–88, 197–98; and government patronage, 2, 19, 21, 68–69, 74–88, 128, 170, 189, 192, 195–97, 200–11; historic responsibilities and limitations of, 76–77; and involvement in pan-Indian meetings, 177, 180. *See also* Aniceto; Apoena (Chief of Pimentel Barbosa community); Apoena (Chief of São Marcos community); Babatti; Celestino; Loazo, Benedito; Urubuenã; Zé Tropeiro

Xavante migrations: map of, 61. *See also* Xavante communities: fissure and dispersal

Xavante oral histories: 3, 6, 58, 75, 77, 122–23, 126, 175, 184, 186

Xavante political economy: and adaptation to cerrado, 70–73; and hunting and gathering, 1, 6, 11, 19, 70–73, 75–77, 81–83, 116, 123, 127–29, 158, 160, 169, 181, 187, 193, 195, 198, 201; and kin-ordered mode of production, 72, 76–79, 83; and swidden agriculture, 11, 19, 70–73, 76, 82, 160, 193; and systems of exchange, 73, 126, 194

Xavante political mobilization: and allies in civil society, 21, 133, 161, 163–64, 177–80, 198–200, 214–15; and Constituent Assembly, 212–14; and importance of historical narratives, 173–74; and manipulation of indigenista discourse, 16, 21, 134–36, 144–45, 161, 164, 174–75, 216; and pressuring of military officials, 20, 113, 147, 160–61, 164–67, 170–71, 177, 180–81, 185–86, 197–200, 205–8; and use of stylized violence, 21, 161, 183, 185, 205–6

Xavante population: between 1950 and 1990, 6, 66, 117, 189, 203; compared with indigenous population of Mato Grosso and Brazil, 18

Xavante Project, 21, 171, 187–221; and cattle grazing, 188, 203, 206, 209; and education, 188, 195; and rice production, 188–89, 192–96, 201, 208–9. *See also* Fundação Nacional do Índio: Xavante communities; Xavante leadership: government patronage; Xavante social structure

Xavante reservations: 1, 6, 88, 165, 187–88, 211; area of, 189; maps of, 166, 182, 191; Mato Grosso's policy towards, 65, 88, 95, 98–99, 103, 142, 145, 164–70, 176, 184, 187, 197, 257 n.18; reluctance of federal government to create sizable, 67, 142, 154–61, 183, 189, 198; and struggle for Culuene, 165–68. *See also*

835060

Seth Garfield is Assistant Professor in the Department of History at University of Texas at Austin.

Library of Congress Cataloging-in-Publication Data

Garfield, Seth

Indigenous struggle at the heart of Brazil : state policy, frontier expansion, and the Xavante Indians, 1937–1988 / Seth Garfield.

p. cm.

Includes bibliographical references and index.

ISBN 0-8223-2661-2 (cloth : alk. paper)—ISBN 0-8223-2665-5 (pbk. : alk. paper)

1. Xavante Indians—Government relations. 2. Indians of South America—Brazil—Government relations. I. Title.

F2520.1.A4 G37 2001

323.1'1984—dc21   00-061746